THE ARMIES
OF U. S. GRANT

THE ARMIES
OF U.S. GRANT

James R. Arnold

ARMS AND
ARMOUR

Arms and Armour Press
A Cassell Imprint
Wellington House, 125 Strand, London WC2R 0BB.

Distributed in the USA by Sterling Publishing Co. Inc,
387 Park Avenue South, New York, NY 10016-8810

Distributed in Australia by Capricorn Link (Australia) Pty Ltd, 2/13
Carrington Road, Castle Hill, New South Wales 2154

First published 1995
This paperback edition 1996
© Simon Foster, 1994

British Library Cataloguing-in-Publication data: A catalogue record
for this book is available from the British Library

ISBN 1-85409-374-6

Designed and edited by DAG Publications Ltd.
Designed by David Gibbons; edited by Michael Boxall;
Printed and bound in Great Britain by
Hartnolls Limited, Bodmin, Cornwall.

Contents

Introduction

TWENTY-FIVE YEARS AFTER THE END OF THE AMERICAN CIVIL War, William T. Sherman sought to redress an imbalance in the war's history. He believed that the celebrated duels between the eastern armies in Virginia had received so much publicity that they overshadowed more important events in the West. Sherman wrote that the Union victories at Pea Ridge, Fort Donelson and Shiloh were key to all subsequent events: 'They encouraged us and discouraged our too sanguine opponents, thereby leading to all our Western successes.' He went a step further, asserting that, 'The more you study the Civil War, the more you will discover that the Northwestern States saved the Union.' He understood the Northwestern yankees to include soldiers from the core region of Ohio, Indiana and Illinois, and from adjacent, less populated states such as Wisconsin. It went without saying that western born Ulysses S. Grant was their surpassing leader.

Grant began the war as an unremarkable volunteer aide trying to help organize Illinois soldiers for state officials. He ended his military service as a victorious lieutenant general commanding all the Federal armies. He rose to this exalted level for many reasons, having to do with his character and his strategic ability. But first and foremost, he received promotions because he won battles. Yet his first battle was a defeat by any conventional standard and his first victories featured his own poor generalship that permitted the enemy to deliver surprise attacks that nearly drove his army from the field. His soldiers' courage saved the army from the awkward position Grant placed it in at Fort Donelson and from a near-untenable position he assigned to it at Shiloh. The western soldier's fighting mettle overcame these blunders and brought victory, thereby allowing Grant to rise to become the Union's indispensable man.

This book relies on diaries, letters and first-hand accounts gleaned from archives and libraries throughout the United States to tell both the story of Grant's armies and a parallel story about the development of the man himself. It tells how Grant's first command evolved from an eager but totally raw force into the Army of the Tennessee, an army that considered itself invincible. Even today, despite the fact that the Civil War is the most intensely studied American conflict, the imbalance perceived by Sherman remains. The war in the West is still eclipsed by less significant actions in the East. The first part of this book helps rectify that imbalance.

Having triumphed in the West, Grant heads East to meet and lead the Army of the Potomac. Here we will see whether and how the western and eastern styles of war merged to create a military machine capable of overcoming Robert E. Lee and his vaunted Army of Northern Virginia. It is a grim tale of grinding attrition in which the gallantry of the Regulars in the Wilderness or the 1st Maine Heavy Artillery at Petersburg seems to matter not at all. Why does the individual and unit bravery displayed by the eastern soldier fail to produce the dramatic results earned by the similar conduct of the western yankees? Grant's western army made the transition from enthusiastic but inept volunteer force to an aggressive, veteran, mobile striking force. This the Army of the Potomac could not do.

In sum, this book is a story of the development of a great fighting force, the Army of the Tennessee, and the story of how the commander of that army adapts to an entirely different army and a wholly new style of war when he comes East to grapple with his greatest foe.

ACKNOWLEDGMENTS

During Roberta's and my tour of Grant's battlefields, many National Park historians at the National Military Parks and Battlefields kindly shared their knowledge and their archival treasures. Thanks to the entire staff at Fort Donelson who warned us about seed ticks and opened their archival files: Woody Harrell, Shiloh; Terrence J. Winschel, Vicksburg; Jim Ogden, Chickamauga-Chattanooga; Don Pfanz, Fredericksburg-Spotsylvania; Chris Calkins, Richmond-Petersburg.

Carl Teger skilfully reproduced many of the archival photographs that appear herein. Joyce B. Arnold provided research at the Chicago Historical Society. The Chicago Historical Society, Metropolitan Museum of Art, Library of Congress, and National Archives provided visual material. The superb collection at the Military History Institute in Carlisle, Pennsylvania provided many first-hand accounts. Thanks to John Slonaker and his staff. The fine library at Washington and Lee University provided much source material. Ralph Reinertsen examined the issue of Sheridan's use of modern fire and movement tactics.

I am indebted to Roberta Wiener, who once again provided critical editing, research, and proofreading.

James R. Arnold, 1995

1
A Period of Apprenticeship

'I guess I've come to take command.' These words were spoken by 39-year-old Ulysses Simpson Grant to the officers of 'Yates' Hellions', a newly raised regiment of unruly Illinois volunteers, in June 1861. No one present at this time, nor anyone who had known Grant previously, would have suspected that he would become the man to lead the North to victory in the Civil War.

He was born Hiram Ulysses Grant in 1822. Young Grant enjoyed a typical Ohio boyhood. He detested school, preferring nature and its animals, particularly horses. His father ran a tannery and the youth disliked working there. Despite his unexceptional background, he received an appointment to the United States Military Academy at West Point, an appointment he did not welcome. A mix-up during the application process gave him a new name: Ulysses S. Grant, and this name he carried to his grave.

At West Point he was a very average cadet who never seriously applied himself to his studies. He graduated in 1843 with a class rank of twenty-one out of thirty-nine. While a cadet, he had displayed a special aptitude for horsemanship, and this was to stand him in good stead during the war against Mexico where he served competently. He participated in every major battle except Buena Vista and ended up as a captain with two citations for bravery: one gained at Monterrey and the other while storming the gates of Mexico City. After that war he fell in love with Julia Dent and married her. For the remainder of his life she was to be an invaluable anchor against the drift towards his particular demon that was almost his undoing – alcohol. Grant greatly enjoyed its taste but had no head for it. This became apparent during his post-war service on the West Coast, where, separated from his wife and bored by the routine of garrison life, he took to the bottle. Neglecting his duty, he had come near to being court-martialled when he resigned from the army in 1854. For six subsequent years he floundered. The eve of the Civil War found him at Galena, Illinois.

The 10-inch mortar shell fired by South Carolina hotheads to open the bombardment of Fort Sumter on 12 April 1861 led to President Abraham Lincoln's call for 75,000 men to put down the rebellion. By tradition, the United States had always relied upon its militia during times of conflict. Accordingly, after the fall of Fort Sumter, each state received the government's manpower demand. Illinois' quota was six regiments totalling 4,458 men and 225 officers. The latter figure far exceeded the number of experienced officers available, and the total requirement represented more than one-quarter of the entire strength of the 1860 United States Regular Army. Illinois had enjoyed several peaceful decades since a gangly man named Abe Lincoln had chased about the state in pursuit of Indians during the so-called 'Black Hawk War'. As a consequence its militia establishment had atrophied from disuse. In this, Illinois shared the experience of every state east of the Mississippi River. With the exception of the city of Chicago, there were few organized militia companies within state borders, and when the president's call came, everything had to be built from scratch.

So it was that on the night of 18 April 1861, volunteers gathered at the Court House in Galena, Illinois to nominate ex-captain Ulysses S. Grant to chair the recruiting committee. Grant obliged, but when the next logical step took place, and the newly recruited company wanted to elect Grant to lead them, he declined. As a West Point graduate and a captain in the regular army, he considered the rank of militia captain a trifle below his dignity and, like almost every West Pointer in the nation, he hoped for something better.

Illinois Governor Dick Yates accepted the Galena company into the state militia, but stipulated that the company be locally outfitted. Quite simply the state had little in store to equip its militia. Its 'arsenal' of 600 decrepit muskets and 297 horse pistols went to the companies sent to occupy the restive town of Cairo at the southern tip of the state. The Cairo-bound militia marched with four old cannon which, lacking shells and canister, had to use lead slugs, and its infantry carried shotguns and sporting rifles. Meanwhile, Sam Grant (as he was known to friends) helped the Galena company by designing their uniform. Naturally he based his design on the familiar uniform of the regular service. So the Galena company received blue frock-coats with dark gray trousers with blue cords. In addition to dressing the men, Grant helped the 'officers' to learn military drill.

During this time Grant was befriended and assisted by a local lawyer named John Rawlins, and renewed his acquaintance with the 33-year-old Ely S. Parker, a full-blooded Seneca Indian who also happened to be a trained civil engineer. They had known each other when Grant had been a store clerk in Galena in 1857. Both Rawlins and Parker were to figure prominently in Grant's military family. As the Galena company took to the trains en route for their camp of instruction, few remarked upon a small figure in an old slouch hat and a faded blue overcoat, who carried a carpetbag and fell in at the company's rear. Ulysses S. Grant had begun the long journey that would take him to Lieutenant General Commanding the entire United States Army and to two terms in the White House.

It was easy to overlook this restrained, controlled person. When depressed, he was merely silent; when cheerful, he merely smiled. He looked and behaved as a simple, common man. His modesty prevented him from pushing for an inflated rank during the early months of the war. While helping the state of Illinois organize its regiments, he met most of the newly appointed regimental colonels. Convinced that if these men, many of whom had no military experience, could command a regiment he could do the same, he wrote to the Adjutant General of the Army on 24 May 1861 setting out his qualifications for command of a regiment. It is fortunate that his request got lost somewhere in the War Department because, as events would prove, the volunteer service offered a much better opportunity for distinguishing himself and rising rapidly.

As was the case North and South, the militia camp of instruction at Springfield, Illinois was a scene of appalling chaos. Most volunteer companies arrived over-subscribed, and the extra men did not want to be sent home. Politicians seized the opportunity to form new units and appoint new officers. Those with political pull found themselves commanding regiments, but the process sickened honest Sam Grant. Taken in tow by a friendly congressman, he reluctantly entered the governor's office to request a position. He was told that there was no place for him 'as there were now sufficient assistants in the military offices.'[1] Passed over, Grant continued to see unqualified civilians who were good orators, or who had political connections, or were West Pointers who made a good impression become colonels in the Illinois militia. Since Grant was none of these, he took the only employment he could find. He had served as a store clerk. Now he served as a low-level clerk in the governor's office.

Then came a small opportunity. Proud West Pointer John Pope left in a huff when the brigade he had organized failed to elect him to lead it, choosing instead a windy politician named Benjamin Prentiss, whose rendezvous with destiny on the Shiloh battlefield lay less than twelve months ahead. Pope's departure left a vacancy and Governor Yates, finally awakened to Grant's competency, appointed him to command the camp of instruction. During this service, Grant favourably impressed the officers of the newly mustered 21st Illinois Volunteers. The regiment's colonel was a lout and a drunkard, happy to quote Napoleon but ignorant of military reality. The farm boys in the ranks took advantage by robbing hen houses, drinking in local saloons, and earning the name 'Yates' Hellions'. Mortified, Yates appointed Grant colonel.

His arrival at his new regiment was a notable event. The soldiers were unimpressed with their new officer – Grant would fail to make a favourable first impression on everyone he encountered – and began to make fun of this small man dressed in dingy civilian clothes. Some danced behind him while throwing mock punches. Someone pushed a soldier who, in turn, struck Grant and knocked his hat to the ground. Calmly, Grant picked up his hat, turned around, and fixed the men with a stare. The rascal averted his eyes. Much as Napoleon Bonaparte had faced down uppity officers and mutinous men when he took command of the Army of Italy, so Grant, with his firm personality, began to dominate events. He disbanded the unruly camp guards, organized a system of roll-calls, and instituted regular drills. Soon his regiment had begun to acquire the rudiments of discipline.

When the time came for the regiment to re-enlist – Washington authorities had come to realize that the rebellion would not be put down by 75,000 90-day volunteer militia, and Lincoln had called for 300,000 men to serve for three years or the duration of the war – Grant, knowing he was no orator, turned to two men he had just met who seemed able to inspire patriotism. Congressman John A. McClernand would rise to vie with Grant for command of the Vicksburg campaign. In 1861 he delivered an unexceptional speech that failed to rouse 'Yates' Hellions'. The second speaker was different. Congressman John A. Logan was a swarthy, black-moustached man with piercing eyes and an irascible manner. He had served as a volunteer lieutenant in the Mexican War and knew something about the business, but, better still, he knew personally most of the men he was addressing. After stirring his audience with the theme of devotion to the country, he looked at one man and said, 'You can't fall out now. If you go home now to Mary, she will say, "Why, Tom, are you home from the war so soon? How far did you get?"' Rhetorically, Logan supplied the answer: 'Mattoon! [a small Illinois town].' To roars of laughter, 603 men, nearly everyone present, signed up for three years. They demanded a speech from their colonel. Grant rose and said simply, 'Men, go to your quarters.'[2] And they went.

So it was throughout the nation, North and South, as volunteers flocked to the rival banners to go to war, although they had no idea what lay ahead.

Grant quickly whipped the 21st Illinois Volunteers into tolerable shape, and in July 1861 he had his first experience of independent command when, hearing that the rebels had surrounded an Illinois regiment in nearby Missouri, he marched his men to relieve their comrades. In his *Memoirs* Colonel Grant described his feelings:

'My sensations as we approached what I supposed might be "a field of battle" were anything but agreeable. I had been in all the engagements in Mexico that it was possible for one person to be in; but not in command. If some one else had been colonel and I had been lieutenant-colonel I do not think I would have felt any trepidation.'[3]

This affair turned out to be a false alarm, but it had been a test none the less. The nation's rapid mobilization had thrust soldiers who had never previously commanded more than a handful of men into positions of great responsibility where they could not shelter behind a senior officer. They had to take decisions that could cost men's lives and then stand accountable for their decisions – a crushing burden that proved too much for many including George McClellan, Joe Hooker and Henry Halleck. Grant, like many officers North and South, had physical courage, as had been shown conspicuously in Mexico, but the situation along the Illinois–Missouri border in July 1861 required moral courage. Had it been possible he would have dodged the responsibility, but there was no one else and so he went ahead.

A few weeks later he faced an even stiffer challenge. He received orders to march against a reported rebel encampment commanded by a Colonel Thomas Harris. Grant marched his men across 25 miles of deserted countryside where, for all he knew, the enemy might be lying in wait to destroy his regiment:

'As we approached the brow of the hill from which it was expected we could see Harris' camp, and possibly find his men ready formed to meet us, my heart kept getting higher and higher until it felt to me as though it was in my throat. I would have given anything then to have been back in Illinois, but I had not the moral courage to halt and consider what to do; I kept right on.'[4]

He found that Harris had abandoned his camp and his normal calm returned. It had been a pivotal formative experience. Grant reflected that Harris had probably been as afraid of him as he was of Harris. It was a novel thought and one that forever altered his approach to war. He wrote: 'From that event to the close of the war, I never experienced trepidation upon confronting an enemy ... I never forgot that he had as much reason to fear my forces as I had his.'[5]

Before being called upon to face rebel fire, Grant had been tested, had surmounted self-doubt and drawn conclusions that would underlie his command approach.

1   Lloyd Lewis, *Captain Sam Grant*, (Boston: Little, Brown and Co., 1950), p. 415.
2   *Captain Sam Grant*, p. 430.
3   Ulysses S. Grant, *Personal Memoirs*, (New York: De Capo Press, 1982), p. 126.
4   Grant, *Personal Memoirs*, p. 127.
5   Grant, *Personal Memoirs*, p. 127.

2
The Camp of Instruction

CAIRO, ILLINOIS WAS THE SOUTHERNMOST CITY IN THE United States remaining loyal to the old flag. Located near the junction of the Ohio and Mississippi Rivers, Cairo became a staging area for the federal offensive to open the Mississippi. Here, on 20 August 1861, Grant took command. His orders were to clear south-east Missouri of rebel forces.

The North's original strategic plan, formulated by the ageing but still astute Winfield Scott, placed a huge emphasis on the Mississippi, seeing it as a corridor of invasion to bisect the Confederacy. Key to the Mississippi was the border state of Kentucky, which maintained an uneasy neutrality while forces massed just over its borders, north and south. Kentucky had to be handled very, very gingerly, but for the moment it well served Confederate interests by blocking the Mississippi and shielding Tennessee from any Union thrust. Ultimately both sides needed Kentucky and both believed that whichever side crossed Kentucky's borders first would drive the state into the opposite camp.

The Confederate commander, Major General Leonidas Polk, appreciated much of this. While cognizant of the implications of Kentucky's neutrality, this bishop-general began receiving ominous reports about Grant's build-up in southern Illinois and was worried that it foreshadowed a Union advance into Kentucky. He decided to pre-empt Grant by occupying the high bluffs at Columbus, Kentucky. This position offered a fine natural bastion from which to oppose a federal movement down the Mississippi. On 3 September 1861, Polk invaded the neutral ground.[1] It proved a mistake.

On 5 September, the day after Grant assumed command at Cairo, a spy reported that the Confederates had occupied Columbus, a mere twenty miles downstream on the Mississippi. It seemed that they intended to advance upon Paducah, Kentucky, a small town located at the mouth of the Tennessee River. Grant telegraphed the news to his superior and immediately set about organizing an expedition. Instead of moving directly against Columbus, he planned to use the locally available steamboats to move forty miles up the Ohio River to Paducah before Polk's men could get there. By that evening he had yet to receive a response from his superior and telegraphed again to say that in the absence of any orders he would sail at midnight. He promptly loaded 1,800 infantry aboard the steamers and, escorted by the gunboats *Tyler* and *Conestoga*, reached and occupied Paducah on the 6th without opposition. On returning to Cairo he found that he had received permission to do what he had already done.

Because the occupation of Paducah produced no great battle it went largely overlooked, but it was a crucial strategic move. Had the Rebel advance continued unopposed to occupy the line from Columbus to Paducah, they would have interdicted all shipping on the Ohio River, and the yankees would have had to mount an amphibious attack across the Ohio or make a difficult flank march to turn the Confederate position. Such an operation would have long delayed Grant's forthcoming Henry–Donelson campaign with incalculable consequences. That none of this transpired can be attributed to the fact that an obscure federal brigadier used his own initiative to counter immediately the initial Confederate advance.

Grant's initiative in capturing Paducah was unusual at this stage of the war. His prompt and aggressive *riposte* was a direct result of the lesson he had assimilated when advancing on Colonel Harris' camp; that warfare's inherent uncertainty promoted caution among most men and gave opportunity for the bold advance. Paducah was the first flowering of this insight, the first example of what would become the Grant way. Moreover, it soon became clear that the Union Army had more resources to bring to bear in Kentucky than had Polk. Soon other federal forces marched over the Ohio River into the Bluegrass State. Suddenly unshielded, the Confederacy lay vulnerable from the Mississippi River east to the mountains.

Grant's capture of Paducah frightened his superiors as much as it scared his enemy. Although he pleaded to be allowed to advance farther, their cautious frame of mind tethered him to his base at Cairo where he spent his time organizing a staff. He chose a 50-year-old regular artilleryman, Major Joseph D. Webster, as his chief of staff. Grant was impressed by lawyers and his selections included several young attorneys who displayed energy and a glib tongue but who had no military experience. With one exception they would prove unsuitable. That exception was a brilliant young man named John A. Rawlins whom Grant took on to his staff as an aide-de-camp. The 32-year-old Rawlins was an 'honest, unpretending, and unassuming' man, with few educational advantages.[2] He had seen his own father fall victim to alcohol, and he had a lifelong violent antipathy to the demon drink. He was also a sincere patriot, determined to serve his country, and he felt that he could best accomplish this by keeping his general away from alcohol. A firm character, he was not reticent in expressing an opinion, and in time, if he thought Grant was mis-stepping, he would chide the general in no uncertain terms. To the amazement of everyone else on Grant's staff, Rawlins would even curse the general to his face. Other bemused staffers believed Rawlins to be guilty of insubordination many times a day, but his behaviour did not seem to faze the general. Rawlins was to

15

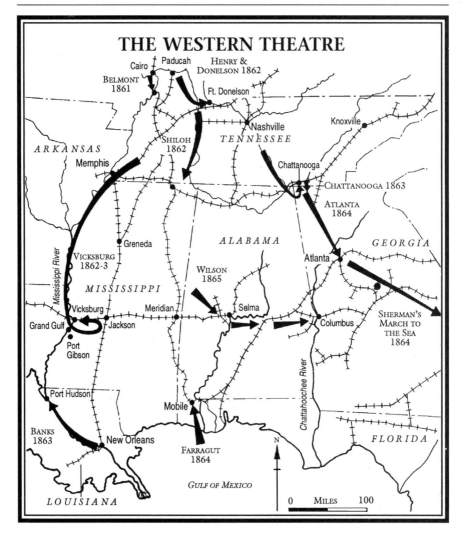

THE WESTERN THEATRE

guide his chief through many political and social entanglements and eventually became an indispensable chief of staff. In 1861, Rawlins, like Grant himself, had to learn his trade in the unforgiving school of battle.

Grant did not choose his chief lieutenant, General John McClernand. McClernand was an important Illinois politician, and Lincoln wanted him placed where he could use his connections to cement potential political rivals to the Northern cause. Since the Cairo region was at best divided in its loyalties – situated so close to the southern states, inevitably there were many in the pro-slavery camp – it seemed to Lincoln to be ideal for McClernand. Little did the president realize that he had saddled Grant with a man who had a deep thirst for military glory, a terrible temper, fondness for intrigue, and a disdain for professional army officers. Among myriad problems, Grant had to handle McClernand with great care. For the time being, McClernand put his considerable energy into organizing an infantry brigade.

Most of Grant's officers had little idea of what constituted the military life. The officers of the 31st Illinois, for example, learned the rudiments of their profession from a private who was a Mexican War veteran. He instructed them in everything from the manual of arms to the correct wording of commands. Perhaps because they realized that their officers knew little more than they did, the volunteers resisted when the officers tried to enforce discipline. The rankers could see little point in the endless, repetitive drill. Complaining of the broiling sun and frequent rain, one private wrote how for the third time in a week, 'We had our knapsacks on ... with everything we could get in them and had to take them off and open them out and then repack them again.'[3] Such foolishness made little sense to strong-willed farm boys who had joined up to fight the Rebels.

Even junior officers objected to the drill routine. Three company officers in the 27th Illinois asked their regimental commander to resign because, they claimed, he drilled the regiment too hard. An Indiana volunteer spoke for many when he said: 'We had enlisted to put down the Rebellion, and had not the patience with the red-tape tomfoolery of the regular service.'[4] Those who complained too loud, or simply were too stupid to master the basic drill, were assigned to 'awkward squads' where they received yet more drill as punishment.

Grant himself had stood near the bottom of his West Point class in the study of tactics. Since his graduation he had never opened a manual on the subject. Once the war began, he obtained a copy of Hardee's *Tactics* and quickly perceived that it was a translation from the French with Hardee's name attached, and thus was merely an updated version of Scott's system which he had learned at West Point. In Scott's system, every change in the order of march began with the command *'Halt!'* After stopping the men, an officer could re-orient the ranks by ordering a change such as *'Right Face!'* Once properly aligned, the movement could resume after the command *'Forward March!'* The French system as compiled by Hardee did away with the need to halt, and allowed changes in a unit's facing to be made while the unit was in motion. Thus, Grant experienced 'no trouble in giving commands that would take my regiment where I wanted it to go and carry it around all obstacles.'[5] This was an ability shared by virtually all the officers from the old regular service and one that non-military men had to struggle to learn.

Mastery of basic drill was necessary so that a unit could manoeuvre on the battlefield. As the first battles would show, hesitation and confusion had lethal consequences. But little of this was yet apparent to the new army. Officers dimly perceived that drill was the only way to ensure that the men would learn the habit of obeying orders. The men

17

had little idea that discipline was a military necessity. So it was that petty conflicts between green troops and equally green officers dominated the first months at Cairo.

Worse, few officers had any idea how to care for their men. Most of the young soldiers had never been far from home, had little skill at caring for themselves, and no immunity to common diseases. Even diligent officers found the independent-minded western volunteer resistant to basic hygiene. One such volunteer informed his officer that he had joined up 'to put down the Rebellion, not to pick up garbage, sweep streets, clean out sinks [latrines]'.[6] Such attitudes made poor sanitation worse. When coupled with exposure to the weather they produced raging diseases – measles and dysentery were prime killers – that felled hundreds before anyone ever came close to facing the enemy.

But the organization continued slowly and painfully, and the unit took on a veneer of military competence. The arrival of uniforms, equipment and weapons made the men feel more like soldiers, but the western yankees had no idea that their government was giving them some of the world's poorest firearms.

The shortage of weapons plagued the federal war effort during the first two years of the conflict. After the burning of Harpers Ferry, the only federal arsenal operating was at Springfield, Massachusetts, and because Springfield's output was so slow many volunteer regiments in 1861 and 1862 received older United States weapons, the best of which were the Model 1855 rifle and rifle-musket, the Model 1841 rifle, and Model 1842 musket. All these were percussion firearms. Before the war, ordnance workers had converted the 1816 and 1835 flintlock muskets to percussion weapons. Many regiments had to make do with these poor substitutes because there was nothing else available.

To meet the shortfall, purchasing agents went to Europe to buy weapons. There, they had to compete with Confederate agents in furious bidding wars. It was a delightful situation for the officers representing the armies of Europe. They were only too eager to empty their arsenals of obsolete weapons by selling at a high price to the desperate Americans. By the summer of 1862, the US government had purchased 738,000 rifles, muskets and carbines from foreign sources. Only 116,740 were the first-rate British-manufactured Enfields. Enfields were much prized because shortly before the war Enfield had re-tooled using machinery directly copied from the Springfield Arsenal. The Enfield was one-hundredth of an inch smaller in calibre than the Springfield, and thus Enfield .57 calibre ammunition could be loaded into Springfield .58 calibre weapons. The balance of the imports were inferior weapons, detested by the men who nicknamed them 'European stovepipes', and prone to inaccuracy and explosive defects. The hapless 101st Illinois were armed with the .72 calibre Russian musket, surely one of the poorest firearms of the era.

The western volunteer did not realize that eastern regiments had first claim on both domestically produced and imported weapons. On the eve of the Shiloh campaign, one typical Indiana regiment armed itself with Belgian muskets that had been rejected first by Pennsylvania and then Ohio. Quite simply, the farther west a unit mustered, the less likely it was to receive adequate weapons. Western cavalry particularly suffered from inadequate weapons. In the summer of 1863 many of Grant's men exchanged their own altered flintlocks and inferior imports for captured Enfields that had been brought through the blockade to arm the Confederate defenders of Vicksburg. Later in the war, many of them traded one last time, exchanging their Enfields for Springfields.

Illustrative of the variety of shoulder firearms used to equip the volunteers of 1861 and 1862 is the following list of weapons issued to 136 New York regiments. It should be remembered that New York was a wealthy state, close to the sources of domestic manufacture and imports. Still, there are sixteen different models ranging from .71 to .54 in calibre:

Model	Calibre	Number of regiments to whom issued
Long Enfield	.577	57
1842 Musket	.69	31
French Vincennes	.69	11
US Rifle-Musket	.58	11
Austrian Rifle	.54	7
1840 altered smoothbore	.69	7
Austrian Rifle	.58	4
Austrian Rifle	.55	3
French Rifle-Musket	.69	3
Short Enfield	.577	3
Remington Rifle	.54	3
1822 altered musket	.69	3
Prussian smoothbore	.71	2
Short Austrian Rifle	.69	2
French Liège Rifle	.58	1
Prussian altered musket	.69	1

This enormous variety of weapons required a wide assortment of ammunition and proved a quartermaster's nightmare. McClernand's division fought at Fort Donelson and Shiloh with a mix of six different types of firearms, all of different calibre. Too often in the first engagements a regiment fired off its ammunition and then found it could not find an ammunition wagon carrying the appropriate calibre. However, it should also be noted that the cry of 'out of ammunition!' served as an all too convenient excuse for a unit to retreat. In response to combat experience, officers burdened their men with ever increasing ammunition loads. It was not uncommon for a soldier to have his cartridge box stuffed with the standard 40 rounds of ammunition and to carry another 40 or 60 loose in his pockets or haversack. Over time, veterans learned to husband their ammunition more carefully.

The difficulties of ammunition supply had eased considerably by the end of 1863 when most Union foot soldiers had Springfield rifle-muskets. The last two years of the war also saw increasing numbers of infantry receive breechloading weapons, which brought about its own special challenge for the officers charged with maintaining an uninterrupted supply of ammunition to the firing line.

However, Springfields and breechloaders were weapons for the future. At Cairo in 1861 men were happy to receive a firearm of any type. Once given guns they began their weapons drill. Taught according to the manual of arms, this involved a sequence of actions: taking the paper cartridge from the cartridge box; biting off the end of the cartridge; placing it in the gun barrel; drawing the ramrod; ramming the cartridge home; returning the ramrod; placing the percussion cap on the nipple of the musket (capping the musket). With practice, men could become adept at all of this but it was not easy, particularly for the shorter men who had to grapple with weapons nearly as tall as themselves.

Having 'mastered' the mechanics of loading, the men next learned how to aim and fire. Many volunteers were poor marksmen when they enter the service, and the first muskets they received did little to improve matters. Instead of the coveted Springfield muskets, most of the volunteers at Cairo received heavy, inferior Austrian weapons. Together with the equally disliked Belgian muskets, these imports had a tremendous recoil and were prone to burst when fired. An Illinois colonel boasted that he always knew which of his men carried the Belgian musket: 'I count the men on the ground; it never deceives me. It is fire and fall flat.'[7] These characteristics did not lend themselves to sharpshooting accuracy. An Ohio soldier recalls that his comrades, who were experienced shooters, considered the Belgian muskets '... both ominous and onerous'.[8]

In the hands of skilled marksmen, however – and the western armies had more than a few of them – even the Belgian musket could be deadly. A Wisconsin private remarked that although they were heavy, with careful loading they were 'good shooting guns'.[9] He saw an Indian soldier armed with this weapon return to camp one night with an armful of squirrels. Using his Belgian musket, he had shot all of them cleanly through the head. Of course hunting squirrels was a bit different from a battle line, but the point is, in the hands of a marksman the inferior weapons were still formidable.

A handful of men at Cairo received better weapons. The two flank companies of 7th Iowa were issued Springfields with tape self-primers (a transitional weapon on the developmental ladder toward the percussion cap). The other eight companies had to make do with modified 'buck and ball' Springfield muskets. This 'buck and ball' ammunition consisted of a one-ounce round ball in a paper cartridge with three large buckshot attached. Unless the soldier held the musket tightly into his shoulder, the heavy discharge could literally knock him down. All these weapons were heavy: the Springfield with 16-inch bayonet attached weighed 10 pounds. Most of them had a fearful kick which caused the soldier to cringe at every discharge. A recruit recalled: 'Quite a number of the men had never fired a gun in their lives; and several of them, when commanded to fire, would shut their eyes, turn their heads in the opposite direction, and blaze away.'[10]

Regardless of the weapons they received, marksmanship seemed to be a gift. Most skilled shooters had learned while still young. An Illinois private who was an experienced hunter and comfortably able to shoot the head off a squirrel at some distance, relates that he always tried to take careful, deliberate aim during battle. However, 'many a time the surroundings were such that the only thing to do was to hold low, and fire through the smoke in the direction of the enemy. I will say here that the extent of wild shooting done in battle, especially by raw troops, is astonishing.'[11] After the battle of Shiloh, this private noticed that the trees behind his battle line were thickly pock-marked by musket balls up to a height of 100 feet. Although the enemy had been but a short distance away across a dead level field, their fire had been wildly inaccurate. This was typical.

An Ohio veteran recalled that most of the men in his unit were experienced hunters, except for the officers who came from a higher social class. These officers did not know 'the difference between a rifle and a shotgun'. Some regiments had more than their fair share of inexperienced shooters for whom no amount of drill or practice could overcome their innate gun-shyness: 'They would invariably shut both eyes and turn the head on pulling the trigger.' It was as if they were 'more afraid of their musket than the enemy'. The difference between the experienced and the gun-shy showed up during target practice. When the sharpshooter platoon aimed at a row of cracker barrels set up at a distance of 200 yards, the boxes invariably flew into splinters with each volley. The inexperienced men fired volleys that 'cut through the tree tops, [and] made the dirt fly not a hundred feet in front with not a bullet mark on the box, and no amount of coaching produced any better results'.[12]

Advances in weapons technology yielded ever increasing accuracy. A man firing a smoothbore musket, the type of weapon used by most western soldiers on both sides at the start of the war, had little chance of hitting an enemy soldier standing 200 yards away. At 50 yards the same weapon was deadly. A better weapon, such as an old-style rifle-musket like the Model 1841 'Mississippi' Rifle – a weapon made famous by a Mississippi colonel named Jefferson Davis during the war against

Mexico; in fact it was a Northern-manufactured gun – fired a round ball that could consistently hit a head-sized target at 100 yards. It was still a dangerous weapon at 200 yards, but at 300 accuracy fell off to about one in four shots hitting an 8-foot square target. Lethal at close ranges, by the standards of 1861 these were obsolete weapons. The reason was that a French officer had invented something vastly superior.

The improvement in infantry weapons came when a certain Captain Minié invented a conical bullet with a tapered hollow, the base of which was fitted with a small iron cap. When the trigger was squeezed the force of the explosion drove the cap into the hollow, thereby expanding the bullet so that it engaged the rifling tightly. This process reduced windage (the difference between the bullet's and the gun-bore's diameter). Using one of Minié's weapons, a trained rifleman could hit a man-sized target 500 yards away at least five times out of ten. Naturally, Minié's invention stimulated a host of modifications, some of which improved upon the original. A British inventor designed a conical bullet for the Enfield that was so well-machined that a skilled marksmen put 98 out of 100 shots into a 7-foot target circle at 600 yards' range on a windy, rainy day! Tests with the American manufactured Model 1855 Rifle-Musket showed an average 15-inch vertical and 13-inch horizontal deviation at 500 yards, a performance even better than the Enfield. Rifled muskets like the Springfield and Enfield could fire out to more than 1,000 yards, although at that range they could only put a volume of fire into a broad target area.

Three major factors kept the weapons used by Grant's army from killing every enemy encountered. First, the accuracy a tester achieved on the firing range was very different from that achieved when men were under fire. Secondly, because the Civil War-era weapons had low muzzle velocity in comparison with modern weapons, one had to aim high in order to reach a distant target. Author and gun enthusiast Jack Coggins explains:

'Ranges had to be correctly estimated and sights carefully adjusted for anything but the very closest ranges. A bullet fired by a kneeling man at the belt buckle of a man running toward him at an estimated range of 300 yards would just pass over the head of a man 250 yards away [because the bullet had to be 'lobbed' toward the target to overcome the effects of gravity]. Thus, if the shooter had overestimated the range by as little as 50 yards he would have missed.'[13]

Applying this to a combat situation, a rifled musket sighted for 300 yards fired from a kneeling position would hit any enemy soldiers who had closed to within 75 yards. Thereafter, the bullet would rise for the next 165 yards and thus create a safe zone. From about 240 to 350 yards the bullet would sink below man height and thereby create a second danger zone. If the same weapon were sighted for longer ranges, the bullet had to pass along a much higher trajectory, thus greatly decreasing the depth of the danger zone. In comparison, the standard Springfield rifle used by American soldiers in both world wars had a much higher muzzle velocity which enabled the bullet to travel in a relatively straight line for the entire time it passed through the same 350 yards, and thus create a much deeper killing zone.

Lastly, regardless of theoretical ranges, most Civil War battles took place in wooded, uneven terrain where sighting distances were far less than the weapon's theoretical range. This overlooked fact (overlooked until historian Paddy Griffith delved into the subject in the mid-1980s) greatly reduced the tactical impact of Captain Minié's invention during the American Civil War.

When the war began, no American general knew much about ballistics, and in the scramble to mobilize they were happy to find weapons of any sort to equip their men. Their men, in turn, of course wanted to obtain the most modern weapons possible, not because they perceived it would give them a tactical advantage but rather because, like most people anywhere, something modern exerted considerable attraction simply because it was new. Had Grant's soldiers practised their shooting regularly, some no doubt would have become better marksmen. But throughout the war, target practice tended to be neglected. Experienced hunters and natural marksmen could and did hit their targets (when they could see them) at much greater ranges than had been the case hitherto, but their ability was largely independent of the type of weapon they used. On the other hand, the average infantryman had little chance to hit anyone more than 200 yards away. Over time, Grant's soldiers would became proficient killing machines, but not in 1861 as they learned about war in Cairo's camp of instruction.

Poor shots many of Grant's infantry may have been, but his carbine-armed cavalry troopers were even worse. At the end of 1861, an Illinois cavalry unit practised their 'marksmanship' on a life-sized target of Jefferson Davis at 200 yards' range. Many of these men were firing their carbines for the first time. Companies of 30 men, picked by their captains for their presumed skill, fired at the target. One company missed entirely; the best company managed only seven hits.

In theory an even more lethal killer than the firearm was the bayonet. Experienced Mexican War officers rightly believed that a spirited bayonet charge would win the day, but they held this belief for the wrong reason. A close order bayonet charge presented a terrifying spectacle to anyone on the receiving end. In the overwhelming number of cases a defender would not wait to feel a bayonet rammed home, but, very wisely, would run away. Officers did not understand that a bayonet charge was formidable because of the psychological stress it forced upon the defender. Many had seen the Mexican infantry run from their trenches when the American infantry pressed home a bayonet charge. Some had seen the fancy bayonet drill performed by a travelling Zouave team that toured the nation just before war began. These officers were obsessed with the physical aspects of bayonet drill without realizing that the usefulness of the drill was to teach the recruit a confident, disciplined state of mind. They put their men through too much bayonet drill (to the exclusion of more useful rifle practice) simply because they believed that the superior wielding of the bayonet would cause their men to triumph.

In the camps at Cairo, bayonet drill could take on the appearance of comedy theatre rather than hard preparation for killing. An observer watching company bayonet drill said that the soldiers looked '... like a line of beings made up about equally of the frog, the sand-hill crane, the sentinel crab, and the grasshopper; all of them rapidly jumping, thrusting, swinging, striking, jerking every way, and all gone stark mad'.[14]

While the men laboured at drill, the more conscientious officers pored over such tomes as Wilcox's *Evolutions of the Line* (a translation of an Austrian manual), and Scott's *Military Dictionary*. To their chagrin they quickly found that there was a huge difference between paper manoeuvres and tactics on the drill ground. Many embarrassed themselves as they tried to march their awkward volunteers about the drill field. In one case, when his horse shied from the music of the regimental band, the colonel of the 5th Wisconsin dropped his drill notes. They scattered to the wind, forcing the helpless colonel to rely upon his subordinates to march the regiment back to camp. Had they had more time, everyone would have learned much, including the fact that drill ground manoeuvres only partially prepared men for deployment on a fire swept battlefield. But in 1861 everyone was in a hurry to join battle, whip the Rebels, and return home.

As the American volunteers took their cram courses in military affairs, certain regimental commanders at Cairo rose in prominence. Notable was Colonel John A. Logan, a politician who enjoyed immense popularity in southern Illinois. It was said that he knew virtually everyone in the regiment he recruited. Like McClernand, Logan was ambitious and distrusted professional officers. He was a charismatic leader who was to become, in the words of William T. Sherman, ' ... a brave, fierce fighter, full of the passion of war ... perfect in battle'.[15]

Colonel Napoleon Buford, as befitting his name, wanted his regiment to be a model unit and, putting his West Point education to work, drilled the 27th Illinois incessantly. After a hard day's drill, in the old army style, he would summon his companies to his quarters where they were required to sing patriotic and religious songs for him and his wife. Since many of his men were Germans, often they sang in their native tongue. What the rough-hewn, English-speaking Illinois farm boys thought of this can only be guessed.

An enthusiastic businessman named Jacob Lauman had been appointed colonel of the 7th Iowa which regiment also had a large number of Germans including its lieutenant-colonel, Augustus Wentz. Wentz had been born in Germany and had emigrated to the United States in time to serve in the regular artillery during the Mexican War. Wentz provided veteran leadership while Lauman learned the rudiments of command. Many of the soldiers in the 7th Iowa had already fought at the Battle of Wilson's Creek in Missouri. Elements of other regiments also had some combat experience, but except for a small number of Mexican War veterans, none of the rest of Grant's men had ever been exposed to enemy fire.

During his two months at Cairo Grant would send his men out on scouting expeditions into 'enemy' territory and, though seldom coming under fire, officers and men learned the arts of campaigning. By the beginning of November 1861 the men had become restless and bored and were threatening to desert if not sent into battle soon. On the morning of 6 November they were marched down to the Cairo levee, filed across wooden planks on to the decks of steamboats, and headed out into wide water. They did not know whether they were heading up the Ohio or down the Mississippi. When the steamers turned downstream the word spread rapidly: 'We are going to attack Columbus.' This electrifying intelligence caused the men to cheer and wave their caps. At last they were going to war.

1 United States War Department, *War of the Rebellion: A Compilation of the Official Records of the Union and Confederate Armies*, Series I, Vol. 4 (Washington: Government Printing Office, 1880-1901), Polk to Harris, September 4, 1861, p. 180. Hereafter cited as *Official Records*.
2 Gideon Welles, *Diary of Gideon Welles*, Vol. 1 (Boston: Houghton Mifflin Co., 1911), p. 386. Described by Welles on July 31, 1863.
3 Nathaniel C. Hughes, *The Battle of Belmont*, (Chapel Hill: University of North Carolina Press, 1991), p. 16.
4 Stephen Z. Starr, *The Union Cavalry in the Civil War*, Vol. 2 (Baton Rouge, LA: Louisiana State University Press, 1985), p. 10.
5 Ulysses S. Grant, *Personal Memoirs*, New York: De Capo Press, 1982), p. 129.
6 Michael C. Adams, *Our Masters the Rebels: Speculations on Union Military Failure in the East, 1861-1865*, (Cambridge, MA: Harvard University Press, 1978), p. 30.
7 Francis A. Lord, *They Fought for the Union*, (New York: Bonanza Books, 1960), p. 96.
8 Richard A. Baumgartner and Larry M. Strayer, eds., *Ralsa C. Rice: Yankee Tigers: Through the Civil War with the 125th Ohio*, (Huntington, WV: Blue Acorn Press, 1992), p. 26.
9 Byron R. Abernethy, ed., *Private Elisha Stockwell, Jr. Sees the Civil War*, (Norman: University of Oklahoma Press, 1958), p. 32.
10 Lord, *They Fought for the Union*, p. 27.
11 Leander Stillwell, *The Story of a Common Soldier of Army Life in the Civil War 1861-1865*, (Franklin Hudson Publishing Co., 1920), p. 55.
12 *Yankee Tigers*, p. 28.
13 Jack Coggins, *Arms and Equipment of the Civil War*, (New York: Doubleday & Co., 1962), p. 39.
14 Lord, *They Fought for the Union*, p. 27.
15 Hughes, *The Battle of Belmont*, p. 19.

3
First Fire at Belmont

TOWERING SOME 150 FEET ABOVE THE MISSISSIPPI, THE CONfederate position on the bluffs around Columbus, Kentucky, was formidable indeed. At the bottom of the bluffs was a line of coastal batteries with 10-inch Columbiads and 11-inch howitzers. Halfway up the slope was a second line of batteries. Crowning the heights was a string of earthen forts, one of which contained the largest artillery piece in the entire Confederacy; a 128-pound Whitworth rifled gun known fondly to its crew as the 'Lady Polk'. Polk's position, already referred to as the 'Gibraltar of the Mississippi', contained about 140 guns sited to prevent the passage of any ship in the river, and its defences were manned by a garrison of about 17,000 men. Instead of attacking this formidable position, Grant determined to land on the bank opposite Columbus where he hoped to surprise and capture a smaller Confederate camp.

In support of this effort he mounted an elaborate series of probes and diversions to occupy Confederate attention, and assigned no fewer than seven columns comprising 12,000 men to this task. Grant himself accompanied the force that marched on Belmont where, on 7 November 1861, it landed at Hunter's Farm on the west bank of the Mississippi. The Belmont expedition numbered 3,113 men divided into five infantry regiments, two cavalry companies, and the six-gun Chicago Light Battery.

Because he had 'no staff officer who could be trusted' with the duty, Grant personally led an *ad hoc* battalion of 350 men along the river and so positioned them as to be able to block any enemy thrust against his landing site.[1] Having secured his line of communications, he led the remainder of his force towards the Confederate camp, his two cavalry companies scouting ahead. Meanwhile the timber clad gunboats *Lexington* and *Tyler* manoeuvred at long range in front of the Confederate batteries to divert attention from the land thrust.

Confederate cavalry pickets soon spotted Grant's advancing troops who, pushing on, got to within about two miles of their objective. At 10 a.m. the five infantry regiments managed to deploy though not without a certain amount of confusion. Grant himself had to intervene in order to get one regiment to deploy its skirmishers correctly. He had ordered a colonel to advance his skirmishers, and the colonel selected Company B because its captain was the only one 'who had paid any attention' to skirmisher drill. The captain asked if he should deploy by section, platoon or company. While the perplexed colonel pondered these choices, Grant ordered the captain to deploy his entire company and develop the enemy's line.[2] Meanwhile, under the careful tutelage of Augustus Wentz, the more experienced 7th Iowa managed its deployment successfully without recourse to the commanding general. It meticulously followed the drill book, even to the extent of carefully positioning its ten band members so that there was one man behind each of the ten combat companies ready to assist the wounded to the rear.

None of the green troops knew how they would behave in this their first exposure to battle. Believing firmly in the connection between oratory and war (this much at least the former politicians and lawyers had learned), officers gave short speeches to rouse the troops. One captain told his men that if he '... should show the white feather, shoot me dead in my tracks'. Then the men discarded packs and heavy coats and rolled up their sleeves to prepare for work. Finally the line completed its deployment, shook out its skirmishers, and advanced.

Because the half-mile-long line had to cross a tangle of woods and swamp, the men quickly lost their alignment. They could see little but could hear the 'long roll' coming from the rebel camp. Then the rival skirmish lines engaged and the fight devolved into a disjointed series of small unit actions. Drill was forgotten as many men dispersed behind the available cover and fought 'Indian fashion'. Many of the soldiers used up a tremendous amount of ammunition before they actually saw any enemy troops. Colonel Lauman of the 7th Iowa paused in the heavy timber, listened to the crash of musketry off to his right, raised his sword and shouted to his men, 'There's fighting, boys!' and led his unit towards the sound of the guns.[3]

The five Rebel regiments occupying Belmont had been surprised by Grant's approach. General Gideon Pillow was in command of them, and although he was a high-ranking Mexican War veteran he was no combat leader. As inexperienced as the enemy, the Confederates had managed a disorderly deployment in front of their camp. A back and forth fight ensued in which tangled terrain played havoc with parade ground manoeuvres. Units groped blindly toward an unseen enemy and fired whenever they themselves came under fire. Typical was the experience of Logan's 31st Illinois. Nearing the Confederate line, Logan folded his three skirmisher companies into his battle line, and at a range of about 125 yards opened fire at the enemy's line. From a forested ravine, the rebels returned fire and dropped two company commanders and Logan's horse in the first exchange. Discarding formal drill, Logan ordered his men to lie down and fire while prone. Taking cover behind trees, fallen logs and underbrush, the 31st duelled with the unseen enemy. Recognizing that this was wild, unaimed shooting, Grant sent orders to cease fire to conserve ammunition. In another sector of the field, Colonel Lauman shared Logan's response to enemy fire and had his men lie on the ground to shelter from an enemy

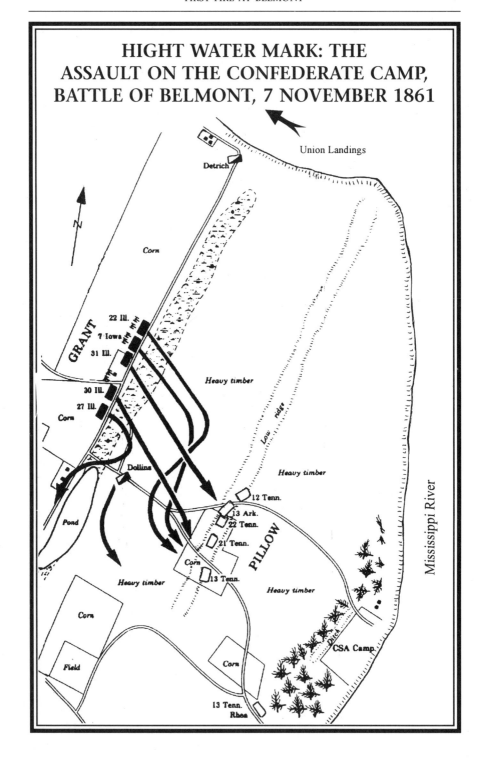

HIGHT WATER MARK: THE ASSAULT ON THE CONFEDERATE CAMP, BATTLE OF BELMONT, 7 NOVEMBER 1861

Union Landings

Detrich

Corn

GRANT

22 Ill.

7 Iowa

31 Ill.

30 Ill.

27 Ill.

Corn

Dollins

Pond

Heavy timber

Heavy timber

Corn

Heavy timber

Corn

Field

Corn

Low ridge

12 Tenn.

13 Ark.
22 Tenn.

21 Tenn.

PILLOW

13 Tenn.

Heavy timber

CSA Camp

13 Tenn.
Rhea

Mississippi River

volley, then crawl forward and when sure of a target get up and fire.

A Confederate artillery battery dominated the action from the middle of the rebel line until Taylor's Chicago Battery, with its four 6-pounders and two 12-pound howitzers, reached the federal position to challenge it. Taylor ordered them into battery 200 yards in front of the infantry line from where it had a short-range opportunity against the Confederate guns. A yankee artillery lieutenant, Patrick White, told his gunners to '... cover themselves the best they could and to fire low and to fire direct at their flash'.[4] Although they fired fast, and some shots told, the green gunners had trouble shooting accurately. In the excitement one gunner rushed to sponge out a tube just as the gun discharged and thereby lost an arm. But after about thirty minutes the Chicago Battery's fire superiority forced the Confederate battery to abandon one gun and withdraw. This retreat marked the collapse of the Confederate line. It was 2 p.m. and Grant's army surged forward to their objective.

The Chicago Battery occupied a commanding knoll a mere 300 yards from the enemy camp. Already demoralized by its retreat, the Confederate infantry wavered under this shelling. Then Grant's infantry charged forward through the abatis surrounding the camp, sending the rebels 'skedunking from their den ... strewing the ground as they went with guns, coats, and canteens'.[5] Had the battle ended there, Belmont would have been a memorable first victory for Grant's Army, but his men fell to celebrating their success, swarming around the camp's flag-pole 'like bees around an overturned hive'.[6] Colonel Lauman led a small force in pursuit of the fleeing rebels only to fall wounded in the thigh, and without his leadership the pursuit fizzled out. Meanwhile, despite Grant's efforts to rally them, the yankees remained a disorderly mob, happy at the thought of victory. Confederate reinforcements began arriving by steamboat from across the river at Columbus, and their timely intervention revitalized the rebel soldiers who launched a counter-attack.

Again the Northern artillery, reinforced by captured brass pieces, formed a canister-firing line which held hard. Its men were tired, one gunner fell to the ground saying 'I'm played out; I must rest if I am shot for it.'[7] One gun crew continued to fire with a mere four men repelled the counter-attack and a lull ensued.

During the next thirty minutes the Union troops cavorted and huzza'd, believing the battle over and won. General McClernand found the sight of a tree stump in the midst of the rebel camp irresistible to his political soul, clambered onto it and delivered an impromptu victory speech. Simultaneously the band played, the men sang patriotic tunes, and fired a volley into the air to celebrate their victory. Soon the ranks dissolved yet more as the men went in search of souvenirs. Only the army's chief doctor retained his composure. He managed to gather most of the wounded at a field hospital and had them brought back to the transports. In hopes of restoring order, Grant ordered the rebel camp burned. This did little good, and when more enemy reinforcements crossed the river he ordered a retreat back to his transports.

The withdrawal threatened to turn into a rout: 'We were demoralized. Officers would call their men to fall in but the men would pay no attention. Every man was trying to save himself, some would throw down their arms and part of a regiment would take one rout [sic] and the other part start another way.'[8]

When Confederate reinforcements threatened the flank of the retreating Union column, disaster seemed imminent. Men began to shout that they were surrounded. Grant responded coolly, telling the men, 'we cut our way in and could cut our way out just as well'.[9] His attitude had a bracing effect. McClernand ordered Logan to place the artillery on a rise from where it could deliver a telling fire against the Confederate line. The rise was devoid of any cover. There Taylor's Chicago Battery took up position and 'opened on them with double shot on top of canister. They could not stand that, so their lines broke; then we limbered up and pushed on and I remember unlimbering again to give them another discharge when a staff officer called on me to hasten and get out.'[10]

Once the artillery had blown a hole in the Confederate line, Logan led his 31st into the breach. Handing the flag to a captain, he told him to carry it to victory or die with it. Then, shouting to the men to follow him and the flag, Logan ordered the charge. Many men recalled how Logan's inspirational presence lifted their morale. During the breakout, 'Black Jack' Logan had his horse shot from under him, his pistol shattered at his side by a bullet, and a third shot nicked his hand. Front line leadership was the norm. McClernand had two shots hit his holster while another struck his pistol. His body servant dismounted to help a wounded officer who had been struck while just next to McClernand. A Confederate officer suddenly appeared to demand his surrender and the servant blew his brains out with a revolver shot.

As the retreat continued, Confederate soldiers fired at the retreating column from the safety of the adjacent woods. It was as easy as shooting deer they later reported. During the retreat, rebel sharpshooters 'spotted' Grant (as they later reported to a Union officer) but were unable to bring down their man. In the long run, however, the deadly enfilade fire took its toll. Grant's chief medical officer had tried to improvise an ambulance train with ammunition wagons, but overwhelmed by the increasing number of wounded and hard pressed by the pursuing rebels, this expedient collapsed and many wounded had to be left behind. Shedding stragglers and some of the captured cannon, Grant's men reached the place where Grant had left his flank guard earlier in the morning. He intended to use this fresh force to cover his embarkation, but to his horror he found that the captain in charge had abandoned the position and returned to the boats. Despondent, Grant said, 'it's no use ... the gunboats must cover our retreat'.[11]

Losing unit cohesion, the survivors rushed to the steamboats. Grant himself had to slide down the bank on his horse and then cross over a single board gang-plank to safety. More than any other army commander during the war, Grant experienced numerous close calls with death. Aboard the transport, he had a second narrow escape. He had returned exhausted, went to the captain's cabin and lay down on a sofa. Roused by the sound of firing, he rose to investigate: 'I had scarcely left when a musket ball entered the room, struck the head of the sofa, passed through it and lodged in the foot.'[12]

Grant survived to see that those men who had managed to board the steamers were trying to cover their comrades by firing from the decks. The Chicago Battery set up a cannon on the deck of one steamer and sent canister whistling into the trees to keep the pursuers at bay. Quite simply, the final stages of Grant's withdrawal had degenerated into a rout and only the presence of the timber clad gunboats saved his force.

Yet Grant refused to see the Battle of Belmont in this light. While steaming back to Cairo, his expedition encountered a boat heading for the action with an eager correspondent aboard. Grant shouted over to him that his men had just won a victory. His attitude changed everything: the fleet's withdrawal became a triumphant victory procession. Union forts along the river fired congratulatory salutes. The entire city of Cairo lit up its lights to greet the returning warriors. At 2 a.m. on the 7th, Grant wired his account of the fight to his superiors:

'We met the rebels about nine o'clock this morning two & half miles from Belmont, drove them step by step into their camp & across the river. We burned their tents & started on our return with all their artillery but for lack of transportation had to leave four pieces in the woods. The rebels recrossed the river & followed in our rear to place of embarkation. Loss heavy on both sides.'[13]

This was a remarkably restrained account, but some of his officers knew better. They wrote that the army had been soundly whipped and that Grant had been at fault. Yet while initial newspaper accounts portrayed a Union defeat, within a week journalists changed their tune and reported a clear victory. Likewise, three days after the battle, President Lincoln sent congratulations to McClernand who, because of his diligent self-promotion, was emerging as the officer who had saved the army from Grant's bungling.

At the Battle of Belmont, Grant's Army lost some 90 killed, 400 wounded (of whom 100 fell into enemy hands), and 100 unwounded men captured. This amounted to 16 per cent of the men engaged. Lauman's 7th Iowa suffered the heaviest regimental losses; 31 killed, 77 wounded, and 114 missing, a loss rate of 43 per cent. During the retreat, the soldiers had discarded most of their equipment, leaving the Confederates happily to glean at least 1,000 rifles, overcoats, knapsacks, two of the Chicago Battery's caissons, the chief surgeon's prized instruments, McClernand's fine iron-framed cot (a curious item to take on a raid deep into enemy territory!) and the commanding general's mess chest and gold pen.

While the Confederates celebrated to the tune of the hastily composed 'Belmont Fast Trot', a song poking fun at the speed of the Federal retreat, they too counted noses and found that their losses were not light. Pillow had about 3,000 men for the fight's duration and another 1,500 joined the battle from across the river at Columbus. Total casualties were 105 killed, 419 wounded, and 117 missing, and two artillery pieces were lost.

The real significance of the Battle of Belmont lay not in the casualties sustained, but rather the impact on those who fought and on the strategic situation in the Mississippi River Valley. Because of Grant's own attitude, the majority of his men recalled the satisfying capture of the rebel camp and forgot about the harrowing retreat to the boats. They had learned that war was a serious business. One sergeant in the 27th Illinois concluded: 'We are not yet veterans only recruits after all.'[14]

Many of the men on the Belmont Expedition would figure prominently in Grant's future:

Colonel Napoleon Buford, 27th Illinois, would rise to brevet Major General and fight at Corinth and Vicksburg where he would be shelved as combat commander.

Colonel Jacob Lauman, 7th Iowa, would become brigade commander at Donelson, fight at Shiloh, and assume divisional command at Vicksburg. Sherman would relieve him when his division suffered heavy loses during the Jackson, Mississippi, campaign.

Colonel John Logan would perform well as brigade, division, and corps commander under Grant and then Sherman.

Brigadier General John McClernand would fight at Donelson and Shiloh, raise a fresh corps in hopes of capturing Vicksburg unaided, and eventually link up with Grant at Vicksburg. There, his constant intriguing would cause Grant to relieve him of command.

Captain Ezra Taylor, Chicago Light Battery, wrote a short, critical after action report. Concerned that his battery had lost two caissons and a baggage wagon, he said: 'The result of the battle is anything but satisfactory to me.'[15] He would fight at Shiloh and Vicksburg, becoming first Sherman's and then McPherson's chief of artillery.

Lieutenant Patrick White, Chicago Light Battery, would become captain of another Chicago battery and win the Medal of Honor at Vicksburg.

Because of Belmont, the Commander-in-Chief, Abraham Lincoln, took note of a hitherto unknown officer named Grant who had

had the fortitude to attack the enemy while most generals found reasons to delay offensive action. Strategically, Grant's thrust at Columbus fixed the attention of the Confederate high command upon the Mississippi River to the exclusion of other potential avenues of federal advance. In the coming months Leonidas Polk would decline to send reinforcements from Columbus to other endangered sectors. Meanwhile Grant gazed elsewhere and saw opportunity on the Tennessee and Cumberland Rivers.

Combat Assessment

Grant: First general to try to co-ordinate with the navy to launch an offensive. Ably conducted advance and capture of Confederate camp and then lost control of army. Calling the battle a victory when other generals would have concluded it was a defeat made all the difference in how his officers and men viewed the action.

Staff: Inadequate in numbers and experience. Totally amateur performance forced Grant to assume multiple duties.

Lieutenants: McClernand behaved well and showed particular understanding of value of artillery. Logan and Lauman excelled.

Infantry: All units responded to inspired personal leadership. Otherwise behaved like the green units they were.

Cavalry: Had a limited role screening the advance and protecting the flank.

Artillery: The Chicago Battery performed magnificently, exhibiting mobile firepower. Key to the battle.

Medical Corps: Lacking ambulances, it proved unequal to the battle's demands.

UNION ORDER OF BATTLE:[16]
Belmont, Missouri, 7 November 1861
Brigadier General Ulysses S. Grant, District of South-east Missouri

First Brigade: Brigadier General John A. McClernand
27th Illinois
30th Illinois
31st Illinois
Dollins' Co. Illinois Cavalry
Delano's Adams County Co. Illinois Cavalry
1st Illinois Light Artillery, Battery B

Second Brigade: Colonel Henry Dougherty
22d Illinois
7th Iowa

Chicago Light Battery
Gunboats *Tyler* and *Lexington*

1   Ulysses S. Grant, *Personal Memoirs* (New York: De Capo Press, 1982), p. 139.
2   Nathaniel C. Hughes, *The Battle of Belmont*, (Chapel Hill: University of North Carolina Press, 1991), p. 86.
3   Hughes, p. 92.
4   Hughes, p. 106.

5 Hughes, p. 119.
6 Hughes, p. 119.
7 Hughes, p. 126.
8 Hughes, pp. 148-149.
9 Grant, *Personal Memoirs*, p. 141.
10 Hughes, p. 152.
11 Hughes, p. 170.
12 Grant, *Personal Memoirs*, p. 143.
13 Ulysses S. Grant, *The Papers of Ulysses S. Grant*, Vol. 3 (Carbondale: Southern Illinois University Press, 1970), p. 128.
14 Hughes, p. 163.
15 *Official Records*, I:3, "Report of Capt. Ezra Taylor," November 8, 1861, p. 290.
16 *Official Records*, I:3, p. 275.

4
River to Victory

AS WAS THE CASE WITH LAND WARFARE, TECHNOLOGICAL advances placed novel demands upon the naval officers of the early 1860s. Rifled artillery, mounted aboard ships and in coastal batteries, offered unprecedented long-range hitting power. At the opposite end of the spectrum, steam-propelled rams provided point-blank lethality. Armour plating rendered obsolete the ships and tactics of earlier times. Riverine warfare along the Mississippi and its tributaries demanded another round of change and innovation. On both sides, naval officers proved much more adaptable than their army peers and thereby avoided the blundering butchery of land battles, and their high degree of skill freed their commanders from the need for detailed supervision of naval warfare.

Combined operations, manoeuvres involving both the army and the navy, are prone to inter-service rivalry and red tape. At the outbreak of the war there were neither formal doctrines nor standard procedures to help overcome these problems. Moreover, a lack of trained professionals resulted in a rather primitive command structure. As a consequence combined operations were particularly inclined to founder at the hands of pettifogging bureaucrats or to collapse in logistical confusion. What was needed were a few dynamic officers with the determination to improvise with the material at hand and to utilize unconventional approaches. Fortunately for Grant's armies, such men were at hand.

After the Battle of Belmont, Grant himself grew in appreciation of the value of naval forces. He benefited from the fact that in the naval arms race along the western rivers, the Federals had a decided edge. Whereas Confederate authorities had to scramble to build even one vessel, Union officials could and did utilize their superior resources to purchase and convert existing boats and to construct new ones. On 16 May 1861 the US Navy sent Commander John Rodgers west, to create a 'brown water navy'. Rodgers purchased three passenger-freight boats and hired a Cincinnati firm to modify them for war. The company lowered the boilers below the deck to protect them from shot and shell, added oak bulwarks, and cut gun ports. From the Navy's Erie, Pennsylvania, depot came ten 8-inch and six 32-pounder smoothbore cannon to equip them. The three: AO *Tyler*, *Lexington* and *Conestoga*, formed the nucleus of the famous 'timberclads' of the Western Flotilla. *Tyler* and

Conestoga campaigned with Grant down the Mississippi to Belmont, and all three would figure prominently in his forthcoming campaigns.

Useful though they were, timberclads could not fight it out with shore batteries mounted behind earthworks. This required a different type of vessel, and naval constructor Samuel A. Pook was equal to the challenge. He collaborated with the chief of the Bureau of Construction and Repair and an experienced civilian steam engineer to design giant ironclads purpose-built for riverine combat. A radical departure from anything previously built, these broad-beamed boats featured sloping armour-plated sides, blackened gunports, and a centre-wheel, twin-engined propulsion system. Their armour was thickest in the bows and stern because it was expected that they would engage bows on to rebel shore batteries and forts. Inventor-engineer James B. Eads of St. Louis won the contract to build the ironclads on the basis of his pledge to complete them in 63 days or less. Eads employed 800 workers who laboured day and night to finish the job. He co-ordinated the work via telegraph, chasing down special machine items, boilers and armour plating.

In the autumn of 1861, Commander Rodgers and an assistant supervised a test to assess the strength of the armour plating. Several sheets of iron plate were firmly bolted to a 16-inch thick oak block and set at a 35 degree angle, the same inclination as the sides of the iron-clads' casemates. At a range of 800 yards, a 10-pound Parrott rifle made a slight dent. At 300 yards it made an indentation one inch thick and loosened the bolts. At 200 yards the artillery piece had the same effect of denting but not cracking the armour. Finally, the testers placed a Parrott a mere 100 yards from its target and stood the armour up at right angles to the gun. Everyone assumed that the Parrott's solid bolt would pierce the armour. Instead, the projectile 'hit fair in the center, knocking the target around out of its place, and shattering the ball in a thousand fragments, many pieces flying back to the gun'.[1] The testers declined to close the range further! Convinced that plate armour could counter at least field artillery, Rodgers ordered Eads to proceed. Soon rolling mills and machine shops from Pittsburgh to St. Louis were turning out the material to construct the so-called City class (they were named after the place of construction; Carondelet, Mound City, Cairo) of ironclads.

Simultaneously, and in sharp contrast, Confederate naval officers were struggling in makeshift dry-docks to fasten railroad iron to cut down, leaky vessels powered by wheezy, unreliable engines. More often than not they failed, usually having to burn their unfinished boats while still on their stocks to prevent them from falling into the hands of the onrushing US Navy. One they did finish, the *Arkansas*, would interfere heroically with Grant's Vicksburg campaign.

In the autumn of 1861, strategists North and South began to focus on the possibilities inherent in the western rivers, particularly the

Cumberland and Tennessee, which cut deep into the Confederate heart-land in western Tennessee. Nowhere was the stereotype of Northern industrial society versus Southern planter society better exemplified than in the efforts of the rival forces to prepare for this riverine campaign. Quickly the North amassed an overwhelming superiority in both battle craft and transports. But it required someone to capitalize on this advantage before its benefits became clear.

The Federal command structure in the West made it difficult for that someone to emerge. Three generals commanded three distinct departments in the West: the Department of Kansas, under Major General David Hunter; the Department of Missouri, under Major General Henry Halleck; and the Department of the Ohio, under Brigadier General Don Carlos Buell, who had replaced one William T. Sherman after Sherman had lost the confidence of Washington authorities. Grant, in Cairo, served in Halleck's domain, but the boundary separating Halleck from Buell was just east of the Cumberland. An offensive down the Tennessee and Cumberland Rivers would inevitably require close co-ordination with Buell. The fact that Halleck and Buell were coequals and that both received orders from Major General George McClellan in Washington meant that such co-ordination would be difficult. By January 1862, there were no less than four separate Union plans for the western theatre. Rather than wait to harmonize theatre operations, Halleck, who had correctly divined that the Confederate forts blocking the Tennessee and Cumberland Rivers were the most important objective, ordered Grant to proceed against Fort Henry. The order nearly cost Grant his life.

Grant believed that gunboats alone could reduce Fort Henry. He planned to use his infantry to cut off the garrison's retreat. The evening of 5 February 1862 found him aboard the ironclad *Cincinnati* as it steamed along the Tennessee. Together with flotilla commander Andrew Foote, he watched closely while sailors hoisted Confederate naval mines from the murky waters of the river. A naval armourer unscrewed a powder cap at one end of the device and a loud sizzling noise ensued. Grant and Foote sprang for the ladder leading to the next deck and collided in their haste. Foote asked Grant, 'General, why this haste?' Referring to Foote's boast that the navy would capture Fort Henry before the army, Grant replied, ' so that the navy may not get ahead of us'.[2] Amidst sheepish laughter, the mine fuze fizzled out and Grant survived the third near lethal incident of his Civil War service.

The next day, while the infantry struggled forward through difficult terrain in an effort to surround Fort Henry, the navy took matters into its own hands and a tough duel ensued between Foote's ironclads and Fort Henry's cannon. For much of the battle the land-based cannon, protected behind 14-foot-thick earthen walls, seemed destined to prove their superiority over the waterborne artillery platform protected by

GRANT'S PERIL

After the capture of Fort Henry on 6 February 1862, a potentially overwhelming force surrounded Grant, comprising: **1**, Polk at Columbus with 17,000; **2**, Fort Donelson garrison of 5,000; **3**, Clark at Hopkinsville with 2,000; **4**, Pillow at Clarksville with 2,000; **5**, Floyd and Buckner at Russelville with 8,000; **6**, Hardee at Bowling Green with 14,000

plate armour. Foote's flagship, the *Cincinnati*, took at least thirty hits. The *Essex* suffered 72 hits, including one 128-pound Columbiad blow that exploded a boiler, scalding the captain and many of the crew. But the Confederates in turn suffered disheartening equipment problems and crew losses, and eighty minutes later the small garrison surrendered, the majority of the defenders having escaped to Fort Donelson before the naval action began. The army's only contribution to the battle occurred when Grant's cavalry pursued Fort Henry's garrison to snap up stragglers along the route to Fort Donelson. Had Grant co-ordinated matters better, his forces would have completed the investment of the fort before the naval attack. Still it was an important victory and gave promise for something more. Foote called it 'A good day's work.'[3] Grant wrote to his wife to announce that the day after tomorrow he would advance on Fort Donelson.

Grant was very 'impatient' to get to Donelson before the rebels could reinforce the fort.[4] He sensed something that was unappreciated by any other Union leader: Federal forces had seized the initiative in the West. In the event, high water, poor logistics, and the need for the fleet to refit prior to tackling Fort Donelson caused a six-day delay before the army could close upon Donelson. Most generals would have been extremely uncomfortable given the situation in which Grant found himself. The fleet departed, leaving a single ironclad to guard the river. Grant's army huddled in crowded, wet terrain with its back against a fast flowing, unfordable river. He was deep in enemy territory and a glance at the map would show how vulnerable was his position. Unperturbed, the general wrote to his sister that the enemy was badly scared and he had no worry about ultimate success. He told a departing newspaper man that he might want to wait around another day or so because the army was going to capture Fort Donelson. The reporter asked whether Grant knew the Confederate strength and the general replied that he did not, but he still thought that he could take the fort. This was U. S. Grant: an aggressive, risk-taking commander not prone to take counsel of his fears.

On 9 February, riding 'Old Jack', a clay bank stallion of fighting mettle, Grant accompanied a cavalry patrol to ascertain the condition of the Telegraph and Ridge roads that led to Fort Donelson. Such preparations for advance alarmed his cautious superior, Henry Halleck. His contribution to the campaign at this point had been to send entrenching tools and reinforcements so that Grant could 'Hold on to Fort Henry at all hazards.'[5]

Grant largely ignored Halleck and prepared for the march on Fort Donelson. His logistical organization was so sparse that he even lacked a quartermaster. Having served in this branch in Mexico, Grant felt confident that he could overcome logistical limitations. In the event, logistics almost undid him. His supply train had to be transported by ship, leaving his men to make do with what they could carry. This amounted to two days' rations in their haversacks and 40 rounds of ammunition in their cartridge boxes. The army was embarking on a mid-winter campaign and had no tents or camp equipment. Grant had requested that the regimental trains be forwarded to Fort Henry, but someone made a mistake and failed to comply. The reinforcements Halleck had sent came downriver by raft and steamer and they too had left their wagons behind. The few wagons on hand trailed the column and hauled an extra three days' rations. The contractors for fresh beef could not procure the transportation to ship the cattle to the army, which forced the men to live off salt meat and contributed to an outbreak of dysentery. Grant ordered that the countryside be scoured for supplies,

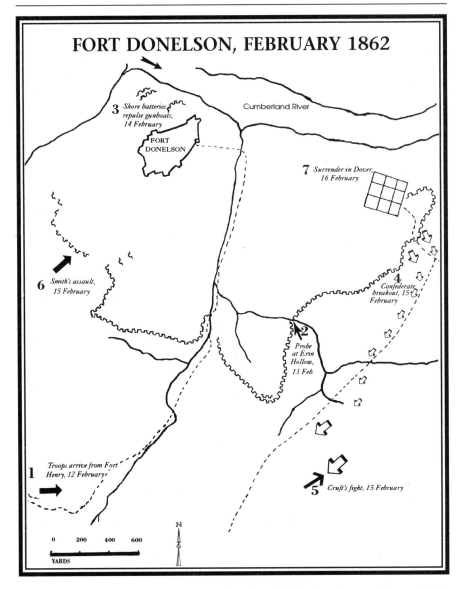

FORT DONELSON, FEBRUARY 1862

3 Shore batteries repulse gunboats, 14 February

Cumberland River

FORT DONELSON

7 Surrender in Dover, 16 February

6 Smith's assault, 15 February

4 Confederate breakout, 15 February

2 Probe at Erin Hollow, 13 Feb.

1 Troops arrive from Fort Henry, 12 February

5 Cruft's fight, 15 February

0   200   400   600

YARDS

N

but this part of Tennessee was a hardscrabble farming region, thinly populated, so there was little to find.

None the less, by 14 February his men had invested Fort Donelson. His army numbered about 25,000 men (eight times more men than he had ever commanded previously) divided into three infantry divisions. Only one of his divisional leaders, McClernand, had served with Grant before. Likewise, all his brigade commanders except Jacob Lauman were new. Included in his army's ranks were three regiments that had fought at Belmont together with Battery B, 1st Illinois Light

Artillery and Dollins' Company of Illinois cavalry. Most of the rest of his force had never seen combat.

Among the reinforcements Halleck had provided for the expedition were 'Birge's Western Sharpshooters'. Wearing distinctive gray coats and gray sugarloaf-shaped hats with three black squirrel tails, these rough-hewn men gave Grant a unique force of sharpshooters. They were armed with Dimmock plains rifles and target rifles of great accuracy. Each man carried a whistle and understood a set of signals to direct movements. In front of the trenches at Fort Donelson, the 'Western Sharpshooters' were in their element amidst the thick forest and brush as they stalked the Confederate defenders. They advanced through the cover like Indians and 'wanted no better fun than to creep through the underbrush and pick off the Rebels'. This was not a risk-free activity however. Confederate cavalry colonel Nathan Bedford Forrest borrowed a Maynard rifle to drop one of Birge's men from his treetop sharpshooter's perch.

The Union troops investing the fort spent several miserable nights. Many had discarded their blankets during the warm day, and when the weather changed found themselves utterly unprepared. A soldier in the 12th Iowa wrote to his mother: 'Just as we halted it commenced raining and we huddled down as best we could, one of the boys and my self got down on a bunch of wet leaves and covered our blankets over us. But had not laid very long before the rain abaited [sic] and it grew cold and it commenced snowing – I tell you it was cold. I shaked like I had the ague if not worse.'[6] Exposure to the elements was one of the major factors that contributed to the terrible non-battle attrition that whittled away the ranks of the Civil War fighting men. For Grant's western army, the bad weather at Fort Donelson marks the beginning of a steady attrition that would claim thousands.

While Grant tightened his embrace of Fort Donelson, he waited for the navy to repeat its Fort Henry performance. Donelson was different. Its outer line of field fortifications overlooked rugged terrain featuring steep slopes and wooded ravines. The fort itself was a 15-acre structure built to protect a coastal battery that interdicted the Cumberland River. The rebels had carved artillery positions into the bluffs. Confederate gunners from various field batteries and an infantry detachment from a Tennessee regiment had volunteered to serve the coastal battery guns. Their accurate fire badly battered Foote's four ironclads on the 14th, forcing them to withdraw for repairs. The losses suffered by the navy during its victory at Fort Henry and its drubbing before Fort Donelson put a brake on the infantry's willingness to serve aboard gunboats and ironclads. Always short of crews, hitherto the navy had appealed to the army for men. Grant's soldiers, sensing a chance to escape the infantryman's lot of hard marches and uncomfortable encampments, volunteered enthusiastically, but news of the fearful carnage a ricocheting cannonball could wreak inside an iron casemate and of the scald burns inflicted by a pierced steam drum curtailed this enthusiasm for service afloat. It also caused Grant to revise his plans. He realized that if the fort was to be taken, it would have to be taken by the infantry.

He entrusted the task to his most experienced unit. McClernand tested the defences by advancing up the Erin Hollow, a ravine on the south-eastern sector of Fort Donelson's outer line of works that bisected the Confederate perimeter. To defend this sector, Confederate engineers had designed artillery redoubts to enfilade any advance through the hollow, thereby turning a weakness into a killing ground. So it proved when McClernand's assault collapsed against the cleverly configured works. With this repulse, and the failure of the gunboats, Grant reluctantly decided to begin siege operations, but the Confederates struck first.

The fort's commander – an inept officer named General John B. Floyd – had decided to stage a breakout by switching most of his 15,000 men to Grant's right flank to deliver a surprise assault along the Forge Road. Meanwhile, McClernand, whose division stood in the path of the planned Confederate attack, reported that his own right flank was within 400 yards of an impassable water obstacle. Grant paid no attention and allowed this dangling flank to go unattended.

At daybreak on the 15th, the Confederates attacked the open flank and after several hours of hard combat, much of it at ranges as close as thirty yards, the attackers forced McClernand's division from its position. Losses were heavy as typified by the 8th Illinois Volunteer Infantry of Oglesby's Brigade. The regiment's Company C comprised 99 country boys, volunteers all, half of whom were under 22 years of age and only eight of whom were over 30 years of age. Two of the volunteers were foreign born, an Irishman and an Englishman. Although belonging to an Illinois regiment, only 36 men had been born in the state. The balance came from eleven other states including fifteen men who hailed from the South. Three out of every four listed farming as their occupation. Sixty-seven of 78 privates were unmarried. All in all, Company C was much like many midwestern units raised from rural areas. So devastating was its first exposure to combat, that when an officer called roll on the morning after the battle, only seventeen men answered the call.

McClernand's shattered division withdrew before the rebel onslaught, and reinforcements failed to restore the line. A soldier in 12th Illinois recalls that the near rout of the federal forces angered his commander Colonel John McArthur. Scottish-born McArthur had come to America at the age of 23. Trained as a blacksmith, he was a classic American success story. A self-made man, he parlayed his iron-working skill first to become a foundry foreman and then to start up his own manufacturing plant. At the age of 35 he volunteered for war, becoming colonel of his regiment. Accustomed to success brought on by hard work, what he saw in his first battle at Fort Donelson infuriated him: 'Colonel McArthur was very mad, very angry. He said it [the retreat of the 41st Regiment] was because of their cowardly officers.'

Meanwhile, farther to the left, the men in the adjacent units also wondered what was happening to McClernand's division. A major of the 12th Iowa reported: 'The men of this division had heard the terrible roar of the conflict ... had listened with bated breath and clasped musket waiting orders which would send them to the help of their comrades.'[7]

The reason for the hesitation and confusion became apparent when messengers arrived at Grant's headquarters to report the Confederate attack and found the general absent. He was off consulting Foote about how best to coordinate with the next naval attack. Worse, Grant had left no one at headquarters to control matters until his return. Left to their own devices, some officers performed better than others. On his own initiative, General Lew Wallace dispatched Cruft's Brigade, the 25th Kentucky and 44th Indiana, towards the sounds of McClernand's fight. They arrived in time to buttress McClernand's wavering line, but in the smoky confusion delivered their first volleys into several Illinois regiments. Soon the entire line collapsed carrying Cruft's men along with them. The Confederates had achieved their breakout.

So far, command confusion had plagued the yankee defence. Now it beset both armies. On the Confederate side, most of the army stood still while officers wondered what to do to capitalize on their success. Cavalryman Bedford Forrest was not hampered by such indecision. Co-operating closely with the most advanced Confederate units, Forrest led his troopers forward in a charge against the flank of the 11th Illinois. Countering him was Colonel Thomas Ransom, an officer who would rise far in Grant's esteem. Ransom led a desperate defence featuring vicious hand-to-hand fighting and the capture and recapture of the 11th's regimental and national Colours several times. Finally Ransom fell wounded and his regiment collapsed under the weight of Forrest's combined arms assault. Colonel John Logan's 31st Illinois, veterans of the fight at Belmont, stood next in line. With its flank exposed, the 31st began to break despite the former politician's pretty words: 'suffer death men, but disgrace never, stand firm'.[8]

The attackers continued onward, striking a small earthen redan defended by the 24-pound howitzers of McAllister's Battery E, 1st Illinois Artillery. Again Forrest used his cavalry to take the position in flank and rear while the superb Confederate 2d Kentucky Infantry attacked the redan from the front. By 1 p.m. Grant's crisis was at hand. McClernand's division was no longer an effective fighting force. Many men were out of ammunition. At this stage in the war their officers had not learned how to keep a continuous flow of ammunition arriving at the front. Having expended what was in their cartridge boxes, the volunteers figured they had performed their duty and could honorably retire.

Thus the Federal right flank was nothing more than a crowd of broken, dispirited men. It was, recalled one soldier, 'a stampede'. Grant's aide, Captain John Rawlins, encountered the flying bluecoats and watched as a bareheaded officer galloped by shouting 'we're cut to pieces'. Only the restraining presence of General Lew Wallace prevented Rawlins from drawing his pistol and shooting the distraught officer.

Indeed, amidst great confusion Lew Wallace was keeping his balance. On his own initiative he had already sent two brigades to the imperilled flank, and now he sent another: Thayer's brigade supported by the six-gun Battery A, 1st Illinois Light Artillery, the famous Chicago Board of Trade battery. Attorney John Thayer had always had a keen interest in military matters. He was a relative of Sylvanus Thayer, the 'Father of the Military Academy' at West Point. He had seen combat against the plains Indians, experience acquired when serving as the first brigadier general of the Nebraska Territory Militia. When the Civil War began the men of the 1st Nebraska Regiment naturally elected Thayer to be their colonel. Colonel Thayer led his raw brigade through a throng of dispirited soldiers of McClernand's command, and took a position on the slope of a wooded hill where he could block a further Confederate advance against the Union flank. Thick undergrowth channelled any potential attack on to the Wynn's Ferry Road. Here, Thayer stationed his artillery battery. Joining them were some welcome reinforcements, two guns of Taylor's Illinois Battery (the heroes of Belmont) that Wallace had sent galloping along the Wynn's Ferry Road to provide some veteran steadiness. To the artillery's left stood one company of the 32d Illinois. Next to this company were the 58th Ohio. The 1st Nebraska were on the battery's right, with the 58th Illinois completing the front line farther to the right. Skirmishers linked this line with McClernand's survivors. Lying down in close support, 50 yards behind the first line, were the 76th Ohio. Farther back along the road were the 46th and 57th Illinois Regiments massed in columns of companies. The 68th Ohio deployed at right angles to this line, guarding against any surprise attack from the direction of Fort Donelson.

Using slightly overblown language (after all he was to write *Ben Hur!*), Lew Wallace relates how, 'Scarcely had this formation been made when the enemy attacked, coming up the road and through the shrubs and trees on both sides of it, and making the battery and the First Nebraska the principal points of attack. They met the storm, no man flinching, and their fire was terrible. To say they did well is not enough. Their conduct was splendid.'[9] For the next 45 minutes, Thayer's brigade repulsed three determined rebel attacks. The Confederate breakout attempt had shot its bolt.

In contrast to Lew Wallace's commendable initiative was C. F. Smith's performance. Smith's division remained inert until about 1 p.m. when Grant finally returned to the battlefield. Only after receiving a direct order did Smith dispatch reinforcements to the embattled Union right flank. Grant then rode on to Lew Wallace's position where he found the soldiers standing anxiously in small knots, talking excitedly, and reporting that they were getting short of ammunition. Grant observed that there were ample supplies all around. The problem was that the officers seemed incapable of directing events. Grant overheard some men saying that the rebels had attacked with filled knapsacks and haversacks, and this alerted him to the possibility that the enemy was intending to break out. Assessing the situation, Grant ordered his chief of staff to spread the word that the enemy was trying to escape and that the Union soldiers must refill their cartridge boxes and block this attempt. As had been the case after Belmont, Grant refused to describe the situation as rout and defeat. Instead he defined it as the enemy's last desperate effort to flee. It was the perfect tonic to restore confidence. He then rode off to organize a counter-attack. Grant confided to an aide that his men seemed badly demoralized but that the enemy must be badly disorganized as well. Victory, he said, would go to whomever attacked next, and the enemy 'will have to hurry if he gets ahead of me'.[10]

Surmising that the enemy had stripped their own right to attack his right flank, Grant ordered C. F. Smith to assault the works to his front. This was to prove the key decision of the day.

The 60-year-old Smith had once been a West Point instructor. Among his cadets was a middling, lazy student named Grant. Now he proceeded to show his former cadet how a West Point man should perform by organizing his attack carefully and cleverly. He feinted with Cook's small brigade while launching his main effort with Lauman's larger one. Riding to his favourite regiment, the 2d Iowa, Smith explained that the regiment must take the fort and he would lead them. Smith impressed his green troops with his veteran aplomb. Said one volunteer: 'He could ride along a line of volunteers in the regulation uniform of a brigadier general, plume, chapeau, epaulets, and all without exciting laughter.' Another soldier who was facing fire for the first time took comfort from Smith's presence: 'I was scared to death, but I saw the old man's white moustache over his shoulder and went on.' Smith was not entirely happy with the conduct of his men. During the advance he said: 'Damn you, gentlemen, I see skulkers, I'll have none here. Come on, you volunteers, come on. This is your chance. You volunteered to be killed for love of country and now you can be!'[11]

Storming forward, the yankee attackers confronted a mere three battalions armed with double-barrelled shotguns. To the inexperienced attackers, the defender's fire seemed 'galling', 'murderous' and 'destructive'. Voltaire Paine Twombly, a native of Van Buren County, Iowa, had volunteered as a private in the 2d Iowa when Lincoln issued his first call. By the time of Donelson, he had risen to the rank of corporal. During the advance against the rebel rifle pits he saw three Colour-bearers shot down. Twombly seized the Colour and was almost immediately knocked down by a spent ball. He stood up and bore the Colours for the remainder of the fight, thereby winning the Congressional Medal of Honor. Twombly would rise to captain during four years of service that included Shiloh, Corinth and the Atlanta Campaign.

From General Smith to Corporal Twombly, the 2d Iowa received inspired leadership during its assault. Even the regiment's badly wounded major encouraged the troops as he was carried to the rear by shouting, 'Forward my brave boys! We will gain the fort yet!'[12] Spearheaded by the impetuous charge of the 2d Iowa, Lauman's brigade overran the badly outnumbered defenders.Smith pressed forward, ran into Confederate reserves, and was stopped cold. His men fell back to the captured trenches, counted noses – they had lost 357 killed and wounded – and congratulated themselves on what they had accomplished. 'Right gallantly', said Smith, 'was the duty performed.'[13] By 3 p.m. Fort Donelson's outer defences were in Grant's hands.

At about the same time Lew Wallace followed Grant's orders to retake the Union right. Just as Smith had relied upon the 2d Iowa, so Wallace put his faith in the 11th Indiana Regiment. This had been his own command, and he had given them zouave training. Asking the 11th if they were ready, they replied 'Let 'er rip!' Reminding them to use their special training, Wallace led them to the attack. They fought in loose order, creeping along the ground when the enemy's fire was hottest, lying on their backs to load, and charging forward when the enemy fire slackened. Rapidly Wallace's counter-attack regained the lost ground, supported by a squadron of regular cavalry armed with breech-loading Sharps carbines. So, by the narrowest margin, and aided immeasurably by Confederate command indecision, Grant's army held the line at Fort Donelson. The next day the garrison commander asked for terms:

> Headquarters, Fort Donelson
> February 16, 1862
>
> To Brigadier-General U. S. Grant,
> Com'ding U. S. Forces.
> Near Fort Donelson.
> Sir: In consideration of all the circumstances governing the present situation of affairs at this station, I propose to the Commanding Officer of the Federal forces the appointment of Commissioners to agree upon terms of capitulation of the forces and fort under my command, and in that suggest an armistice until 12 o'clock to-day.
>
> I am, sir, very respectfully,
> Your ob't se'v't,
> S. B. Buckner,
> Brig. Gen. C. S. A.

Advised by his former teacher, General Smith, Grant replied:

Headquarters Army in the Field
Camp near Donelson,

General S. B. Buckner,   February 16, 1862
Confederate Army.
Sir: Yours of this date, proposing armistice and appointment
of Commissioners to settle terms of capitulation, is just
received. No terms except an unconditional and immediate
surrender can be accepted. I propose to move immediately
upon your works.

I am, sir, very respectfully,
Your ob't se'v't,
U. S. Grant,
Brig. Gen.

When Buckner agreed to capitulate, Federal troops moved to occupy the fort. Pride of place went to Colonel Lauman's brigade and the 2d Iowa. Lauman had asked Smith to have the honour of entering the works first and the old general agreed. Led by the 2d Iowa's band and Colour-bearers, his brigade marched past the 'woebegone' looking Confederates to the fort itself where the 2d Iowa planted their 'colors upon the battlements beside the white of the enemy'.[14] It was a proud moment for a great fighting regiment.

Grant rode to meet Buckner at a hotel in the small town of Dover. Although he did not know it, this was the first of three surrenders he would negotiate during the war. In spite of his harsh sounding words, according to Buckner, Grant treated him kindly and politely. The two had been old comrades and they fell to talking. Buckner told Grant that had he been in command, he would never have allowed the yankees to make an unopposed approach on Donelson. Grant replied that had Buckner been in command, he would not have tried it the way he did. Grant then expressed regret that Buckner's superior, General Gideon Pillow – an officer whom he had known in Mexico – had escaped capture: 'If I had captured him, I would have turned him loose. I would rather have him in command of you fellows than as a prisoner.'[15] Joking aside, Grant's accurate assessment of his opponent had been crucial to his conduct of the campaign.

Grant ended the interview with a magnanimous gesture. Back in 1854 Grant had arrived in New York City from the West Coast nearly penniless. He had appealed to his friend, Captain Buckner, who had lent Grant money for room and board. Remembering this incident, Grant said to Buckner, 'You are, I know, separated from your people, and perhaps you need funds; my purse is at your disposal.'[16]

Grant's Army captured about 16,500 men, fourteen heavy guns and 43 field pieces, and a large quantity of supplies at Fort Donelson.

Because of lax security and poor staff work (things got so out of hand that Buckner proffered the use of his own staff to sort matters out), many prisoners escaped to Nashville by simply walking through the porous Union lines. By July 1862, most of the rebels captured at Donelson had been exchanged. They returned South to encounter substantial pressure to re-enlist. By the autumn of 1862 many were back in the ranks and some were holding the line in northern Mississippi against Grant's Army.

After the surrender, in addition to coping with the influx of prisoners, Grant's medical corps had to cope with the wounded, a task that completely overwhelmed them. Grant's Army had travelled light, which meant that ambulances, tents and medical chests had not kept up with the advance. Regulations specified one medical officer per regiment. This officer was supposed to establish a field hospital just behind the battle line. Two-wheeled ambulances, intended to transport the wounded to the field hospitals, proved practically useless. Worse, there was nowhere to accommodate the wounded once the surgeons at the field hospitals had completed their bloody work. There were only a handful of rude farmhouses inside the Federal line, so the wounded had to survive outdoors, on the ground, but at least the diligent medical staff could put hay and straw for bedding, build fires to warm them, and serve tea, coffee and soup.

The wounded men's plight worsened as they travelled farther to the rear. A healthy soldier of the 11th Indiana Zouaves likened the inadequate river transports to 'an open car loaded with hogs in bad weather going to market'.[17] It was a nightmare-like journey for the 1,700 yankee and 1,000 rebel wounded who sailed north aboard these craft. A doctor of the Western Sanitary Commission reported that the men's condition was deplorable with neither clean bandages nor clothes, nor extra blankets. Inadequate rations consisted of cornmeal gruel, hard bread, and bacon. Once the wounded had dispersed to the friendly river towns along the Ohio and Mississippi Rivers, they received much better care from nurses belonging to various religious orders and from concerned citizens. But even so they were victims of the indifferent skills of the surgeons. One mistreated lieutenant had his fractured thigh-bone set to a contraption of hinged splints and brass rivets that dug into his flesh. His kindly physician told him, 'You are in a very precarious condition, and it all depends upon your constitution, and your ability to bear up under treatment.'[18] Given the poor nutrition provided aboard the transports and the crude state of surgical art, this was asking a great deal of a man who had given his all for the cause.

The entirely inadequate provision for the wounded gave birth to a fleet of hospital steamers. In the future, private humanitarian groups would charter and equip these vessels and, together with official government hospital boats, they would partially redress the mistakes exposed during the Fort Henry and Fort Donelson campaign.

The capture of Fort Henry and Fort Donelson had been stupendous achievements. Grant had taken a raw army of men who had little idea about warfare, and, accompanied by only three other West Point officers, taken them deep into enemy territory. The rewards for this boldness were considerable, both for Grant personally and for the cause. Most people overlooked the fact that the navy had captured Fort Henry. Instead, success redounded upon Grant's shoulders. For example, in distant Virginia, General George Meade wrote to his wife, 'Is not the news from Tennessee glorious.'[19] Meade proceeded to explain the great strategical possibilities flowing from Grant's capture of Fort Henry. Grant's success also marked the beginning of a rivalry between western armies and the Army of the Potomac. Meade observed that many people began to ask: 'Why cannot you do in Virginia what has been done in Tennessee?' He feared such talk would spur the eastern army into a premature offensive.

Grant's victory projected him to national status. Throughout the nation people read about his exploits. Newspapers trumpeted that his initials 'U. S.' stood for 'Unconditional Surrender'. The Lincoln administration rewarded his success by promoting him to Major General of Volunteers, which was not bad for a man who had been nearly unemployable in the preceding summer.

There was a substantial cloud on the horizon in the form of Henry Halleck. Upon learning of the fall of Fort Donelson, Halleck wired General-in-Chief McClellan asking for supreme command in the West 'in return for Forts Henry and Donelson'.[20] Here was clearly an ambitious officer eager to take credit for Grant's successes. Halleck proceeded to send his congratulations to a variety of subordinates but sent not a word to Grant. On 11 March 1862 Halleck got what he was looking for, a theatre command entitled the 'Department of the Mississippi'.

Meanwhile, Grant himself was not content merely to capture Fort Donelson. Then and thereafter he sensed a great opportunity. He reflected in his *Memoirs* that had there been unity of action, Federal forces could have marched to Chattanooga, Corinth, Memphis, and Vicksburg with the forces they had already in the field. Capture of these strategic points would have stimulated Northern recruiting and deprived the South of thousands of conscripts from the south-western states who were unenthusiastic about the war. Instead, the North had to pay in blood for each of these cities while Southern conscript officers were able to enlist the region's able-bodied men and thereby prolong the war.

In the event, Grant notified his superiors that unless he received orders to the contrary he proposed to take Clarksville, Tennessee, and march on Nashville. Here again the Grant Way shines through the muddle and indecision that characterized the North's first three years of war planning. In the absence of restraining orders, he would continue his offensive. Ignoring departmental boundaries, Grant followed up his success by advancing on Nashville, a very important city for the Southern war effort. Many Federal commanders recognized its value, but again it was Grant who did something about it. His impetuosity landed him in trouble with the pedantic General Halleck.

None the less, the capture of Forts Henry and Donelson had entirely changed the strategic chessboard in the West. By bluff alone, Confederate General Albert Sydney Johnson had held the long line from the mountains west to the Mississippi River. His aggressive stance had immobilized a much larger Union force. Halleck had conceptually understood what the United States forces ought to do, but it had been Grant who had seen through Johnson's bluff and decided to act by driving a wedge into the Confederate position. This wedge caused Johnson's entire line to collapse. Emboldened by Grant's success, other Federal forces under such cautious commanders as Buell and Halleck suddenly surged forward. Grant had seized the initiative in the West, and despite temporary setbacks, was never to lose it.

The fighting at Fort Donelson also had enormous consequences for the men who made up Grant's Army. Many of the regimental and brigade commanders continued to serve with Grant and would rise to positions of great importance. Their shared experience was a key to their future effectiveness. The growing familiarity among Grant and his lieutenants would help at Shiloh, Vicksburg and beyond. Within the ranks, the battle changed the eager volunteer into a more cynical veteran. One Illinois soldier wrote home that he and his comrades were no longer spoiling for a fight, 'they have seen the fun they were so anxious to see, and are satisfied'. He noted that when a steamboat passed by with new troops, the 'green hands' cheered loudly, something the 'old troops' no longer did.[21] Having faced the enemy's fire and triumphed, they felt like veterans: 'I have heard some men say', recalled an Iowa soldier, 'that they felt a little affraid [sic] the first fire but fils [sic] just as cool as I do now'.[22] The Iowa soldier had identified the beginning of a tradition of victory that was arising among Grant's Westerners.

Combat Assessment

Grant: Commanding a force eight times larger than ever before, he gave a mixed performance. Better coordination with the navy would have bagged the Fort Henry garrison. Careless security on the night of 15 February almost jeopardized the entire campaign. He would have done well to have followed Napoleon's advice: namely, consider what would I do if the enemy unexpectedly appeared on my left, on my right, or in my rear. Napoleon cautioned that if a commander cannot readily meet such eventualities, his dispositions are false. Still, Grant launched an offensive when most generals would have delayed, and in battle on 15 February his moral courage won out where many would have faltered. In sum, Grant is still learning his trade.

Staff: Another wretched performance. His staff is not worthy of the name as indicated by the collapse of command and control both when Grant rides off to visit the navy on 15 February and after the surrender when it fails to supervise the enemy prisoners, thus allowing many to escape.

Lieutenants: McClernand fails to ensure flank security; Smith is inert until receiving positive orders and then proves the man of the hour; Wallace gives a fine performance; Admiral Foote gives exemplary support.

Infantry:

The green soldiers fight surprisingly well.

Cavalry: Not yet adequately armed and still dispersed in penny packets.

Artillery: Limited opportunities, but the Illinois Light Artillery provides fine service when it faces flank during Wallace's stand.

Medical Corps: Overwhelmed by the carnage.

UNION FLEET AT FORT HENRY, TENNESSEE,[23] 6 February 1862
Flag Officer Andrew H. Foote

First Division

Cincinnati (flagship): six 32-pounder, three 8-inch, four rifled army 42-pounder, one 12-pounder boat howitzer

Essex: one 32-pounder, three 11-inch, one 10-inch, one 12-pounder boat howitzer

Carondelet: same armament as *Cincinnati*

St. Louis: seven 32-pounder, two 8-inch, four rifled 42-pounder, one rifled boat howitzer

Second Division

Conestoga: four 32-pounder

Tyler: one 32-pounder, six 8-inch

Lexington: two 32-pounder, four 8-inch

UNION ORDER OF BATTLE:
Fort Donelson, Tennessee,[24] 12–16 February 1862
Brigadier General Ulysses S. Grant, District of Cairo

First Division: Brigadier General John A. McClernand*

FIRST BRIGADE: Colonel Richard J. Oglesby

8th Illinois
18th Illinois
29th Illinois
30th Illinois*
31st Illinois*
Illinois Light Artillery, Batt. A
  (B&L says 2d ILA, Batt. D)
2d Illinois Light Artillery, Batt. E
2d Illinois Cavalry, Cos. A and B
2d US Cavalry, Co. C

4th US Cavalry, Co. I
Carmichael's Illinois cavalry
Dollins' Co. Illinois cavalry*
O'Harnett's Illinois cavalry
Stewart's Illinois cavalry
  (B&L says King's IC)

SECOND BRIGADE:
Colonel William H. L. Wallace
11th Illinois
20th Illinois
45th Illinois
48th Illinois
1st Illinois Light Artillery, Batt. B*
1st Illinois Light Artillery, Batt. D

4th Illinois Cavalry
THIRD BRIGADE: Colonel William R. Morrison; Colonel Leonard F. Ross
17th Illinois
49th Illinois

Second Division:
Brigadier General Charles F. Smith
FIRST BRIGADE:
Colonel John McArthur
9th Illinois
12th Illinois
41st Illinois
THIRD BRIGADE:
Colonel John Cook
7th Illinois
50th Illinois
52d Indiana
12th Iowa
13th Missouri
1st Missouri Light Artillery, Batt. D
1st Missouri Light Artillery, Batt. H
1st Missouri Light Artillery, Batt. K
FOURTH BRIGADE:
Colonel Jacob G. Lauman*
25th Indiana
2d Iowa
7th Iowa*
14th Iowa
Birge's Missouri Sharpshooters
FIFTH BRIGADE:
Colonel Morgan L. Smith
8th Missouri
11th Indiana

Third Division: Brigadier General Lewis Wallace
FIRST BRIGADE:
Colonel Charles Cruft
31st Indiana
44th Indiana
17th Kentucky
25th Kentucky
SECOND BRIGADE:
att. to 3d brigade under Thayer
46th Illinois
57th Illinois
58th Illinois
20th Ohio
THIRD BRIGADE:
Colonel John M. Thayer
1st Nebraska
58th Ohio
68th Ohio
76th Ohio
NOT BRIGADED
1st Illinois Light Artillery, Batt. A
32d Illinois, Co. A

Vessels: Flag Officer Andrew H. Foote
St. Louis (flagship)
Carondelet
Louisville: six 32-pounder, three 8-inch, four rifled 42-pounder, one 12-pounder boat howitzer
Pittsburgh: six 32-pounder, three 8-inch, four rifled 42-pounder
Tyler
Conestoga

* Belmont veterans

1   Edwin C. Bearss, *Hardluck Ironclad: The Sinking and Salvage of the Cairo*, (Baton Rouge: Louisiana State University Press, 1966), p. 25.
2   Benjamin Franklin Cooling, *Forts Henry and Donelson: The Key to the Confederate Heartland* (Knoxville: The University of Tennessee Press, 1987), p. 100.
3   Cooling, p. 111.
4   Ulysses S. Grant, *Personal Memoirs* (New York: De Capo Press, 1982), p. 152.
5   Cooling, p. 116.
6   Letter of Charles Sackett, 12th Iowa Infantry, Archives, Fort Donelson National Battlefield.
7   Archives, Fort Donelson National Battlefield.
8   Cooling, p. 175.
9   Thayer's dispositions are in his after action report, *Official Records*, I:7, p. 252. Lew Wallace's report is on pp. 236-240.
10 Grant, *Personal Memoirs*, p.157.
11 Quotations regarding Smith are from markers at the Fort Donelson National Battlefield.

12 Letter of Daniel P. Donnell, Archives, Fort Donelson National Battlefield.
13 Cooling, p. 185.
14 Edwin C. Bearss, *Unconditional Surrender: The Fall of Fort Donelson*, (Eastern National Park and Monument Assoc., 1991), p. 29.
15 Bearss, *Unconditional Surrender*, p. 35.
16 Bearss, *Unconditional Surrender*, p. 39.
17 Cooling, p. 252.
18 Cooling, p. 255.
19 George Meade, *The Life and Letters of George Gordon Meade*, vol. 1 (New York: Charles Scribner's Sons, 1913), p. 245.
20 Bearss, *Unconditional Surrender*, p. 45.
21 Cooling, p. 252.
22 Letter of Charles Sackett, 12th Iowa Infantry, Archives, Fort Donelson National Battlefield.
23 *Battles and Leaders of the Civil War*, Vol. I (New York: Thomas Yoseloff, 1956), p. 362.
24 *Official Records*, I:7, pp. 167-169.

5
Shiloh:
The Painful Lessons

PART 1. ARMY ORGANIZATION

On 4 March 1862, Major General Halleck relieved Grant of command because of alleged neglect and inefficiency. Grant's senior divisional commander, General C. F. Smith, replaced him and began a march south from Fort Donelson in the direction of the important rail hub of Corinth, Mississippi. As Smith advanced along the Tennessee River he called upon a newly raised division under the command of William T. Sherman to raid downstream to cut the Memphis and Charleston Railroad. Foiled by torrential rains, Sherman returned downstream and landed at the first place above water. Located on the western bank of the Tennessee River, its name was Pittsburgh Landing. About four miles further south was a small place of worship known as Shiloh Church. The ground from the landing to this church was soon to be the scene of a terrible battle.

Fortunately for the army, Halleck's coup against the only Union general who had won a major victory failed when he ran up against a higher authority. President Lincoln had heard that Halleck had relieved Grant, and was not about to lose his best (and at this point in the war apparently his only) fighting general. Halleck was ordered to provide the Army Adjutant General with detailed, specific information about the basis for his decision to relieve Grant. Halleck quickly backed down and wrote to Grant: 'Instead of relieving you, I wish you as soon as your new army is in the field to assume the immediate command and lead it on to new victories.'[1] Halleck also managed to fool Grant into thinking that someone else had tried to take his command away and that he, Halleck, had interceded on his behalf!

With characteristic energy, Grant began forwarding troops to the camps about Pittsburgh Landing. If the battle at Fort Donelson had proven anything, it was that the soldiers badly needed instruction and discipline. So he and his chief lieutenant, Sherman, set about building the Army of the Tennessee.

Infantry Organization

When someone asked a Civil War soldier what unit he belonged to he replied by naming his regiment. Soldiers took pride in their regiment and the regiment, in turn, was the fundamental tactical entity on the battlefield. Regular Army regiments comprised three battalions, one of which served as a depot unit. Regular battalions had eight companies, each having an authorized strength of 100 men. In contrast, the volunteer regiments which made up the preponderance of the Federal fighting force had no battalion structure. Instead they featured ten companies (a legacy of the nation's British military heritage) with overall command exercised by a colonel, lieutenant colonel, and major. A captain commanded each company, supported by a first and a second lieutenant, one first sergeant, four sergeants, and eight corporals. Eighty-two privates stood at the bottom of the totem pole. An average volunteer regiment went to the front with about 1,000 men, but attrition quickly reduced strengths to 200 to 300 men. The volunteer regiment's ten companies were lettered according to their captain's seniority. Again in keeping with British tradition, two companies – A and B – served as semi-élite flank companies. Company A had pride of place on the right, since this was the position that would meet danger first when the regiment marched by the right flank. Company B stood on the left flank. Often, especially early in the war, the flank companies received superior weapons and performed hazardous duties.

No duty was more hazardous than that of carrying the Colours. Each regiment's Colour guard composed non-commissioned officers chosen for their courage. When the regiment formed line, the Colour guard stood in the centre. By regulation they carried two Colours; the Stars and Stripes and the solid blue national flag. Informally, many regiments carried a third state banner. Whether on defence or attack, the Colour guard was the target of enemy fire.

First of all, when the initial volleys had shrouded the battlefield in smoke, the flags towered above and were often the only thing that could be seen by men engaged in a firefight. The Colours were visible evidence showing where an enemy regiment was aligned. In such circumstances, unable to see individual targets, everyone blazed away in the general direction of the flags. This fact, coupled with the great prestige associated with capturing an enemy Colour, caused a tremendous weight of hot lead to be directed at the Colour-bearers. Likewise during an assault, the marksmen among a defending line would target the Colour-bearers. In a typical letter describing an action fought at a range of 100 feet, a captain describes how his men went about 'picking out the Colours first' as they shredded an attacking regiment.[2] It was all too common for an assault to feature a succession of Colour-bearers felled by enemy fire, but there was never a lack of volunteers to carry the Colour.

Picked non-commissioned officers served as the Colour guard. Given their brief life expectancy, the wisdom of assigning the best corporals and sergeants – the backbone of a regiment – to this position of greatest danger is questionable. Much like duty with a forlorn hope in times past, service with the Colour guard did offer the possibility of rapid advancement if one survived. A Wisconsin private relates the altogether typical story of a Colour sergeant remarking on the eve of battle,

'I'll come out a dead sergeant or a live lieutenant.' This sergeant, although repeatedly knocked down by enemy fire, held onto his flag although it was covered with his own blood and shredded by hostile fire. The private concluded that indeed the sergeant 'came out the live field lieutenant' but he was 'a cripple for life'.[3]

The Civil War was the last American conflict in which music played a prominent role on the battlefield. The War Department authorized regular companies to have two musicians (typically a fifer and drummer) while the regiment as a whole possessed a drum major, two principal musicians, and 24 band members. Each company in a volunteer regiment had a drummer and fifer, while at the regimental level there was a drum major, fife major, and 24 band members. This made for an impressive musical presence in camp and, when the band members were not serving as stretcher-bearers and surgeon's assistants, a morale boosting battlefield presence. But to cold-eyed clerks in the War Department, the bands were an expensive waste of manpower. On 27 July 1862, the War Department ordered that regimental bands be discontinued in favour of drummers and fifers. Henceforth only larger formations could have a band.

To provide medical care, each regular battalion had one hospital steward. Volunteer regiments had one surgeon and one assistant surgeon appointed by the governors of the states. Here was another fine opportunity to dispense political patronage. Far too many medical practitioners serving in the volunteer ranks were former country physicians with little practical experience and no knowledge of military medical administration or battlefield surgery. Each brigade had a brigade surgeon who frequently ran the general hospitals in the larger cities or served in field hospitals while on campaign. If he were talented, or politically well-connected, this man could advance to become 'medical director' of a division or corps. At this level he served on the staff of a general. If asked, he could provide general information about the health of the command and offer guidance about camp sanitation and hygiene.

During the war's earliest battles, the regiment was the largest tactical entity. As we have seen, at the Battle of Belmont individual regiments operated with little regard to one another. As armies grew larger, the need for higher levels of organization became apparent. Soon the brigade became the smallest tactical unit capable of independent operation. Four or five regiments composed a brigade. Nominally, a brigadier general led a brigade, but the practice of leading from the front produced such heavy losses that many colonels actually commanded a brigade in combat. Reflecting the systematic formality of the eastern armies, brigades were numbered serially within their division. In the West, the brigades were numbered without reference to their divisional structure. By 1863, all Federal armies had assumed a uniform organization. Also by War Department order, and unlike the Confederate practice, there was no effort to create brigades composing regiments from the same state. Because of the high turnover in brigade leadership and the presence of regiments from different states, there was little brigade-wide *esprit de corps* in the Federal service.

On 3 August 1861, the War Department decreed that three brigades would form a division and each division would be led by a major general. Few yankee soldiers felt any strong attachment to the particular division in which their regiment served. The divisional structure greatly eased the general's problems of command and control. Thus we saw Grant at Fort Donelson no longer concerned with individual regiments, but thinking in terms of divisions. Even the divisional structure was soon subsumed by the higher organization of the army corps. McClellan introduced the corps to the Army of the Potomac in March 1862. As with everything else, the western armies were much slower to adapt to modern practice. Western generals including Grant did not adopt the corps structure until October 1862. Thus Grant fought the Battle of Shiloh as a divisional battle. From a practical standpoint, this meant that he had to express his desires through five divisional commanders. Had he been in the East, his army would have composed two corps. On the Shiloh battlefield this made a great difference. The existence of five basically independent divisional commands impaired coordination. One division might hold hard while the two adjacent divisions would (and did!) retreat and thus expose the tenacious division to attack in flank. Instead, if the divisions had been bound by a corps level attachment, there would have been greater harmony of manoeuvre.

The corps structure never caught hold in the West to the extent that it did in the more sophisticated East. As early as 1862, many eastern soldiers took pride in their corps, particularly if they belonged to a formation like the Army of the Potomac's Second Corps, a renowned fighting formation. Regardless of the theatre, most corps featured three divisions. Senior major generals commanded the Federal army's corps. They had a staff of lieutenant-colonels assigned to the duties of Assistant Adjutant General, Quartermaster, Commissary of Subsistence, and Assistant Inspector General. In addition, each corps commander had a major and two captains as aides-de-camp, positions appointed by the President based upon the corps commander's recommendations and confirmed by the Senate. In 1862, the Federal army organized infantry corps that numbered one to eighteen. In 1863 it added corps nineteen to twenty-three, and in 1864 completed the task with corps twenty-four and twenty-five. The twenty-fifth corps was a Negro unit.

To promote corps-wide spirit, the Army of the Potomac began the practice of issuing corps badges, which were generally worn on the cap or left side of the hat. When, in 1863, two corps went west to Chattanooga, the western soldiers saw the corps symbol emblazoned on virtually everything capable of holding an image including wagons, tents and ammunition boxes. Legend has it that one eastern soldier asked a westerner what his corps badge was and the westerner slapped his cartridge box and replied, 'this is my corps badge'. In any event, the Fifteenth Army Corps did adopt the cartridge box with its inscription 'Forty Rounds' as its corps badge. Soon all the western corps had followed this eastern practice.

Two or more corps formed an army (again, this was the theory and was more applicable during the early war to the eastern armies) commanded by a major general. Assisting him were regular army officers serving as Chiefs of Cavalry, Artillery, Engineers and Topographical Engineers. An Assistant Adjutant General handled the business of keeping records. An Inspector General was in charge of army discipline and training and, curiously, supervised picket and outpost duties. Often this officer also took over intelligence duties. Army commanders nominated their own aides-de-camp.

Because divisional, corps and army commanders were almost always major generals, there was a great deal of command friction caused by questions of seniority. Frequently qualified officers refused assignment because they perceived that they would be forced to serve under an officer whom they believed they outranked. Further clouding the issue was the question of rank in the old pre-war army. In addition, there was often little love lost between West Point-educated regular officers and volunteers who had risen to general's rank. Thrown into the mix were the political generals who earned their appointments not because of their military prowess but thanks to their political connections. These factors, plus simple jealousy, combined all too often to inhibit battlefield performance.

Once the organizational kinks had been worked out, the Federal forces that campaigned to crush the rebellion were reasonably modern entities. They did not compare in professionalism to Europe's standing armies, particularly in regard to the composition of their staffs. But this lack of military professionalism reflected the fact that the America of the 1860s was not nearly as warlike as its European peers.

Cavalry Organization
Napoleon had taught the world how to wield a combined arms force that included a formidable shock assault cavalry. For geographical reasons, the United States had never featured a prominent cavalry arm. When the Civil War began, the Federal government had the First and Second Dragoons, First Mounted Rifles, and the First and Second Cavalry Regiments in service. Each of these units had ten companies. In May 1861, a newly raised cavalry regiment of twelve companies joined the regular service. In the autumn of that year, the dragoons and mounted rifles were renamed as cavalry regiments with a minimum strength of 997 and a maximum strength of 1,189 men. From May 1861 the War Department reluctantly began to tolerate the creation of volunteer cavalry regiments of average initial strength of 1,200 men.

Regular cavalry regiments had three battalions of two squadrons each. Two companies made up a squadron. By regulation, each company included a captain, first lieutenant, second lieutenant, first sergeant, a company quartermaster sergeant, four sergeants, eight corporals, two musicians (usually buglers) two farriers, a saddler, a wagoner, and 56 privates. The fact that twelve sergeants and corporals were deemed necessary to manage 56 cavalry privates (the same number of non-commissioned officers who controlled 82 infantry privates) indicates that the authorities recognized that mounted men required more control than their foot-slogging brethren. The battalion featured 316 company officers and men, plus a major, an adjutant, quartermaster/commissary lieutenant, sergeant major, quartermaster sergeant, commissary sergeant, hospital steward, saddler sergeant, and a veterinary sergeant giving a total minimum strength of 325 men. The regiment added a colonel, lieutenant colonel, adjutant, quartermaster and commissary lieutenant, two chief buglers, and a 16-man band.

The volunteer regiments consisted of four to six squadrons, each of two companies. Except for the absence of the battalion structure, the internal composition of the volunteer regiments was much the same as in the regular service. During the entire war, a total of 258 cavalry regiments and 170 independent cavalry companies served in the Federal service.

Artillery Organization

The basic field artillery unit was the battery. Its minimum authorized composition included a captain, first lieutenant, second lieutenant, first sergeant, company quartermaster sergeant, four sergeants, eight corporals, two musicians, two artificers, one wagoner, and 58 privates. The authorities recognized that the artillery, being the most technical of the three branches, needed a greater proportion of non-commissioned officer control than did the infantry. A field artillery battery had four or six artillery tubes, these being a mix of guns and howitzers.

Regular artillery regiments consisted of eight to twelve batteries, each having a minimum of 80 and a maximum of 156 officers and men. Volunteer artillery regiments had a 12-battery organization, each battery having 144 officers and men. Heavy artillery regiments had the same organization as the field artillery except in the substitution of the term company for battery. For both the field and heavy artillery, the regimental structure was purely an administrative convention. The Regular United States Army provided nineteen batteries for the war. The volunteer service contributed 1,647 batteries.

PART 2. 'NOT BEATEN YET BY A DAMN SIGHT'

During the second half of March 1862, the Union camps around Pittsburgh Landing had expanded away from the river as additional troops arrived. General Sherman selected the camp sites without consideration of tactical merit, choosing rather sites favoured by proximity to good water and open fields where the men could drill. His superior shared his overconfident attitude.

On the eve of battle, Grant had committed a host of errors that threatened his army's destruction. He had selected his position at Pittsburgh Landing because its road net offered a springboard for a march on the Confederate base at Corinth. He never considered that the reverse was equally true, that Albert Sidney Johnston's army could use the same roads to advance on the yankee army, so he declined to fortify his camps. He had three veteran divisions (commanded by W. H. L. Wallace, Lew Wallace and McClernand) – veterans by the standards of 1862 in that they and their officers had already participated in battle – yet placed his rawest division (Sherman's) closest to the enemy. He maintained his own headquarters nine miles away from the army in the comfortable town of Savannah, and neglected to nominate any divisional general for overall field command, which meant that the divisions would fight without co-ordination. Lastly, neither he nor his lieutenants, particularly Sherman, took routine security precautions including picketing the roads between the Union camps and the enemy. On the night of 5 April Grant telegraphed Halleck, 'I have scarcely the faintest idea of an attack (a general attack) being made upon us.'[4] Quite simply, the rebel assault came as a colossal surprise.

At 6 a.m. on 6 April, forty thousand Confederate soldiers caught the 33,000 ill-prepared Union men in their camps. War correspondent Whitelaw Reid wrote of the attack:

'Some, particularly among our officers, were not yet out of bed. Others were dressing, others washing, others cooking, a few eating their breakfasts. Many guns were unloaded, accoutrements lying pell-mell, ammunition was ill-supplied – in short, the camps were virtually surprised.'

A surviving soldier confirms Reid's account: 'Shells were hurtling through the tents while, before there was time for thought or preparation, there came rushing through the woods the line of battle sweeping the front of the division camps.'[5]

The absence of the commanding general meant that co-operation among the defending generals was haphazard. At dawn an enterprising Missouri colonel named Everett Peabody had conducted a reconnaissance in force and engaged the picket line protecting the Confederate assault force. His initiative bought a precious hour of warning for those defenders wise enough to take advantage, including some of the men belonging to Brigadier General Benjamin Prentiss's division who managed to form up before the attack began. It also brought down upon him the wrath of his commander. Ben Prentiss had attended a military school during his youth and then participated in the campaign against the Mormons during the Mexican War. Thereafter he became an attorney. He spurred to the front and angrily demanded if Peabody had provoked the enemy's attack by his unauthorized mission: 'Colonel Peabody,' shouted Prentiss, 'I will hold your personally responsible for bringing on this engagement.'[6] Here was a man looking for a scapegoat! Yet he was scarcely alone in his inability to understand the gravity of what was taking place.

The previous day, Sherman had received reports of an enemy build-up and had caustically dismissed them, calling the men who furnished these reports 'badly scared'. Although he would claim in both his after-action report and in his *Memoirs* that his division was in line of battle when the Confederates struck, this was not true. An officer in his 53d Ohio relates that the men were attending to their normal Sunday morning duties: 'Officers' servants and company cooks were preparing breakfast, sentinels were pacing their beats, details for brigade guard and fatigue duty were marching to their posts, and ... the sutler shop was open.'[7]

Sherman appeared at his camp line at about 7 a.m. Accompanied by his staff, he calmly gazed through his field glasses at an unknown force some half a mile away. He failed to notice some Confederate skirmishers advancing out of the brush only 50 yards away. A yankee officer shouted to him to look to his right. Turning, Sherman saw a line of riflemen with weapons aimed directly at him. He exclaimed 'My God, we are attacked!'[8] The rebels fired, hitting Sherman in the hand and killing his cavalry orderly. Shouting to a nearby officer, 'Appler, hold your position; I will support you,' Sherman galloped off to organize a defence.

It is revealing to observe how Sherman described this event in his official report. He acknowledges the death of his orderly at 7 a.m. Then he writes, that 'About 8 a.m. I saw the glistening bayonets of heavy masses of infantry to our left front in the woods ... and became satisfied for the first time that the enemy designed a determined attack on our whole camp. All the regiments of my division were then in line of battle at their proper posts.'[9] Thus is official history written!

In the event, Sherman's raw division fought tenaciously at their tent line. Key to the camp's defence was the performance of Captain A. C. Waterhouse's Battery E, 1st Illinois Light Artillery. This battery had been in camp a mere week, had drilled only three times, and had not even had time to break in the horses to their artillery harness. None the less, under the guidance of Sherman's chief of artillery, Battery E took up a commanding position on a slight rise from where its six James rifles controlled the approach to Sherman's camp. Sherman's division managed to hold on until reinforced by McClernand.

On Sherman's left, Prentiss – supported by Steven A. Hurlbut's division – likewise experienced the shock of the surprise Confederate assault. The 61st Illinois had only been in service for two months and had never seen combat. At about 7.30 a.m. a wild-eyed officer rode through camp on a foam-flecked horse. Halting abruptly, knocking over mess tins in the process, he shouted, 'My God! This regiment's not in line yet! They have been fighting on the right for over an hour!'[10] Hastily the scared men strapped on their equipment and prepared for battle. Private Leander Stillwell describes waiting at his camp as the attackers approached. Although his comrades were firing (disregarding orders, they had begun firing at long range as soon as they saw the first enemy soldiers) Stillwell was an experienced hunter accustomed to husbanding his ammunition until a good shot presented itself.

'... the Confederates halted and began firing also, and the fronts of both lines were at once shrouded in smoke. I had my gun at the ready, and was trying to peer under the smoke in order to get a sight of our enemies. Suddenly I heard some one in a highly excited tone calling to me just in my rear – "Stillwell! shoot! shoot! Why don't you shoot?"'[11]

Obeying his wildly excited lieutenant, Stillwell blazed away through the smoke, all the while doubting he could possibly hit anything. The volume of unaimed fire astonished him. The return fire passing overhead sounded like a swarm of bees. The defenders dispersed behind whatever cover was available. Soon Stillwell saw his first dead soldier:

'There was a man just on my right behind a tree of generous proportions, and I somewhat envied him. He was actively engaged in loading and firing ... But, all at once, there he was lying on his back, at the foot of his tree, with one leg doubled under him, motionless – and stone dead! ... The event came nearer completely upsetting me than anything else that occurred during the battle – but I got used to such incidents in the course of the day.'[12]

Whereas Stillwell and the majority of the surprised yankees held their ground at first contact, hundreds of others fled to the rear. By 9 a.m. the federal forces had ceded their first line.

Where was Grant? As had been the case at Donelson, he was absent from the field during the first hours of the enemy attack. He abandoned his breakfast at his sumptuous headquarters in Savannah and reached the field at about 8.30 a.m. During his steamboat journey to the scene of the fight he passed Crump's Landing where he alerted Lew Wallace's detached division. Disembarking at Pittsburgh Landing he organized a straggler line to roust out the faint-hearted soldiers who had fled to the shelter of the steep bank along the Tennessee and then rode forward to see his lieutenants.

He found Sherman coolly directing his defence on the Union right. Reassured by Sherman's conduct, he left him pretty much alone for the rest of the engagement. Grant's troubles rested along his centre and left centre. Whenever heavy enemy pressure forced one of his divisions to retire, it exposed the flanks of the adjacent divisions. They in turn would retreat, and this pattern of progressive withdrawals threatened to cause the collapse of the entire line. There was a hidden advantage to the manner in which Grant's divisions had been dispersed in their camps. A system of unfordable creeks and rivers narrowed the front, limited manoeuvre, and thus favoured the defender. The manner in which the Union divisional camps were stacked from Pittsburgh Landing outward, gave the yankees a natural series of defensive positions to which they could retire. Thus, inadvertently the army had a layered defence (a defence in depth). Secondly, in this war the normal response for inexperienced troops and their commanders in battle was to march to the sound of the guns. For the Confederates, this meant packing the front with massed targets and taking losses. For the Federals, it often meant reinforcing a wavering line just when it needed help. Thus the battle featured Confederate assaults against a succession of backstopping positions, and this process took the starch out of the rebel effort.

But none of this would have been of any consequence had not Grant's men fought hard. Grant himself laboured mightily to restore a line parallel to the original position along the Purdy–Hamburg Road and sent word to both Lew Wallace and Brigadier General William Nelson (of Buell's army) to hurry to the field. But the lack of cohesion among his divisions threatened to undo this effort. The battle hinged on what became known as the 'Hornets' Nest', a sunken farm lane blocking a direct Confederate thrust to Pittsburgh Landing. Grant ordered Prentiss to 'maintain that position [the Hornets' Nest] at all hazards'.[13] One of the units on which both commanders had to depend was Battery A, 1st Illinois Light Artillery. The battery historian recalls:

'Sunday morning, April 6, 1862, dawned upon us clear, warm, and bright ... Our camp was up and astir at the usual early hour. The postilions had taken the horses to drink in a creek near by, and were letting them nibble at the new grass on their way back to camp. [The battery was immobilized when the battle began.] The sound of skirmish firing suddenly was heard and in short order the crack of musketry and the booming of artillery followed. We knew this meant business. [The battery had been engaged at Fort Donelson and thus was combat experienced.] ... numbers of wounded began passing our camp, reporting their regiments "all cut to pieces". We ridiculed them and shamed some of them to turning back to the front ... We were put in a position as a reserve, and began to receive a severe shelling which we could not return. Two horses were killed under their riders, and brave, handsome Sergeant Jerry Powell had his right arm taken off by a shell ... [The battery was receiving effective long-range counter-battery fire.] We were soon moved forward ... and opened fire on the rebel battery that had been firing at us, and, after some fifteen minutes of lively firing with solid shot and shell, we silenced it completely ...[Batteries often believed they had 'silenced' an opposing battery; frequently this was erroneous. The target battery would either cease fire to avoid wasting ammunition in a long-range duel or switch to a different target. However, in this case Battery A did cause its foe to displace.]

'We were getting short of ammunition. The infantry supporting us had been lying in the hollow, now charged forward with a yell. They delivered one volley which was returned with terrible effect, causing them to fall back. [Here was classic Civil War defensive tactics. Much like Wellington's Army in the Napoleonic Wars, infantry often relied upon a close-range volley fired from concealed ground, followed by an instant bayonet attack. Unlike Wellington's foe, the attacker was usually in line and thus could return the fire effectively. Typically, it was during these counter-attacks and ensuing short-range firefights that the defender suffered the heaviest losses.] This gave the rebels courage, and they made a charge for our guns ... we continued firing as long as prudence allowed, and then limbered up and fell back to a new line ... Here, after a short fight, we were obliged a second time to fall back. In this stand we suffered severely. [This was the action at the Hornets' Nest.]

'Our infantry support was all broken up into squads and were fighting desperately, while we were firing solid shots and a few shells, having exhausted our cannister [*sic*] ... the enemy had succeeded in turning our left, and on they came from front and left flank, in solid line to scoop us in. Then Lieut. Wood's voice rang out clear and strong, "Limber to the rear, Get your guns out of this."'[14]

During the withdrawal the battery suffered fearfully from point-blank Confederate fire (the writer notes that he could plainly see the attackers' brass buttons). Initially only four of the six pieces could withdraw; losses among horses and men temporarily immobilized the other two guns. One gun squad lost five of seven men and all but one horse within seconds. Men from the other guns rallied to try to haul this gun to the rear. The surviving horse balked until hit by a bullet which prodded it into motion. The battery later participated in the last ditch defence at the landing where it went into battery next to the siege guns.

In sum, during the first day of battle the battery engaged for eight hard hours and performed exceptionally well. It fired 838 rounds and lost four men killed outright, 26 wounded including several mortally, and 48 horses killed or disabled, without losing a single gun or man taken prisoner.

As Grant understood matters, his battlefield task reduced itself to surviving until reinforcements arrived. He did not know that the anticipated reinforcements from Wallace and Buell would not arrive in time to save him. Whatever could be done would come from the efforts of the five divisions that had begun the battle. In the face of disaster, Grant maintained his composure. He remembered the experience at Fort Donelson, where the Confederate assault had disrupted the attacker as much as the defender. If here at Shiloh the Federal force could hold on, he believed that tomorrow they could counter-attack and win the battle.

Although badly battered, Sherman and McClernand managed to retire slowly to a pre-selected final position along the Hamburg–Savannah Road, inflicting heavy losses on the attacker during this process. At about 3 p.m. heavy Confederate assaults accomplished exactly what Sidney Johnston had planned, the crumbling of the Union left flank. The two left-flank Federal brigades under Colonel David Stuart and Brigadier General John McArthur had fought a lonely battle against overwhelming numbers. Along this front the 9th Illinois suffered 365 casualties, a loss rate of 59 per cent and the highest sustained by any Federal unit during the battle. But here as elsewhere it was the same story of disjointed, uncoordinated resistance leading to defeat in detail. When the two brigades retreated all the way back to the landing, a marvellous opportunity for the rebels to cut behind Grant's line and destroy his army emerged. The lack of Confederate reserves coupled with the confusion stemming from Johnston's mortal wounding prevented southern exploitation.

Instead, for five hours some twelve separate rebel assaults struck the Hornets' Nest which was easily the best defensive position along any part of Grant's line. An Illinois marksman describes the action here. He could clearly see a Confederate Colour-bearer some 200 yards distant waving a large flag. He carefully aimed his musket and fired. The marksman ducked under the smoke to see if he had hit his target, 'but the blamed thing was still flying'. He fired four more careful rounds and still could not drop his target. Concluding that the enemy must be sheltered behind a stump, he shifted his aim to a diagonal battle line 250 yards from his position. Because of a breeze that dispersed the smoke:

'The Confederate line of battle was in plain sight. It was in the open, in the edge of an old field ... It afforded a splendid mark. Even the ramrods could be seen flashing in the air, as the men, while in the act of loading, drew and returned the rammers.'[15]

'There was a battery of light artillery on this line, about a quarter mile to our right, on a slight elevation of the ground. It was right flush up with the infantry line of battle, and oh, how those artillery men handled their guns! It seemed to me that there was the roar of a cannon from that battery about every other second. When ramming cartridge, I sometimes glanced in that direction. The men were big fellows, stripped to the waist, their white skins flashing in the sunlight, and they were working like I have seen men doing when fighting a big fire in the woods.'[16]

Supported on his left by Hurlbut and on his right by W. H. L. Wallace, Prentiss's solid artillery and infantry line repulsed all attacks. Along this sector Hurlbut provided sterling combat leadership. Just the previous winter, Sherman had advised the hard-drinking lawyer-politician (another of Lincoln's Illinois Republican cronies) to read and study the art of warfare. Then he had been amused to overhear Hurlbut practising battalion drill in his room with an experienced lieutenant who knew the proper procedure. Sherman listened while Hurlbut worked on the words of command and the proper tone of voice, ordering units to 'Break from the right, to march to the left!' and 'Battalion Halt! Forward into line.'[17] This earnest preparation paid off in the Hornets' Nest. For four hours he rode along his line conducting a determined defence, ignoring a spent musket ball which struck him in the arm, showing a cool indifference to a rifle bullet that hit a tree within a few feet of his head. But there was nothing he could do when the Confederates managed to mass a grand battery of 62 artillery pieces against his position.

This battery was the greatest North American concentration of field artillery to date. It presented a stupendous arc of fire from rising ground overlooking the Hornets' Nest and pinned the defenders to the ground. To an officer in the 2d Iowa (the regiment that had gallantly stormed Fort Donelson's outer works), the bombardment was '... like a mighty hurricane sweeping everything before it'.[18] But still the yankees held their ground. During this fighting, one regiment – the 44th Indiana Volunteers, a Fort Donelson veteran unit serving in Jacob Lauman's brigade – lost seven Colour-bearers and one officer and 33 men killed; six officers and 171 men wounded of the total strength of 478 men.

Along the left flank of the Hornets' Nest position 'Black Jack' Logan's 32d Illinois Volunteers were heavily engaged. The regiment had already helped repel the Confederate frontal attacks when Hurlbut ordered then out of line and sent them to buttress the imperilled left flank. Logan arrived at his new position and, together with another Illinois regiment, the 28th, beat off a Confederate frontal attack. But he had no support on his own left flank and the rebels began manoeuvring to envelop him. Logan faced one company to flank, and then disaster struck. For no apparent reason the 28th broke and fled, leaving Logan's right flank exposed as well. 'Black Jack' rode along his front to steady his men, who responded by continuing to fire until they ran out of ammunition (the series of improvised Union defensive positions had played havoc with any effort to provide a regular flow of ammunition to the fighting regiments). Hearing that they were out of cartridges, he ordered them to 'Fix bayonets!', being determined, as he later wrote, 'to fight them in every way possible'.[19] Outflanked left and right, attacked in the centre, Logan at last gave the order to retreat, but not until the charging rebels were within forty feet of his position. He was the last man to retire and received a serious shoulder wound as he withdrew.

Logan's defeat on Prentiss's left and the retreat of Sherman and McClernand on his right left the defenders of the Hornets' Nest isolated and vulnerable. The Confederates who had been engaging McClernand and Sherman changed face to bore in against this position and shortly after 4 p.m. the majority of the Confederate army had surrounded the Hornets' Nest defenders. W. H. L. Wallace tried to cut his way out and managed to extricate some of his men but fell mortally wounded. For the remainder, some 2,200 men, there was no choice but to surrender.

Earlier in the afternoon, Grant's chief of staff, Colonel Joseph Webster, had received his permission to prepare a last-ditch position on a steep ridge overlooking the Dill Branch. By the time Prentiss surrendered, Webster had collected some fifty artillery pieces to form this last position. Anchoring it was a battery of 32-pound siege guns that had been brought to Pittsburgh Landing in the optimistic belief that they would be needed to batter Confederate entrenchments at Corinth. About 4,000 semi-organized infantry from a variety of commands supported the gun line. After a day of punishment and retreat, it required considerable valor even to attempt to hold the line. 'The most trying situation in battle', wrote a soldier who was there, 'is one where you have to lie flat on the ground, under fire ... without any opportunity to return it.'[20] The strain was almost intolerable and a last hard push might have overcome this position.

Thousands of officers and men thronged to safety below the crest of the riverbank behind the gun line. Some officers rode among these dispirited troops in a vain effort to rally them. When Nelson arrived in the van of his division at dusk, he rode through the packed crowd waving his hat and shouting 'Fall in, boys, fall in and follow me! We shall whip them yet!'[21] Finding that his entreaty was to of no avail, Nelson set to with the flat of his sword, but nothing could force the badly frightened men back into the ranks. They had seen terrible slaughter up close and wanted nothing more to do with it.

But the attackers themselves were much fatigued and badly hurt. The terrain they had to surmount, the Dill Branch, was a rugged ravine, steep and wooded. The physical stamina needed to attack at this point was enormous. In the event, a piecemeal attack did strike the Dill Branch position at nightfall, only to collapse against the heavy artillery fire and the enfilade fire from the gunboats *Tyler* and *Lexington*. Simultaneously Nelson's reinforcements reached the field. By the narrowest margin, Grant's army had survived.

Grant himself observed the last Confederate charge, chewing a cigar 'imperturbably' according to an eye-witness, even while a cannon shot beheaded one of his staff ten feet away.[22] Another staffer saw him gazing toward the retiring Confederates while speaking, as if to himself. Uncertain, the staffer rode closer and heard Grant mutter, 'Not beaten yet by a damn sight!'[23]

That night was a testing time for the battered men of Grant's army. At Pittsburgh Landing, regimental bands played throughout most of the long, rainy hours of darkness in an effort to hearten and rally the hundreds of dispirited soldiers sheltering along the river bank. Repeatedly they played the popular ballad 'The Girl I Left Behind Me'. The fighting soldiers had altered the last stanza:

> 'If ever I get through this war,
>   And a Rebel ball don't find me,
>   I'll shape my course by the northern star,
>   To the girl I left behind me.'

Overnight, the balance of Buell's Army together with Lew Wallace's fresh division joined Grant's men. Recalling the lesson of Fort Donelson, Grant reasoned that here too the side that struck first would gain a great morale advantage. When young James McPherson of his staff asked whether he intended to retreat, Grant replied decisively, 'No! I propose to attack at daylight and whip them.'[24] However, his own fatigue and the army's confused alignment kept him from issuing specific instructions for the attack. Nor did he go to meet Buell who had arrived at Pittsburgh Landing and was supervising the disembarkation of his own army. Buell was contemptuous that the Army of the Tennessee was apparently a defeated force, and made no effort to see Grant, even though he was planning an offensive of his own.

On the morning of 7 April, re-envigored by the presence of these 25,000 reinforcements, the yankees pushed forward all along the line. It was not a well co-ordinated advance. Grant and Buell's failure to communicate with each other resulted in a disjointed series of divisional attacks. Grant moved about the battlefield to inspire his men, and even appeared in a few places where he did not belong.

General Buell's signals officer, Lieutenant Joseph Hinman, had established a signal station on a rise from where he could transmit Buell's orders, but stragglers kept obstructing his line of sight and he got an infantry detachment to clear them away. Peering through his telescope he became furious when all he could see was a pair of cavalry boots. 'Git out of the way there! Ain't you got no sense?' He saw through his lens the offending boots approach and a voice say, 'I am very sorry. Please accept my apology. You were perfectly right in reprimanding me.'[25] The figure departed and to Hinman's amazement he made out first the shoulder-straps of a major general, and then the face of General Ulysses S. Grant.

Later, while he was reconnoitring in front of his troops, hidden enemy artillery and riflemen opened a brisk fire at Grant and the two staff officers who were with him. The three rode rapidly for shelter. In the brief flurry of fire a bullet mortally wounded one staffer's horse and another struck Grant's sword scabbard. This was his fourth close call of the war.

Most of the fresh troops who were engaged on the second day at Shiloh had never been in action before. They repeated the mistakes of the previous day. One of Wallace's men, Private Elisha Stockwell, described how on taking his place on the firing line he had been ordered not to begin firing until his regiment's skirmishers had cleared the front. Stockwell had to grab his adjacent comrade's musket to prevent him firing prematurely. Then:

'We were ordered to fire, and as soon as I let go of Ned's gun, he stuck it up in the air, shut both eyes, and fired at the tree tops [at battle's end soldiers examined Ned's musket and found it half full of cartridges with the balls put in upside down] ... Schnider did the same. But

Schnider was in rear rank and behind Curly [the company bully] and he cut a lock of Curly's hair off just above the ear, and burned his neck. I thought Curly was going to strike him with his gun. He told him, "You might have killed me." And Schnider said, "Makes me not much difference, I not like you very well anyhow."'

After enduring a barrage, the waiting out of which proved harder than fighting, Stockwell reports, the regiment received orders to charge:

'We were going down hill when someone hit me in the back with his bayonet quite severely [the men were advancing in two-deep line] ... I turned around to give him a piece of my mind, but there lay the poor fellow shot in the forehead ... I turned and went on. We had lost all formation, and were rushing down the road like a mob [a characteristic of most Civil War charges regardless of the men's level of training and experience] ... We stopped [at a small stream] ... and I got behind a small tree. I could see the little puffs of smoke at the top of the hill on the other side some forty rods [more than 200 yards] from us, and I shot at those puffs. [The assault had collapsed into a medium-range firefight, another typical characteristic of a Civil War charge.] The brush was so thick I couldn't see the Rebs, but loaded and fired at the smoke until a grape shot came through the tree and knocked me flat as I was putting the cap on my gun. I thought my arm was gone, but I rolled on my right side and looked at my arm and couldn't see anything wrong with it, so got to my feet ... and saw the Rebs coming down hill just like we had. [The Confederates were defending their position with the customary tactic of firing and counter-charging.]

'The road was full ... and I shot for the middle of the crowd and began loading. But as they were getting so close, I looked behind me to see what the rest [of the company] were doing. I saw the Colours going out of sight over the hill, and only two of our men in sight. As I started to run, I heard several shout "Halt!" But I knew it was the Rebs, and I hadn't any thought of obeying them.'[26]

Despite such setbacks, the Union armies' weight of numbers held sway. By 2.30 p.m. Johnston's successor, General Beauregard, had ordered a retreat. There was no effective pursuit that day.

Largely because it had been dispersed amid the various infantry commands, Grant's cavalry had had little chance to show what it could do during the 2-day battle. The Union generals had used the cavalry primarily as a provost force to halt the flood of stragglers. A soldier recalled that 'cavalrymen were riding in all directions with sabres drawn and revolvers threatening to shoot and "Cut men's heads off" if they did not stop'.[27] On 8 April, the cavalry received the chance to try their steel on Confederate heads instead. It was an ideal assignment: to pursue a defeated enemy. Sherman led the 4th Illinois Cavalry and two infantry brigades towards Corinth. At a crossroads he paused while the cavalry scouted alternative routes. A half-mile further on, the road ran through a cleared field and then into a 200-yard expanse of fallen timber. Beyond lay a Confederate camp.

Sherman deployed two infantry companies into skirmish formation and ordered them to advance cautiously. The remaining eight companies formed line 100 yards behind to support the skirmishers. Sherman reported: 'Taking it for granted that this disposition would clear the camp, I held Colonel Dickey's Fourth Illinois Cavalry ready for the charge.'[28] But the enemy cavalry charged first!

They were Forrest's men, and cared not a hoot for the fact that Sherman considered the muddy, log-strewn ground unsuitable for cavalry. Led by Forrest in person, the 350 Confederate horsemen broke through the infantry skirmishers and advanced upon the men in line. These infantry of the 77th Ohio were much depleted by two days' fighting and they broke badly, threw away their weapons, and fled. Dickey's cavalry began a nervous carbine fire, but it seemed to make no impression upon Forrest's men. On they came and, after a brief hand-to-hand mêlée, the Illinois cavalry broke as well. Thoroughly alarmed, Sherman sent an aide back to order the entire brigade to form line of battle. Then he and his staff rode for their lives. Behind the shelter of the infantry brigade, Sherman, the 77th Ohio, and the Illinois cavalry reformed. Sherman resumed his cautious advance, occupied the Confederate camp (where he captured some 180 Confederate wounded and freed fifty Union wounded) and went no farther. This was the sum total of the Union 'pursuit' after Shiloh.

Quite evidently, Grant's cavalry were not equal to the opportunity. Sherman had been unwilling to deploy his cavalry in the van, and it had stood passively to receive the shock of Forrest's attack. The blue troopers were not yet battle cavalry.

The Battle of Shiloh had been fought between two raw armies. By and large, given that they were new to their trade, both sides had done extremely well and had displayed a determined stubbornness that typified the western battles during the first three years of the war. The inexperience of officers and men alike, coupled with the difficult terrain, reduced the battle to a series of disjointed frontal charges. The absence of tactical acumen contributed to the heavy losses. Grant and Buell lost about 13,700 men while the Confederates suffered 10,700 casualties. At least one Union soldier expressed surprise that losses had not been heavier. Elisha Stockwell, a 15-year-old private in the 14th Wisconsin Volunteers, whose exploits have just been recounted, had fought bravely during this, his first, battle. He had received two wounds in addition to the accidental bayonet cut from his fallen comrade. After the battle he complained to his company (who had lost about 40 per cent of its strength in its first battle) that he was disappointed so many rebels got away. He had supposed that once a battle began everyone continued firing until all on one side of the other were killed!

Afterwards, Grant lamely defended his decision not to fortify his campsite by saying that 'drill and discipline were worth more to our men than fortifications'.[29] This disingenuously overlooks the fact that his raw troops could have acquired drill and discipline while digging breast-works. The fact was that Grant never for one moment anticipated an enemy strike against his camp. Civilians living behind his lines had reported his failure to fortify to probing Confederate cavalry, and this report helped encourage Johnston to launch his attack.[30] Overconfident, ill-prepared, Grant was most fortunate to win the battle. Had Nelson not gone ahead of Buell's Army and thereby arrived when he did, or had the Confederates not suffered a 24-hour delay during their approach march, or had any number of other seemingly trivial events not occurred, Grant would have been badly defeated with incalculable consequences. Almost certainly defeat at Shiloh would have blocked his subsequent rise. To his credit, Grant learned from the experience. Never again would he make the same mistake. During the Battle of Shiloh much of the command confusion stemmed from the unwieldy division-based organization. Henceforth, Grant's armies would fight within a corps structure.

The men who had fought at Shiloh began to think of themselves as veterans. Simultaneously, the military establishment began imple-menting appropriate measures for what now seemed would be a long war. Individual training remained largely unchanged, except that every-one took it more seriously. Gone were the days when a bored volunteer could shout out to the drill sergeant, 'Let's stop this fooling and go over to the grocery.'[31] The War Department's re-publication of Willard's *System of Target Practice* underscored the seriousness of the Federal war effort. It specified individual firing practice at a man-sized target (6 feet high, 22 inches wide) at 150-yards' range and a platoon-sized target (6 feet high, 264 inches wide) at 1,000 yards' range. In spite of such prac-tice, at best only about one-third of the men in a typical regiment man-aged to hit the target at 150-yards' range.

Soldiers continued to practise company and regimental drill and became much more proficient. But the drill itself remained unrealistic and seldom was there combined arms training. A Wisconsin soldier who served from Shiloh until the end of the war observed that so infrequent were they, that only once did he ever participate in a divisional manoeu-vre. Even with the most professional of the arms, the artillery, training lacked realism. As late as 1864, when drilling in preparation for the com-ing campaign, a gunner noted that his unit practised on dry, flat ground, even though 'Every enlisted man in the army knew that we were to fight in a rugged, wooded country.'[32] Lacking a systematic approach to realistic training, throughout the war most soldiers learned by bitter experience.

How different this all could have been was demonstrated by Colonel William Hazen. Among the units to reinforce Grant at Shiloh was the remarkable 41st Ohio, Hazen's Brigade, Nelson's Division. Probably no volunteer regiment surpassed the 41st in professionalism and this was due to Hazen, who had been its first colonel. A martinet tried and true, who believed that 'one button neglected may lead to the loss of an army', Hazen insisted that when in camp his regiment, and later his entire brigade, be fully occupied with *useful* exercise. He established schools to train both officers and men. Hazen personally conducted officers' drill, which commenced with daily, hour-long lessons in the School of the Soldier and progressed to more sophisticated studies. He divided the officers into small study sections for an additional hour of recitation beginning with Scott's *Infantry Tactics*. Officers recited aloud their lessons while Hazen listened and criticized. Upon becoming brigade commander, he had his instructors keep a written record of each officer's performance, which he used to conduct weekly evaluations. In this way, inefficient officers 'soon made their unfitness evident' and were dismissed.[33]

In addition to their own studies, the officers drilled their soldiers in squads and then progressed to company and battalion drill. So rigid was Hazen's approach that he demanded that battalions march to and from drill in precise platoon or section columns. His demanding discipline extended throughout the regiment. He ordered that regimental chaplains, with the officer of the day and the medical officers, inspect the messes each day to verify that cooking was performed in a sanitary and wholesome manner. Such attention to detail ensured that the 41st Ohio became a crack, fighting regiment. It was one of the few units on the battlefield that delivered volley fire. In many engagements, including an important defence of Thomas's position at Chickamauga, its steady volley firing was heard above the general din of battle.

Had Grant's armies been more professionally inclined, had Grant been more attentive to practical detail, a realistic system of instruction and drill could have been installed. The absence of any formal system to pass on hard-learned tactical lessons doomed too many men to death or maiming.

Combat Assessment

Grant: The most poorly conducted campaign of his career. Very fortunate to win. However, his calm composure and refusal to admit defeat did contribute to victory.

Staff: With the exception of Webster's concentration of the artillery, another extraordinarily amateurish performance. In one typical bit of ineptitude, Grant had to send three staff officers to direct Lew Wallace to march to his relief and Wallace still managed to head in the wrong direction and so fail to reach the field during the battle's first day.

Lieutenants: Woeful pre-battle security. During the battle, the divisional commanders exhibited amazing personal bravery, a must with an inexperienced army. When given a line to hold, they performed well. The need to conduct a fighting withdrawal, a difficult operation for even a veteran force, overtaxed them.

Infantry: Subjected to a surprise shock assault, often fighting with one or both flanks exposed, called upon to retire before a charging enemy, the infantry offered determined resistance. An altogether remarkable performance that is becoming characteristic of the western yankee.

Cavalry: The cavalry fail to provide a security cordon around the camp. Because of unfavourable terrain, Grant breaks his mounted forces into penny packets without regard to regimental or even company attachments, and uses then to intercept stragglers. After the battle, they prove unable to pursue a shattered enemy force.

Artillery: Another fine display of energy and courage. Often the batteries are the tactical key to a defensive position. When massed at the end of the first day, they prove invincible.

Medical Corps: Overwhelmed by the bloodshed.

UNION ORDER OF BATTLE:
Shiloh, Tennessee,[34] 6–7 April 1862
Major General Ulysses S. Grant, Army of the Tennessee

First Division:
Major General John A. McClernand*
FIRST BRIGADE:
Colonel Abraham M. Hare, Colonel
   Marcellus M. Crocker
8th Illinois*
18th Illinois*
11th Iowa
13th Iowa
2d Illinois Light Artillery, Batt. D*
SECOND BRIGADE:
Colonel C. Carroll Marsh
11th Illinois*
20th Illinois*
45th Illinois*
48th Illinois*
THIRD BRIGADE:
Colonel Julius Raith, Lieutenant
   Colonel Enos P. Wood
17th Illinois*
29th Illinois*
43d Illinois
49th Illinois*
Illinois Cavalry Co.
UNATTACHED
Stewart's Co. Illinois Cavalry*
1st Illinois Light Artillery, Batt. A*
2d Illinois Light Artillery, Batt. E*
Ohio Light Artillery, 14th Batt.

Second Division:
Brigadier General William H. L.
   Wallace,* Colonel James M. Tuttle
FIRST BRIGADE:
Colonel James M. Tuttle
2d Iowa*
7th Iowa*
12th Iowa*
14th Iowa*
SECOND BRIGADE:
Brigadier General John McArthur,*
   Colonel Thomas Morton
9th Illinois*
12th Illinois*
13th Missouri*
14th Missouri
81st Ohio
THIRD BRIGADE:
Colonel Thomas W. Sweeny, Colonel
   Silas D. Baldwin
8th Iowa
7th Illinois*
50th Illinois*
52d Illinois
57th Illinois*
58th Illinois*

CAVALRY
2d Illinois, Coys. A and B
2d US, Co. C
4th US, Co. I*

ARTILLERY
1st Illinois Light, Battery A
1st Missouri Light, Batts. D, H, K*

Third Division:
Major General Lewis Wallace*
FIRST BRIGADE:
Colonel Morgan L. Smith*
11th Indiana*
24th Indiana
8th Missouri*
SECOND BRIGADE: Colonel John M.
    Thayer*
23d Indiana
1st Nebraska*
58th Ohio*
68th Ohio*
THIRD BRIGADE:
Colonel Charles Whittlesey
20th Ohio*
56th Ohio
76th Ohio*
78th Ohio
ARTILLERY
Indiana Light, 9th Batt.
1st Missouri Light, Batt. I
CAVALRY
11th Illinois, 3d Bn.
5th Ohio, 3d Bn.

Fourth Division:
Brigadier General Stephen A. Hurlbut
FIRST BRIGADE:
Colonel Nelson G. Williams, Colonel
    Isaac C. Pugh
28th Illinois
32d Illinois*
41st Illinois*
3d Iowa
SECOND BRIGADE:
Colonel James C. Veatch
14th Illinois
15th Illinois
46th Illinois*
25th Indiana*
THIRD BRIGADE:
Brigadier General Jacob G. Lauman*
31st Indiana*
44th Indiana*
17th Kentucky*
25th Kentucky*
CAVALRY
5th Ohio, 1st & 2d Batts.

ARTILLERY
Michigan Light, 2d Batt.
Missouri Light, Mann's Batt.
Ohio Light, 13th Batt.

Fifth Division:
Brigadier General William T. Sherman
FIRST BRIGADE:
Colonel John A. McDowell
40th Illinois
6th Iowa
46th Ohio
Indiana Light Artillery, 6th Batt.
SECOND BRIGADE:
Colonel David Stuart, Lieutenant
        Colonel Oscar Malmborg, Colonel
        T. Kilby Smith
55th Illinois
54th Ohio
71st Ohio
THIRD BRIGADE:
Colonel Jesse Hildebrand
53d Ohio
57th Ohio
77th Ohio
FOURTH BRIGADE:
Colonel Ralph P. Buckland
48th Ohio
70th Ohio
72d Ohio
CAVALRY
4th Illinois, 1st & 2d Battalions
ARTILLERY:
Major Ezra Taylor
1st Illinois Light, Batts. B* and E

Sixth Division:
Brigadier General Benjamin M. Prentiss
FIRST BRIGADE:
Colonel Everett Peabody
12th Michigan
21st Missouri
25th Missouri
16th Wisconsin
SECOND BRIGADE:
Colonel Madison Miller
61st Illinois
16th Iowa
18th Missouri
CAVALRY
11th Illinois (8 companies)
ARTILLERY
Minnesota Light, 1st Batt.

Ohio Light, 5th Batt.
UNATTACHED INFANTRY
15th Iowa
23d Missouri
18th Wisconsin
UNASSIGNED TROOPS
15th Michigan
14th Wisconsin

1st Illinois Light Artillery, Batts. H and I
2d Illinois Light Artillery, Batts. B and F
Ohio Light Artillery, 8th Batt.

*Veterans of previous battles

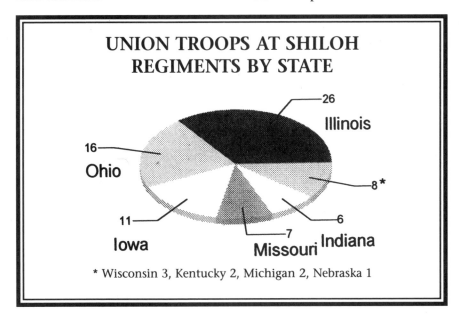

UNION TROOPS AT SHILOH
REGIMENTS BY STATE

26 — Illinois

16 — Ohio

8 *

11 — Iowa

7 — Missouri

6 — Indiana

* Wisconsin 3, Kentucky 2, Michigan 2, Nebraska 1

1 Wiley Sword, *Shiloh: Bloody April*, (Dayton: Morningside Bookshop, 1988), p. 17.
2 Robert Garth Scott, ed., *Fallen Leaves: The Civil War Letters of Major Henry Livermore Abbott*, (Kent, OH: Kent State University Press, 1991. Abbott relates this description in his letter of July 6, 1863.
3 Byron R. Abernethy, ed., *Private Elisha Stockwell, Jr. Sees the Civil War*, (Norman: University of Oklahoma Press, 1958), pp. 48-49.
4 US. Military Academy, *The West Point Atlas of American Wars, Volume I, 1689-1900*, (New York: Frederick A. Praeger Publishers, 1959), Map 33.
5 These quotes are from monument inscriptions at the Shiloh National Military Park.
6 Sword, p. 151.
7 Sword, p. 173.
8 Sword, p. 176
9 Sherman includes his official report in his Memoirs. William Tecumseh Sherman, *Memoirs of General W. T. Sherman*, (New York: Library of America, 1990), p. 256.
10 Sword, p. 155.
11 Leander Stillwell, *The Story of a Common Soldier of Army Life in the Civil War 1861-1865*, (Franklin Hudson Publishing Co., 1920), p. 54.
12 Stillwell, p. 56.
13 *West Point Atlas*, Map 35.
14 Charles B. Kimbell, *History of Battery "A" First Illinois Light Artillery Volunteers*, (Chicago: Cushing Printing Co., 1899), pp. 41-45.
15 Stillwell, p. 60.
16 Stillwell, p. 61.

17 *Memoirs of General W. T.. Sherman*, p. 237.
18 Sword, p. 292.
19 Sword, p. 280.
20 Stillwell, p. 59.
21 Henry Villard, *Memoirs of Henry Villard*, Vol. I (Boston: Houghton, Mifflin Co., 1904), p. 244.
22 See Kimbell, pp. 44-45.
23 Sword, p. 368.
24 Sword, p. 379.
25 G. Allen Foster, *The Eyes and Ears of the Civil War*, (New York: Criterion Books, 1963), p. 5.
26 *Private Elisha Stockwell, Jr. Sees the Civil War*, p. 18-19.
27 Joseph Allan Frank and George A. Reaves, *"Seeing the Elephant": Raw Recruits at the Battle of Shiloh*, (New York: Greenwood Press, 1989), p. 105.
28 *Memoirs of General W. T. Sherman*, p. 264.
29 Ulysses S. Grant, *Personal Memoirs*, (New York: De Capo Press, 1982), p. 186.
30 *Official Records*, I:10/2, Chalmers to Garner, April 2, 1862, p. 384.
31 *Battles & Leaders of the Civil War*, Vol. I, p. 153.
32 Michael C. Adams, *Our Masters the Rebels: Speculations on Union Military Failure in the East, 1861-1865*, (Cambridge, MA: Harvard University Press, 1978), p. 34.
33 W. B. Hazen, *A Narrative of Military Service*, (Boston: Ticknor & Co., 1885), p. 8.
34 *Official Records*, I:52/1, pp. 16-20.

6
Towards a Veteran Army

PART 1. LESSONS FROM BATTLE:
SURGEONS, CAVALRYMEN AND GUNNERS

The Battle of Shiloh marks a watershed in the evolution of Grant's armies. Everyone who participated in this, the war's most bloody battle to date, considered himself a veteran thereafter. For them, the war lost all romance. They would carry on without illusion, visions of glory replaced by stoic determination. The battle also represents a major strategic turning-point in the war. The South had strained every nerve to concentrate a striking force at Corinth. Led by the man whom Jefferson Davis considered his most able general, Sidney Johnston, this force had delivered an assault against the North's most successful commander. Even with the advantage of surprise and superior numbers, the Confederates had failed. With the armies resting in post-battle shock and exhaustion, it is a convenient time for us to pause to consider some of the lessons of Shiloh.

Immediately apparent was the wretched inadequacy of medical care for the wounded. An Iowa soldier described the chaotic scene around Pittsburgh Landing after the battle: '... wagons were hurrying off to the battlefield after wounded, soldiers were running around hunting comrades ... I went up the hill to a lot of tents and a log house, but all were full of the wounded ... every inch of shelter afforded by tents, houses, or wagons was occupied and used as [a] hospital.'

It was no better on the transports anchored in the Tennessee River. 'The scene upon the boat was heart-rending,' wrote a wounded soldier, 'men wounded and mangled in every conceivable way ... some with arms, legs, and even their jaws shot off, bleeding to death and ... no surgeons to attend us.' And so it was downstream in the small town of Savannah where the transports deposited the wounded. Savannah's post commander wrote to his wife: 'You can have no conception of the amount of suffering here. Men lay out in stables and die without their wounds dressed.'

Grant's chief medical officer, Surgeon J. H. Brinton, acknowledged that his medical officers were involved in 'most arduous' work performed 'under every disadvantage'.[1] Why was this so? First, there were not enough medical officers. Secondly, too many did not know what they were doing. Lastly, the organization of the casualty clearing personnel and medical attendants was poor.

After Shiloh, the pressing need for additional medical personnel led to the practice of hiring men to serve as contract surgeons. While this increased numbers it did not necessarily increase the quality of medical attention. The payment of 80 to 100 dollars per month attracted many who had but the slightest knowledge of medical practice. As in all human endeavours, much depended upon the individual. Patriotic, well-intentioned men might or might not be capable of performing battlefield surgery. Charlatans, impostors and drunkards – and of these there were many, particularly among the ranks of the contract surgeons, and particularly in the more rural West – cared little about their patients' fate. A soldier relates:

'While there were some noble, humane and self-sacrificing physicians in the army, who were an ornament to the class and a God-send to the poor, broken down, fever-stricken or wounded soldier, unfortunately they formed a minority to the unskilled quacks whose ignorance and brutality made them objects of detestation to the soldier. Many of these fellows, if compelled to depend upon their profession in civil life, would have starved, but having, through the influence of political friends, been appointed army surgeons as soon as they donned the shoulder straps, blossomed out into miserable tyrants. Brutal as well as ignorant and careless of the poor soldiers placed in their care, they helped to fill many graves.'[2]

Slowly, the reorganization of the hospital service led to a more efficient casualty-clearing system. In theory, each corps' ambulances were under the guidance of a captain who served under the corps' medical director. Beneath him was a lieutenant directing the divisional ambulances and a second lieutenant who commanded the brigade ambulances. On the march, the ambulances converged to follow in the division's wake. On the battlefield they dispersed to their respective units. Each ambulance had a driver and two stretcher-bearers. Regimental stretcher-bearers, aided by bandsmen and cooks, brought a wounded man to the ambulance which then carried him to the divisional hospital. These two-horse ambulances had one stuffed, leather-covered seat along each side, and a third, hinged seat that could be reclined to carry a third prostrate victim. Under the seats was a keg of water, and under the driver's seat was a supply of beef stock and hospital stores. Attached to each side of the ambulance was a canvas-covered stretcher.

If the patient survived the trip by stretcher-bearer and jolting, stiff sprung ambulance ('a carriage, which a perfectly healthy man would find exceedingly uncomfortable') to the divisional hospital, he entered the surgeon's realm.[3] Here the surgeons performed rudimentary triage, and assistant surgeons dealt with first aid which, if they were competent, was fairly sophisticated; ligatures, compresses, bandages and tourniquets being used to control bleeding. They would sort the wounded and prepare the chosen ones for surgery. Medical statistics for the whole war show that bullets caused 94 per cent of all wounds and artillery fire was responsible for most of the rest. So infrequent was hand-to-hand fighting that edged weapons produced only 0.4 per cent of the casualties. Statistics also show that 71 per cent of the wounds were to the limbs. If these were not immediately life threatening, the injured men would have to wait. Because of the nature of the era's ammunition, the more serious limb wounds were likely to involve shattered bones, for which the surgical response was amputation. Surgeons understood that amputations were best performed quickly before shock set in, so these men received top priority. The Civil War image of amputated legs and arms stacked like cordwood outside the field hospital is accurate, simply because this type of wound predominated and it was one that the surgeons could take care of, albeit in a crude manner.

The next more common type of wound, 18 per cent, was to the torso, with chest wounds three times as frequent as abdominal wounds. Surgeons considered virtually any gut-shot man as being incurable, so the hospital assistants shoved these unfortunates aside for later attention. Face and head wounds constituted 11 per cent of the wounds a surgeon was likely to see. Any serious head wound was usually considered hopeless.

Federal surgeons, unlike their southern brethren, had ample anaesthetics. They used chloroform, ether, opium, or some mixture of the three, which was well and good. The problem was that they used the same soaked handkerchief mask over and over again. Likewise, having no knowledge, bacteriology, they used the same surgical tools repeatedly without any kind of sterilization other than wiping the most blood-encrusted knife or saw. About one in five patients developed post-operative infections (gangrene, pyemia, erysipelas) as a consequence of the unsanitary conditions under which surgeons operated. Nevertheless a wounded man had a very fair chance of surviving surgery (the post-operative mortality rate was about 14 per cent) if he received timely attention. Here lay the rub. In every battle of any size, the number of wounded swamped the number of medical attendants.

In the system improvised at Shiloh and perfected by Colonel Jonathan Letterman in the Army of the Potomac lay the seeds of the modern casualty-clearing system: first aid station; divisional sorting and care; field hospital; transport to permanent hospital. Although as the war progressed Grant's armies would become more efficient and sophisticated in the care of the wounded, overall medical attention was unnecessarily inadequate. The Federal government invested enormous amounts of energy and money first to attract volunteers and then to conscript recruits, but all too often that same government and its generals turned a blind eye when it came to dealing with the wounded.

A variety of religious orders and samaritan groups tried to alleviate the soldiers' suffering. Foremost among these was the United States Sanitary Commission, a volunteer group which did much to rectify the government's neglectful stance. It raised money to recruit physicians and nurses, inspected camps with a view to improving sanitation, and worked to better the soldiers' diet. The Commission maintained a soldiers' home in Washington and various transient lodges throughout the North, and their lists of hospital inmates were often the only way for families to locate their loved ones.

In addition to highlighting the appalling inefficiency of the medical services, the Battle of Shiloh revealed a cavalry arm unworthy of the name. On the surface this is hard to understand because, compared to eastern formations, western cavalry included a greater number of country boys who were familiar with the rudiments of horse management. Moreover, whereas in the East cavalry service brought out volunteer officers of a higher social class who were well versed in the romance of the mounted arm, in the West it tended to bring out men who were more practical. Despite these advantages, western cavalry did not fare well during the early years of the war. Given that European cavalry schools reckoned that it took some years to turn a recruit into a good trooper, it is not surprising that Grant's green cavalry did not initially distinguish themselves, but their failures can be attributed to more than just rawness.

During the first years, few Union cavalry units anywhere received adequate weapons. As was the case with the infantry, western troopers particularly suffered. Even a well-supplied regiment such as the 3d Ohio had three different carbines: the Sharps, Burnside and Remington. At least these were modern weapons. More typical was the 4th Iowa, a unit armed with a heavy sabre, the unreliable Starr's revolver, a Mexican War era smoothbore holster-pistol, and Austrian rifles! The hapless 7th Kansas Cavalry, virtually at the bottom of the Federal supply line, went to war with a motley collection of armaments including cumbersome muzzle-loading pistols and Prussian rifles. At the end of 1861, when a typical Illinois cavalry detachment scouted enemy territory in Kentucky, it had to borrow rifles from several infantry regiments in order to perform this duty.

The arming of the western trooper proceeded slowly. In October 1862, when Major General William S. Rosecrans badly needed effective cavalry in order to co-operate with Grant as the two generals tried to repulse a series of attacks against their lines of communication, Rosecrans explained his troopers' needs: 'Third Michigan Cavalry requires 690 revolvers, 294 Colt's revolving rifles; Fifth Ohio Cavalry, 88 revolvers, 170 Sharps' carbines; Second Iowa, 30 revolving rifles; Seventh Kansas, 250 revolvers, 500 Colt's revolving rifles; Company A, Second US Cavalry, 60 revolvers, 60 carbines – all with slings, pistol-pouches, cap-boxes, and ammunition complete.'[4] Not until the autumn of 1863 was the western cavalry even moderately well armed, and it was not until 1864 that most troopers could be termed properly armed.

In addition, most officers' concept of cavalry operations came from the Napoleonic wars, where the mounted sabre charge was the supreme manoeuvre. In those wars, troopers who tried to defend themselves with firearms were lost against a determined enemy who closed in order to use the sword and sabre. Therefore, both the Cavalry Bureau and Union cavalry officers worked to arm their men with edged weapons, hoping to replicate the great feats of Murat, Nansouty and La Salle. They failed to realize that important advances in firearms technology had rendered edged weapons obsolete. Southern cavalry officers – with the notable exceptions of John Mosby and Bedford Forrest – shared their enemy's faith in swords and sabres, but for once southern equipment shortages worked to the benefit of the Confederacy. Unable to equip their troopers with edged weapons, southern officers led their men into battle armed with pistols, shotguns and carbines. They soon learned that these were superior weapons in a close-quarters cavalry brawl. A Mississippi trooper described the fight between his unit and an Illinois cavalry unit. Although both sides fought bravely and with determination, 'pistols in the hands of the Mississippians proved superior to sabres wielded by the hardy sons of Illinois'.[5] During the first years northern troopers fighting with edged weapons were frequently bested by their pistol-wielding opponents.

Moreover Grant had little idea how best to organize and utilize his mounted arm. Even while fellow western general John Pope was organizing his cavalry into a divisional grouping, and simultaneously beginning the association of an obscure captain named Phil Sheridan with the cavalry, Grant persisted in scattering his cavalry throughout his infantry formations. The cavalry received their orders from whichever infantry officer they happened to be serving with. Dispersed in penny packets, the cavalry found itself on Grant's early battlefields consigned to provost duty.

Union cavalry suffered greatly from the poor quality of their horses. The army's rapid expansion provided great opportunity for unscrupulous civilian contractors to foist off shoddy material and nowhere was the abuse greater then in the matter of horseflesh. The phrase 'sharp as a horse trader' passed into American slang because everyone recognized that dealers in horseflesh were particularly unethical businessmen. As late as 1864, Secretary of War Stanton complained: 'My life is worried out of me by the constant calls of the generals in the field for more cavalry horses, and by the dishonesty of the contractors who supply us with inferior horses.' These contractors were, concluded the Secretary, 'a set of unmitigated scoundrels'.[6] Concern about horses reached all the way up to the man at the top. In early 1864, while preparing for the pending contest against Lee, President Lincoln interviewed the chief of the Cavalry Bureau and gave his celebrated comment: 'I don't care so much for brigadiers; I can make them. But horses and mules cost money.'[7]

The conduct of the business sharpies who supplied the Federal service with mounts meant that the trooper in the field was likely to have a weak or lame horse incapable of standing a campaign's hardships. At a minimum, most of the horses offered for use in the West were untrained, a debilitating weakness in battle. Finally, it must be said that the western troopers suffered more than most from the twin vices afflicting Civil War cavalry: straggling and marauding. All these factors caused Grant to over-look the potential usefulness of his mounted arm until 1864, when a leader and a force combined to produce a superior battle tool.

In contrast to the cavalry, Grant's artillery consistently con-tributed to his victories on the battlefield. As the surgeons in the field hospitals could plainly see, musketry was the big killer on the battle-field. More then one veteran recalled that artillery fire was noisy and frightening, 'but didn't kill often unless at close range and firing grape and canister'.[8] Although artillery did cause fewer than 5 per cent of total losses, most of the casualties came from canister-fire at close range when the tactical battle hung in the balance. As we have seen, at Belmont the intervention of one Union battery consistently dominated the infantry firefight. At Fort Donelson, a well-sited battery was the linchpin in Thayer's defence that thwarted the Confederate effort to overwhelm Grant's exposed right flank. At Shiloh, time and again artillery batteries blasted apart charging masses of Confederate infantry, and during the final stand at Pittsburgh Landing artillery virtually unaided defended the Dill Branch line.

American officers had learned artillery theory at West Point from Professor Dennis Hart Mahan. Had they been about to refight the Napoleonic wars, these officers would have been well prepared. Mahan recommended the deployment of artillery in such a manner as to silence the enemy's guns and pave the way for the infantry assault. This was reasonable as far as it went. Where Mahan went astray was in his advice to have cannon accompany the assault infantry by positioning some guns on the infantry flanks and a 2-gun section 100 paces ahead of each advancing infantry column. This would have been difficult on a Napoleonic battlefield (as French infantry found to their cost during the Peninsula campaign) and was quite suicidal on a Civil War field.

Fortunately for the Union cause, in 1858 a board of officers con-vened to revise artillery instruction. The War Department adopted their resultant manual, *Instruction for Field Artillery*, in March 1860. Conse-quently, in contrast to the infantry and cavalry branches which did not have a uniform system of tactical instruction, the artillery benefited from having one manual from the very onset. The overall excellence of this manual contributed to the generally excellent performance of the Federal regular and volunteer batteries.

It was not without its flaws however. It prescribed a deployment well suited for the Napoleonic wars. The individual gun occupied a front of two yards and a depth of five yards. Fourteen yard intervals separated each piece, giving a 6-gun battery an 82-yard frontage. Six yards farther back was the limber with its ready-use ammunition chest and six horses occupying a depth of eleven yards. Another 11-yard interval separated the limber from the caisson with its extra ammunition chests and horse teams that occupied a depth of fourteen yards. In sum, a single gun, caisson and limber occupied a space 47 yards deep extending from the gun's barrel back to the reserve teams. A 6-gun battery presented a target box 82 yards wide by 47 yards deep. This was too much valuable material packed into too small an area. Counter-battery fire, particularly from rifled artillery, could accurately bombard a target box of this size. The regulation deployment of a battery failed to take into account the accuracy of modern artillery, the improvement in explosives, and the extended range of the rifled musket.

In practice, Grant's gunners quickly dispensed with deployment by the book. Instead, they sought firing positions where the vulnerable limbers, caissons and teams could remain conveniently close but well sheltered from enemy fire. Reverse slopes, small ravines and woodlots usually filled the bill. Of course the most important component of a good firing position was a good field of fire. If necessary gunners would sacrifice defensive security in order to obtain a better field of fire. Battle accounts are full of reports of aggressive battery commanders deploying on some naked knoll in order to achieve oblique or enfilade fire against enemy infantry. Much depended upon the battery commander's sense of the ground. Ideally, his position was far enough away from covered terrain that could harbour lurking enemy marksmen and had access to an escape path should things go badly.

In Grant's western armies there was little central direction of the artillery arm. Although each division had a chief of artillery, individual batteries operated in association with infantry brigades where they were under the control of infantry brigade commanders. One of the prime evils stemming from this dispersal of the batteries was that they often had to deploy wherever chance dictated that the infantry deploy. Typically, a brigade would be groping blindly in wooded terrain, encounter enemy skirmishers, and deploy. As an afterthought, the colonel or brigadier would order his accompanying battery to join the firing line. Forced into a location with a restricted field of fire, the battery would be exposed to concealed enemy infantry. If an adjacent infantry regiment retired or broke totally, the battery could be taken in flank or rear before it knew what had happened. Forced into hasty flight, the gunners might or might not be able to extricate their weapons.

This happened repeatedly at Shiloh. Captain A. C. Waterhouse, who commanded Battery E, 1st Illinois Light Artillery, had to insert his battery directly into the infantry firing line at the start of the battle. Initially, his six James rifles severely punished several rebel formations that had the misfortune to pass obliquely across its front. Then Confederate pressure increased and the supporting infantry broke. Suddenly enemy infantry approached from the battery's flank and Waterhouse gave the order to limber up and withdraw. Confederate fire downed Waterhouse even as he gave this order. Hastily, the battery scrambled to the rear through the woods where a caisson became jammed between trees and had to be abandoned. Next it encountered Sherman's Chief of Artillery, Ezra Taylor, the hero of Belmont and now a major. Major Taylor believed Waterhouse's withdrawal to be precipitous, and ordered the battery 'to contest every foot of ground'.[9] Battery E unlimbered and soon was firing canister at masses of Confederate infantry approaching from both front and rear. As the supporting infantry again disintegrated, an enemy regiment approached through the woods to within fifty yards of the battery's flank. When Waterhouse's lieutenant ordered a retreat, it was too late. Men and horses were falling so fast that it was impossible to rehitch all the guns. It didn't help matters that the battery had found itself ordered into position on a muddy slope where several of the depleted teams became bogged down. Abandoning three guns, the survivors barely managed to escape.

Another of Sherman's batteries had a somewhat similar misfortune. At the beginning of the battle, the 6th Indiana Battery found itself galloped forward through the shattered ranks of some broken infantry where it encountered General Sherman. Sherman ordered it to unlimber immediately and come into battery, action right. As the gunners began to unhitch their pieces, musketry from nearby woods shot down the battery commander. Then, infantry emerged to charge the guns. Having had no time to get set, suddenly deprived of their leader, the gunners abandoned their guns and fled in disorder.

The fate of the artillery in McClernand's division was even worse. When he marched forward to support Sherman, he stationed two infantry brigades in line in wooded, brush covered ground. The accompanying artillery had to conform. McAllister's battery of four 24-pound howitzers took position between the two infantry brigades. Burrows' 14th Ohio Battery unlimbered in the middle of one of the brigades, and Dresser's Illinois battery protected McClernand's right flank. As the combat intensified the infantry supporting McAllister withdrew, allowing a Tennessee regiment to attack the battery's flank. McAllister narrowly escaped with the loss of only one gun. Next, the infantry supporting Burrows' battery broke, which again permitted enemy troops to outflank the gunners. Confederate fire downed 70 of the battery's horses and made it impossible to limber and withdraw. The subsequent charge captured all six of the battery's 6-pound and 12-pound Wiard rifles. Shortly thereafter, the same infantry that had overrun Waterhouse's position, turned to flank Dresser's battery. This time there was no concealed approach. Dresser's gunners killed and wounded a tremendous number of attackers, but the absence of infantry supports allowed the rebels to flank the battery, shoot down gunners and horses alike, render it nearly immobile, and capture four of the six guns.

These experiences underscored the perils inherent in attaching batteries directly to infantry brigades. If they were thoughtful about it, infantry generals usually positioned the batteries wherever they deemed there was a critical position requiring defence. Otherwise, they tended haphazardly to deploy the guns as an afterthought. In contrast, when guided by experienced artillerymen, guns in support of an attack could be arranged with multiple batteries trained at the same target from an extended baseline. This was known as converging fire. Better yet was enfilade fire where the artillery took position on the target's flank. In all events, the gunners sought to fire at an oblique angle to the target since this maximized the likelihood of inflicting damage. When employed on the defensive, veteran gunners sited their pieces to obtain overlapping fields of fire with their solid shot and shell. The artillery became a truly effective weapon at canister range — 300 yards and closer. Here they performed like giant shotguns. A 12-pound Napoleon sent its short, thick canister round out from the muzzle in a 20-yard-wide swathe of flying lead balls. Because of this canister-firing ability, regulations specified that a battery should be able to defend its front from charging infantry. The problems came, as we have seen, when infantry took advantage of cover to work around a battery's flanks.

Battle experience proved that Civil War artillery was more useful in a defensive rather than an offensive role, but it was a bit galling for gunners to resign themselves to this reality. Colonel Wainwright, a gunner in the Army of the Potomac, recalled how his ambitions early in the war to 'gallop half a dozen batteries into position at the decisive moment, as General Senarmont did at the battle of Friedland [one of Napoleon's best gunners who greatly contributed to victory over the Russians in 1807] ... were soon dispersed by the densely wooded country in which all our fighting has been done'.[10]

A word here is in order about the ordnance used by Grant's gunners. At the outbreak of the war, there were only seven 4-gun batteries in the entire United States Army and all their guns were smoothbores. Naturally, the Army of the Potomac had first call on modern rifled artillery and on the preponderance of the expanded Regular Artillery. Whereas McClellan took twenty regular batteries with him during his Peninsula Campaign, Grant had no regular batteries in his Army of the Tennessee at Shiloh.

As was the case with infantry weapons, the gunners out West got second call on available ordnance. At the onset, the three types of gun that were to become most common – the 12-pound Napoleon smoothbore, the 3-inch Ordnance Rifle, and the 10-pound Parrott rifle – were scarcely available. The entire United States Army had only five

Napoleons in service when the war began. Most of Grant's gunners at Shiloh fought with 6-pounder smoothbores, James rifles, cast-steel Wiard rifles, and 12- and 24-pound howitzers. By the 1864 campaign, he went into the Wilderness with the Army of the Potomac's gunners who manned an even proportion of Napoleons and 3-inch rifles.

PART 2. LEADERS OF MEN

America's mobilization for war was so rapid that it overwhelmed the nation's pool of trained officers. Necessity dictated that virtually anyone with military experience would command a regiment at a minimum. Thus the ranks of company grade officers were filled with untutored civilians. These were the positions in the pre-war army, as well as in the professional European armies, that had been occupied by trained and experienced officers who typically remained at this level for years. Moreover, in a professional army a junior officer had the advantage of serving under an experienced mentor. The radically different situation at the beginning of the Civil War had much to do with the characteristic lack of discipline of the Civil War soldier.

In the volunteer regiments it was a lucky captain indeed who had a qualified colonel to teach him how to command a company. More likely a captain would be one of ten company leaders trying to learn his job with little guidance from any senior officers. Beneath the captains were twenty clueless lieutenants also striving to master military duty. A Wisconsin private provides one view of what constituted good company leadership. During the advance on Corinth in 1862, this soldier was unable to march because of a hugely swollen foot (a consequence of shoddy uncured cowhide army shoes). Whereas his captain refused to allow him to remain behind in camp, a lieutenant told him to not join the march. When the private explained that he had had direct orders from the captain, the lieutenant replied, 'I don't give a damn what the captain says.' Regardless of the fact that it was the lieutenant who was more sympathetic to his condition, the private did not think him a good leader. The private explained that 'there wasn't any style of military pomp about him'.[11]

At the beginning of the war recruits had no idea what constituted effective leadership. Since they themselves elected their officers, they tended to vote for men who were their social superiors in civilian life – the town lawyer, the factory owner – or for men who displayed 'military pomp'. The brilliant orator had far greater chance to command a company than a quiet natural leader. So, green regiments received their all important initial military education from junior officers of unproven ability.

The first battle weeded out most of the cowards and charlatans. But simultaneously, enemy fire disproportionately killed the bravest men both because they led from the front and because it was the habit of company officers to remain standing while the men lay down or knelt when under fire. After the first battle, the ranks of the fallen officers were filled from within the regiment. Sergeants became lieutenants, lieutenants became captains and so on, all the way up the chain of command at least to regimental level and often to brigade level. But these newly promoted men knew nothing of formal military training, and their notions of what constituted soldiering were based on their experience of a confused engagement between two groups of utterly unruly amateurs. Like the killed and wounded officers they replaced, they had to grapple with the intricacies of formal drill, and having mastered it they considered themselves qualified because this was the only requirement for leadership they had ever seen. The ability to instruct men to look good while marching in formal review became the proof that a regiment was well trained. This was most particularly true in the Army of the Potomac. Memoirs of junior officers in both the eastern and western armies usually feature a proud mention that the company or regiment looked good during the review. Ability to emulate Napoleonic review standards was the *sine qua non* of leadership.

The fact that a regiment's senior leaders included combat veterans did not guarantee that useful lessons would be imparted to the junior officers. An Ohio soldier relates his experience in 1862 when an inexperienced captain began drilling the raw recruits. The captain gave his orders in a coaxing tone of voice, as if afraid of giving offence (an unsurprising incident given that most junior officers were in that position because they were the most popular, accommodating men in a company group that largely composed neighbours and friends). A veteran colonel passing by offered the distilled wisdom of his combat experience. He admonished the captain to use a firm tone of voice when giving orders: 'Like the crack of a gun, sir! Bite them off!'[12] So the cycle continued throughout the war: men learning their trade by observing their superiors who, in turn, had learned from men ignorant of military training. The process ensured that such bad habits as straggling during a march and losing all order during a charge, would continue unabated for the duration of a regiment's service.

In broad terms there were two types of combat leader: swaggering, boastful men who felt compelled to perform daring deeds in order to gain promotion (or find their names mentioned in the papers); and modest men who obeyed orders because it was their duty. Modest officers were not always the best soldiers and braggarts not always the worst. Many of the Union army's most dashing soldiers – Sheridan for example – were relentless self-promoters.

No officer at the rank of brigade command or below could be an effective officer unless he exhibited bravery. A veteran Confederate officer spoke for leaders on both sides when he said that 'every atom of authority had to be purchased by a drop of your blood'.[13] Thus, Logan at

Belmont or W. H. F. Smith at Fort Donelson led from the front on horse-back, exposed to more hostile fire than the lowly privates. At least until the end of 1863, even divisional leaders such as Sherman at Shiloh felt compelled to ride the lines amid a fearful storm of shot and shell, calmly smoking a cigar, setting an example for the raw troops. After the fighting was over (if they survived) such leaders would be respected and obeyed.

An artillery colonel in the Army of the Potomac reflected on the nature of courage following a close call on the battlefield. While he conspicuously displayed himself on a fireswept knoll in an effort to site his batteries, a shell fragment cut through his trousers at the knee. Fearing the worst, he briefly thought about what life would be like on one leg. Realizing that he was unharmed, the colonel kept at it. Two days later he was back on the same field, this time on foot instead of on horseback. For thirty minutes he was under fire which reduced him to crawling about on his hands and knees, but he felt far more frightened than he had two days previously. He concluded, 'Could there be a stronger proof that courage is merely a non-realization of the danger one is in owing to excitement, responsibility, or something of the sort.'[14]

This imperative for front-line leadership produced a terrible loss rate among regimental and brigade leaders. Early in the war, leaders threw away their lives with reckless abandon. Experience showed that effective leaders had to exhibit balance:

'The man who knows when to use his brains instead of his sword, when to put his command in and follow its movements with a watchful eye, and when to place himself at the post of danger, resolved to win or lose it all by his personal leadership, is a far more useful officer than the reckless and thoughtless man who undertakes to do all the fighting himself.'[15]

The rise to a higher command level required luck to survive exposure at an inferior level and good fortune again (or good political connections) to endure the initial blunders that typified the apprenticeship to command. No general on either side provided an outstanding performance the first time he took the field with an independent command. Three of the Confederacy's greatest leaders – Lee, Jackson and Longstreet – all failed the first time out. Grant narrowly averted disaster at Belmont, was temporarily relieved after Fort Donelson, and put on the shelf after Shiloh. During his first large independent command, Sherman experienced a bloody repulse at Chickasaw Bluffs outside Vicksburg. Likewise, Sheridan accomplished little beyond the fortuitous killing of Jeb Stuart during his Yellow Tavern Campaign. Quite simply, experience was the only teacher.

Experience did not necessarily produce an aggressive leader. Rarer still was the officer who would be aggressive while on independent duty. Almost every officer, with the notable exception of Ulysses Grant, experienced self-doubt. Such doubt could cloud judgement, leaving the officer vulnerable to fears about what the enemy might be up to just across that river, just behind that hill, just within those woods. James Wilson, whose well-thought-out ideas on combat leadership are cited above, demonstrated this fear when he led his Third Cavalry Division in advance of the Army of the Potomac during the Wilderness Campaign. Wilson was an intelligent officer who would prove amply aggressive in subsequent commands. But, having hitherto served in engineering and staff positions, the spring of 1864 marked the first time that he held an independent field command. He led his troopers to an important cross-roads in advance of the army. In the absence of infantry supports, with night approaching, he decided to withdraw even though he was not being pressed by the enemy. He explained his decision: 'It was now late in the afternoon, and, fearing that my exposed position far in front might invite the enemy to concentrate heavily against me, I resolved to make my way to Todd's Tavern.'[16] In other words, to retreat.

One debilitating influence upon the development of effective leadership was the role of politics. State governors retained the power to appoint and promote officers. The United States Senate confirmed the appointments. All of this was a commendable legacy of the great conflict of the 1780s between supporters of centralized federal power and ardent states' righters. Its impact on the United States fighting man in the Civil War was devastating. Skilled, valorous officers who lacked political clout were passed over in favour of those to whom politicians felt obligation or those with whom they wished to curry favour. Too often the assessment of tactical prowess was secondary to political patronage.[17] Sometimes, as in the case of 'Black Jack' Logan, the political appointee proved an able combat leader. But others, such as John McClernand for example, served effectively until their hometown ambitions got the better of their military judgement. And too often, campaign strategy foundered and men died under the leadership of out-and-out incompetents such as Ben Butler or Franz Sigel, generals who continued in command simply because the Lincoln Administration believed it could not retain control of the country without their assistance.

The North's shock over the heavy losses at Shiloh threatened a political firestorm. Rumours of men caught unawares in their camps and killed in the resultant carnage came to the attention of state governors and congressmen whose electorate were either serving in the army or had relatives who were serving. Sensitive to the possibility of political repercussions, Grant's superior, General Henry W. Halleck, carefully distanced himself from the man he suspected would take the fall. Moreover, Halleck had never had much use for his unintellectual, untidy (and worse!) impetuous subordinate. So, after Shiloh Grant passed into a period of partial eclipse. Halleck installed Grant as nominal second in command during the slow advance from Shiloh to Corinth. Halleck, entrenching securely at every halt (determined that his army would not be surprised in their camps) and laying miles of corduroy road to create a secure line of communications, took four weeks to advance twenty miles to Corinth. He all but ignored Grant during this advance. It was the first, and last, time that Grant had to labour in the presence of a superior officer, and Grant found it 'unbearable'.[18]

After the Confederates abandoned Corinth, the western yankees had a great chance to strike decisively. Grant saw it. As he later related: 'a movable force of 80,000 men, besides enough to hold all the territory acquired, could have been set in motion for the accomplishment of any great campaigns ... a bloodless advance to Atlanta, to Vicksburg, or to any other desired point south of Corinth'.[19] Instead, Buell's Army of the Ohio marched east while the balance of the Federal host dispersed to guard towns and railroads in western Tennessee. As had been the case after Fort Donelson, another tremendous strategic opportunity had been fumbled.

One good thing resulted from the break-up of Halleck's army after Corinth. Authorities in Washington summoned Halleck to become the new general in chief (where he proved to be little more than a first-rate clerk). Before departing, however, Halleck again reinstated Grant to field command. Henceforth he would be more concerned with grand tactical and strategical manoeuvre. Yet success or failure continued to hinge on the outcome of numerous tactical encounters.

On 22 February 1865 Robert E. Lee, Grant's greatest adversary, described his notion of tactical warfare:

'Disastrous surprises and those sudden panics which lead to defeat and the greatest loss of life are of rare occurrence among disciplined troops. It is well known that the greatest number of casualties occur when men become scattered, and especially when they retreat in confusion, as the fire of the enemy is then more deliberate and fatal. The experience of every officer shows that those troops suffer least who attack most vigorously [Lee entirely overlooks the consequences of trench warfare. European generals in the First World War would adopt the Lee method.] and that a few men retaining their organization and acting in concert accomplish far more with smaller loss than a larger number scattered and disorganized. [Experience on many fields vindicated this analysis. The ability of a small number of organized men to overthrow a much larger body by delivering a sharp counter-attack was the basis of most defensive tactics.] The appearance of a steady, unbroken line is more formidable to the enemy, and renders his aim less accurate and his fire less effective. [Lee apparently learned nothing from Pickett's charge.] Orders can be readily transmitted [So many battles took place in heavily forested terrain that communication within a regiment, let alone between adjacent units, was extremely difficult. Lee recalls his Mexican War experience and reveals that he is out of touch with tactical realities on the Civil War battlefield.], advantage can be promptly taken of every opportunity, and, all efforts being directed to a common end, the contest will be briefer and success more certain.'[20]

Besides showing his unyielding commitment to the offensive and lack of appreciation of the consequences of trench warfare, Lee's analysis is sound. Support for his views on the potency of a sharp counter-attack comes from many soldiers' memoirs and diaries. Colonel Charles Wainwright served with the Army of the Potomac's artillery throughout the war. During its final campaign he wrote in his diary about how often he had seen a battery force an enemy charge to hesitate and thus give the defending infantry a chance to rally. 'Then', he concluded, 'if you can get a counter-charge, all is safe.'[21]

1 Wiley Sword, *Shiloh: Bloody April*, (Dayton, Morningside Bookshop, 1988), pp. 429-430.
2 Francis A. Lord, *They Fought for the Union*, (New York: Bonanza Books, 1960), p. 99.
3 Lord, p. 101.
4 *Official Records*, I:17/2, Rosecrans to Watson, October 22, 1862, p. 287.
5 Stephen Z. Starr, *The Union Cavalry in the Civil War*, vol. 2 (Baton Rouge: Louisiana State University Press, 1985), p. 143.
6 James Harrison Wilson, *Under the Old Flag*, vol. 1 (New York: D. Appleton and Co., 1912), p. 327.
7 Wilson, vol. 1, p. 349.
8 Leander Stillwell, *The Story of a Common Soldier of Army Life in the Civil War 1861-1865*, (Franklin Hudson Publishing Co., 1920), p. 58.
9 Sword, p. 196.
10 Allan Nevins, ed., *A Diary of Battle: The Personal Journals of Colonel Charles S. Wainwright, 1861-1865*, (New York: Harcourt, Brace & World, 1962), pp. 471-472.
11 Byron R. Abernethy, ed., *Private Elisha Stockwell, Jr. Sees the Civil War*, (Norman: University of Oklahoma Press, 1958), p. 45.
12 Richard A. Baumgartner and Larry M. Strayer, eds., *Ralsa C. Rice: Yankee Tigers: Through the Civil War with the 125th Ohio*, (Huntington, WV: Blue Acorn Press, 1992), p. 21.
13 James R. Arnold, *Chickamauga 1863: The River of Death*, (London, Osprey Publishing, 1992), pp. 21-22.
14 *A Diary of Battle: The Personal Journals of Colonel Charles S. Wainwright*, p. 426.
15 Wilson, vol. 1, p. 425.
16 Wilson, vol. 1, p. 383.
17 For an interesting example of how this worked, see Robert Hunt Rhodes, ed., *All For the Union: The Civil War Diary and Letters of Elisha Hunt Rhodes*, (New York: Vintage Books, 1992), pp. 208-209.
18 Ulysses S. Grant, *Personal Memoirs*, (New York: De Capo Press, 1982), p. 200.
19 Grant, *Personal Memoirs*, p. 199.
20 A. L. Long, *Memoirs of Robert E. Lee*, (Secaucus, N. J.: Blue and Grey Press, 1983), p. 686.
21 *A Diary of Battle: The Personal Journals of Colonel Charles S. Wainwright*, p. 508.

Impressions of Grant

'His features did not indicate any very high grade of intellectuality. He was very indifferently dressed, and did not at all look like a military man.' An aide to Illinois Governor Yates when Grant applied for a position in 1861.

'Grant has personal bravery but no capacity ... Take the least and feeblest of the Circuit Judges of Illinois, and Grant was less than he.' Colonel Napoleon Buford, one of Grant's regimental commanders, at Cairo, Illinois in 1861.

'I could not help feeling rather disappointed by the commonplace appearance of the man.' Newspaper correspondent Henry Villard, on meeting Grant after the surrender of Fort Donelson early in 1862.

'Grant ... is a jackass in the original package. He is a poor drunken imbecile.' Matt Halstead, editor of the Cincinnati Commercial, in early 1863.

'He was a man in whom the army had confidence, but they did not love him.' A soldier's post-war reminiscence.

'Grant is the most unassuming officer I have ever seen.' One of Grant's headquarters guards.

'After the debonair McClellan, the cocky Burnside, rosy Joe Hooker, and the dyspeptic Meade, the calm and unpretentious Grant was not exciting.' A Maine officer, on Grant's arrival in Virginia, 1864.

'He looks like a plain common sense man, not to be puffed up by position or abashed by obstacles.' A Wisconsin officer, describing Grant's appearance at the Headquarters of the Army of the Potomac in March 1864.

'General Grant is not a very fine-looking General, but he has the appearance of a man of determination. He seemed to be thinking of something else than reviews.' Colonel Robert McAllister, after a review in April 1864 before the campaign began.

'He is a man of a natural, severe simplicity, in all things – the very way he wears his high-crowned felt hat shows this: he neither puts it on behind his ears, nor draws it over his eyes; much less does he cock it on one side, but sets it straight and very hard on his head. His riding is the same: without the slightest "air" ... he sits firmly in the saddle and looks straight ahead, as if only intent on getting to some particular point.' Colonel Theodore Lyman, a member of Meade's staff, in April 1864.

'General Grant is a short thickset man and rode his horse like a bag of meal. I was a little disappointed in the appearance, but I like the look of his eye.' Captain Elisha Hunt Rhodes, after a review on 21 April 1864.

'He seems entirely reckless as regards the lives of his men. This, and his remarkable pertinacity constitute his sole claim to superiority over his predecessors. He certainly holds on longer than any of them.' Walter Taylor [Lee's aide de camp], after Spotsylvania, May 1864.

'I hate to see that old cuss around. When that old cuss is around there's sure to be a big fight on hand.' A Vermont veteran, on seeing Grant visiting Sheridan's headquarters in September 1864.

'Grant is a good General and a great man.' Colonel Robert McAllister, in August 1864, during the siege of Petersburg.

'There was a vein of carelessness and indolence running through General

Grant's character, plainly discernible to those who knew him intimately, which seemed at variance with his other qualities of mind.' Sylvanus Cadwallader.

'... his prominent quality of unflinching tenacity of purpose, which blinds him to opposition and obstacles'. General George Meade, at Petersburg in 1864.

'Grant was undoubtedly a great commander. He was the first which the Army of the Potomac ever had who had the moral courage to fight the army for what it was worth.' Confederate Brigadier General Porter Alexander, 1899.

'I believe the chief reason why he was more successful than others was that while they were thinking so much about what the enemy was going to do, Grant was thinking all the time about what he was going to do himself.' General William T. Sherman.

'He was the steadfast centre about and on which everything else turned.' General Philip Sheridan, in 1888.

In His Own Words

On his West Point years: 'I did not take hold of my studies with avidity, in fact I rarely ever read over a lesson the second time during my entire cadetship.'

On seeking an appointment in 1861: 'I felt some hesitation in suggesting rank as high as the colonelcy of a regiment, feeling somewhat doubtful whether I would be equal to the position.'

Pertaining to the entrenchments required to defend Cairo, he informs his superior: 'On the subject of fortifications I scarcely feel myself sufficiently conversant to make recommendations.'

On being presented with a fine dress coat in 1864: 'There have been times in my life when the gift of an overcoat would have been an act of charity. No one gave it to me when I needed it.

Now when I am able to pay for all I need, such gifts are continually thrust upon me.'

In response to a reporter's query as to what he should write about another bloody, futile day of combat at Spotsylvania in 1864: 'We have lost a good many men, and I suppose I shall be blamed for it. I do not know of any way to put down this Rebellion ... except by fighting, and fighting means that men must be killed.'

'The only way to whip an army is to go out and fight it.'

'My object in war was to exhaust Lee's army. I was obliged to sacrifice men to do it. I have been called a butcher. Well, I never spared lives to gain an object; but then I gained it, and I knew it was the only way.'

On General Lee:

'The natural disposition of most people is to clothe a commander of a large army whom they do not know with almost superhuman abilities. A large part of the National army, for instance, and most of the press of the country, clothed General Lee with just such qualities, but I had known him personally, and knew that he was mortal; and it was just as well that I felt this.'

The Art of War :

'The art of war is simple enough. Find out where your enemy is. Get at him as soon as you can. Strike at him as hard as you can and as often as you can, and keep moving on.'

'If men make war in slavish obedience to rules, they will fail.'

The Future of War

'The laws of successful war in one generation would ensure defeat if applied during the next generation.'

7

Grant's Greatest Campaign

PART 1. THE STRATEGY OF THE VICKSBURG CAMPAIGN

In a democracy the people and their leaders are often notably short of patience when they perceive that their generals are making a poor job of it. So it was at the beginning of 1863 when it appeared that Grant had butted up against a stone wall. The *New York Times* observed: 'Grant remains stuck in the mud of northern Mississippi, his army of no use to him or anybody else.' The influential and hostile *Cincinnati Commercial* declared that Grant had accomplished nothing since Iuka and Corinth and had 'botched the whole campaign'.[1] The paper's editor took advantage of Grant's misfortunes to write to his friend Salmon P. Chase, Lincoln's Secretary of the Treasury, to warn that Grant was incompetent, a drunk and a menace to the nation. Grant's position as army commander hung by a narrow thread.

In fact, Grant had accomplished little since the capture of Corinth. Braxton Bragg's invasion of Kentucky dominated the Western theatre during the summer and autumn of 1862. Grant loyally dispatched reinforcements to assist Buell in defending Kentucky. He had to disperse his remaining troops to guard the railroads of western Tennessee. His forces were confronted by two Confederate armies commanded by General Earl Van Dorn and General Stirling Price. Price's mission was to prevent Grant from reinforcing Buell while Grant's mission was to prevent Price from reinforcing Bragg. At the beginning of September Price advanced on Corinth with some 16,000 men. Grant perceived an opportunity to eliminate Price's command before he linked up with Van Dorn, and devised a two-pronged converging attack aimed at the town of Iuka, Mississippi. Grant brought Major General Edward Ord's command by rail and sent them to attack Iuka from the north-west. Meanwhile, he ordered General William S. Rosecrans to attack from the south to cut off Price's escape. Both columns were to begin the assault at dawn on 19 September. This admirably conceived pincers attack shared the flaw of most such plans that require converging columns to unite on the battlefield: it necessitated close co-ordination between columns that were geographically separated. Rosecrans experienced delays, some caused by the weather and some by his own errors, leaving Ord's column to mark time while awaiting Rosecrans' arrival. Finally, at 4 p.m., a good ten hours later than planned, Rosecrans began his assault. A fluke weather system prevented Grant and

Ord from hearing the sounds of the firing and as a consequence Ord failed to join the fight. Price was able to escape the imperfectly drawn cordon that night and unite with another Confederate force led by Van Dorn. The unsuccessful Iuka campaign had been remarkably similar to Robert E. Lee's efforts in western Virginia, where Lee too had designed an overly complex converging attack.

Grant spent most of the following week trying unsuccessfully to obey Halleck's orders to destroy rebel gunboats that were being built along the Yazoo River. When Van Dorn dashed his command senseless against Rosecrans' entrenched men at Corinth on 3 and 4 October, the ensuing Confederate retreat left Grant with the initiative. During this complicated series of manoeuvres, Grant had not personally conducted a battle, but had maintained his composure during a confusing sequence of events and ably supervised the defence of his district against a twin-pronged enemy advance. Short of manpower, he had utilized railroads to concentrate his forces to repulse the Confederate thrust. At the time, the Battle of Corinth appeared to many to be just another engagement in the bewildering swirl of battles triggered by Bragg's invasion of Kentucky. General William T. Sherman explained the significance of the battle: 'It was indeed, a decisive blow to the Confederate cause in our quarter, and changed the whole aspect of affairs in West Tennessee. From the timid defensive we were at once enabled to assume the bold offensive.'[2] That offensive would be of Grant's design, the objective, the Confederate bastion at Vicksburg.

Vicksburg was one of the most important strategic positions the South had to hold if it were to endure. More important than the fact that it interdicted northern navigation down the Mississippi River was the town's access to supplies, particularly cattle and horses, west of the river. Nature had favoured Vicksburg from a military standpoint. It was situated on a high bluff overlooking a bend in the river from where artillery could rake any ships that tried to pass, and a complicated maze of bayous and swamps would prevent a direct thrust from the north. Finally, any yankee land offensive would have to rely on long and vulnerable north-south railroad lines, the Mississippi Central running from Memphis to Jackson, and the Mobile & Ohio running from Corinth to Meridian. The 85 miles of single-track Mobile & Ohio Railroad extending south from Columbus, Kentucky, the line that would have to support a land campaign against Vicksburg, was subject to interdiction from bushwhackers, guerrillas, partisan rangers and organized bodies of rebel cavalry.

To defend against their depredations, Grant had rely upon some very indifferent cavalry of his own. They were 'green and badly organized'.[3] McClernand had only 'two small companies of German cavalry poorly armed'.[4] Sherman reported that his mounted regiment was so used up that he could not push them more than seven or eight miles.

Grenville Dodge, the garrison commander at Corinth, had to supplement his weakened 4th Illinois Cavalry with three companies of infantry mounted on untrained horses. With such as these it was difficult effectively to oppose Confederate raiders whose repeated successes led Sherman to describe the Confederate horse as 'saucy and active, superior to ours', and to despair of ever being able to defend the Union line of communications.[5]

Had Grant's 5,530 cavalry – out of a total force of 61,000 as of 10 November 1862 – been better organized and aggressively handled, they could have accomplished much more. But he mistakenly persisted in breaking down his mounted troops into regiments and companies and distributing them to the various infantry commands. Typical was Hurlbut's command which included the 4th and 11th Illinois, the latter minus one company, the 6th Tennessee Cavalry, one company from each of three separate cavalry regiments (2d Illinois, 12th Illinois, 4th Ohio) nine companies from the 5th Ohio Cavalry, Hawkins' Horse, and Stewart's Independent Cavalry.

When Grant did finally organize a cavalry division it proved to be a division in name only. He assigned each of the three cavalry brigades to three different infantry commands and gave them orders to screen his front. It is probable that he lacked confidence in his mounted arm, and if so it may have been justified. An intelligent young officer named James Harrison Wilson, then merely a lieutenant in the Regular service, who had joined Grant's headquarters as his chief topographical engineer, gave his impression of the newly organized cavalry division: '... excellent material, but all untrained and badly deficient in discipline ... The entire organization was lacking in coherence, cooperation, and steadiness.'[6] Eighteen months later Grant would organize his cavalry into an independent corps and allow Sheridan to lead it off to a death struggle with Jeb Stuart, but at the end of 1862 he and his troopers were not yet prepared for such missions.

Still there were glimmers of promise. At one point while pursuing his overland advance toward Vicksburg, Grant sent the entire cavalry division forward as an advance guard. Overconfident, they fell victim to a cleverly concealed infantry and artillery ambush on 4 December. The 7th Kansas Cavalry acted as rearguard while the balance of the division extricated itself. Dismounted troopers fell back through alternating bands of woods and fields. Facing heavy infantry pressure, they ran to their horses, mounted, galloped across a cleared field into the edge of the next woods, dismounted, and opened fire. While they held off the hard-pressing rebel infantry, the horse holders led their mounts through the woods. When the pressure became too intense, the troopers again ran to their horses for a quick gallop across the next field, dismounted, and fanned out into skirmish formation. They repeated this procedure until the division had successfully withdrawn.

Above: Second Lieutenant Grant was present at most Mexican War battles, including Chapultepec. He considered the war unjust. (Library of Congress)

Below: Grant's infantry storms the Confederate camp at Belmont. (Library of Congress)

Left: Grant's superior and nemesis, General Henry Halleck. (National Archives)

Right: View from the coastal battery at Fort Donelson towards the approach route of the Federal fleet. (Author's collection)

Left: One of Grant's friends was not satisfied with any photograph of the general: 'He seemed constrained and unnatural when sitting for pictures, and was too stiff and austere in appearance to do himself justice. In his everyday life he was inclined to carelessness in dress and attitude.' (National Archives)

Right: Interior view of coastal battery at Fort Donelson. (Author's collection)

Above: Storming the rebel trenchline at Fort Donelson. (Author's collection)

Below: The inner line of fortifications at Fort Donelson. The 2d Iowa marched here to raise the national flag after the surrender. (Author's collection)

Above: The hotel in Dover where Grant accepted the Confederate surrender. (Author's collection)

Below: A western cavalry unit proudly displaying their swords, though these proved inadequate against pistol-armed rebel horsemen. (Library of Congress)

Above: Divisional drill with dispersed skirmishers (nearest to camera), skirmish supports, the main body of the regiment assigned to skirmish duty, and the division drawn up in brigade lines with artillery on the flank. (Library of Congress)

Above right: Cherry Mansion, Grant's headquarters at Savannah. Here he awoke to the sounds of distant battle at Pittsburgh Landing. (Author's collection)

Right: The defence of the Hornets' Nest during Shiloh's first day. (Library of Congress)

Left: From the distant treeline, the greatest bombardment to date in North American history pelted the defenders of the Hornets' Nest, who took shelter in the lane behind the fence line. Then the Confederate infantry charged across this field. (Author's collection)

Centre left: The final gun line on top of the bluff at Pittsburgh Landing at dusk on Shiloh's first day. (Author's collection)

Below: Charge of the 14th Wisconsin Volunteers to capture a rebel battery on Shiloh's second day. (Library of Congress)

Above: Grant observed: 'The navy gave a hearty support to the army at Shiloh, as indeed it always did both before and subsequently when I was in command.' The business end of the iron-clad ram *Benton*. (Author's collection)

Right: Despite *Benton*'s sloping armour, it was far from invulnerable. On 29 May 1863 Admiral Porter sent seven gunboats against the upper battery at Grand Gulf. For six hours his vessels tossed nearly 3,000 rounds of heavy 9- and 11-inch explosive and shrapnel shells against the battery. In an effort to knock it out the gunboats closed for a bombardment at the amazing range of 50 yards. After suffering con-siderable damage – plung-ing 100-pound shot dis-abled *Benton* and knocked the plate armour off *Tuscumbia* – Porter ordered their recall. (Author's collection)

Right: Ratliff Road on the Champion's Hill battlefield, showing typical close terrain. (Author's collection)

Left: The Big Black River where Irish Mike Lawler stormed the rebel bridgehead. (Author's collection)

Below left: Valiant standard-bearers managed to plant their Colours on the Confederate works during the 22 May general assault against Vicksburg, but the infantry could not storm the position. (Library of Congress)

Below: Confederate marksmen on a ridge 300 yards away made movement along the skyline extremely dangerous. To avoid this fire, Thayer's men tunnelled under the ridge, but they still had to cross another 150 yards of open ground to approach the 26th Louisiana Redoubt. (Author's collection)

Left: Grant's men conducted a very active siege at Vicksburg. The defenders' view of Hovey's approach trench. (Author's collection)

Centre left: Reciprocal view showing how near to the goal Hovey's men had come by 3 July. (Author's collection)

Below: View from Confederate Stockade Redan. The markers paralleling the road signpost the inexorable progress of the Union sap. The large white marker on the right of the road indicates the position of a supporting Union battery. The two light blocks on the redan's lip mark the Union position when Pemberton surrendered. (Author's collection)

Above: Just after the surrender, a yankee photographer took this picture of a dominating Confederate redoubt, now flying the national flag. (Library of Congress)

Below: Following a harrowing trip, Grant warms his feet at Thomas's headquarters at Chattanooga. Standing on the left is Rawlins, Grant's indispensable shadow. Rawlins' important talents included a firm ability to screen his chief from office seekers and to keep him from the bottle. Rawlins said of Grant, 'I regard his interest as my interest.' In an army of champion cursers, Rawlins excelled and was not beyond turning his profane tongue on Grant himself. Because Grant knew that he needed this man to restrain him from his weakness for alcohol, he tolerated his terrible temper. (Author's collection)

Above: Although cut off from supplies, Chattanooga remained in telegraphic contact, allowing Grant to supervise the convergence of forces from the Army of the Potomac and the Army of the Tennessee. A telegraph crew plants poles and strings wire. (Library of Congress)

Opposite page, top: A mobile field telegraph office. The wagon on the right contains the wire spool while the set itself is on the cracker barrel beneath the tent. (Library of Congress)

Right: Grant on Orchard Knob watching the Army of the Cumberland storm Missionary Ridge. (Library of Congress)

Above: Grant in dress uniform at the conclusion of his western operations and before his promotion to Lieutenant General. (Library of Congress)

On this field the 7th Kansas Cavalry, one of Grant's better formations, particularly distinguished itself. The unit included veterans of the pre-war fighting in 'bloody Kansas', an Ohio company raised by the eldest son of John Brown, and three companies of Illinois troopers who, having found their own state's quota already met, travelled all the way to Leavenworth, Kansas, in 1861 in order to join the cavalry. These highly motivated troopers showed how cavalry could combine mobility and dismounted firepower to oppose enemy infantry. A Confederate general who witnessed their performance pronounced that their tactics 'did them great credit'.[7]

As Grant's Army assembled for the down-river campaign, it received many reinforcements. While there were various reasons for a man to volunteer for the army in 1862, unalloyed patriotism remained a powerful motivation. A typical volunteer explained in a letter to his family back in Wisconsin that: 'I am contented with my lot ... for I know that I am doing my duty ... If I live to get back, I shall be proud of the freedom I shall have, and know that I helped to gain that freedom. If I should not get back, it will do them good that do get back.'[8]

It was difficult at first for new recruits to settle down alongside the veterans. The 124th Illinois for example faced a typical shakedown at their hands because, although they could not yet perform any of the evolutions required on the battlefield, they had new arms and equipment. The veterans quickly set about relieving them of these impedimenta. One night they organized a 'raid' on the 124th and stole the very tents from over the heads of nearly half the regiment. Later, when a detachment of the 124th returned from a very successful foraging expedition, the veterans tried them before a 'court', charged them with a breach of military discipline, and took not only the fowl, sheep and butter, but collected fines as well! But these antics of 1862 were gentle compared to 1864, when a recruit's introduction to the front usually took place in the inferno of a fire-storm from rebel breastworks.

After the Fort Donelson campaign, Grant had reorganized his baggage column. He limited his officers to 100 pounds each, including mess kits, to be carried in wagons. In practice, the officers had to make do with less because they had to store their baggage aboard the one wagon Grant allowed to each company. This company wagon hauled camp equipage along with the officers' baggage. Each regiment received three additional wagons, one each for headquarters, medical and quartermaster supply. Lean as this allocation was, it still meant that a regimental train consisted of thirteen wagons, and a brigade train for the infantry alone (assuming four regiments) had 55 wagons (counting three extra wagons for brigade-level support).

As Grant laboriously collected draft animals and supplies and tried to secure the north-south railroad lines necessary for an overland expedition against Vicksburg, his enemy toiled with equal industry to interrupt his labours. At the beginning of November 1862, as Grant marched south, Confederate raiders shredded his fragile line of communications. His cavalry was not up to stopping them and it proved exceedingly difficult to block a quick-moving mounted force with infantry alone. Typical was the experience of one Colonel Marsh of the 20th Illinois. He was known as a brave, aggressive officer and stood high on the list for promotion to brigadier general. He had agitated for the opportunity to distinguish himself in independent command. Sent by Grant to deal with raiding Confederate cavalry who had just attacked Holly Springs, Marsh suddenly discovered caution. Although no enemy was in sight, he de-trained his command some seven miles from Holly Springs, formed his men in full battle array, and marched slowly toward the enemy. It was nightfall before he arrived, by which time the base had been thoroughly looted and burned. This was just another example of how command responsibility could unman an otherwise competent officer.

By the end of 1862, Grant had to digest the news that Earl Van Dorn had struck behind him to destroy his major supply base at Holly Springs on 20 December, that Forrest (the only Confederate raider whom Grant really feared) was loose deep in his rear capturing garrisons and destroying the railroad, and that Sherman had failed in a direct assault against the Confederate defences of the Chickasaw Bluffs just north of Vicksburg. He also learned that his former subordinate, Abraham Lincoln's neighbour and friend General John McClernand, was preparing to sail down the Mississippi with a newly raised corps to capture Vicksburg himself. All of this, coupled with Confederate opposition and the many natural obstacles blocking a direct advance toward Vicksburg, persuaded Grant to abandon his campaign and shift his base west to the Mississippi.

He had learned one valuable lesson during the preceding weeks. When Van Dorn ransacked Holly Springs, Grant's Army had to live off the land and the quantity of supplies thus obtained 'amazed' him.[9] Northern Mississippi was a far richer farming area than the area around Shiloh and Fort Donelson. Grant realized that had it been necessary, his men could have subsisted for two months simply by foraging. He would remember this when plotting his final, campaign-winning approach to Vicksburg.

Having decided to base himself on the Mississippi instead of on the more vulnerable railroad lines, Grant collected the many scattered garrisons that hitherto had been assigned to defend his line of communications. Indeed, the need to defend railroad lines, bridges, tunnels and the like plagued every Federal general throughout the war. From Virginia to Missouri an advancing field army had to detach a tremendous number of men to garrison the occupied territory. It represented another factor in the calculus of strategic consumption that inhibited the North from bringing its superior manpower to bear. By ruthlessly abandoning non-essential points, Grant proved more able than his peers to concentrate his manpower. Yet even he had to leave the entire 16th Corps, under General Hurlbut of Shiloh fame, back in western Tennessee to guard hard-won gains.

After numerous failures during February and March 1863, Grant planned to bypass Vicksburg by marching downriver along the Mississippi's western bank and then recross the river below the city. The navy was willing, but Admiral David Porter emphasized that once his ships had run the gauntlet of Vicksburg's batteries, they could not return upstream – against the current they could only make one or two knots – until the army captured the batteries. This meant that it would be an all or nothing gamble. Sherman vigorously opposed Grant's notion, pointing out that Grant would be placing himself between the twin fortresses of Vicksburg and Port Hudson with the great river, an impassable barrier, directly to his rear. Grant replied that he understood the risks, but that to retreat would perhaps fatally dishearten the nation. He explained that the national situation – the last election had gone against Lincoln's party, volunteering had virtually ceased, no other field army was accomplishing anything – demanded that something must be done. So, against the advice of his most respected lieutenant, he ordered the attempt to be made.

PART 2. APPROACH MARCH

The march south from Grant's base at Milliken's Bend traversed bayou country, waterlogged ground that might well be considered 'impassable' to a major military force. It was the time for Lieutenant P. C. Hains of the Engineer Corps to shine as he supervised bridge construction, including one bridge spanning a distance of more than 600 feet. Using locally procured materials and enlisting the native genius of the yankee soldier, Hains' efforts enabled Grant's Army, complete with artillery and trains, to march nearly forty miles through the bayous to reach Perkins' Plantation on the west bank of the Mississippi. Grant later observed: 'I found that volunteers could be found in the ranks and among the commissioned officers to meet every call for aid whether mechanical or professional.'[10] When he needed lumber, men came forward who could improvise a sawmill. When he needed men to crew the steamers that were to run Vicksburg's formidable batteries (the civilian crewmen refused because it was too dangerous), experienced Mississippi rivermen from Missouri and Illinois regiments volunteered.

On 20 April Grant issued Special Order No. 110 to regulate the capture of a bridgehead on the Mississippi's opposite bank. It covered everything from the order of march for the army's three corps to the number of tents each unit could carry. He ordered the establishment of field hospitals and assigned good drill officers to organize the convalescent soldiers, without regard to regiment, into detachments capable of guarding the army's line of communications. In this way the campaign's normal attrition would serve a useful purpose. Grant intended to march light and fast. His trains would carry only ammunition. The men would live off the land.

While Sherman's XVth Corps feinted above Vicksburg, Grant's planned crossing at Grand Gulf failed when rebel shore batteries outfought Porter's gunboats. Grant hastily improvised a new crossing below Grand Gulf. Early on the morning of 30 April, when McClernand's XIIIth Corps crossed successfully, Grant experienced 'a degree of relief scarcely ever equalled since ... I was now in the enemy's country, with a vast river and the stronghold of Vicksburg between me and my base of supplies. But I was on dry ground on the same side of the river as the enemy.' Writing with the value of hindsight, and ignoring the fact that he would have much preferred to march upon Vicksburg directly from the north had logistics and terrain permitted, he added, 'All the campaigns, labors, hardships, and exposures ... [since December] that had been made and endured, were for the accomplishment of this one object.'[11]

At this point, Sherman urged him to stop and consolidate his gains. Grant himself had intended to continue south and join General Nathaniel Banks in a campaign against Port Hudson, but news that Banks was ill-prepared for such a campaign convinced Grant to revise his plan. In one of the war's great decisions, he decided to operate against Vicksburg alone by abandoning his own line of communications in order to sever Vicksburg's links with the rest of the Confederacy. Then he planned to turn to deal directly with the fortress. He put his faith in rapid movement to avoid the overwhelming concentration that the enemy could bring to bear if given time.

Although he depended greatly upon his army's mobility, when Grant crossed to the enemy's side of the Mississippi he took along relatively few cavalry troopers. They amounted to only one complete cavalry regiment, the 4th Iowa, five companies of the 2d Illinois, four belonging to the 3d Illinois, seven companies from the 6th Missouri, Thielemann's 2-company 'battalion' of Illinois Cavalry, and the single-company Kane County (Illinois) Independent Cavalry. He used them in a classic and conservative light cavalry role to scout the roads and help preserve communications between his columns. Not until mid-June did he summon three more regiments to join him. Once the siege began he still used these troopers to patrol the rear and carry messages.

The most celebrated cavalry action of the Vicksburg campaign was the raid led by Colonel Benjamin H. Grierson of the 6th Illinois. Grant intended this raid to serve as a diversion to help cover his downstream crossing of the Mississippi. Begun at dawn on 17 April on the Mississippi-Tennessee border, Grierson's mission was to cut Vicksburg's rail connections with the rest of the eastern Confederacy. Although poorly mounted – some of his men rode horses taken from the wagon-trains just three days earlier – and poorly armed – about half the troopers carried dubious Union and Smith's carbines – Grierson and his 1,700 troopers more than made up for this with boldness. For the minimal loss of three killed, seven wounded, five taken ill and left, and seven missing, Grierson marched some 600 miles through Mississippi and Louisiana killing and wounding about 100 enemy soldiers, capturing another 500, destroying more than fifty miles of railroad and telegraph, and seizing large quantities of supplies and arms.

According to Confederate General Pemberton, who was in command at Vicksburg, the raid failed to distract him from Grant's manoeuvres. According to Grant, it succeeded famously in attracting 'the attention of the enemy from the main movement against Vicksburg'.[12] What is certain is that Grierson did tie down at least 2,000 scarce Confederate infantry, whom Pemberton ordered off to protect certain installations, and most of the available Confederate cavalry — which left him almost blind from the point of view of intelligence. Furthermore, it was the first time in the West that a yankee mounted force had driven deep into enemy territory and emulated the tactics of such Confederate cavaliers as John Morgan, Van Dorn and Forrest.

PART 3. CHAMPION'S HILL, THE DECISIVE BATTLE

On 1 May, the day after a crossing had been secured, Grant sent two corps marching inland towards the small town of Port Gibson in order to expand his bridgehead. At Port Gibson, a small Confederate force commanded by the exceptionally able Brigadier General John S. Bowen conducted a stout 18-hour fight against odds of more than three to one in the yankees' favour. After defeating Bowen, Grant had the choice of moving north directly on Vicksburg or of striking inland to drive a wedge between Pemberton's army and the rest of the Confederacy. Conventional wisdom favoured the cautious first course of action, which would lead to the capture of one of the last two rebel bastions interdicting the Mississippi. The alternative risked much by placing Grant deep in enemy territory between hostile field armies. But it also promised much: if Grant could gain a central position between Pemberton and Johnston, he could defeat the Confederates in detail and perhaps drive Pemberton back into Vicksburg's defences, which would allow the capture of the city and of Pemberton's army. Exhibiting again the audacity of a great captain, Grant chose to forego a direct advance on Vicksburg.

After being joined by Sherman's Corps, Grant began his march into the interior of Mississippi. His men marched hard and fast through suffocating dust which caked the sweat-soaked troops.[13] For the first time in the war, and despite their officers' efforts, many soldiers delighted in burning civilian dwellings along the way. They had become veterans, and one of the consequences was that they now showed a callous indifference to civilian suffering. On 11 May, McPherson collided with a 3,000-strong Confederate brigade at Raymond. Once more the yankees outnumbered the rebels by about three to one, and although the Confederates put up a stiff fight, Union weight of numbers overwhelmed them. In fact, so well had the rebels fought that McPherson exaggerated their numbers to the extent that Grant revised his plan. Instead of turning to deal with Vicksburg, he resolved to continue against the rail hub of Jackson in order to scatter thoroughly the defenders and sever the east-west railroad line leading to Vicksburg.

On the 13th Grant's Army stood interposed between Pemberton and outside help. If the Confederates forces co-operated, there was the real chance that they could crush Grant. The theatre commander, Joseph E. Johnston, saw this chance and urged Pemberton to attack an isolated wing of Grant's forces. On the night of the 13th, Johnston wrote to Pemberton: 'If practicable, come up in his rear at once. To beat a detachment would be of immense value. All the troops you can quickly assemble should be brought. Time is all-important.'[14] Indeed, time was all important. Fortunately for the Federal cause, because of some clever Union espionage work, Grant knew about the intended blow before Pemberton.

Johnston sent his dispatch in triplicate to ensure that Pemberton received it. One of the couriers was a Union-loyal man who had been foisted upon the Confederates. Several months earlier, amid great ceremony, the garrison commander of Memphis, Tennessee, General Hurlbut, had evicted a man because he entertained rebel sentiments. Hurlbut publicly proclaimed that he was taking this action as a warning to the inhabitants of federal-occupied territory not to trifle with Federal forces. Having thus established his pro-South credentials, this man had little trouble worming his way into Confederate service as a special courier with local knowledge of the land. He was one of the three couriers entrusted to carry the message through Grant's lines for delivery to Pemberton. He brought it directly to Grant who, forewarned of the planned Confederate combination, was able to make appropriate dispositions to parry the enemy thrust.

On 14 May McPherson's and Sherman's Corps advanced through a driving rainstorm against Mississippi's state capital at Jackson. This offensive forced Johnston to cede Jackson, and for Grant, temporarily cleared the board of any outside enemy interference. Leaving Sherman to wreck the railroads at Jackson, Grant turned his other two corps east towards Pemberton and Vicksburg.

By the end of the 15th, Grant had concentrated 32,000 men in position for the drive on Vicksburg. In contrast to his opponent, he had perfected this concentration without subjecting the men and draft animals to long, hard marches. His units had finished each day's march early so that they would have time to forage and rest. Grant anticipated a battle on the 16th and, because of his deft handling of the Army of the Tennessee, had a fresh, vigorous force with which to fight.

Early in the morning of the 16th, he interviewed two railroad workers who had just come from Edwards, a station on the Southern Railroad. They told the general that Pemberton had gathered a force of 49 regiments and fifteen batteries, amounting to 25,000 men, to attack Grant's Army. This remarkably accurate intelligence – in fact Pemberton had 23,000 men – confirmed the information brought to him previously by his double agent. Grant sent a courier spurring to Jackson to recall Sherman and ordered McClernand to advance along two routes, the Raymond and Middle Roads, which headed west towards Pemberton's reported position. McPherson was to move his men along the Jackson Road, which lay north of McClernand's twin routes. Grant's last orders included the warning to 'move cautiously with skirmishers to the front to feel for the enemy'.[15] Then the general mounted his horse and, accompanied by his staff and young son, rode towards the anticipated battle.

Even before receiving Grant's orders, McClernand had his troops marching toward the enemy. Moreover, he had met General James McPherson, the commander of the XVII Corps, to arrange a converging attack against Pemberton. It was a commendable display of initiative. The arrival of Grant's orders did little to change this plan. Screened by cavalry detachments, the Union columns approached the Confederate position. Pemberton had arrayed his men along a 3-mile line atop Champion's Hill, a commanding height overgrown with thick brush and trees. This line blocked any advance along the Raymond and Middle Roads. A plantation road running behind the Confederate position would permit the rapid shift of Pemberton's reserves to any threatened sector. Recognizing the strength of his position, Pemberton felt sanguine about his prospects. He did not yet know that the yankees were also advancing via the Jackson Road.

McClernand's columns collided with rebel roadblocks at about 7 a.m. In a classic small-unit outpost battle, McClernand's men deployed into battle line and slowly advanced. On the Middle Road, divisional commander Brigadier General Peter Osterhaus, a graduate of a Berlin military school before emigrating to the United States in 1848, personally oversaw the deployment of his advance brigade and even selected the firing positions for the 7th Michigan Battery to site its 10-pound Rodman rifles. At Jackson Creek, the van division on the Raymond Road found the bridge burned. Efforts to build a bridge faltered when rebel artillery opened fire from a height 1,200 yards away. Up came the 17th Ohio Battery and its six 10-pound Parrotts. The resultant artillery duel demonstrated the superior accuracy of rifled artillery. For thirty minutes

THE BATTLE OF CHAMPION'S HILL
16 MAY 1863

the Ohio gunners pounded the rebel position and knocked out two 12-pound smoothbore Napoleons while suffering few losses in return. Bearing in mind Grant's admonition to exercise caution, McClernand spent the next two hours getting his four divisions off the roads and into the tangled terrain. Meanwhile, worried that McPherson might not hear the sounds of battle, he sent messengers to inform his fellow corps commander that the fight had begun. At 9.45 he also sent a courier to Grant asking whether he should hold or bring on a battle.

Grant, riding along the Jackson Road, did not receive McClernand's query until noon. He replied with a message telling McClernand to attack 'if an opportunity occurs'.[16] So rugged was the ground that it took the courier eighty-five minutes to ride the three miles back to McClernand to deliver this message. Exercising his discretion, McClernand did little fighting for the rest of the day. His caution, which almost cost the battle, rankled Grant then and thereafter, but by fixing Pemberton's attention on the threat to his front, McClernand had performed a valuable service.

The battle hinged on what transpired along Pemberton's left flank, the sector facing the Jackson Road. Here, General Alvin Hovey – an officer who had been promoted to divisional command after displaying superb gallantry at Shiloh – and his men sighted the rebels atop Champion's Hill at 9.45 a.m. Hovey's leading brigade deployed, skirmishers well to the front, with three regiments in a first line and two more in a second. The brigade commander personally took a cavalry patrol forward to within 200 yards of the enemy position to assess the situation. He returned to find Hovey accompanied by the army commander who had just arrived. Grant received a detailed, accurate description of this sector of Pemberton's position: thick timber and a precipitous slope extended east of the Jackson Road while the west of the road featured a more gentle slope and several cleared and cultivated fields. Hovey wanted to attack immediately, but Grant ordered him to wait until Logan's Division of McPherson's Corps arrived.

Dressed in full uniform, mounted on a splendid white horse, 'Black Jack' Logan reached the field at 10 o'clock and, after conferring with McPherson and Grant, had completed his deployment in 25 minutes. Characteristic of the energy displayed by the troops of the Army of the Tennessee was one of Logan's subordinates, Brigadier General Mortimer D. Leggett. He had been on furlough when he learned that the army had crossed the Mississippi. He dropped everything and hurried back to resume brigade command, arriving on the morning of the battle. The skirmishers in one of Leggett's regiments spotted Logan and asked him if they could not unsling their knapsacks before advancing. Logan snapped back, 'No, damn them, you can whip them with your knapsacks on!'[17] Notified that Logan had completed his deployment, Grant handed tactical control of the battle to McPherson. At 10.30 McPherson gave the signal and Hovey's and Logan's men charged with a cheer.

Screened by a heavy skirmish line, Logan's division advanced with two brigades in front and one in reserve. The division made slow progress as the men scrambled up the steep slope. Confederate fire, including shelling from the well-positioned 10-pound Parrotts of the Cherokee Georgia Artillery which enfiladed Logan's line, thinned their ranks and the advance sputtered to a halt. Logan saw that the enemy's left flank appeared not to be anchored on anything substantial and ordered his reserve brigade to move forward at the double and form up to strike the exposed flank. Seeing this threat develop, the Confederates responded with a double-time movement of their own that shifted a brigade to the imperilled flank in the nick of time. This brigade then surged down the slope in an impetuous counter-attack.

Meanwhile, Hovey's men had passed through musket and canister fire to within 75 yards of the hill crest. Sheltered in a ravine, a yankee brigadier ordered his men to fix bayonets. He knew that the defenders would only get off one volley before his men were on them. Accordingly, he told them that after they had advanced a few paces he would chop his sword downwards, a signal to them to fall flat and, it was hoped, the volley would pass overhead. Then the men would get up and charge. The scheme worked perfectly. After a desperate, but brief, hand-to-hand grapple, the brigade overran the Confederate position and captured four guns. Better still, it retained its order. The 11th Indiana – the zouave unit that had distinguished itself at Fort Donelson – turned to the left to enfilade the defenders' line. The 24th Indiana and 29th Wisconsin wheeled to the right to do the same. The Confederates skilfully fell back some 500 yards and established a new line of resistance.

Hovey's men assaulted this new line. An Iowa soldier recalls: 'We moved on the enemy in good order, passed an open field and a house, fired a few rounds, and them made a most gallant charge.'[18] In fact, these 'few rounds' killed the horses of the rebel battery just as it was trying to limber up and withdraw. The ensuing charge captured the entire 4-gun battery. But it was not done without cost. An Ohio soldier relates: 'After entering the field a short distance, the first of our company, Henry Richards, fell shot through the brain. A little further along, as we halted to give them a volley, my brother, John Henry Williams, was shot through the heart ... The comrade on my left had his arm shot off. Other comrades in the company were being hit, but there was no halt. Closing up rank we pressed on.'[19]

At about the same time, over on Logan's front, the battle along the Confederate far left flank reached a climax. Logan's reserve brigade managed to repulse the rebel counter-attack. It was well positioned to take the entire enemy position in flank, but first had to cross a very deep ravine and deal with eight Confederate guns on the far slope. Undaunted, the brigade crossed the hollow, cheered, and charged. Double-shotted canister smashed through their ranks. Individual rebel gunners displayed amazing valour, including one Mississippi captain who served his gun single-handedly until he fell, having been hit six times. His battery lost 74 of 82 men in its desperate defence. Spearheaded by the 8th Illinois and 32d Ohio, the Union soldiers sent the supporting infantry flying and overran the guns. They advanced further to cut one of the two routes Pemberton needed to retreat towards Vicksburg.

At this time, back at the Champion house, a surgeon saw Grant dismount. The roar of battle clearly indicated that Logan's flank attack was succeeding. The surgeon saw Grant remove a cigar from his mouth and heard him say to an aide: 'Go down to Logan and tell him he is making history today.'[20] So far, this history included the thrashing of one full Confederate division and the capture of sixteen cannon. The first phase of the battle of Champion's Hill was over.

Pemberton responded to his crisis with soldierly resolve. Using the plantation road that ran behind his position, he shifted about 5,000 troops from the sector confronting McClernand, and, at about 2.30

p.m., sent them to attack the Union breakthrough. This time it was the yankees who were taken in flank. Pemberton's counter thrust smashed into Hovey's left flank. One Ohio lieutenant describes the scene:

'The enemy's line overlapped ours, as far as I could see on our left. The open timber in our front gave us a good view of them as they came on. Their skirmishers sprang from tree to tree until some of them were just across the road from us [The Confederates were using western-style assault tactics, employing a heavy skirmish line to spearhead the attack through covered terrain.]. The first line, under the withering fire we were giving them from our strong position at the fence, veered off to the right and left. On our right the Twenty-fourth Iowa, being in open timber, was pushed back after the most desperate hand-to-hand fighting. [The fence line served the defenders as a rudimentary breastworks, providing them with some shelter and, more importantly, the confidence to aim accurately and repel the attack. The neighbouring regiment, having no such cover, could not withstand the attack.]

'Our right being uncovered, and having no support on our left, our regiment was forced to leave the fence, for which the enemy made a rush. [The claim that the flanks were 'uncovered' is the standard explanation given in most diaries and post-action reports for any setback. In this case, it happened to be true.] In a moment we were under the most scorching fire from two or three sides. Under this fire our men fell thick and fast ... Loading and firing, we fell slowly back, it being the first time for the Fifty-sixth Ohio to turn their backs to the enemy. Halting at every favorable opportunity, we would give them a few rounds.'[21] [Despite being taken in flank, this was no rout. The soldiers responded with a stubborn and disciplined fighting withdrawal.]

The ferocious Confederate counter-attack recaptured the crest of Champion's Hill, four guns that had been lost earlier and two more Union guns to boot. The hitherto successful yankees retreated three-quarters of a mile. Pemberton's stroke threatened to split Grant's army in two. At this juncture, Grant's first order to McPherson, namely to push his trains to the side of the road to allow trailing units an unimpeded march, paid dividends. Just as Hovey's division collapsed, two brigades in Marcellus Monroe Crocker's Division arrived at the Champion house. Crocker was yet another lawyer in Grant's service. He had attended West Point (although not graduated), begun the war as a captain, served with distinction in the 2d Iowa, and fought at Shiloh. He would go on to make a name for himself during Sherman's Atlanta Campaign when his brigade received the nickname the 'Greyhound Brigade' for its impressive marching ability. Temporarily in command of a division here at Champion's Hill, Crocker intended to take advantage of his opportunity. He formed his two brigades and advanced towards the fighting.

One of Grant's aides arrived to interrupt Crocker's approach march with news that Hovey's division had broken and that one of

Crocker's brigades must hurry to his aid. Crocker galloped to Colonel George Boomer and yelled, 'For God's sake put this brigade into this fight.'[22] Boomer's brigade turned about immediately and marched at the double to the crest where they saw McGinnis' defeated brigade fleeing before the Confederate counter-attack. Resisting the temptation to join the panic, Boomer's men formed into line of battle and began firing at the oncoming rebels. So impetuous was this Confederate assault – it featured Bowen's men, the best division in Pemberton's army – that the issue hung in the balance until Hovey massed sixteen guns on a nearby rise from where they could fire into Bowen's flank. Sheltered by the guns and by Boomer's infantry, Hovey's division began to reform with veteran resolve.

The near-rout of Hovey's Division had presented Grant with the day's crisis. He responded with celerity, sending units to fill the gap and carefully positioning two batteries to block any additional enemy advance.[23] Seeing the last of Crocker's division arriving on the field, he asked, 'What troops are these?' On being told that they were Crocker's rearguard, Grant sent an aide to instruct its colonel to 'move forward as he was [in column of fours] until his front was as far west as the westerly battery ... and then move by his left flank, at double quick, and advance until stopped by the enemy.'

'The General seemed to realize the true state of affairs and said: "Hovey's division and Boomer's brigade are good troops, and if the enemy has driven them, he is not in good plight himself. If we can go in again here and make a little showing, I think he will give way."'[24] Here was the Fort Donelson and Shiloh lesson again: in a difficult battle, with both sides ground down by hard fighting, the man who committed his reserves at the right time and right place would triumph. Grant had probably never read Napoleon who once said that 'the last battalion will decide the issue', but it was a sentiment that he heartily endorsed and frequently put into practice.

Crocker's first two brigades, aided greatly by Hovey's artillery concentration, had stabilized the situation. His last brigade sent to the flank by Grant's direct order, tipped the balance back to the Federal side. Hovey's division rallied and returned to the fray. Logan's division again began to gain ground. McClernand's Corps finally began to advance as well. The fought-out Confederates could resist no longer. Bowen's gallant rebels ceded the crestline for a last time, and the yankees reclaimed the four guns they had captured previously.

Grant tried to pass McClernand's fresher troops through McPherson's tired men in order to pursue the defeated enemy, but McClernand was a trifle slow, and Pemberton's mauled army escaped. Ransom's brigade was one of the units that arrived too late to participate in the battle. Traversing the battlefield, the soldiers crossed a ravine full of dead Confederates. They were Georgia men and many had been wearing large white hats which had proved their downfall. Ransom's soldiers observed that 'nearly all were shot in the head'.[25]

At the Battle of Champion's Hill, the Army of the Tennessee lost 410 killed, 1,844 wounded and 187 missing. This was about 7 per cent of the total engaged and the casualties clearly showed who had done the fighting. The four divisions that fought in McClernand's wing suffered only 158 casualties. Hovey's division lost 1,189 men, about one-third of the division, and Boomer's 4-regiment brigade lost another 510 men. Ever afterwards, Grant believed that had McClernand pulled his weight the campaign would have ended right there on Champion's Hill: 'Had McClernand come up with reasonable promptness, or had I known the ground as I did afterwards, I cannot see how Pemberton could have escaped with any organized force.'[26] Nevertheless, Grant's men had captured 27 cannon and inflicted at least 3,800 casualties (Confederate returns were incomplete) on the enemy army.

The significance of the battle lay not in the losses suffered by the respective armies. Champion's Hill was one of the most crucial encounters of the Civil War: arguably, it was *the* decisive battle of the entire war. The great British historical analyst, J. F. C. Fuller, concluded that: 'The drums of Champion's Hill sounded the doom of Richmond.'[27] Grant's victory drove a wedge between Pemberton and Johnston and permanently separated Pemberton's army from outside help. It sent Pemberton reeling back to the safety of Vicksburg, removing his men from active participation in any subsequent field battles. Once Grant had invested Vicksburg, Pemberton's surrender became merely a matter of time. The only other Confederate stronghold on the Mississippi, Port Hudson, could not (and did not) stand once Vicksburg had fallen. A total of 37,000 men surrendered at Vicksburg and Port Hudson. After securing the line of the Mississippi, the Union host could (and did) turn inward, to campaign against the South's heartland, to defend which, in the absence of the rich resources of the Trans-Mississippi, the South had to rely upon a much attenuated logistical base which proved inadequate. In 1864, the combination of logistics and Grant's unrelenting pressure kept Robert E. Lee's Army of Northern Virginia from delivering the offensive rejoinder to the Army of the Potomac's implacable advance. Forced into a static position, Lee could only sit helplessly and watch while the war continued to be lost elsewhere.

All this flowed from the Battle of Champion's Hill. After 16 May 1863, the South could no longer win the war through their own generals' initiative. Champion's Hill reduced Jefferson Davis to reliance upon Union bungling to confer Southern independence. If a decisive battle is defined as one in which a nation perishes or fatally wounds its foe, Champion's Hill was indeed a decisive engagement.

Victory came to Grant because of his own sound strategic manoeuvring, the sterling service provided by his lieutenants – in particular the brigade and divisional officers in McPherson's Corps – and most of all because of his soldiers' veteran combat performance. The Army of the Tennessee earned victory because the men expected to win when they fought under Grant. As a Wisconsin soldier plainly explained: 'Grant is the only man that can whip the rebs every time.'[28]

1   Dan Bauer, "Who Knows the Truth About the Big Bender?" *Civil War Times Illustrated* (December 1988), p. 40.
2   William Tecumseh Sherman, *Memoirs of General W. T. Sherman*, (New York: Library of America, 1990), p. 284.
3   James Harrison Wilson, *Under the Old Flag*, vol. 1 (New York: D. Appleton and Co., 1912), p. 143.
4   Stephen Z. Starr, *The Union Cavalry in the Civil War*, vol. 2 (Baton Rouge: Louisiana State University Press, 1985), p. 126.
5   *Memoirs of General W. T. Sherman*, p. 279.
6   Wilson, vol. 1, p. 143.
7   Starr, vol. 2, p. 138.
8   Margaret Brobst Roth, ed., *Well Mary: Civil War Letters of a Wisconsin Volunteer*, (Madison: University of Wisconsin Press, 1960), p. 15.
9   Ulysses S. Grant, *Personal Memoirs*, (New York: De Capo Press, 1982), p. 226.
10 Grant, *Personal Memoirs*, pp. 247-248.
11 Grant, *Personal Memoirs*, p. 252.
12 Grant, *Personal Memoirs*, p. 257.
13 Jim Huffstodt, *Hard Dying Men: The Story of General W. H. L. Wallace, General T. E. G. Ransom, and their "Old Eleventh" Illinois Infantry in the American Civil War (1861-1865)*, (Bowie, MD: Heritage Books, 1991), p. 140.
14 Grant, *Personal Memoirs*, p. 266.
15 Grant, *Personal Memoirs*, p. 269.
16 Edwin C. Bearss, *The Campaign for Vicksburg*, vol. 2 (Dayton: Morningside, 1986), p. 593.
17 Bearss, vol. 2, p. 596.
18 Bearss, vol. 2, p. 603.
19 Bearss, vol. 2, p. 604.
20 *Battles & Leaders of the Civil War*, vol. III, p. 511.
21 Bearss, vol. 2, p. 610.
22 Bearss, vol. 2, p. 615.
23 For an eyewitness account, see Sylvanus Cadwallader, *Three Years with Grant*, (New York: Alfred A. Knopf, 1956), p. 79.
24 Related in U. S. Grant, III, "General Ulysses S. Grant: A Close-Up," *Military Analysis of the Civil War: An Anthology by the Editors of Military Affairs*, (Millwood, NY: KTO Press, 1977), pp. 131-132.
25 *Hard Dying Men*, p. 141.
26 Grant, *Personal Memoirs*, p. 272.
27 Bearss, vol. 2, p. 637.
28 Roth, *Civil War Letters of a Wisconsin Volunteer*, p. 21.

8

'We Had Caught Our Rabbit'

PART 1. CLOSING IN

On 17 May the soldiers of the Army of the Tennessee rose early in their campsites on Champion's Hill and set off in pursuit of Pemberton's army. Grant next encountered Pemberton on the Big Black River where he had retained a fortified bridgehead on the east bank, manned by three brigades with eighteen cannon. Grant began a close-up reconnaissance of the bridgehead. Confederate marksmen spotted him and opened a heavy fire. Putting spurs to hs horse, Grant galloped to safety, but he had seen enough. He ordered Sherman and McPherson to cross upstream of this position while McClernand feinted against the bridgehead itself. At this point a hard-riding courier arrived to interrupt him.

The courier had a message from his superior in Washington, his old nemesis Henry Halleck. Dated 11 May, it ordered Grant to go to Banks' assistance and capture Port Hudson first before proceeding against Vicksburg. Grant told the courier that Halleck's order was out of date and he intended to ignore it. Then cheering from the front attracted his attention. He looked through his glass and saw General Mike Lawler – a big, fat, fighting Irishman whose cherished maxim was the Tipperary one: 'If you see a head, hit it!' – stripped down to his shirt sleeves, leading an improbable charge though the swamps against cotton-bale breastworks protecting the bridge over the Big Black River. Seeing the Confederate rearguard in a false position, Lawler had impetuously led the troops of his brigade through water up to their armpits to storm the enemy works with irresistible force. An eye-witness who saw much of the war relates: 'It was at the same time the most perilous and ludicrous charge I witnessed during the war.'[1]

Irish Mike Lawler's charge routed the defenders and captured 1,700 men and all eighteen cannon. After burning the bridges, Pemberton's demoralized army retired back to Vicksburg. The river proved a small barrier to Grant's army. In a familiar western performance, supervised by their energetic general, Ransom's men tore down buildings adjacent to the river for usable timber. They then felled several huge trees so that they dropped across the river to serve as makeshift trusses. Decking the trees with the timber, the men passed quickly on towards Vicksburg.

By noon on the 19th, just twenty days after crossing the Mississippi, Grant's army had completely invested Vicksburg. The speed of the advance astonished his enemies. Three days later General Joseph Johnston was to tell a British visitor that 'Grant had displayed more vigour than he had expected'.[2] Grant did not believe that the time for vigorous activity was at an end. Having recently seen how easily his men had assaulted well-manned works on the Big Black River, he thought that an immediate hard push would capture the city. Accordingly, he ordered a general assault for 2 p.m. His main effort went in against a Confederate works called the Stockade Redan, which blocked one of the principal roads leading into Vicksburg. Frank Blair's Division had served under McClernand at Champion's Hill and had barely participated in that battle. Returned to Sherman's command, Blair drew the assignment of assaulting the Stockade Redan. A narrow, winding road – aptly named Graveyard Road – led to the Redan. The ground fell off sharply on both sides of Graveyard Road. Kilby Smith deployed his regiments on each side of the road and started forward. The precipitous slopes, littered with stumps and felled trees, made it impossible to maintain any order. Three times Kilby Smith halted his brigade to dress ranks, under heavy fire all the while. Pinned down, he sent a courier to Sherman to ask what to do. Back came the unhelpful order to advance his men 'as close to the parapet as possible, and be ready to jump in when they begin to yield'.[3]

On Kilby Smith's right flank, Colonel Giles A. Smith saw the attack falter. He ordered his 8th Missouri to cover the advance with musket fire and led his remaining four regiments into a hollow that led to the Stockade Redan. Despite the covering fire, the defenders had little trouble pelting the yankees with a punishing fire of their own. The attackers paused briefly behind an embankment to get their breath after a difficult uphill climb. Then Giles Smith ordered them forward. The 1st Battalion, 13th United States Infantry – the only regular infantry then serving in Grant's Army – crossed the rise and immediately ran into a deadly crossfire of canister and shell. The captain in command fell mortally wounded, but still managed to cheer his men forward as he lay dying. A shot through the head killed the Colour sergeant. Another soldier picked up the fallen Colour and he too fell dead. In quick succession, five Colour-bearers were hit and dropped. The regulars pressed on and got to within 25 yards of the Stockade Redan, could advance no further, and went to ground behind felled timber and stumps. Another captain seized the Colour and ran ahead to plant the flag on the redan's exterior slope. A bullet hit the flagstaff and carried away one of his fingers.

This torn standard marked the farthest advance of the day. Unable to go forward, unwilling to retreat, the attackers held their ground throughout the long afternoon. When the yankees ran out of ammunition, brave volunteers searched the cartridge boxes of the dead and wounded to replenish. Soldiers particularly admired the efforts of 14-year-old musician Orion Howe. Young Howe dashed across the fire-swept ground to collect cartridges and bring them to the firing line. He then volunteered to go to the rear to bring up a reserve supply. He ran along the Graveyard Road, was struck by a bullet in the leg, but continued on to Sherman's headquarters to tell the general that the men needed ammunition. Seeing blood dripping from the boy's leg, Sherman asked what was the matter. Howe replied, 'They shot me in my leg, sir; but I can go the hospital. Send the cartridges right away.' Sherman promised him he would arrange it. As Howe limped off, he turned to shout out 'caliber 54!', the unusual calibre required by his regiment's Austrian rifles. For this exploit Orion Howe was awarded the Medal of Honor.

At nightfall the yankees fell back a short distance and dug a trench on the Graveyard Road a mere fifty yards from the rebel ditch. Although this was a slight gain, there was no disguising the fact that the assault had been a botched, hastily arranged affair. It had cost 157 men killed, 777 wounded and eight missing. After the battle, the regulars counted 55 bullet holes in the 13th US Infantry's flag. Because of its gallant charge, Sherman authorized the regiment to have inscribed on its Colour the legend 'First at Vicksburg', which hardly made up for the 43 per cent losses incurred during the charge. Accustomed to success, Grant's men were angered by the failure. Typical was the response of the colonel of the 47th Ohio. The regiment had lost a stand of Colours (one of two standards lost this day) in front of the rebel works. The colonel questioned the Colour-bearer who displayed his wounded hand and said that he had dropped the Colour when hit and could not lift it back up because there were so many dead men lying on top of it. The colonel cursed the soldier, called him a coward, and threatened to use his sword to cut off the man's head!

Grant himself was unconvinced that Vicksburg could not be carried by assault. There seemed to be compelling reasons to make the effort. Joe Johnston was lurking just over the horizon around Jackson, where he was known to be receiving reinforcements for the relief of Pemberton's army. Grant lacked the manpower for a siege. His line of communications was precarious. He also believed that the men would not settle down to the monotony of a siege until it became apparent to all that this was the only way to capture Vicksburg. Indeed, the men were in the full flush of victory and considered themselves near unbeatable. The army's chief engineer told Grant that the men were not just ready to assault, they were eager to do so. Lastly, Grant rightly believed that the enemy troops were demoralized.[4] Accordingly, the Army of the Tennessee spent two days making careful preparation. Where appropriate, the men built scaling ladders so that they could clamber up the steep sides of the Confederate earthworks. Gunners brought up extra ammunition and carefully sited their weapons. Grant made arrangements for covering fire from his field guns as well as co-ordinating a bombardment with Admiral Porter's fleet. When all was ready, at 10 a.m. on 22 May 1863, the army delivered a general assault against Vicksburg.

Within minutes it became clear that Confederate morale had recovered. An eye-witness describes the scene. The Union line:

'... had been so mercilessly torn to pieces by Confederate shot and shell that it had lost nearly all resemblance to a line of battle, or the formation of a storming column. Officers and men were rushing ahead pell-mell without much attention to alignment ...

'When they crossed the deep ditch in front of the earthworks and began to ascend the glacis, they were out of musketry range [because the defenders could not depress their rifles] ... A straggling line, continually growing thinner and weaker, finally reached the summit, when all who were not instantly shot down were literally pulled over the rebel breastworks as prisoners. One stand of our colors was planted half way up the embankment and remained there till a daring Confederate ventured over, and carried it back inside. Many stragglers took refuge in the ditch outside the earthworks and remained there till they could crawl away covered by darkness.'[5]

The steep slopes leading up to the Confederate ridgetop line combined with natural and manmade obstructions to make any advance very difficult. None the less, at many points, standard-bearers planted their Colours on the forward slopes of the Confederate works. But with one exception, nowhere could the yankees penetrate the rebel position. For hours they lay pinned in the ditches in front of the enemy position. Typical of their plight was the experience of the 11th Illinois. Their brigadier, General Ransom, formed the regiment '... in columns of companies right in front'. They managed to approach stealthily to within sixty yards of the defenders' works. Ransom made his way to their front and ordered a charge. The regimental officers picked up the cry. The colonel of the 11th cried, 'Now men, charge with a will!' and fell mortally wounded. Murderous Confederate fire mowed the men down 'like grass ... for no matter where we might appear, the rebels, from their works, would have a cross fire upon us'. As quickly as they could, this veteran brigade crawled back a few yards to find cover.

Their repulse was intolerable to Ransom. He seized the Colour of the 95th Illinois and shouted, 'Forward men! We must and will go into that fort!' Inspired, his men charged forward and reached the parapet. Here they planted four Colours, but could go no further. After being pinned down for perhaps ten minutes, Ransom yielded to the inevitable. Climbing onto a stump, he addressed his troops: 'Men of the Second Brigade! We cannot maintain this position. You must retire to the cover of that ravine, one regiment at a time, and in order. Move slowly. The first man who runs or goes beyond the ravine shall be shot on the spot. I will stand here and see how you do it.' While one regiment provided covering fire, the other regiments withdrew as ordered. So fierce was the enemy fire that a captain *crawled* up to Ransom's stump to beg him to take shelter. 'Silence!' snarled Ransom in reply.[6]

The unit that came closest to breaking into Vicksburg was Irish Mike Lawler's brigade whose men, in the predawn darkness, had stealthily approached the enemy works by way of a hillside thicket. When the general assault began, they were a mere fifty yards from their objective. Led by a gallant Iowa sergeant named Griffith, elements of the brigade captured a Confederate redan and held it against all comers, but there were no supporting troops available to exploit the breach, and at nightfall Griffith and his comrades had to retire. When Grant learned of Griffith's heroic effort, he had him listed for a cadetship at West Point. It was one of the few good things to come of this day's attack.

By 11.30 a.m. Grant had decided that the assault had failed, but on receiving word that McClernand was on the brink of a breakthrough he sent one of McPherson's divisions to reinforce him and ordered Sherman and McPherson's remaining units to attack again. In fact McClernand's reported success had been erroneous, and the renewed assaults merely increased the casualty list so that by the time they were called off the army had lost 3,199 men. Ransom's brigade alone suffered 476 casualties on this day.

While blaming McClernand for at least half the army's losses, Grant acknowledged that the assault of 22 May was one of two during the war that he wished he had never ordered. What had caused his misjudgement? The situation confronting him had been novel. Not since the Mexican War had he confronted enemy troops defending a formidable line of works. In Mexico, a determined bayonet attack had overcome such positions. But here about 13,000 of Pemberton's men had been actively engaged, and from the shelter of their works had repelled a determined assault by 35,000 confident, veteran infantrymen. Even when brave men such as Sergeant Griffith gained a foothold, their efforts were stultified by lack of reinforcements.[7] None of the Federal leaders involved had realized that a frontal assault against a well-defended earthworks demanded tactical innovation; the spade, not the bayonet, would be the tool to capture Vicksburg.

PART 2. SIEGE

For the next 43 days, the Army of the Tennessee first invested, and then besieged Vicksburg. Except for the contemporaneous action at Port Hudson – another Confederate stronghold on the Mississippi, some 120 miles downstream – the siege of Vicksburg was unlike any other engagement of the Civil War. To the west, Porter's fleet ccontrolled the Mississippi. Simultaneously, Grant's army blocked all land approaches to the city. The resultant total isolation of Vicksburg made it different from a somewhat similar campaign against Petersburg the following year. Also in contrast to operations at Petersburg, Grant's men pressed the siege of Vicksburg quite vigorously, employing the full range of classic siege techniques.

No sooner had the second assault against Vicksburg failed, than Grant began to prepare for the siege. He realized that he required additional forces to man the trenches facing the city and to maintain a field force to thwart any Confederate effort to relieve it. He called up reinforcements from Hurlbut's XVIth Corps that had been left behind to guard his communications running back to western Tennessee. Thus did Jacob Lauman – once the inexperienced but enthusiastic colonel at Belmont, then the aggressive leader of shock troops at Fort Donelson, and now a divisional commander – rejoin Grant with his infantry division on 28 May. From Missouri on 11 June came General Francis Herron, the hero of Prairie Grove, and his division. General John Parke, once Burnside's chief of staff, brought the IXth Corps, an old Army of the Potomac unit, from Ohio on the 14th. Together with another of Hurlbut's divisions and a provisional division made up of odds and ends, the IX Corps under Sherman protected the Army of the Tennessee from any attack in rear from Joe Johnston. By the time his build-up was complete, Grant had 71,000 men under command, about half of whom were protecting his rear.

He had also managed to get rid of General John McClernand. For six months he had known that McClernand was scheming to supplant him. Grant knew that McClernand had important political connections to the Lincoln Administration, but he could play the army political game as well as anyone. He carefully compiled a list of McClernand's errors – not hard to do after the Illinois politician's inert performance at Champion's Hill and faulty report of breakthrough during the great assault of 22 May 22 – and bided his time. On 30 May, McClernand issued a congratulatory order of the day to his corps that claimed most of the credit for the campaign to date. It proved the last straw. On 18 June Grant happily relieved him of command. He gave the corps to West Point educated General Edward Ord. With the notable exception of Phil Sheridan – who in the summer of 1863 commanded an infantry division in Rosecrans' army – Ord's arrival marks the completion of the Grant team. Here at Vicksburg he had assembled the key lieutenants – Sherman, McPherson, Logan, Blair, Wilson, Ord and Parke, who were to lead the most important units in the campaign of 1864, and go on to lead corps and armies in the final 1865 campaign.

The Confederate engineers had laboured for seven months to design and build the 9-mile-long defensive system protecting Vicksburg against a landward attack. These defences followed the crest of a steep ridge overlooking deep ravines. Numerous gullies cut into the ridge. Rather than build a continuous line along each of these spurs, the engineers had constructed their line from near the head of one gully in a more or less straight line to the head of the next gully. They built triangular outworks on the spurs that extended toward the Union line, from where a few defenders could command the approaches to the main line.

Slaves cleared fields of fire in front of these earth and log fortifications and used the felled trees to create abatis, dense interlocking obstructions of sharpened timber. The roads leading to Vicksburg naturally followed the lie of the land and provided the easiest access to the city. To block these roads, the Confederates had built nine forts. During the siege, the action focused on these forts and on the outworks protecting them. Every slight rise in the ground, each spur jutting toward the enemy lines, acquired an immense tactical significance as a firing position for artillery and sharpshooters.

The successful prosecution of siege operations requires engineers and heavy siege artillery, and Grant had precious few of either. Having only four engineer officers at his disposal, he directed that all West Point graduates – who had been obliged to study military engineering – be drafted in to lend a hand, but for most of the siege there were only five West Pointers besides himself, and one of them declined to serve in the lines. This was the army's chief commissary officer, a short, fat man who weighed more than 220 pounds. This gentleman begged off, explaining that there was nothing in engineering he was good for unless he would do for a sap-roller!

As regards siege artillery, Grant had only had one battery of six 32-pounders. Underscoring the point that the Union generals in the West had to make do with far less in the way of logistical support than the Army of the Potomac was the fact that nowhere else in the West were there any siege guns available. To provide offensive punch, Admiral Porter lent a battery of large-calibre naval guns including 30-pound Parrotts and an 8-inch Columbiad.[8]

Lacking a formidable siege train, Grant's gunners realized that they would have to improvise. They took logs of the hardest wood, bored them out to the size of 6- or 12-pound shells, wrapped the tube with iron reinforcing bands, and blasted away with these 'trench mortars'. Since their field guns did not have the hitting power of a siege gun, the gunners compensated by dragging their guns up to point-blank range. On the sector facing the Great Redoubt, they dug approach trenches through a very deep and rugged ravine, dismantled two 12-pound cannon, and hauled them to within 100 yards of the redoubt. On another sector, a lieutenant in the 8th Battery, Michigan Artillery supervised an effort that carried a 12-pound howitzer to within 100 yards of the 3d Louisiana Redan. Likewise, the gunners of Battery L, 2d Illinois Light Artillery had a daily detail to carry a James rifle forward to the most advanced rifle pits from where it could fire point-blank at the enemy works. Most impressive of all was Captain Patrick White. He had been a lieutenant in the Chicago battery that had fought so prominently at Belmont. At Vicksburg he earned the Medal of Honor when he '... carried with others, by hand, a cannon up to and fired it through an embrasure of the enemy's works'.[9] By the end of the siege, there were some 220 guns bombarding the rebel works.

Since the army did not have the artillery to batter down the fortifications, the troops laboured to dig through and under them. The yankees employed classic siege techniques that had changed little since Roman times. The soil was very favourable for digging; side cuts for the trenches held firm without collapsing, tunnel and mine ceilings did not even require timber supports. The abundant grape vines and sugar cane provided wickerwork for gabions – open-ended cylindrical baskets stuffed with earth – and fascines, bundles of tightly bound brush or stakes. The gabions were used for constructing infantry and artillery firing positions and the fascines for temporary protection in the forwardmost trenches. The gunners protected their embrasures with mantelets – heavy rope or timber shields – another siege device from antiquity. These could be raised for firing and then quickly lowered while reloading.

After establishing their own trench system facing the enemy lines, Grant's men began digging a network of trenches leading to the Confederate lines. The excavation of these saps was dangerous work because the open end faced the enemy, so it was necessary to construct sap-rollers, wicker cylinders that could be pushed to the head of the sap to give protection against smallarms fire. Ever innovative, Logan's men constructed one sap-roller by piling cotton bales on top of a railroad flat car! When it came within 75 yards of the 3d Louisiana Redan, the defenders fired turpentine-soaked musketball coverings into the cotton (a slight advance over Roman fire arrows). Soon the cotton bales were blazing vigorously while rebel sharpshooters stood poised to bring down any yankee bold enough to try to put the fire out. Within minutes the rail car had burned down to its iron axles and wheels. Unfazed, Logan's men built a new sap-roller, five feet in diameter and ten feet long, and continued their advance. So it was all along the front:

'Every man in the investing line became an army engineer day and night. The soldiers worked at digging narrow, zigzag approaches to the rebel works. Entrenchments, rifle pits, and dirt caves were made in every conceivable direction ... Every day the regiments foot by foot, yard by yard, approached nearer the strongly armed rebel works. The soldiers got so they bored like gophers and beavers, with a spade in one hand and a gun in the other.'[10]

It was a hard grind for these soldiers under the hot Mississippi sun. There were no light uniforms for summer wear. The men could discard their heavy frock-coats but could do nothing about their flannel underwear, overshirt, felt hat, and heavy woollen trousers. An Ohio soldier's diary describes daily life:

'May 29. On fatigue duty, making a sap, heavy cannonading in front. May 31. I worked on the sap 6 hours to-night. June 2. Our men are sapping and mining every night. We are bound to dig them out. June 9. The duty of the pickets is sharp shooting daytime and advance at night to within 50 yards of the rebel works and watch their movements while our working parties dig trenches or saps to advance. June 19. On fatigue duty all day pulling grape [vines] to make gabions.'[11]

Many men quickly grew bored with the routine. Officers noted that the work performed by line troops in the trenches was deficient compared to that of the special pioneer detachments or the hired black labourers. None the less, inexorably the saps advanced towards the rebel works.

The action in front of the 3d Louisiana Redan typified siege operations at Vicksburg. This redan blocked the Jackson Road, one of the main entrances to the city. It was here that Logan's men employed their railroad car sap-roller to approach the rebel works and then substituted a more conventional sap-roller when the defenders burned the railroad car. Under the direction of the corps' chief engineer, Captain Andrew Hickenlooper, the effort had begun on 23 May, the day after the failed second assault. That night Hickenlooper stationed workmen at 5-feet intervals, gave each a pick, shovel and gabion, and told them to cover themselves securely and connect with their neighbours before daylight! The prospect of being exposed to close-range Confederate sharpshooters served as a stimulus to their digging. During the day, relief parties deepened and widened the sap and the next night the effort began anew. On 25 May, the opponents arranged a truce in order to bury the men killed during the 22 May assault. Hickenlooper took advantage of this to stroll between the lines to study the terrain.

Traditionally, the defensive counter to Hickenlooper's 'flying saps' is artillery, but the Federal artillery, particularly two 8-inch guns from the naval battery, silenced the Confederate guns in the redan and the work continued. On 3 June the sap had reached a commanding knoll 130 yards east of the objective. Hickenlooper had selected this site for a breaching battery during his reconnaissance on 25 May. His workers spent two days building a formidable, 8-foot-thick earthworks named Battery Hickenlooper, and then continued on towards the 3d Louisiana Redan.

By 16 June the yankees had sapped to within 25 yards of the redan's exterior slope. They then dug two support lines of rifle pits from where marksmen could fire against the defenders. Any Confederate soldier who tried to fire at the sappers was silhouetted against the skyline and offered a prime target for riflemen sitting 25 to 50 yards below them. On the 17th fatigue-parties carelessly left a cotton bale near the sap-roller. The Louisiana defenders quickly torched it with their turpentine-soaked charges and the fire spread to consume the sap-roller. The yankees built a third roller and by the 21st had reached to within a few yards of the redan's exterior slope. The defenders resorted to hurling artillery shells as hand-grenades into the Union trench and this made further work impossible. Hickenlooper called for men who had been coal-miners to volunteer to tunnel directly into the redan.

The miners divided themselves into 6-man teams and worked in 1-hour shifts, two men picking, two shovelling and two passing sacks of spoil back out of the tunnel. Working non-stop, the miners drove a 3-foot-wide, 4-foot-high gallery 45 feet under the redan. The defenders, hearing the noise, dug countermines to intercept the yankee mine. Undaunted the northern miners continued with three side branches which they filled with 2,200 pounds of gunpowder. They laid parallel strands of safety fuse (the duplication ensured ignition should one fuse fail) to the powder and on 25 June announced that all was ready.

On the night of 18 June gunners had hauled two 30-pound Parrotts up to Battery Hickenlooper. At a range of only 130 yards, the big Parrotts had quickly punched a breach in the redan's parapet. Unbeknown to the attackers, a rebel major had ordered his men to build a parapet across the open end of the V-shaped redan, and this precaution was to prove crucial.

Grant spent the morning of 25 June co-ordinating efforts to take advantage of the mine's explosion. He prepared a series of diversions to occupy Confederate attention on other sectors and arranged for an artillery bombardment in an endeavour to interdict the movement of enemy reserves. Then he rode to Battery Hickenlooper to observe the attack. He watched the assault troops – the brigade of Mortimer Leggett, who had cut short his furlough to reach the field at Champion's Hill – assemble in column, four ranks wide, in the approach trench. Just in front of them crouched Hickenlooper, another officer and ten pioneers to act as a forlorn hope, a mere 25 yards from the redan. Picked sharpshooters manned the flanking rifle pits. At 3.30 p.m. the mine exploded. 'The burst was terrific,' recalls an eye-witness. 'The air was filled with dirt, dust, stockades, gabions, timbers, one or two gun carriages, and an immense surging white cloud of smoke.'[12] The explosion killed and buried six of the defenders. Before the dust had settled, the assault troops of the 45th Illinois cheered and surged forward towards the newly formed crater.

Led by the forlorn hope who cleared obstacles from their path, they entered a pit 40 feet across and 12 feet deep, and then, to their horror, encountered the newly built,and impressive earthen traverse across the open side of the V-shaped redan. While the mine had demolished the front of the V, it had not touched this traverse. From its parapet, the Louisiana defenders fired at point-blank range into the assault troops who were piling into the crater. The lieutenant-colonel of the 45th, sword in hand, fell mortally wounded while leading his men. The regiment's Colour-bearer managed to plant it on the traverse. Realizing that no one was following his example, this brave man had to run back to shelter.

Only two companies could deploy in the crater. Colonel Maltby, the regiment's commander, divided the men into teams, positioning one team to provide fire support with rifle and hand-grenade while the other team tried to crawl up the slope of the traverse. When this failed, he had one team fire while the other loaded. The riflemen worked their weapons so fast that they overheated and fouled after thirty minutes, so Maltby ordered two fresh companies into the crater to continue the fight. Meanwhile, Hickenlooper and his pioneers carried forward pre-fabricated loop-holed head logs to protect the infantry. It proved a mistake. Confederate artillery fired into the logs at point-blank range. The resultant explosions unleashed a flurry of deadly splinters that killed and wounded a number of attackers including Colonel Maltby. Told of this, General Leggett snarled and ordered the logs removed. Meanwhile, the defenders followed this up with a barrage of hand-grenades and explosive shells dropped by hand. The Union gunners back in Battery Hickenlooper could clearly hear groans and shrieks coming from the closely packed infantry of the 45th Illinois as the grenades exploded among them. General Logan exclaimed, 'My God! They are killing my bravest men in that hole!'[13]

One of the privates in the front ranks managed to throw back some twenty grenades into the rebel lines before falling mortally wounded when one of them exploded in his hand. Leggett directed other men to keep up this dangerous work. Fearing an enemy sortie against his wavering men, a captain ran back to a nearby battery, picked up three 10-pound Parrott shells, cut the fuses to five seconds, returned to the crater, and hurled them over the traverse. The resultant explosions ended any Confederate thoughts about a counter-attack.

From his vantage point at Battery Hickenlooper, Grant had watched the mine explode and the subsequent infantry charge. He said that if Leggett's people could hold the crater through the night, the XVI-Ith Corps could capture a series of nearby rifle pits and pave the way for a decisive breakthrough along the Jackson Road. He ordered Hicken-looper to prepare emplacements at the crater for two artillery pieces so that the guns could breach the traverse at the base of the redan. While Hickenlooper and his pioneers laboured amid exploding grenades and shells, the infantry continued the firefight to cover them. At 6 p.m. Leggett ordered the 20th Illinois to relieve the 45th. The 20th fought until 11 p.m. but could gain no advantage. On came the rest of the brigade in succession until the 45th returned to the fight at daylight. This time the 45th fought until 10 a.m. before leaving the crater. Then the 124th Illinois took up the fight until 5 p.m. of the second day.

When it finally became clear that an advance artillery position could not be built in the crater itself, Grant realized that there was no chance for a breakthrough. Leaving a few men to hold the section of the parapet they had managed to capture, the balance of the attacking force withdrew. The 45th Illinois had lost seven killed and 61 wounded during its two bouts in the crater. Leggett's brigade suffered a total of 34 killed and 209 wounded.

The two-day fight at the 3d Louisiana Redan was one combat among many during the siege of Vicksburg, and was wholly characteristic of the inventiveness, determination and courage displayed by Grant's men at the siege. During the assault on 22 May, Leggett's brigade had charged the same redan and got to within 100 yards before becoming hopelessly entangled in the abatis and cut down by fierce fire. Unable to capture the redan by assault, the next day they had begun to dig forward. They had built a novel sap-roller, lost it; built a second and lost it too; and then built a third. When they could advance no farther above ground, they had tunnelled beneath the ground. And, the fight at the redan did not stop after the failure of the first mine. In subsequent days, Hickenlooper began another tunnel beneath the Confederate traverse which initiated a new round of mine and counter-mine, an activity halted only by Pemberton's surrender. Such was the calibre of the men of Grant's Army of the Tennessee.

At no point along the army's 12-mile-long line were the Union trenches more than 600 yards from the enemy works. During the siege both sides engaged in active sniping which made life in the trenches miserable. One moment's inattention could have lethal consequences. An Illinois artilleryman relates, 'Here George Whitier was killed by a sharpshooter. He was washing his hands in a stooping posture behind the works. Getting some soap in his eyes, he called for a towel and holding out his hands, he raised himself a little too high and a rebel bullet went through his heart.'[14]

Because the defenders had to husband their ammunition, casualties among Grant's men were low, but men who were hit were generally either killed or very seriously wounded because the only men shooting at them were marksmen. The Army of the Tennessee lost one of its best gunners to such a sharpshooter. Captain Henry Rogers of Company D, 1st Illinois Artillery, sighted one of his battery's 24-pound howitzers and then mounted the parapet to observe the shot's effect. He lingered here too long. While turning to tell his men how to cut the fuses to adjust the range, a shot rang out and Rogers collapsed backwards into his men's arms and died. As time passed, the men became inured to danger. One veteran recalled that 'Hair-breadth escapes were so common occurrences in our experience that they called forth no more remark among us than would a needle's prick in a sewing circle.'[15]

Grant himself had two narrow escapes during the siege. While conferring with Sherman and directing infantry to close up on the enemy outworks, a shell exploded and killed a soldier standing next to him. Later, in an uncharacteristic display of foolhardy bravery, he stood atop the trench to supervise construction of a redoubt while rebel bullets filled the air around him.

Unlike their counterparts, yankee marksmen had the advantage of unlimited ammunition and targets who manned ridgetop positions where they presented an easily visible silhouette against the skyline. The yankees could lurk in the hollows and wait their chance. Other Federal sharpshooters occupied every commanding point along their lines, and even built wooden towers to give them good firing positions. One of these structures received the name Coonskin Tower in honour of the army's best marksman. Lieutenant Henry C. Foster of the 23d Indiana was a deadly shot who was known army-wide as 'Coonskin' from the raccoon fur cap he wore. 'Coonskin' would collect food for several days in his haversack, creep forward into no man's land under cover of darkness and build a burrow with a lookout hole. He would bide his time until an unwary rebel showed himself. When 'Coonskin' fired he seldom missed. Men like Foster stalked the enemy without orders, apparently for the sport of it. Clearly the war had hardened them. James Wilson relates that '... no one seemed to feel any more compunction in taking a good shot at an unknown enemy than at a deer'.[16]

Grant honored one such prominent marksman, Private Lorain Ruggles, with a gift of a Henry 15-shot repeating rifle. Ruggles spent his days wandering the trenches searching for an advantageous perch. He would return to his Ohio regiment to relate his day's exploits. One day he reported to his colonel and seemed quite dejected. Ruggles explained, 'Colonel, I aint had no kind of luck to-day. I haint killed a feller.'[17]

Unlike these cold-blooded sharpshooters, the common soldier sent out on picket duty with orders to fire at will, generally considered only enemy soldiers who were trying to hide (and prominent officers!) fair game. Otherwise, their attitude was one of live and let live. The pickets in the advance posts punctiliously observed an informal truce. In typical behaviour the soldiers of the 37th Illinois met regularly with their foes even though specifically ordered not even to talk to enemy soldiers. They exchanged news and traded for tobacco. When the rebels seemed to violate the terms of the truce by bringing up a working-party to improve their rifle pits, the Illinois soldiers objected and began firing. However, before the unofficial armistice ended, they warned the enemy that they were about to open fire. A private recalls, 'the cry along the front was "Hunt your holes!"' and the war resumed.[18]

Having served him for many months, Grant's staff began to notice how his personal habits reflected his command style. He was, wrote at aide, 'distressingly reluctant to waste any time in bed when there was work to do'.[19] Even during campaign lulls, he slept only four or five hours each night. Likewise, he kept a frugal mess table devoid of most luxuries. But the 47-day siege was not to Grant's taste. It bored him, and when bored he became vulnerable to his great vice, the demon drink for which he had a near fatal attraction. But he could not hold his liquor. Rawlins understood this and forbade any officer to give him a drink. Rawlins threatened anyone who connived at Grant's drinking with public humiliation, disgrace, reduction in rank and even dismissal.

The hapless staffer who liked to imbibe had to do so behind closed tent-flaps, 'with the utmost caution and secrecy'.[20]

On 6 June Ulysses S. Grant evaded the vigilant Rawlins and went on a tour of inspection by boat up the Yazoo River. It turned into a two-day drinking spree. Newspaper writer Sylvanus Cadwallader accompanied Grant and later wrote: 'I was not long in perceiving that Grant had been drinking heavily, and he was still keeping it up. He made several trips to the bar room of the boat in a short time, and became stupid in speech and staggering in gait ... I was greatly alarmed by his condition, which was fast becoming worse.' After two days Cadwallader managed to haul Grant back to his headquarters aboard an ambulance. They arrived at about midnight and Cadwallader watched with near stupefaction as Grant 'shrugged his shoulders, pulled down his vest, shook himself together, as one just rising from a nap, and seeing Rawlins and Riggen [one of Grant's staff officers] bid them good-night in a natural tone and manner, and started to his tent as steadily as he ever walked in his life.'[21] His act did not fool Rawlins. The next day, citing his great solicitude for the army's safety, Rawlins demanded that either Grant pledge not 'to touch a single drop of any kind of liquor' no matter what or he would resign.[22] Grant accepted Rawlins' ultimatum. For the remainder of the war he stayed sober while in the field.

Grant's bender had been innocent enough. No active operations were under way during his absence, and he had issued no orders while under the influence of alcohol. But had news of the escapade reached his superiors the consequences could have been devastating for his career. In the past, particularly after the surprise at Shiloh, hostile newspapers had declared that Grant had been drunk on the field. One of the reasons a War Department official named Charles Dana was visiting Vicksburg was to investigate rumours of Grant's drinking. In the event, a conspiracy of silence among Grant's loyal aides, newspaper journalist Sylvanus Cadwallader, and Dana himself – who had come to recognize that Grant was indispensable to the North's war effort – kept anyone from learning about Grant's binge until more than twenty years later.

By the end of June, yankee sapheads all along the front were very close to the Confederate works. To cite three examples: Thayer's approach had reached the stockade outside the 26th Louisiana Redoubt; at the Stockade Redan a mere 25 feet separated the saphead from the stockade; another mine had all but destroyed the 3d Louisiana Redan. Chief Engineer Comstock informed Grant that the heads of all of the approaches were 5 to 120 yards from the Confederate trenchline. The approaches had been widened and deepened so that assault troops could advance in perfect safety right up to the sapheads. The pioneers prepared planks and sandbags to cross the ditches so that field artillery could move up in the wake of the assault troops. Numerous mines had been dug beneath key forts and charges were ready for detonation.

Quite literally, Vicksburg was a powder keg waiting to explode. Grant scheduled a final assault for 6 July. On the 3rd, General Pemberton wisely asked for terms before the final assault could be delivered.

During the afternoon of 3 July 1863 the two commanders met to discuss surrender terms. They had known each other back in Mexico, but this did little to ease the meeting's tension. Northern-born Pemberton was acutely uncomfortable with his situation, stood Grant up for twenty minutes before appearing, and gave no indication that he had ever met him before. Even after a staff officer had introduced the two generals and they had shaken hands, an awkward silence prevailed. Finally, Pemberton asked what terms Grant proposed and Grant replied that they were those he had already demanded in writing, namely unconditional surrender. Angrily, Pemberton refused. Fortunately for everyone, the two generals stood aside while their staffs discussed matters. That evening Grant offered to allow the Confederates to sign paroles not to fight until exchanged and to let the officers retain their sidearms. Pemberton accepted these terms and the two met again the next day. The surrender ceremony lacked drama, in large part because Pemberton wanted nothing to do with it. Grant reached the designated house and began climbing the stairs when Pemberton emerged. Without any salutation, the Confederate general pulled his sword from his scabbard and thrust it toward his victor. Grant placed his hand on the proffered sword and told Pemberton to retain his sidearm. Embarrassing silence ensued so Grant offered Pemberton a cigar. Somewhat hesitatingly, Pemberton accepted, but this gesture too did little to thaw the chilly scene. As quickly as possible Pemberton departed, his surrender complete.

During the siege, federal troops had boasted loudly to the nearby Confederates that they would eat their 4 July dinners in Vicksburg. In response, the *Vicksburg Daily Citizen* wrote that in cooking a rabbit the best recipe was 'First ketch your rabbit.' After the surrender Grant exulted, 'We had caught our rabbit!'[23] Never one to waste time, the same day he sent Sherman marching east to try to bag Joe Johnston and his army. Although that effort failed, it did little to detract from the campaign's stupendous achievement.

The Army of the Tennessee lost 1,514 men killed, 7,395 wounded and 453 missing from the time Grant led it east across the Mississippi until Vicksburg surrendered. This total of 9,362 men was one more casualty than the army had suffered at Shiloh. During the twenty days of open manoeuvring from 1 April to 19 May, the army marched more than 200 miles through enemy territory and operated between two enemy forces which, had they combined, outnumbered the Army of the Tennessee. In those twenty days, Grant's army inflicted more than 8,000 Confederate battle casualties and captured 88 cannon and howitzers. At Vicksburg itself, Pemberton surrendered 29,491 men and 172 cannon and howitzers, 60,000 muskets, and more than 2,000,000 rounds of ammunition. Five days later, as a direct consequence of Vicksburg's surrender, the Confederate garrison at Port Hudson also surrendered, which struck another 6,500 men from the southern inventory. These were losses of men and *matériel* that the South could not afford. In Grant's words: 'The fate of the Confederacy was sealed when Vicksburg fell.'[24]

Secretary of the Navy Gideon Welles brought President Lincoln the news that Vicksburg had capitulated. He describes the President's reaction:

'His countenance beaming with joy; he caught my hand, and, throwing his arm around me, exclaimed ..." cannot, in words, tell you my joy over this result. It is great, Mr. Welles, it is great!"'[25]

The fall of Vicksburg opened the way for an offensive that would win the war. Grant clearly saw the opportunity and pressed Halleck for permission to transport his army by ship down the Mississippi, out into the Gulf of Mexico, and to land near the strategic port of Mobile, Alabama. At this time Mobile was defended by artillery alone, and Grant had no doubt that he could capture it. Then he intended to operate against the Confederacy's underbelly, the region that supplied most of the necessities for both Lee's and Bragg's armies. In all likelihood this plan would have been successful. Instead, as he had done following the capture of Donelson and again after the capture of Corinth, Halleck frittered away the strategic opportunity earned by Grant's army. Responding in part to Lincoln's concerns about French pressure along the Rio Grande, he scattered Grant's troops to a variety of secondary fronts and by so doing prolonged the war.

For all Northerners living west of the Appalachian Mountains, Vicksburg was a tremendous victory. Pemberton's surrender reduced the Confederacy to only one remaining major army in the West. Neither soldier nor civilian would have believed that the war would last for almost two more long years.

Combat Assessment

Grant: His greatest campaign, worthy of Napoleon.

Staff: Much improved, ably handled difficult manoeuvres and logistics. James Wilson's performance marks him as a coming man.

Lieutenants: Sherman doubted Grant's strategy but loyally supported him. McPherson proved equal to the challenge of corps command. Ransom had attracted Grant's favourable attention and, although a mere brigadier, also seemed equal to corps command. Grant considered Logan and Crocker to be fully competent divisional commanders and their performance justified his faith. By the end of the campaign he believed them ready for army command.

Infantry: A magnificent veteran performance by an army accustomed to victory. The brigadiers and colonels particularly displayed great energy and courage.

Artillery: At Champion's Hill provided critical support when the issue hung in the balance. Enthusiastically converted from field to siege operations.

Cavalry: With the exception of Grierson's raid, still used in penny packets as scouts, couriers and military police.

Engineers: Having only four officers of the Engineer Corps, Grant orders all West Point-educated officers – who had to have studied engineering as a discipline – to assist in actively pressing the siege. This order and the resultant effort greatly contributes to the siege's success.

The Navy: In Grant's words, 'The navy under Porter was all it could be', its service indispensable.[26]

UNION FORCES, Vicksburg, Missouri,[27] 18 May–4 July 1863
ARMY OF THE TENNESSEE: Major General Ulysses S. Grant
Escort: 4th Illinois Cavalry, Co. A
Engineers: 1st Bn. Engineer Regiment of the West

NINTH ARMY CORPS:
Major General John G. Parke

First Division:
Brigadier General Thomas Welsh
FIRST BRIGADE: Colonel Henry Bowman
36th Massachusetts
17th Michigan
27th Michigan
45th Pennsylvania
THIRD BRIGADE:
Colonel Daniel Leasure
2d Michigan
8th Michigan
20th Michigan
79th New York
100th Pennsylvania
ARTILLERY: Pennsylvania Light, Batt. D

Second Division:
Brigadier General Robert B. Potter
FIRST BRIGADE:
Colonel Simon G. Griffin
6th New Hampshire
9th New Hampshire
7th Rhode Island
SECOND BRIGADE:
Brigadier General Edward Ferrero
35th Massachusetts
11th New Hampshire
51st New York
51st Pennsylvania

THIRD BRIGADE:
Colonel Benjamin C. Christ
29th Massachusetts
46th New York
50th Pennsylvania
ARTILLERY: 2d New York Light., Batt. L
ARTILLERY RESERVE: 2d US, Batt. E

THIRTEENTH ARMY CORPS:
Major General John A. McClernand,
    Major General Edward O.C. Ord
Escort: 3d Illinois Cavalry, Co. L
Pioneers: Kentucky Infantry (Independent Co.)

Ninth Division:
Brigadier General Peter J. Osterhaus
FIRST BRIGADE:
Brigadier General Albert L. Lee,
    Colonel James Keigwin
118th Illinois
49th Indiana
69th Indiana
7th Kentucky
120th Ohio
SECOND BRIGADE:
Colonel Daniel W. Lindsey
54th Indiana
22d Kentucky
16th Ohio
42d Ohio
114th Ohio

CAVALRY:
2d Illinois (five companies)
3d Illinois (three companies)
6th Missouri (seven companies)
ARTILLERY: Captain Jacob T. Foster
Michigan Light, 7th Batt.
Wisconsin Light, 1st Batt.

Tenth Division:
Brigadier General Andrew J. Smith
Escort: 4th Indiana Cavalry, Co. C
FIRST BRIGADE: Brigadier General
  Stephen G. Burbridge
16th Indiana
60th Indiana
67th Indiana
83d Ohio
96th Ohio
23d Wisconsin
SECOND BRIGADE:
Colonel William J. Landram
77th Illinois
97th Illinois
130th Illinois
19th Kentucky
48th Ohio
ARTILLERY:
Illinois Light, Chicago Mercantile
  Batt.
Ohio Light, 17th Batt.

Twelfth Division:
Brigadier General Alvin P. Hovey
Escort: 1st Indiana Cavalry, Co. C
FIRST BRIGADE: Brigadier General
  George F. McGinnis
11th Indiana
24th Indiana
34th Indiana
46th Indiana
29th Wisconsin
SECOND BRIGADE:
Colonel James R. Slack
87th Illinois
47th Indiana
24th Iowa
28th Iowa
56th Ohio
ARTILLERY:
1st Missouri Light, Batt. A
Ohio Light, 2d Batt.
Ohio Light, 16th Batt.

Fourteenth Division:
Brigadier General Eugene A. Carr
Escort: 3d Illinois Cavalry, Co. G
FIRST BRIGADE:
Brigadier General William P. Benton,
  Colonel Henry D. Washburn,
  Colonel David Shunk
33d Illinois
99th Illinois
8th Indiana
18th Indiana
1st US (siege guns)
SECOND BRIGADE:
Brigadier General Michael K. Lawler
21st Iowa
22d Iowa
23d Iowa
11th Wisconsin
ARTILLERY:
2d Illinois Light, Batt. A
Indiana Light, 1st Batt.

FIFTEENTH ARMY CORPS:
Major General William T. Sherman

First Division:
Major General Frederick Steele
FIRST BRIGADE:
Colonel Francis H. Manter, Colonel
  Bernard G. Farrar
13th Illinois
27th Missouri
29th Missouri
30th Missouri
31st Missouri
32d Missouri
SECOND BRIGADE:
Colonel Charles R. Woods
25th Iowa
31st Iowa
3d Missouri
12th Missouri
17th Missouri
76th Ohio
THIRD BRIGADE:
Brigadier General John M. Thayer
4th Iowa
9th Iowa
26th Iowa
30th Iowa
ARTILLERY:
Iowa Light, 1st Batt.
2d Missouri Light, Batt. F

Ohio Light, 4th Batt.
CAVALRY:
Kane County (Illinois) Independent
   Co.
3d Illinois, Co. D

Second Division:
Major General Frank P. Blair
FIRST BRIGADE:
Colonel Giles A. Smith
113th Illinois
116th Illinois
6th Missouri
8th Missouri
13th US
SECOND BRIGADE:
Colonel Thomas Kilby Smith,
   Brigadier General Joseph A. J.
   Lightburn
55th Illinois
127th Illinois
83d Indiana
54th Ohio
57th Ohio
THIRD BRIGADE:
Brigadier General Hugh Ewing
30th Ohio
37th Ohio
47th Ohio
4th West Virginia
ARTILLERY:
1st Illinois Light, Batts. A, B, H
Ohio Light, 8th Batt.
CAVALRY:
Thielemann's (Illinois) Battalion, Cos.
   A and B
10th Missouri, Co. C

Third Division:
Brigadier General James M. Tuttle
FIRST BRIGADE:
Brigadier General Ralph P. Buckland,
   Colonel William L. McMillen
114th Illinois
93d Indiana
72d Ohio
95th Ohio
SECOND BRIGADE:
Brigadier General Joseph A. Mower
47th Illinois
5th Minnesota
11th Missouri
8th Wisconsin

THIRD BRIGADE:
Brigadier General Charles L. Matthies,
   Colonel Joseph J. Woods
8th Iowa
12th Iowa
35th Iowa
ARTILLERY: Captain Nelson T. Spoor
1st Illinois Light, Batt. E
Iowa Light, 2d Batt.

UNATTACHED CAVALRY: 4th Iowa

SIXTEENTH ARMY CORPS (Detachment): Major General Cadwallader C. Washburn

First Division: Brigadier General
   William Sooy Smith
Escort: 7th Illinois Cavalry, Co. B
FIRST BRIGADE:
Colonel John M. Loomis
26th Illinois
90th Illinois
12th Indiana
100th Indiana
SECOND BRIGADE:
Colonel Stephen G. Hicks
40th Illinois
103d Illinois
15th Michigan
46th Ohio
THIRD BRIGADE:
Colonel Joseph R. Cockerill
97th Indiana
99th Indiana
53d Ohio
70th Ohio
FOURTH BRIGADE:
Colonel William W. Sanford
48th Illinois
6th Iowa
ARTILLERY: Captain William Cogswell
1st Illinois Light, Batts. F and I
Illinois Light, Cogswell's Batt.
Indiana Light, 6th Batt.

Fourth Division:
Brigadier General Jacob Lauman
FIRST BRIGADE: Colonel Isaac C. Pugh
41st Illinois
53d Illinois
3d Iowa
33d Wisconsin

SECOND BRIGADE: Colonel Cyrus Hall
14th Illinois
15th Illinois
46th Illinois
76th Illinois
53d Indiana
THIRD BRIGADE:
Colonel George E. Bryant, Colonel
    Amory K. Johnson
28th Illinois
32d Illinois
12th Wisconsin
CAVALRY:
15th Illinois, Cos. F and I
ARTILLERY:
Captain George C. Gumbart
2d Illinois Light, Batts. E and K
Ohio Light, 5th, 7th, 15th Batts.

Provisional Division:
Brigadier General Nathan Kimball
(composed of first and second
brigades of the Third Division and
four regiments from the Sixth Division)
ENGELMANN'S BRIGADE:
Colonel Adolph Engelmann
43d Illinois
61st Illinois
106th Illinois
12th Michigan
RICHMOND'S BRIGADE:
Colonel Jonathan Richmond
18th Illinois
54th Illinois
126th Illinois
22d Ohio
MONTGOMERY'S BRIGADE:
Colonel Milton Montgomery
40th Iowa
3d Minnesota
25th Wisconsin
27th Wisconsin

SEVENTEENTH ARMY CORPS:
Major General James B. McPherson
Escort: 4th Co. Ohio Cavalry

Third Division:
Major General John A. Logan
Escort: 2d Illinois Cavalry, Co. A
FIRST BRIGADE: Brigadier General John
    E. Smith, Brigadier General Mor-

timer D. Leggett
20th Illinois
31st Illinois
45th Illinois
124th Illinois
23d Indiana
SECOND BRIGADE: Brigadier General
    Mortimer D. Leggett, Colonel
    Manning F. Force
30th Illinois
20th Ohio
68th Ohio
78th Ohio
THIRD BRIGADE:
Brigadier General John D. Stevenson
8th Illinois
17th Illinois
81st Illinois
7th Missouri
32d Ohio
ARTILLERY: Major Charles J. Stolbrand
1st Illinois Light, Batt. D
2d Illinois Light, Batts. G and L
Michigan Light, 8th Batt.
Ohio Light, 3d Batt.

Sixth Divison:
Brigadier General John McArthur
Escort: 11th Illinois Cavalry, Co. G
FIRST BRIGADE:
Brigadier General Hugh T. Reid
1st Kansas
16th Wisconsin
SECOND BRIGADE: Brigadier General
    Thomas E. G. Ransom
11th Illinois
72d Illinois
95th Illinois
14th Wisconsin
17th Wisconsin
THIRD BRIGADE:
Colonel William Hall, Colonel
    Alexander Chambers
11th Iowa
13th Iowa
15th Iowa
16th Iowa
ARTILLERY: Major Thomas D. Maurice
2d Illinois Light, Batt. F
Minnesota Light, 1st Batt.
1st Missouri Light, Batt. C
Ohio Light, 10th Batt.

Seventh Division: Brigadier General Isaac F. Quinby, Brigadier General John E. Smith
Escort: 4th Missouri Cavalry, Co. F
FIRST BRIGADE: Colonel John B. Sanborn
48th Indiana
59th Indiana
4th Minnesota
18th Wisconsin
SECOND BRIGADE: Colonel Samuel A. Holmes, Colonel Green B. Raum
56th Illinois
17th Iowa
10th Missouri
24th Missouri
80th Ohio
THIRD BRIGADE:
Colonel George B. Boomer, Colonel Holden Putnam, Brigadier General Charles L. Matthies
93d Illinois
5th Iowa
10th Iowa
26th Missouri
ARTILLERY: Captain Frank C. Sands, Captain Henry Dillon
1st Missouri Light, Batt. M

Ohio Light, 11th Batt.
Wisconsin Light, 6th and 12th Batts.

Herron's Division:
Major General Francis J. Herron (from Department of the Missouri)
FIRST BRIGADE:
Brigadier General William Vandever
37th Illinois
26th Indiana
20th Iowa
34th Iowa
38th Iowa
1st Missouri Light Artillery, Batts. E and F
SECOND BRIGADE:
Brigadier General William W. Orme
94th Illinois
19th Iowa
20th Wisconsin
1st Missouri Light Artillery, Batt. B

UNATTACHED CAVALRY:
Colonel Cyrus Bussey
5th Illinois
3d Iowa
2d Wisconsin

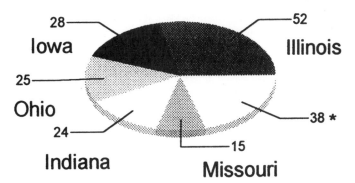

UNION TROOPS AT VICKSBURG
REGIMENTS BY STATE

28 — Iowa
52 — Illinois
25 — Ohio
24 — Indiana
15 — Missouri
38 *

* Michigan 7, Louisiana 5, Pennsylvania 4, Kentucky 3, Massachusetts 3, Minnesota 3, New Hampshire 3, New York 3, Mississippi 2, Arkansas 1, Kansas 1, Rhode Island 1, West Virginia 1, US Regulars 1

DISTRICT NORTH-EAST LOUISIANA:
Brigadier General Elias S. Dennis

DETACHED BRIGADE:
Colonel George W. Neeley
63d Illinois
108th Illinois
120th Illinois
131st Illinois
10th Illinois Cavalry, Cos. A, D, G, K

AFRICAN BRIGADE:
Colonel Isaac F. Shepard

Post of Milliken's Bend, LA:
Colonel Hiram Scofield
8th Louisiana
9th Louisiana
11th Louisiana
13th Louisiana
1st Mississippi
3d Mississippi

Post of Goodrich's Landing, LA:
Colonel William F. Wood
1st Arkansas
10th Louisiana

1 Sylvanus Cadwallader, *Three Years with Grant*, (New York: Alfred A. Knopf, 1956), p. 83.
2 Walter Lord, ed., *The Fremantle Diary*, (Boston: Little, Brown and Co., 1954), May 22, 1863, p. 98.
3 Bearss, vol. 3, p. 762.
4 See *Official Records*, I:24/3, Pemberton to Davis, May 19, 1863, pp. 891-892 in which he reports his "army was much demoralized."
5 Cadwallader, p. 90.
6 Jim Huffstodt, *Hard Dying Men: The Story of General W.H.L. Wallace, General T.E.G. Ransom, and their "Old Eleventh" Illinois Infantry in the American Civil War (1861-1865)*, (Bowie, MD: Heritage Books, 1991), pp. 143-145.
7 For an interesting discussion of this point, see James Harrison Wilson, *Under the Old Flag*, vol. 1 (New York: D. Appleton and Co., 1912), p. 181.
8 Battery Selfridge at the Vicksburg National Military Park displays fine specimens of these cannon.
9 Monument inscription at Vicksburg National Military Park.
10 Edwin C. Bearss, *The Campaign for Vicksburg*, vol. 3 (Dayton: Morningside, 1986), p. 954.
11 Bearss, vol. 3, p. 893.
12 Cadwallader, p. 121.
13 Earl S. Miers, *The Web of Victory: Grant at Vicksburg*, (Baton Rouge: Louisiana State University Press, 1955), p. 283.
14 Charles B. Kimbell, *History of Battery "A" First Illinois Light Artillery Volunteers*, (Chicago: Cushing Printing Co., 1899), p. 64.
15 Bearss, vol. 3, p. 895.
16 Wilson, vol. 1, p. 219.
17 Bearss, vol. 3, p. 912.
18 Michael A. Mullins, *The Fremont Rifles: A History of the 37th Illinois Veteran Volunteer Infantry*, (Wilmington, NC: Broadfoot Publishing, 1990), p. 207.
19 "Samuel H. Beckwith: Grant's Shadow," in John Y. Simon and David L. Wilson, eds., *Ulysses S. Grant: Essays, Documents*, (Carbondale: Southern Illinois University Press, 1981), p. 89.
20 Cadwallader, p. 118.
21 Cadwallader, pp. 103-109.
22 Dan Bauer, "Who Knows the Truth About the Big Bender?" *Civil War Times Illustrated* (December 1988), p. 39.
23 Grant, *Personal Memoirs*, p. 295.
24 Grant, *Personal Memoirs*, p. 297.
25 Gideon Welles, *Diary of Gideon Welles*, vol. 1 (Boston: Houghton Mifflin Co., 1911), p. 364.
26 Grant, *Personal Memoirs*, p. 300.
27 *Official Records*, I:24/2, pp. 148–158.

9
'A Controlling and Regulating Mind'

PART 1. THE NEW COMMAND

'All reports indicate the necessity of a controlling and regulating mind.'[1] So concluded Secretary of War Stanton when apprised of the difficult situation confronting the Army of the Cumberland. Badly defeated at the battle of Chickamauga in September 1863, Major General William S. Rosecrans' men held on to the key rail centre of Chattanooga by the narrowest of margins. The Confederates held the high ground overlooking the city. With its back to the river, and only a tortuous single mountain path linking it with the rear, by October the Army of the Cumberland was in deadly peril. Forage was scarce, horses sickened and died. With few horses capable of hauling wagons and guns – even empty wagons had to be double teamed, so weak were the remaining horses – the army was virtually immobile. Rations for the men had been cut, and cut again. The first cases of scurvy were reported.

Some units had fared better than others. General Phil Sheridan had sent a company of the 2d Kentucky Cavalry with his trusted scout/spy, James Card, behind enemy lines to forage for food. Under Card's direction, this company successfully secreted itself in a mountain valley from where it collected corn, eggs and fowl to supplement the division's scanty rations. Despite Card's efforts, low morale afflicted even Sheridan's division. Periodically this hard man assembled his men to witness the execution of deserters.

The Army of the Cumberland, from its Chief of Staff down, had lost confidence in Rosecrans. The generals fell to quarrelling while their men went uncared for. Rosecrans himself was no longer sure that he could hold on to Chattanooga. To the president, Rosecrans' behaviour seemed '... stunned, like a duck hit on the head'.[2] Recognizing that a crisis was at hand, Lincoln, Halleck and Stanton agreed to summon their reliable troubleshooter to set things right.

Newly promoted to Major General in the Regular Army as a reward for Vicksburg, on 18 October 1863 Grant assumed command of the Military Division of the Mississippi, a vast area encompassing most of the armies west of the Alleghanies. He hastened to Louisville to meet Stanton and received *carte blanche* to deal with the crisis as he saw fit. His first decision was to replace Rosecrans. Grant had worked with Rosecrans during the Iuka campaign. Then and thereafter, Rosecrans had shown flashes of brilliance. But his excitable nature made him unsteady under pressure.

At Chickamauga he had collapsed entirely and fled the field even while the unflappable and stubborn Major General George H. Thomas was fighting to save the army. Already the men were calling Thomas 'The Rock of Chickamauga'. It was this man whom Grant selected to command the Army of the Cumberland. The day after becoming theatre commander, Grant sent an order to Thomas to hold Chattanooga at all costs. Thomas replied, 'We will hold the town until we starve.'[3]

Grant's transfer to Chattanooga underscores the fact that this city was now the war's strategic centre. From the Atlantic to the Mississippi and beyond, no other sector gave promise of dynamic manoeuvre or decisive battle. Even though the Virginia theatre continued to attract more attention, the armies there were again stalemated. In partial recognition of this fact, both sides had sent substantial forces west to fight for Chattanooga. Yet here too, because of Rosecrans' lethargy and Bragg's inability to cobble together a capable command structure, stalemate reigned. On the Federal side, if anything were going to happen during the rest of 1863, it would be up to Grant.

He learned that Rosecrans' staff had a fully prepared plan, designed by a skilled engineering officer, to open a new supply line. Briefed on this plan by Rosecrans himself, Grant thought it gave promise of relieving the situation. Simultaneously, he wondered why Rosecrans had not carried it out himself.[4] Pondering Chattanooga's dire peril, the general set off across the mountains towards Chattanooga.

The journey showed Grant everything he needed to know. The so-called supply line was a mountain track littered with broken down wagons, abandoned supplies, and the carcasses of dead mules and horses. Recently, Confederate cavalry had raided this line, wrecking the entire train of the XIVth Corps. Along much of the track, mud came up to the horses' bellies. Heavy rains had washed out the track in many places, forcing even individual riders to dismount to lead their horses across. In Grant's case, his aides had to carry him across some of the worst of these washouts because the general had a lame leg caused by a recent fall. Grant could not help but notice that it was hardly a fit track for the scores of draft teams and wagons needed to supply the army in Chattanooga. Progress was slow, so Grant and his staff halted for the night.

Staff duties under Grant were simple: do your job promptly and don't worry about formalities. Typically Grant would rise and leave his headquarters with little fanfare. Woe to the staffer who was not ready, for he would not wait. 'We who served him', recalls his telegraph officer, Captain Samuel H. Beckwith, 'were supposed to be "on the job" at the stroke of the clock.'[5] But so hard had been the previous day's journey that Beckwith overslept. He awoke to find that Grant, who was as exhausted as anyone, was an older man, and was suffering a badly swollen leg, had already departed, so anxious was he to reach Chattanooga. It took an entire day for Beckwith to catch up with him.

Arriving at Chattanooga in the evening of 23 October, Grant limped into Thomas's headquarters, wet and filthy. He declined an offer of dry clothes, sat in front of a fire, lit a cigar and asked each of Thomas's staff officers to describe and assess the situation. Grant knew that the first order of business had to be to find a more secure supply line. He called it 'opening up the cracker line'. So he paid particular attention when General William F. 'Baldy' Smith, the army's chief engineer, started to describe the region's complicated topography. An eye-witness recalls that when Smith began speaking, Grant straightened in his chair, became very animated, and 'began to fire whole volleys of questions'.[6] At the conclusion of the briefings, Grant stayed up another hour to write messages and orders.

At first light next morning, Grant began a thorough tour of inspection. 'Baldy' Smith showed him the lie of the land and described in detail his plan to re-open a supply line.[7] This reconnaissance confirmed Grant's favourable impression, and he told Smith to get on with it. As he neared Chickamauga Creek, the Union pickets recognized him and the duty officer began to call out the guard. Disliking such ostentation, Grant told them to desist. But his authority only stretched so far. Across the stream a Confederate officer recognized Grant and ordered, 'Turn out the guard! The commanding General!' Dutifully the rebel pickets lined up and presented arms. Courteously, Grant acknowledged them with a salute and then resumed his study of the Confederate lines. Later he encountered a blue-clad soldier sitting on a log and asked him what unit he belonged to. The soldier turned out to be one of Longstreet's men who was wearing a uniform gleaned from the Chickamauga battlefield. Unperturbed, Grant and this rebel private enjoyed an amiable chat. As soon as was appropriate both men would resume the business of trying to kill each another.

That evening Grant sent out another flurry of telegrams designed to implement Smith's plan. Within 24 hours of arriving in Chattanooga, Grant had adopted a campaign scheme and set it in motion. One of Thomas's aides wrote that, based on Grant's performance at Vicksburg, everyone expected to meet an able soldier, 'but hardly anybody was prepared to find one who had the grasp, the promptness of decision, and the general administrative capacity' that Grant displayed as soon as he arrived.[8]

Not everyone in the Army of the Cumberland was so favourably impressed. At the command level, Clausewitz's 'friction' of war often reduces to personality conflicts among ambitious men. So it was at Chattanooga (and so it would be again in Virginia) when the senior leadership of the Army of the Cumberland made themselves awkward to their new commanding general. Thomas himself probably wondered why Grant, a man whom he had outperformed at West Point and arguably outperformed on the battlefield, was in charge instead of himself. At any rate, an attitude of this sort took hold and was most pronounced in the behaviour of Thomas's chief of staff, an old line Regular officer named Whipple. He kept raising technical objections to Grant's plans, an obstructionism that bordered on rudeness. People had reacted to Grant in this way all his life, so the unassuming Grant shrugged it off. Not so his hot-tempered chief of staff Rawlins. Rawlins fought Whipple tooth and nail and the resultant friction between the staffs impeded preparations to relieve the difficult situation afflicting the army in Chattanooga. Fortunately for the Union cause, on the heights overlooking Chattanooga, the Confederate Army of Tennessee was experiencing more than its own share of personality clashes. These conflicts led Bragg to deplete his army by sending off major detachments simply because he wanted to rid himself of difficult subordinates.[9] It left the rebels vulnerable if Grant could restore his supply line and take the offensive.

Now that Grant was a theatre commander, he had to rely upon the military telegraph to get in touch with his far-flung forces. Although Chattanooga was almost surrounded, it still had telegraphic links to the rest of the North. Indeed the telegraph system had come a long way since the war started. Back in 1861, the United States Army had gone to war in full expectation of employing the tried and true manual signals system which featured men waving a white flag with a red square in the centre for use against a dark background, a red flag with a white square for use against a light background, and torches for nocturnal use. A man with a telescope could read the flags or torches from a distance of up to twenty miles. Useful though it was, the manual system quickly gave way to the electronic field telegraph.

In the summer of 1861, the Army's Signals Officer, the able and energetic Major A. J. Myers, created a 'flying' telegraph train designed for quickly stringing temporary telegraph lines. These trains hauled hand-carried reels with several miles of light wire, lightweight lance poles fitted with insulators, telegraph sets, and tool kits. But the need of heavy storage batteries to provide the electricity constrained mobility.

Myers sought improvement and found the Beardslee magneto-electric telegraphic instrument. This device had a hand crank to generate electricity and a dial with a plainly marked alphabet. It eliminated the need of a skilled Morse Code operator. The inclusion of insulated wire gave the system a range of several miles. On 3 March 1863, Congress established the Signal Corps. It grew from Myers' essentially one-man operation to a force of 300 officers and 2,000 men by the end of the war.

While Myers struggled to perfect his system, he ran into competition from the civilian military telegraph organization. With their batteries and Morse sets, the civilians could transmit signals faster and along greater distances than could Myers' field telegraph. But the military, being the military, went ahead and purchased thirty Signal Corps trains equipped with the Beardslee system. In the East, General Hooker had become so frustrated with the slow signalling along a 10-mile Signal Corps line that he turned it over to the civilian telegraphers. The civilians rigged up their Morse keys and batteries and, using the same Signal Corps line, quickly restored prompt service. Finally, by late 1863 the civilian organization had proved so superior – it had designed increasingly portable Morse equipment – that the Secretary of War turned over all telegraphic signalling responsibility to it. When Grant recommended his cipher operator, Samuel Beckwith, for a commission in the Army Signal Corps, Beckwith declined, preferring to remain a civilian employee of the US Military Telegraph.

Except for the Vicksburg Campaign, Grant was in direct telegraphic communication with his superiors during most of his field operations. Via telegraph he kept them informed and received information about enemy movements. As he became increasingly important to the Federal war effort, Washington provided him with a secret cipher that could not be broken by the enemy even if they intercepted any of his messages. Only Beckwith had access to the key. He was strictly enjoined not to share the cipher with anyone, including members of Grant's staff. Grant would write out his orders longhand and then Beckwith would encode and transmit them. Beckwith describes how messages were kept secret:

'Arbitrary words were used to represent proper names and also many ordinary military phrases. The words of the entire body of the despatch, after being concealed in this manner, were then arranged in one of over a thousand possible combinations, the particular combination being indicated by a key word, and as each combination had several key words, it was not necessary to use the same one twice in succession. As a feature of the combination blind words were interspersed at regular or varying intervals, which in translation were of course discarded. When finally prepared for transmission the despatch was wholly unintelligible to the transmitting or receiving operator, and no case can be recalled of the enemy having translated a Federal despatch.'[10]

Soon after Grant's arrival at Chattanooga, the West's telegraph lines were humming with coded instructions summoning key forces to the relief of Chattanooga.

PART 2. VINDICATION ON MISSIONARY RIDGE

In Chattanooga itself, the Army of the Cumberland reorganized, ridding itself of two feeble corps commanders, Majors General Alexander McCook and Thomas Crittenden. Amazingly, Crittenden would return to command a division in Burnside's Corps during Grant's Virginia campaign of 1864. Extensive shuffling and consolidation reduced the army from four to two corps. John Palmer, an indifferent leader with important political connections, stepped up to command Thomas's old

XIVth Corps, while Gordon Granger – an officer whose commendable march to the sound of the guns had saved Thomas at Chickamauga – took over the IVth Corps.

At the opposite end of the spectrum, the men in the ranks were little different from those who served in the Army of the Tennessee. With the exception of three Pennsylvania regiments, they hailed from the Midwest and Northwest states. About three-quarters of the regiments came from Ohio, Indiana and Illinois. Typically the soldiers had been farmers or mechanics. Like the Army of the Tennessee, their regiments included far fewer immigrants than did the eastern armies. What separated them enormously from Grant's veterans was the absence of a tradition of victory.

Some had served alongside the Army of the Tennessee during the second day at Shiloh. Thereafter, they had chased Bragg through Kentucky, fought a bloody tactical draw at Perryville, been surprised in their camps at Stones River – a colossal bloodbath 'won' only by Rosecrans' tenacity and Bragg's vacillation – and been routed at Chickamauga where the army lost more than 16,000 men and about 50 field guns. Hungry and discontented, they manned the fortifications defending Chattanooga and waited to see what fate would bring.

At a minimum, it would bring reinforcements. Even before the disaster at Chickamauga, Halleck had ordered troops to be sent to Rosecrans from Memphis and Vicksburg. By 15 November 17,000 men would travel 675 miles by boat, railroad and on foot to arrive at Bridgeport, some 25 miles downstream on the Tennessee River. Even more impressive was the fact that Lincoln, on learning of Chattanooga's peril, had decided to send two corps from the Army of the Potomac. Naturally that army's commander, Major General George Meade, had nominated his two poorest corps, the XIth and XIIth. Still, in an awesome display of the North's *matériel* advantages and the strategic mobility provided by railroads, 20,000 men and 3,000 draft animals were moved 1,157 miles to Bridgeport in less than three weeks. 'Fighting Joe' Hooker was in command of them, but welcome though they were, whether he and they were equal to the challenge of western combat remained to be seen.

The men Grant really awaited were his old reliables, the Army of the Tennessee's XVth and XVIIth Corps. Under the command of Sherman, they left Vicksburg in late September. But Halleck had ordered them to rebuild the railroad as they marched, so their progress was snaillike. Finally, Grant countermanded Halleck's order and Sherman's pace accelerated and his command reached Bridgeport on 15 November. Sherman himself had ridden ahead to Chattanooga. Although aware of the Army of the Cumberland's dire straits, when Grant took him on a tour of the lines he was appalled. Gazing up at the Confederate-held heights, he blurted out, 'Why, General Grant, you are besieged!' Grant nodded and replied, 'It's too true.'[11] Then the general explained to his friend how he intended to lift the siege.

It was 'Baldy' Smith's plan, and Grant rewarded the engineer by allowing him to carry it out. Smith's plan called for a simultaneous thrust by Hooker's force at Bridgeport and Thomas's men at Chattanooga, the idea being to drive away the Confederate infantry and artillery that controlled the river and roads between those two points. Characteristic of the Grant way, Grant ordered Hooker to leave his trains behind in order to move rapidly. He elaborated that Hooker's men should carry forage, three days' rations, and sixty rounds of ammunition. Hooker obediently began with a stealthy crossing of the Tennessee River at Bridgeport on the night of 26 October. At 3 a.m. a picked force of 1,500 men commanded by General Hazen silently cast loose from Chattanooga aboard pontoon rafts and drifted past sleeping rebel sentinels to Brown's Ferry where they landed, secured the heights, repulsed a Confederate counter-attack, and began building a pontoon bridge to establish land communications with Chattanooga while waiting for Hooker's column to link up with them. Hooker pressed forward while one of his divisions beat off a determined Confederate counter-attack on the night of 28/29 October. The link-up complete, Federal quartermasters filled a small steamer with 40,000 rations and sent her off to Chattanooga.

Reports of Hooker's movement toward Chattanooga had lifted the morale of the Army of the Cumberland's soldiers. Somebody was doing something to make things better, and they correctly attributed the new-found energy to General Grant. Grant did not impress the Army of Cumberland veterans with his appearance. He wore a dust-stained uniform and hat that made him virtually indistinguishable from a corporal. What did impress them was the resumption of regular rations. When the steamer reached Chattanooga, the word spread quickly, 'The Cracker line is open. Full rations, boys!'[12] An Ohio veteran recalled, 'It was apparent to all, that there was a mastermind now at the head of our army.'[13]

It took three more weeks for the build-up to be completed. Then, on 23 November, Grant ordered Thomas to conduct a reconnaissance in force to determine whether Bragg were withdrawing. This phase of the campaign featured a panoramic advance by two Army of the Cumberland divisions to Orchard Knob, a low ridge halfway between the city and the Confederate lines on Missionary Ridge. It was one of a handful of occasions when a general could cast his eye right and left and see an entire division arrayed for battle. Perhaps because divisional commander Thomas Wood knew that his advance would take place beneath the watchful eyes of his corps, army and theatre commanders, he took particular care with his dispositions.

Wood placed two brigades forward and one in reserve. Each of the two front brigades formed in two lines, the regiments in the first line deployed in line, the regiments in the second 'in double column, closed en masse.' Behind the leftmost brigade the reserve brigade also formed

139

'in double column, closed en masse,'[14] Wood anticipating that any Confederate counterstroke would come against his left, and the reserve brigade's compact columns could be rapidly deployed to protect the left flank if needed. Otherwise, it could pass to the front and deploy to support the attack. Each of the front assault brigades had a very heavy skirmish line, the equivalent of an entire regiment, deployed to lead the charge.

Although under fire for most of the advance, Wood's men marched at the double for the first mile and then accelerated for the final, quarter-mile bayonet charge to Orchard Knob. So unexpected and sudden was their advance, and so determined was their final charge, that they captured virtually an entire regiment of Alabama troops who were defending the works on Orchard Knob. It was a textbook assault and showed what the officers and men were capable of when manoeuvring unimpeded by dense woodland.

The capture of Orchard Knob gained Thomas's men some elbow-room to manoeuvre, and the high command a vantage point to study the enemy lines at close range. Drawing up plans to complete his breakout from Chattanooga, Grant sent 'Baldy' Smith to reconnoitre the northern end of Missionary Ridge. He reported that this sector of Bragg's position beyond his right flank lay unoccupied and vulnerable. Accordingly, Grant ordered Sherman to move with his four Army of the Tennessee divisions towards this position. Once Sherman started to roll up Bragg's flank, Grant intended that the Army of the Cumberland would attack Bragg's centre. Meanwhile Hooker would advance against Bragg's left.

On 24 November the movement began. Hooker captured Lookout Mountain in the celebrated 'Battle Above the Clouds' while Sherman crossed the Tennessee River beyond Bragg's right flank. Gazing at Lookout Mountain from the valley below, Grant and his staff glimpsed Hooker's men through intermittent gaps in the fog. They thrilled to the spectacle of one intrepid standard-bearer who kept well in front of his unit, constantly waving his flag to urge the line upward. Suddenly, the rebels turned on him in an effort to capture his standard, but alert to this possibility, the valiant, unknown soldier ran back unscathed to his own lines. In what amounted to little more than a hard skirmish, Hooker captured Lookout Mountain. The next morning a party from the 8th Kentucky scaled the peak to plant a Stars and Stripes banner where everyone could see it.

Lookout Mountain may have seemed a dramatic affair and Hooker and his men made much of it, but after ceding the height, the Confederates burned the bridges in the valley, effectively isolating Hooker's command from any intervention during the next day. At the time Grant did not know this. In later life, when the action rose in national myth, Grant sniffed, 'The Battle of Lookout Mountain is one of the romances of the war. There was no such battle and no action even worthy to be called a battle on Lookout Mountain. It is all poetry.'[15]

While Hooker's men were climbing Lookout Mountain, the main effort of the day involved Sherman. After crossing the Tennessee on pontoons that had been carefully hidden in a nearby creek, Sherman cautiously paused to concentrate his forces before continuing. It proved a mistake. By 4 p.m. Sherman had seized the northern end of Missionary Ridge only to find himself in possession of an isolated hill, and an unsuspected, wide ravine separated him from the Confederate main line. Worse, in the fading light he could see veterans of Cleburne's division, the best unit in Bragg's army, beginning to file into position to counter any attack from across the ravine.

Accordingly, Grant recast his plans for 25 November. Instead of a single, powerful flank attack delivered by Sherman alone, he called for a double envelopment featuring simultaneous attacks by Sherman and Hooker. At the appropriate time Thomas would assault the centre. When the day began, Grant and his lieutenants –Thomas, Granger, Wood, W. F. Smith and Rawlins – rode to Orchard Knob to await news. Here they spent most of the day under shell fire from a Confederate 10-pound Parrott rifle battery on Missionary Ridge. Worse, couriers brought information that Hooker could not advance because of the burned bridges and Sherman's attacks had stalled against fierce Confederate opposition.

At 10 a.m. Grant shifted Howard's two divisions to reinforce Sherman. At noon he sent another. Sherman attacked repeatedly but could make no progress. Finally, in mid-afternoon observers on Orchard Knob thought they could detect Confederate reserves moving towards Bragg's right. Although it transpired that they were mistaken, at the time Grant thought that he must order the Army of the Cumberland forward to relieve pressure on Sherman, specifically an assault against the trenches at the base of Missionary Ridge. What happened next proved that the westerners of the Army of the Cumberland had merely been waiting for a leader equal to their mettle.

Because of the depleted strengths of the regiments in his corps, Gordon Granger had arranged some of his units into 'demi-brigades', an innovation divisional commander Phil Sheridan found 'awkward'.[16] Despite the complications of the unfamiliar structure, Sheridan deployed his division using a variation of the form employed two days earlier by General Wood. Preferring a thinner formation, Sheridan had two brigades in double lines at the front and a third brigade formed in column of attack as a reserve. Screened by a heavy line of skirmishers, Sheridan's division – one of the four that took part in the assault – set off across the plain towards Missionary Ridge.

Because the Confederate defences on Missionary Ridge were poorly sited (along the geological, not the military, crest), their artillery had a narrow fire zone. Although passing through this zone was dangerous – a typical regiment, the 5th Kentucky, lost thirteen men to one shell burst – once the attackers were through they had only musketry from the trenchline at the ridge's base with which to contend. This trench they stormed relatively easily, driving the defenders back up the slope.

As per orders, having captured the line of works at the base of Missionary Ridge, many units halted to consolidate their position, but a handful of men, excited to see the backs of their enemy, went on. Moreover, the annoying fire from the two lines of trenches above made the position at the ridge's base untenable. Soon soldiers all along the line surged upwards. This classic display of small-unit level initiative was wholly characteristic of the American volunteer. In their own language, 'when they saw a good thing, they knew it, and took it'.[17]

Back on Orchard Knob, Grant had an excellent view of what was taking place. He commented that it was contrary to his plan, he intended to have the men dress ranks and form assault columns before continuing, but since the men had gone so far he would not order them back. Anxious officers pointed out the gaps in the charging line and Grant responded that they were not as badly scattered as it seemed. Patiently he explained that the perspective looking up the ridge revealed more bare ground between them than would be the case if the observer were on the same level as the assault troops. He concluded: 'The boys feel pretty good. Let them alone awhile.'[18]

An apprehensive officer approached and commented that the men were not even stopping to reform. Grant replied, 'Let 'em go, Sheridan will come out all right.'[19] Then he issued orders for the entire 2-mile line to charge the heights. Sheridan himself describes his advance and how 'there seemed to be a rivalry as to which color should be farthest to the front; first one would go forward a few feet, then another would come up to it, the color bearers vying with one another as to who should be foremost.'[20]

An Ohio sergeant describes the assault and the dramatic role played by Sheridan:

'We started up with one of the best lines of battle that it was possible to muster, with the shot and shell, grape and canister flying in our faces, over our heads and under our feet, where it tore holes in the ground big enough to bury an ox in. We succeeded fairly well until we got within 30 yards of that battery, when some of the more nervous comrades started to retreat. As luck would have it, at this critical moment along came General Phil Sheridan on his famous black charger, and as he had already taken in the situation, and seeing that many of the boys were about to retreat, cried out: "For God's sake, men, don't go back!" They all rushed forward, and the 125th Ohio [soon] had the United States flag flying over the battery.'[21]

All along Missionary Ridge, although the rebel fire was fierce, it was a plunging fire and less effective than it should have been. The Army of the Cumberland veterans continued their climb. One colonel relates how, 'When within ten yards of the crest, our men seemed to be thrown forward as if by some powerful engine, and the old flag was planted firmly and surely on the last line of works.'[22] Reaching the summit, the assault troops found that many of the defenders were less then keen. Numerous Confederates turned the butts of their muskets toward the yankees in token of surrender. Among the first trophies seized by Sheridan's men were two cannon named 'Lady Breckenridge' and 'Lady Buckner'. To capture these cannon and the heights on which they stood, Sheridan's intrepid division lost 123 officers and 1,181 men killed, wounded or missing from an initial strength of 6,000 men.

Grant rode forward to the crest of Missionary Ridge to take a close look at the situation. Sporadic fighting continued along the ridge and he came under fire once more, but he and his staff deployed the men to sweep along the ridge to take the remaining defenders in flank. Bragg's army broke in ignominious rout, abandoning 37 cannon and howitzers. The entire affair had lasted about 60 minutes. At a cost of 5,824 men, Grant's combined armies had driven the enemy from what should have been an impregnable position and inflicted losses of 6,667 men. The army's quartermaster general noted in his journal that evening: 'Another laurel leaf is added to Grant's Crown.'[23]

In subsequent years, when the Union charge up Missionary Ridge grew into the stuff of legend, it became a story of thousands of men advancing on their own initiative to the consternation of their commanders. In fact, Grant and his lieutenants had planned the breakout from Chattanooga with consummate skill. During the campaign, Grant had displayed great flexibility, shifting units and assignments as the situation warranted, recasting plans when unexpected events occurred.

Above all, the assault on Missionary Ridge had been sweet revenge for the Army of the Cumberland. Many regiments had charged to the chant, 'Chickamauga! Chickamauga!' Their reward had been the sight of their longtime enemies in the Army of Tennessee fleeing before their bayonets. The former Army of the Potomac units had also fought creditably. The fact that a previously dispirited force had gallantly conducted an amazing frontal assault, and that two cast-off eastern formations had contributed useful service, highlights what Grant meant to the Union cause. When handled with a sure touch, the Union soldier was the equal of his opponent. On a level playing field, the North's numerical and logistical superiority would have to tell.

After Chattanooga, Grant had to turn immediately to the relief of Burnside in Knoxville. In part, this accounts for his one major misstep during the campaign, his failure to pursue Bragg's army. Grant knew that Knoxville was a strategic side-show, but the pitiful plight of the Union-loyal citizens of that region had long won Lincoln's attention. Dutifully, Grant dispatched Sherman north-east towards Knoxville, even while recognizing that the true strategic path lay south-east towards Atlanta and east from Vicksburg against Mobile.

So ended 1863, a year in which Grant had more to do with planning strategy and organizing victory in the West than any other general or politician. Ahead lay promotion to commanding general of all of the nation's armies.

Combat Assessment

Grant: Wonderful flexibility, inspiring leadership.

Staff: In a complicated situation involving multiple commands, difficult logistics, and adverse topography the staff rises to provide solid, professional support. William F. Smith shines.

Lieutenants: Sherman blunders; Hooker performs ably; after initial hesitation, Thomas is excellent. Missionary Ridge marks Sheridan as a coming man.

Infantry: A veteran exhibition, with gallantry spread throughout the ranks.

Artillery: Lack of mobility caused by horses' starvation coupled with unfavourable terrain reduces its role to near insignificance.

Cavalry: Absent because of shortage of forage.

CHATTANOOGA Campaign,[24] 20 November 1863
Major General Ulysses S. Grant commanding

ARMY OF THE CUMBERLAND: Major General George H. Thomas

General Headquarters
1st Ohio Sharpshooters
10th Ohio Infantry

FOURTH ARMY CORPS:
Major General Gordon Granger

First Division:
Brigadier General Charles Cruft
Escort: 92d Illinois, Co. E
SECOND BRIGADE:
Brigadier General Walter C. Whitaker
96th Illinois
35th Indiana
8th Kentucky
40th Ohio
51st Ohio
99th Ohio
THIRD BRIGADE: Colonel William Grose

59th Illinois
75th Illinois
84th Illinois
9th Indiana
36th Indiana
24th Ohio

Second Division:
Major General Philip H. Sheridan
FIRST BRIGADE:
Colonel Francis T. Sherman
36th Illinois
44th Illinois
73d Illinois
74th Illinois
88th Illinois
22d Indiana
2d Missouri
15th Missouri

24th Wisconsin
SECOND BRIGADE:
Brigadier General George D. Wagner
100th Illinois
15th Indiana
40th Indiana
51st Indiana
57th Indiana
58th Indiana
26th Ohio
97th Ohio
THIRD BRIGADE:
Colonel Charles G. Harker
22d Illinois
27th Illinois
42d Illinois
51st Illinois
79th Illinois
3d Kentucky
64th Ohio
65th Ohio
125th Ohio
ARTILLERY:
Captain Warren P. Edgarton
1st Illinois Light, Batt. M
10th Indiana Batt.
1st Missouri Light, Batt. G
1st Ohio Light, Batt. I
4th US, Batt. G
5th US, Batt. H

Third Division:
Brigadier General Thomas J. Wood
FIRST BRIGADE:
Brigadier General August Willich
25th Illinois
35th Illinois
89th Illinois
32d Indiana
68th Indiana
8th Kansas
15th Ohio
49th Ohio
15th Wisconsin
SECOND BRIGADE:
Brigadier General William B. Hazen
6th Indiana
5th Kentucky
6th Kentucky
23d Kentucky
1st Ohio
6th Ohio
41st Ohio

93d Ohio
124th Ohio
THIRD BRIGADE:
Brigadier General Samuel Beatty
79th Indiana
86th Indiana
9th Kentucky
17th Kentucky
13th Ohio
19th Ohio
59th Ohio
ARTILLERY: Captain Cullen Bradley
Illinois Light, Bridges' Batt.
6th Ohio Batt.
20th Ohio Batt.
Penn Light, Batt. B

FOURTEENTH ARMY CORPS:
Major General John M. Palmer
Escort: 1st Ohio Cavalry, Co. L

First Division:
Brigadier General Richard W. Johnson
FIRST BRIGADE:
Brigadier General William P. Carlin
104th Illinois
38th Indiana
42d Indiana
88th Indiana
2d Ohio
33d Ohio
94th Ohio
10th Wisconsin
SECOND BRIGADE:
Colonel Marshall F. Moore, Colonel
    William L. Stoughton
19th Illinois
11th Michigan
69th Ohio
15th US, 1st Bn.
15th US, 2d Bn.
16th US, 1st Bn.
18th US, 1st Bn.
18th US, 2d Bn.
19th US, 1st Bn.
THIRD BRIGADE:
Brigadier General John C. Stark-
    weather
24th Illinois
37th Indiana
21st Ohio
74th Ohio
78th Penn

145

79th Penn
1st Wisconsin
21st Wisconsin
ARTILLERY:
1st Illinois Light, Batt. C
1st Michigan Light, Batt. A
5th US, Batt. H

Second Division:
Brigadier General Jefferson C. Davis
FIRST BRIGADE:
Brigadier General James D. Morgan
10th Illinois
16th Illinois
60th Illinois
21st Kentucky
10th Michigan
14th Michigan
SECOND BRIGADE:
Brigadier General John Beatty
34th Illinois
78th Illinois
3d Ohio
98th Ohio
108th Ohio
113th Ohio
121st Ohio
THIRD BRIGADE:
Colonel Daniel McCook
85th Illinois
86th Illinois
110th Illinois
125th Illinois
52d Illinois
ARTILLERY:
Captain William A. Hotchkiss
2d Illinois Light, Batt. I
Minnesota Light, 2d Batt.
Wisconsin Light, 5th Batt.

Third Division:
Brigadier General Absalom Baird
FIRST BRIGADE:
Brigadier General John B. Turchin
82d Indiana
11th Ohio
17th Ohio
31st Ohio
36th Ohio
89th Ohio
92d Ohio
SECOND BRIGADE:
Colonel Ferdinand Van Derveer

75th Indiana
87th Indiana
101st Indiana
2d Minnesota
9th Ohio
35th Ohio
105th Ohio
THIRD BRIGADE: Colonel Edward H.
Phelps, Colonel William H. Hays
10th Indiana
74th Indiana
4th Kentucky
10th Kentucky
18th Kentucky
14th Ohio
38th Ohio
ARTILLERY: Captain George R. Swallow
Indiana Light, 7th Batt.
Indiana Light, 19th Batt.
4th US, Batt. I

Engineer Troops:
Brigadier General William F. Smith
ENGINEERS
1st Michigan Engineers (det.)
13th Michigan Infantry
21st Michigan Infantry
22d Michigan Infantry
18th Ohio Infantry
PIONEER BRIGADE:
Colonel George P. Buell
1st Battalion
2d Battalion
3d Battalion

Artillery Reserve:
Brigadier General John M. Brannan

First Division: Colonel James Barnett
FIRST BRIGADE:
Major Charles S. Cotter
1st Ohio Light, Batt. B
1st Ohio Light, Batt. C
1st Ohio Light, Batt. E
1st Ohio Light, Batt. F
SECOND BRIGADE:
1st Ohio Light, Batt. G
1st Ohio Light, Batt. M
Ohio Light, 18th Batt.
Ohio Light, 20th Batt.

Second Division:
FIRST BRIGADE:

Captain Josiah W. Church
1st Michigan Light, Batt. D
1st Tennessee Light, Batt. A
Wisconsin Light, 3d Batt.
Wisconsin Light, 8th Batt.
Wisconsin Light, 10th Batt.
SECOND BRIGADE: Captain Arnold
  Sutermeister
Indiana Light, 4th Batt.
Indiana Light, 8th Batt.

Indiana Light, 11th Batt.
Indiana Light, 21st Batt.
1st Wisconsin Heavy, Co. C

Post Of Chattanooga: Colonel John
  G. Parkhurst
44th Indiana
15th Kentucky
9th Michigan

ARMY OF THE TENNESSEE: Major General William T. Sherman

FIFTEENTH ARMY CORPS:
Major General Frank P. Blair, Jr.

First Division:
Brigadier General Peter J. Osterhaus
FIRST BRIGADE:
Brigadier General Charles R. Woods
13th Illinois
3d Missouri
12th Missouri
17th Missouri
27th Missouri
29th Missouri
31st Missouri
32d Missouri
76th Ohio
SECOND BRIGADE:
Colonel James A. Williamson
4th Iowa
9th Iowa
25th Iowa
26th Iowa
30th Iowa
31st Iowa
ARTILLERY: Captain Henry H. Griffiths
Iowa Light, 1st Batt.
2d Missouri Light, Batt. F
Ohio Light, 4th Batt.

Second Division:
Brigadier General Morgan L. Smith
FIRST BRIGADE:
Brigadier General Giles A. Smith,
  Colonel Nathan W. Tupper
55th Illinois
116th Illinois
127th Illinois
6th Missouri
8th Missouri
57th Ohio
13th US, 1st Bn.

SECOND BRIGADE: Brigadier General
  Joseph A. J. Lightburn
83d Indiana
30th Ohio
37th Ohio
47th Ohio
54th Ohio
4th West Virginia
ARTILLERY:
1st Illinois Light, Batt. A
1st Illinois Light, Batt. B
1st Illinois Light, Batt. H

Fourth Division:
Brigadier General Hugh Ewing
FIRST BRIGADE: Colonel John M.
  Loomis
26th Illinois
90th Illinois
12th Indiana
100th Indiana
SECOND BRIGADE:
Brigadier General John M. Corse,
  Colonel Charles C. Walcutt
40th Illinois
103d Illinois
6th Iowa
15th Michigan
46th Ohio
THIRD BRIGADE:
Colonel Joseph R. Cockerill
48th Illinois
97th Indiana
99th Indiana
53d Ohio
70th Ohio
ARTILLERY: Captain Henry Richardson
1st Illinois Light, Batt. F
1st Illinois Light, Batt. I
1st Missouri Light, Batt. D

SEVENTH ARMY CORPS:

Second Division:
Brigadier General John E. Smith
FIRST BRIGADE: Colonel Jesse I.
Alexander
63d Illinois
48th Indiana
59th Indiana
4th Minnesota
18th Wisconsin
SECOND BRIGADE: Colonel Green B.
Raum, Colonel Francis C. Deim-
ling, Colonel Clark R. Wever
56th Illinois
17th Iowa

10th Missouri
24th Missouri
80th Ohio
THIRD BRIGADE:
Brigadier General Charles L. Matthies,
Colonel Benjamin D. Dean,
Colonel Jabez Banbury
93d Illinois
15th Iowa
10th Iowa
26th Missouri
ARTILLERY: Captain Henry Dillon
Cogswell's (Illinois) Batt.
Wisconsin Light, 6th Batt.
Wisconsin Light, 12th Batt.

1   John M. Hoffman, ed., "First Impressions of Three Days' Fighting: Quartermaster General Meigs' 'Journal of the Battle of Chattanooga'," in John Y. Simon and David L. Wilson, eds., *Ulysses S. Grant: Essays, Documents*, (Carbondale IL: Southern Illinois University Press, 1981), p.60.
2   James Lee McDonough, *Chattanooga: A Death Grip on the Confederacy*, (Knoxville: University of Tennessee Press, 1984), p. 44.
3   Ulysses S. Grant, *Personal Memoirs*, (New York: De Capo Press, 1982), p. 312.
4   See Grant, *Personal Memoirs*, p. 313. Referring to these plans, Grant relates, "My only wonder was that he had not carried them out."
5   "Samuel H. Beckwith: "Grant's Shadow," in *Ulysses S. Grant: Essays, Documents*, p. 99.
6   Horace Porter, *Campaigning with Grant*, (New York: The Century Co., 1897), p. 5.
7   W.F. Smith, *From Chattanooga to Petersburg Under Generals Grant and Butler*, (Boston: Houghton Mifflin, 1893), p. 9.
8   Porter, p. 8.
9   For a description of this friction, see James Harrison Wilson, *Under the Old Flag*, vol. 1 (New York: D. Appleton and Co., 1912), p. 275.
10 "Samuel H. Beckwith," in *Ulysses S. Grant: Essays, Documents*, p. 84.
11 Shelby Foote, *The Civil War: Fredericksburg to Meridian*, (New York: Random House, 1963), p. 836.
12 *Battles & Leaders of the Civil War*, vol. 3, p. 678.
13 Richard A. Baumgartner and Larry M. Strayer, eds., *Ralsa C. Rice: Yankee Tigers: Through the Civil War with the 125th Ohio*, (Huntington, WV: Blue Acorn Press, 1992), p. 75.
14 Wood's description of this assault is in *Official Records*, I:31/2, p. 254. His regimental commander's reports follow.
15 Grant, *Personal Memoirs*, p. 336.
16 Philip H. Sheridan, *Personal Memoirs of P. H. Sheridan*, vol. 1 (New York: Charles L. Webster & Co., 1888), p. 298.
17 Sylvanus Cadwallader, *Three Years with Grant*, (New York: Alfred A. Knopf, 1956), p. 151.
18 Cadwallader, p. 151.
19 "Samuel H. Beckwith," in *Ulysses S. Grant: Essays, Documents*, p. 103.
20 Sheridan, vol. 1, p. 311.
21 *Yankee Tigers*, p. 214.
22 Sheridan, vol. 1., p. 321.
23 "First Impressions of Three Days' Fighting: Quartermaster General Meigs' 'Journal of the Battle of Chattanooga,'" in *Ulysses S. Grant: Essays Documents*, p. 76
24 *Official Records*, I:31/2, pp. 15-24.

10
Warfare in Transition

PART 1. INFANTRY TACTICS AT THE DAWN OF TRENCH WARFARE
By the end of 1863 there was ample evidence for the discriminating observer that the era of open battle was giving way to a new kind of warfare in which the defender fought exclusively from behind fieldworks and fortifications. In the West, at Stones River in December 1862, the Army of the Cumberland had foregone the opportunity to entrench, preferring to fight in traditional 'stand-up' style. After the first day of its next battle, along Chickamauga Creek in September 1863, it had spent the night felling trees and preparing a long line of breastworks. In the East, neither side had prepared extensive fieldworks during the Battle of Gettysburg. Less than five months later, Lee's Army of Northern Virginia responded to a Federal advance by immediately constructing an imposing line of fieldworks along Mine Run and challenging Meade's Army of the Potomac to attack.

This transitional period offers a useful opportunity to reflect upon tactical developments in Grant's armies after two years of war, and how they would apply to the rest of the conflict.

Most of the typical battles fought by Grant's armies in the West had taken place in closed, wooded terrain and at extremely close range. Cavalry contributed little, artillery was a supporting arm. It was the rival infantry who decided the day. Until the soldiers started making extensive use of fieldworks in late 1863, combat in the Civil War centred around the infantry firefight. This was an affair of opposing lines – both deployed in loose, 2-deep formation – blazing away at one another until one or both wavered and withdrew. It was a time, recalls one officer, 'when all consideration for tactics is lost'.[1] Under these conditions there was no substitute for raw courage.

Habitually, the fighting took place at point-blank range and most losses were incurred during the opening minutes. The colonel of the 20th Ohio describes his perspective of the Battle of Raymond in 1863 during Grant's approach to Vicksburg. His men halted in a field in front of a wooded hill. An unseen battery began shelling them, and the regiment advanced into the woods while another brigade came up to support their right flank. 'All at once the woods rang with the shrill rebel yell, and a deafening din of musketry.' The 20th rushed forward to the shelter of a stream bank and opened fire. A firefight ensued and the regiment lost all track of time. Recalls the colonel: 'I cannot tell how long the battle lasted. I remember noticing the forest leaves, cut by rifle balls, falling in thick eddies ... At one time the enemy in our front advanced to the border of the creek, and rifles of opposing lines crossed while firing. Men who were shot were burned by the powder of the rifles that sped the balls.'[2]

Emory Upton, who served in all three combat arms, wrote about his introduction to the infantry firefight and noted that 'Nearly the whole loss [his regiment lost 227 killed and wounded out of 453 men engaged] was inflicted at a range varying between four and eight rods [24 to 48 yards] and in the space of about five minutes.'[3] Because the infantry weapons rapidly fouled, and the clouds of black smoke quickly obscured the target, after those first minutes the rate of loss decreased tremendously.

Even on the infrequent occasions when rival lines engaged in open terrain, the decisive firefight took place at very close range. A Massachusetts company commander describing Pickett's charge at Gettysburg notes that his regiment could see the enemy during its three-quarters of a mile approach march, but he chose to 'let the regiment in front of us get within 100 feet of us, & then bowled them over like nine pins ... In two minutes there were only groups of two or three men running round wildly.'[4]

The firefight's characteristics changed very little until the custom of entrenching began. Consider the following two accounts, the first in the West in 1862 and the second in Virginia two years later. At Shiloh a soldier in the 55th Illinois wrote that his regiment went forward in the attack, encountered hostile fire, and then, 'We would lay on the ground and load our guns stand up and fire sometimes behind a tree or running from one tree to the other ... the hardes [sic] thing to do was to get a sight of a rebel before they move ... It seemed to me that they were all deers but they was a good deal worse for while I was looking for them they were firing at me.'[5]

During the Battle of the Wilderness, curiosity prompted a yankee gunner to head towards the firing line to see an infantry fight: 'Then, partially obscured by a cloud of powder smoke, I saw a straggling line of men clad in blue ... not standing as if on parade, but ... taking advantage of the cover afforded by trees, and they were firing rapidly. Their line officers were standing behind them or in line with them. The smoke drifted to and fro, and there were many rifts in it. I saw scores of wounded men. I saw many dead soldiers lying on the ground, and I saw men constantly falling on the battle line ... I could not see the Confederates.'[6]

The hallmark of the regimental firefight was that it began unexpectedly. The attackers groped their way through the woods until they collided with the enemy, and the battle began. Theoretically, it was the mission of the skirmish line to operate in front of the regiment in order to detect the enemy's line and provide warning of imminent encounter. In reality, once the skirmishers contacted the enemy, distances between rival battle lines were already so short that tactical commanders had little chance to make adjustments before their units became thoroughly involved in extremely close-range fighting.

Nor did this situation change from year to year. Writing a typical post-action report, Colonel Charles Cruft explained that at Fort Donelson in 1862: 'The ground on which the action occurred is a succession of hills and ravines, covered with a thick undergrowth of oak bushes. The deadened leaves of the oak shrubs were almost identical in color with the brown jean uniforms of the enemy, and rendered *it almost impossible to distinguish their line* [author's emphasis] until a fire revealed its locality.'[7]

A Rhode Island officer whose unit participated in a unexceptional assault in the Wilderness in 1864 wrote:

'As our Brigade reached the line of fire we were formed in two lines with the 2nd R. I. [Rhode Island] and 10th Mass [Massachusetts] in front and the 7th and 37th Mass. in the rear line. We remained in line until between 3 and 4 o'clock p.m. when we were ordered to advance to the attack. The woods and brush were so thick and dark that the enemy *could not be seen* [author's emphasis], but we knew they were in our front from the terrible fire we received ... The line surged backwards and forwards, now advancing and now retreating until darkness put an end to the carnage.'[8]

By the end of 1863, Civil War tactical combat had assumed a certain stereotypical quality. Regiments deployed in line, brigadier generals placed half their units in a front line and the balance in a supporting line. The soldiers would advance through the woods while their officers tried to maintain order and direction. A crackling of fire announced that the skirmish line had encountered the enemy. The skirmishers came tumbling back and the soldiers took cover to begin a firefight against a nearly invisible foe. They scrambled through the 9-point re-loading sequence while trying to avoid exposing themselves to hostile fire. After firing fifteen or twenty rounds – something the veteran could accomplish in less than ten minutes – the rifles began to foul. The act of tearing open the cartridges with their teeth was like sucking on charcoal, so the soldiers became thirsty at the very moment when whatever water was to hand was needed to clean their rifles. Regardless of whether the unit drove the enemy back or merely stood and traded volleys, the physical exertion of advancing and loading, the tension caused by imminent peril, the need to master terror while seeing one's comrades dropping all around, and the raging thirst all combined to make the men vulnerable to counter-attack. Since the regimental firefight took place amid blinding conditions and consumed all attention, the officers and men had little idea of what was taking place on adjacent sectors. If they sensed that a neighbouring unit was caving in, or that one or both flanks had become unprotected, regardless of reality they were likely to fall back. Thus, post-action reports are replete with claims that the unit held its ground until the enemy turned its flanks.

The feeling within a regiment that it was fighting in isolation made it especially susceptible to renewed enemy pressure. Whichever side committed reserves would gain a temporary advantage until those reserves, in turn, encountered an opposing battle line. This phenomenon accounts for the to and fro nature of tactical Civil War combat before the advent of trench warfare.

The brigade and divisional commanders did appreciate the value of reserves and usually deployed their assault formations with half the regiments in a first wave and the remainder in a second. But the problem of maintaining a proper interval between front-line troops and reserves was seldom mastered. If the supports did not stay close to the leading troops they quickly lost sight of them as they disappeared into the forest. Colonel Rufus Dawes' 6th Wisconsin was in the second line at the Battle of The Wilderness. His mission was to follow the 7th Indiana at an interval of 100 paces. Dawes recalls: 'It was with the greatest difficulty that we could keep in sight of them in the brush. We soon lost connection on our right, but we followed the colors of the seventh Indiana. When tangled in a thicket we heard Colonel Grover order his regiment to advance at a double quick. Colonel Bragg directed me to hasten forward with our regiment as fast as practicable through the brush, while he ran ahead to keep in sight the colors of the seventh Indiana.' The 6th Wisconsin, a veteran Iron Brigade unit, had not even received fire and had already lost its alignment, the right half of the regiment was out of control, and high-ranking officers were running about desperately trying to restore order.

The need to remain within sighting distance meant that the initial firestorm that consumed the first wave also took its toll of the reserve. Dawes again: 'As we hurried along there was a great outburst of musketry. Major Plummer shouted to me: "Look to the right!"' These were Plummer's last words. While Dawes tried to change front to confront the enemy, a devastating volley killed Plummer, a captain and a lieutenant, and struck 40 to 50 more men. All this happened to the 6th Wisconsin while it was nominally in the second, supporting line.

Time and again generals blamed their failure either on the absence of a timely commitment of reserves or a bunching of first line and reserve formations that led to unmanageable disorder.

How well did instruction and standard tactical doctrine prepare officers and men for this pattern of combat? The answer is, not very well at all. Most striking is the fact that the drill manuals offered little useful guidance for officers confronting combat. Consider the matter of marching pace. The manuals called for the soldiers to march at one of three speeds: common time at 70 yards per minute; quick time at 86 yards per minute; double-quick time at 109 yards per minute. Accordingly, officers drilled their men in this procedure only to find that on the battlefield it was irrelevant. In combat, numerous factors affected pace including the men's fatigue, whether they were carrying packs, temperature and the nature of the terrain. Common time became a comfortable walk, quick time a fast walk and double-quick a jogging pace. In other words, the men walked or ran as the situation demanded and no one bothered about counting steps.

Likewise, there was the business of close-shoulder formation. On the drill ground officers toiled to have the men stand and move in uniform ranks. Drill manuals specified with great detail frontages, intervals and the like. An average soldier standing in battle formation occupied about two feet of frontage and one foot of depth. With a spacing of 16 inches between ranks, the standard 2-deep line had a depth of three feet four inches. This was all very well if the object were for the men to look good on parade – and in the Army of the Potomac, the Praetorian Guard of the Civil War, this indeed seemed to be the purpose of a great deal of effort and trouble – but, on the battlefield formal shoulder to shoulder manoeuvring was as irrelevant as parade ground pacing. To take one example among hundreds: at Shiloh when the 30th Indiana received fire for the first time, the entire regiment 'treed' itself; the men scattering to take shelter behind tree trunks.[9]

This scattering for shelter was not a consequence of lack of drill or rawness, but quite the opposite; veteran units learned how to disperse to take advantage of all available cover while retaining sufficient cohesion to respond to their officers' orders. But the drill manuals never reflected such tactical realities. Thus a general like William T. Sherman could and did recommend that recruits should not spend much time being instructed in rear echelons. Rather, he wanted them sent to the front where experience would serve as the teacher. The consequence of this attitude, as we will see, was that generals employed the inexperienced regiments of 1864 as shock troops because, unlike the veterans, they did not know any better than to make frontal charges against enemy fieldworks.

As early as the Battle of Fort Donelson, Colonel Morgan L. Smith's brigade employed modern assault tactics to charge the Confederate works. In his youth Smith had served in the regular army as a sergeant and drill instructor. When the war began he raised a Missouri regiment from roughneck St. Louis rivermen, who had the good sense to vote him colonel. He commanded the 8th Missouri and 11th Indiana at Fort Donelson. Ordered to retake the ground lost by McClernand during the morning, Smith sent forward one company in skirmish formation to draw Confederate fire and ascertain the enemy position. Then he deployed four more companies in skirmish order with intervals of two paces between each man, and had them advance while taking advantage of woods, brush, and folds in the ground. A picked force of sharpshooters supported the skirmish advance. When his remaining fifteen companies came under fire as they advanced toward a clearing, he ordered them to lie down while the skirmishers engaged the enemy. As soon as a lull occurred, Smith sent his formed companies forward at the run. They re-absorbed the skirmishers and drove back the wavering enemy troops. Then he sent the skirmishers out again, repeating the entire process several times until closing the fort's entrenchments. For the final charge, he deployed his entire force in a heavy skirmish line.[10] Smith's system of advances by rushes and skirmish line resulted in his men suffering only 80 casualties, a proportionally lower loss rate than was sustained by an adjacent brigade that charged in conventional style.

The absence of any system to circulate valuable tactical lessons to the rest of the army meant that experience such as that acquired by Smith's men did not spread. Nor did the combat units comprehensively conduct realistic tactical schooling during lulls at the front. These failures doomed all too many soldiers to
participate in assaults like the one described by a soldier in the 55th Illinois at Vicksburg on 19 May:

'The waiting battle line rushed cheering to the charge – a human wave that seemed irresistible when it began surging onward towards the rebel lines. But as it dashed over stumps and tangled limbs of fallen trees, struggled through deep gullies bristling with brush and cane, and climbed the steep slopes opposite in the face of a roaring, whistling storm of lead and iron rain, men dropped by the tens, stopped behind some sheltering log or bank, slackened speed from sheer want of breath, until all the momentum of the start had worn itself out, and then a line of panting, staggering humanity pressed up and on until a few of the pluckiest and strongest perhaps struggled nerveless into the ditch, attempted to climb the abrupt scarp, and were there either slain, desperately wounded or captured, or escaped by miraculous fortune when the shades of night ... covered them from sight.'[11]

The failed assault of 19 May was a direct consequence of haste and faulty or no reconnaissance. At brigade and divisional level this failure was all too typical. Grant's armies lacked any formal doctrine specifying that a tactical commander should conduct a reconnaissance before sending his men forward. When Grant ordered an assault, the result was a blind surge forward that might or might not break the enemy's line. Against an entrenched foe, as will be seen, it usually accomplished nothing beyond running up the butcher's bill.

From the beginning to the end of the open battle phase of the war (before the comprehensive use of fieldworks), there was little tactical evolution despite the fact that the tactical challenge remained unchanged. No one had figured out how to maintain command and control, and yet generals continued to try to manoeuvre long battle lines through thick woods. This situation reached a terrible climax in 1864 when, for the first time, two utterly determined, bloody-minded army commanders opposed each other. One veteran recalled the fighting in the Wilderness in 1864 with the comment: 'Maneuvering here was necessarily out of the question and only Indian tactics told.'[12]

But the experienced officers of the Army of the Potomac had not even tried to analyse the early battles in order to develop new tactical methods. They had fought on this same ground one year earlier. They had had an entire winter to contemplate three years' accumulated lessons. But it seems that either no one had any tactical insight to provide or that few thought about tactics during the long stay in winter quarters. They continued to train the men with the same tactics used when the war began and to employ the same formations when in battle. Given the paucity of tactical thinking, all the advantages went to the defender. It was a situation exacerbated in 1864 by the advent of trench warfare.

There was one technological innovation available which, had the Federal government availed itself of it, would have profoundly changed the nature of tactical combat and shortened the war considerably. Because of the need to equip immediately large numbers of troops, Brigadier General James Ripley – the Chief of Ordnance from 23 April 1861 until 15 September 1863 – resisted allocating scarce resources to breech-loading weapons. Older officers tended to support Ripley's position on the grounds that breech-loaders, particularly repeaters, encouraged men to throw away their fire, used up too much ammunition, and were expensive. Indeed, throughout the world in 1861, only Prussia had adopted a breech-loader, the celebrated 'needle-gun', for its military. However, once the Union had mobilized its first waves, the failure to exploit breech-loading technology was inexcusable. Ripley can only be seen as a classic hidebound military bureaucrat.

Finally, by December 1864, the Chief of the Ordnance Department acknowledged the fact that breech-loaders had demonstrated their superiority for both infantry and cavalry. Breech-loaders came in both single-shot and repeating models. Both offered the tremendous advantage of allowing a man to load while lying prone. The three best breech-loaders were made by Ballard, Merrill, and Sharps. The Sharps was the most sought-after single-shot breech-loader, and the Federal government purchased 9,141 of them during the war. In addition, a few states equipped picked regiments with these single-shot models. Berdan's Sharpshooters and the flank companies of the Connecticut regiments used them. The reason they wanted these weapons was made clear by a display of marksmanship at Cold Harbor in 1864. Here a yankee sharpshooter tried his aim with a Springfield rifled musket, missed, picked up a Sharps rifle and hit a Confederate soldier at a range of about 800 yards!

Although not superior in accuracy, the three main types of repeating breech-loaders – the 5- or 6-shot Colt revolving rifle, the awesome Henry 16-shot repeater (the father of the Winchester rifle), and the more common Spencer 7-shot repeater – provided unprecedented firepower. A unit such as the 37th Massachusetts, the first regiment in the Army of the Potomac's VIth Corps to receive a repeating weapon, felt honoured to be supplied with the Spencer. During the siege of Vicksburg, General Grant personally bestowed a Henry rifle upon a well-known marksman who stalked the trenches and was the terror of Confederate sentries with this formidable weapon.

Even a handful of men armed with repeaters could have a profound tactical impact. During the fighting in the Wilderness in 1864, the officer commanding the Pennsylvania Bucktails spied a Confederate line poised to take an adjacent unit in flank. He sent a captain and a squad of men through the woods to a place where they could enfilade the rebels. The squad's rapid fire with their Spencers managed to distract the enemy long enough for the Union line to shift to defend its flank.

Utilized in greater numbers, the Spencers had decisive tactical impact. A Confederate officer describes a rebel assault during the Petersburg Campaign. Under Robert E. Lee's watchful eye, the Confederates were driving cavalry and infantry of Benjamin Butler's Army of the James. Then they encountered an infantry picket line armed with Spencer repeaters:

'Field's men were moving forward handsomely, & still cheering, when this skirmish line opened fire & discharged their seven shots apiece in less than a minute. It made quite a hot volley, & gave the idea of a considerable force. It plainly shook up our advancing line of battle, which dropped men here & there all along, but which gathered itself & with fresh cheers & fresh impetus threw itself forward. And then the Federal line of battle opened on them with a roar which told its own story of its deadly power. Our line hardly seemed to last a minute before it became a confused mass of fugitives ... The time had been wonderfully short but our losses are estimated to have been nearly a thousand men killed & wounded.'[13]

The only disadvantage of the repeating rifle was that it used up ammunition at a prodigious rate. Because it required special metallic cartridges, fresh ammunition could only come from appropriate wagons. In the confusion of battle these wagons were not always where they were needed and the fast-firing riflemen would find themselves stranded and out of ammunition. Among many instances, this happened to the 37th Massachusetts during Sheridan's attack on Winchester in 1864. The 37th had pushed forward aggressively, entered an open field, fired off its ammunition, been unable to locate more, and simply gone to ground beneath a hail of Confederate shot and shell to which they had no answer. Fortunately, an alert officer in a supporting unit spotted the ammunition train with its single wagon emblazoned in large lettering '37th Mass'. He opened several ammunition boxes, ordered his men to fill their pockets, and hastened to the front line to succour the 37th Massachusetts. Restocked, the regiment silenced an enemy battery and continued the advance.

Experienced field soldiers (as opposed to sharpshooters) regarded the 7-shot Spencer rifle as the finest weapon available. The Federal government issued at least 12,471 Spencer rifles (not to be confused with the far more common Spencer carbine which was a cavalry weapon) to soldiers during the war. Brigadier General James Ripley and his fellow bureaucrats' myopic failure to arm the yankee soldier with breech-loading repeaters was one of the great tragedies to befall the nation. In adequate numbers, there is no doubt they could have shortened the war with considerably less loss of life to both sides.

PART 2. THE MATTER OF REPLACEMENTS

Shortly after Lincoln issued his call for 75,000 militia to suppress the insurrection in 1861, three regular army officers received orders to recommend a procedure for organizing the volunteers and regulars. They suggested the formation of a 3-battalion regiment in which two battalions would serve at the front while the third remained as a depot battalion to assimilate and drill recruits. Had this been put into practice, the Federal armies would have benefited immensely. It would have ensured a steady transfusion of fresh manpower into veteran regiments and would have enabled those regiments to retain experienced, qualified officers who could have rotated between the line and depot battalions, thus reducing combat fatigue and spreading lessons learned to incoming recruits.

Instead, as so often occurs when a democracy goes to war, political expedience triumphed over practical considerations. In the 1860s, states remained suspicious of a strong central government. Moreover, by retaining control of their volunteer units, state governors could dispense political patronage. Accordingly, Congress enacted legislation on 22 July 1861 that established the volunteer regiment at ten companies and made no provisions for filling depleted ranks. Most new recruits would not flow into veteran units. Rather they would form new regiments and thus provide state governors with the opportunity to appoint entirely new sets of officers and thereby reward political cronies. This policy meant that battle losses and disease inevitably reduced veteran regiments to mere skeletons.

Experienced military men, including both Sherman and Grant, recognized the stupidity of this system, but their appeals for reform fell foul of political necessity. As the conflict dragged on, war weariness undermined public resolve. Lincoln needed the support of key states such as New York and Indiana, and one way to preserve at least their governors' support was by allowing them to continue to form new regiments.

When the war began, the existing Regular Army formations offered experienced cadres from which to draw officers and non-commissioned officers who could have imparted their knowledge to newly raised volunteer formations. The General-in-Chief of the United States Army, Winfield Scott, opposed this laudable idea on the grounds that the Regular service would suffer from the loss of experienced men. As late as 1864, General George Meade retained this attitude. Meade turned down the application of a lieutenant of engineers to become a colonel of volunteers on the grounds that the former was more valuable than the latter!

On 1 January 1861 the Regular Army numbered only 16,402 men. About one in five of the officers were sent South. Amazingly, records show that only 26 of the enlisted men deserted when the war began. On 3 May 1861 Lincoln issued a proclamation that increased the Regular Army by 22,714 officers and men, but it proved difficult to achieve this goal.

Recruiters for Regular Army formations faced especially challenging problems. The discipline that distinguished regulars from volunteers did little to induce a man to join the regular service. Regular recruits had to enlist for longer terms of service, received a smaller monthly wage, unlike the volunteers had no guarantee of pensions for their family should they fall in battle, and collected smaller bounties until the middle of 1863. As if these differences were not enough, many states discouraged regular recruiters from competing within their boundaries for manpower. Furthermore, most men preferred to join locally raised units and took pride in state affiliations. They thought of themselves as Mainers or Hoosiers before they thought of themselves as Americans. These factors combined to make it very hard for recruiters to attract men for the Regular Army, and only 67,000 men enlisted during the war.

In the first month of 1863, the War Department decided that volunteer regiments that had lost half their authorized strength would be consolidated with regiments of the same arm and from the same state. The divisional and corps commanders would decide which regimental officers to retain and who to muster out. In theory this would permit the discharge of incompetents. Virtually every soldier from private to corps commander opposed the consolidation. Among many, William T. Sherman urged that depleted regiments be filled with conscripts, but only the state of Wisconsin followed this sensible advice. Too many qualified officers were lost to the service as a result of the regimental consolidations. On the other hand, the threat of consolidation did induce 3-year volunteers to re-enlist in order to preserve the unit.

Sensible change finally came about in the autumn of 1863 when Lincoln called upon the states for another 300,000 men. Failure to raise the required number would set in motion a Federal draft. This threat returned control over manpower distribution to the United States government. The prospect of a draft encouraged 'volunteering' to the tune of 69,380 recruits beyond the 300,000 the government had called for. The great majority went into established units. The states created only forty new regiments with this manpower. The unintended consequence of this harvest of volunteers was that most new recruits learned the way of war from experienced soldiers. The veterans 'broke them in', a term 'most applicable from the manner in which the educating was conducted' recalls one veteran. He elaborated: 'The unbroken animal if harnessed between two sturdy, well-broken ones can scarcely go amiss, but go he must.'[14] In homey, country language, this soldier pinpointed the value of a regimental cadre system.

But governors sought ways around coercive Federal practices. On 23 April 1864, as Grant was about to begin his campaign against Richmond, five midwestern states offered 85,000 militia for 100 days of military service. Although these militia provided useful line of communications duties, clearly they would have aided the war effort much more had they been used to fill existing regiments.

During the war the Federal government raised a total of 2,047 regiments, of which thirty were Regular Army and 120 were coloured units. A total of 1,696, or 83 per cent, were infantry units; 272, or 13 per cent, were cavalry; 78, or 4 per cent, were artillery. While these totals reflect a tremendous mobilization for war, there is no doubt that several badly misguided decisions – most notably how to utilize existing regular army personnel and how to replace losses – undermined the North's manpower advantage.

Another equally important factor sapped the North's numerical superiority. Throughout the war, little regard was paid to such basic issues as nutrition and sanitation. As late as the spring of 1864, while Grant was straining every nerve to get as many men forward to strengthen his fighting ranks, wretched conditions prevailed at most recruiting depots. New recruits were thrown into prison-like surroundings where the healthy and the sick freely mixed, both usually reduced to sleeping on cold floors. A visitor to a New York depot reported talking with a recent recruit who formerly had been a respectable and healthy man. Now that he was a soldier he lay on an overcrowded warehouse floor, barely covered by a little straw. He was sick, enfeebled and ignored. When the visitor departed he found himself covered with lice![15] Such squalor was scarcely conducive to volunteering. These conditions reduced the number of men who volunteered and killed off a good many more long before they ever got to the front. It was a colossal waste for which a negligent government was responsible.

Even in well-led regiments commanded by officers who paid attention to their men's welfare, disease took a fearful toll. As noted previously, few regiments were as fortunate as William Hazen's 41st Ohio. As early as 16 September 1861, the date Hazen issued his second general order, the 41st Ohio's officers were being strictly enjoined to look to their men's hygiene. These regiment's officers were *sans pareil*. They included Lieutenant Colonel James Garfield, Lieutenant Emerson Opdycke, a second lieutenant who advanced to brevet brigadier general, and a lieutenant who rose to command the regiment itself. All but two of the first lieutenants served through the entire war with credit. All the second lieutenants likewise served honourably. Despite such excellent officers who carried out Hazen's strict orders with regard to welfare, Hazen writes that 'diarroea [sic], fevers, measels [sic], and pneumonia' were extremely common. The 41st Ohio was a quintessential fighting regiment. From Shiloh to Chickamauga through the Atlanta Campaign to Franklin and Nashville it lost eight officers and 168 men killed or mortally wounded, but during the same time 153 men succumbed to disease.

Desertion also weakened the army, and nothing contributed more to the deserters' ranks than the bounty system. From 1863 to 1865, the years of bounty and conscription, a staggering total of 278,644 Federal soldiers deserted. The bounty system was a ready-made field for speculation. The high bounties attracted many men from north of the Great Lakes who offered themselves as substitutes for native-born Americans facing the draft. Nearly 50,000 Canadians served in the Federal armies during the war. Since they enlisted for financial gain, their ranks included a disproportionate number of bounty jumpers. Recalling the Canadians in his regiment, an Ohio soldier explained they 'would join a command, then desert to another camp of instruction, change their names, enlist, secure another bounty, and continued this nefarious practice until their accumulations reached a sum sufficient to satisfy, when they made their desertion final and returned home.'[16]

Home-grown bounty jumpers were common as well. One New Yorker confessed that he had made 32 jumps before finally being arrested. A New England veteran related (with perhaps just a touch of hyperbole) that half the bounty men in his regiment forgot their names at the first roll call. When New Hampshire sent 625 recruits to fill up the ranks of one of its veteran units, 137 deserted during the journey to the front and another 118 ran away within a week of joining their regiment. A disgusted Grant said that not one in eight of the high bounty recruits contributed useful battlefield service.

The Federal armies received a constant trickle of recruits from the ranks of Confederate deserters and prisoners of war. Some of them were men who had been conscripted unwillingly by the Confederate authorities. Typical was a German 'recruit' in the 14th Wisconsin Volunteer Infantry. This man, a tailor by trade, had just emigrated from his homeland and arrived in New Orleans on the eve of the war. When he applied for work he was told to enlist if he wanted to eat. He deserted at the first opportunity during the Battle of Shiloh, enlisted in the 14th Wisconsin, received a wound at Vicksburg, returned to duty as soon as he recovered, and served honourably for his 3-year term of enlistment. Most former Confederates were far less motivated, having joined Federal service to escape the horrors of prisoner-of-war camps. Others signed up for service only on the condition they would not have to fight against their former comrades. Six regiments of these 'galvanized rebels' served in the far West where they garrisoned forts and fought the Indians. By so doing they released other Union soldiers for combat duty against the Confederacy.

On 25 May 1863, Halleck ordered an end to the exchange of prisoners. Up to this point, a captured Federal soldier had had a fair chance of being released from confinement in exchange for the release of a Confederate soldier of equal rank. A system of equivalency specified the exchange value for officers and generals. A general was worth sixty enlisted men, a sergeant, two. The system began to founder in 1862 when the North enlisted black soldiers and the South refused to include them in the exchange agreement. When Grant became supreme commander in 1864, he put an end to all prisoner exchanges. For him it was a simple matter of arithmetic: one soldier was proportionally more important to the outnumbered Southern armies than he was to the Northern forces. Since Grant endorsed attrition's lethal logic, he accepted the consequences of no more prisoner exchange on the grounds that it would bring the conflict to an end more quickly. One of his former soldiers, an Illinois artilleryman, captured in the summer of 1863, describes the reality of Halleck and Grant's decision when he and his squad arrived at Richmond's Belle Island prison: 'Now we realized what hunger was ... breakfast ... 1/2 ounce of meat with a piece of bread not much larger ... Supper ... 1/2 pint of dirty soup, with a small piece of bread. Such was our rations day after day.'[17]

After enduring a winter in an old cast-off tent with seven men sharing two old blankets, surviving members of his squad were shipped to the notorious prison at Andersonville where conditions were much worse. Andersonville was an open stockade prison for enlisted men where prisoners suffered from cruel treatment by their guards (in this war as in all others, maltreatment of prisoners rose as the distance from the front lines increased; front-line soldiers pitied prisoners, rear echelon personnel abused them), exposure, scanty rations, extreme overcrowding, an appalling lack of sanitation (the water source for drinking and the latrines was one and the same) and resultant in lethal epidemics of waterborne diseases. A Massachusetts officer describes what the survivors looked like after liberation:

'Not one in fifty was able to stand. Many were left dead on the cars ... most of them were nearly naked, and their feet and hands were frozen; they had lost their reason; could not tell the State they came from ... I took a little fellow in my arms and carried him across the street; he could not have been over sixteen years old, and did not weigh more than fifty pounds; he died just as I laid him down.'[18]

At least 12,912 soldiers perished at Andersonville. A total of 26,249 Union soldiers died in Southern prisons, one of every seven in confinement, and twice the death rate suffered by Confederate prisoners incarcerated in the North.

Confronted with such horrible conditions, some yankee prisoners chose life over loyalty and joined special units that served in the Confederate army. So desperate was the South for manpower that in 1864 officials began trying to attract recruits. They considered foreign-born soldiers, who presumably had little attachment to the Union, and midwesterners, who presumably shared little in common with New England yankees and might even blame them for starting the war, as likely candidates. So smooth-talking recruiting officers circulated among the prisoners, telling them that their government had abandoned them and that '... if you serve faithfully to the end, you will receive the same rewards as the rest of its [the Confederacy's] soldiers. You will be taken out of here, be well-fed, given a good bounty and, at the conclusion of the War, receive a land warrant for a nice farm.'[19] Prisoners perked up when they heard the words 'well-fed'.

The first efforts in this regard, at a prison in Florence, South Carolina, netted 800 recruits. The Confederacy organized them into the 1st and 2nd Foreign Battalions. As might be expected, they quickly earned a reputation for insubordination, theft and vandalism. The 2nd Battalion 'served' in the defence of Savannah, Georgia, against Sherman's army during that general's march to the sea. Fifty-eight of them 'deserted' to Sherman once his army drew near. Others conspired with a Union emissary to surrender their post. When the Confederates detected the plot, they arrested the ringleaders and executed seven of them. The rest of the men in the battalion were returned to prison.

In sharp contrast was the performance of some 250 ex-prisoners in a little-known engagement in north-eastern Mississippi in December 1864. The Union cavalry general Benjamin Grierson (the same officer who conducted the raid during the Vicksburg campaign) was advancing against a scratch brigade of Confederates. Scheduled to join the ranks of the 10th Tennessee Infantry were a group of former Andersonville prisoners. On the eve of battle they received weapons. Six promptly deserted and told Grierson that the remainder would not fight against their former comrades. The next day Grierson confidently advanced against the sector defended by the former ex-prisoners only to receive a heavy volley at 50-yards' range! For the next two hours the former prisoners fought furiously, refusing to yield until they ran out of ammunition. Their behaviour surprised everyone, North and South. Apparently it was an anomaly, the only recorded occasion when Federal prisoners of war fought hard against their former comrades.

1 Peter S. Michie, *The Life and Letters of Emory Upton*, (New York: Arno Press, 1979), p. 201.
2 Manning F. Force, *Personal Recollections of the Vicksburg Campaign*, (Cincinnati: Henry C. Sherick, 1885), pp. 8-9.
3 *The Life and Letters of Emory Upton*, p. 81.
4 Robert Garth Scott, ed., *Fallen Leaves: The Civil War Letters of Major Henry Livermore Abbott*, (Kent, OH: Kent State University Press, 1991), see Abbott's letter of July 6, 1863.
5 Joseph Allan Frank and George A. Reaves, *"Seeing the Elephant": Raw Recruits at the Battle of Shiloh*, (New York: Greenwood Press, 1989), p. 102.
6 Richard Wheeler, *On Fields of Fury. From the Wilderness to the Crater: An Eyewitness History*, (New York: Harper Collins Publishers, 1991), p. 94.
7 *Official Records*, I:7, p. 245.
8 Robert Hunt Rhodes, ed., *All For the Union: The Civil War Diary and Letters of Elisha Hunt Rhodes*, (New York: Vintage Books, 1992), p. 144.
9 *"Seeing the Elephant,"* p. 101.
10 Smith's report is in *Official Records*, I:7, p. 233.
11 Edwin C. Bearss, *The Campaign for Vicksburg*, vol. 3 (Dayton: Morningside, 1986), p. 762.
12 This observation cited in James I. Robertson, ed., *(The Civil War Letters of General Robert McAllister*, (New Brunswick, NJ: Rutgers University Press, 1965), p. 413.
13 Gary W. Gallagher, ed., *Fighting for the Confederacy: The Personal Recollections of General Edward Porter Alexander*, (Chapel Hill: University of North Carolina Press, 1989), pp. 483-484.
14 Richard A. Baumgartner and Larry M. Strayer, eds., *Ralsa C. Rice: Yankee Tigers: Through the Civil War with the 125th Ohio*, (Huntington, WV: Blue Acorn Press, 1992), p. 85.
15 The story is related in Allan Nevins, ed., *A Diary of Battle: The Personal Journals of Colonel Charles S. Wainwright, 1861-1865*, (New York: Harcourt, Brace & World, 1962), p. 320.
16 *Yankee Tigers*, p. 22.
17 Charles B. Kimbell, *History of Battery "A" First Illinois Light Artillery Volunteers*, (Chicago: Cushing Printing Co., 1899), p. 66.
18 Francis A. Lord, *They Fought for the Union*, (New York: Bonanza Books, 1960), p. 247.
19 Walter Brian Cisco, "Galvanized Rebels," *Civil War*, Vol. VII:5 (September-October 1990), p. 51.

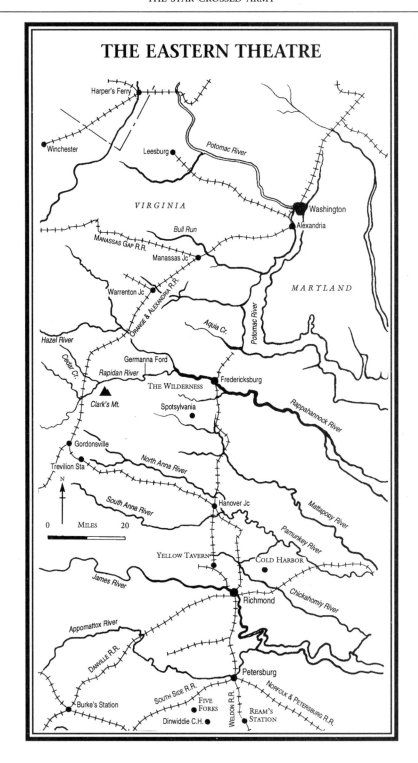

THE EASTERN THEATRE

11
The Star-Crossed Army

PART 1. THE BURDEN OF COMMAND

Lincoln had twice brought western generals to the capital to help him win the war. Boastful Major General John Pope had been thoroughly outfoxed by Lee back in 1862 during the Second Bull Run campaign. In a different way, Major General Henry Halleck had proven an even greater disappointment. Lincoln understood his own shortcomings as grand strategist, but he also understood that Union forces greatly outnumbered the enemy, and that if they could pull in harness they could not be stopped. He had hoped that Halleck, 'Old Brains' as he was known, would give the war effort the decisive strategic direction to take advantage of this fact. Instead, Halleck accepted the promotion to General in Chief while declining to assume the responsibility of command. He proved little more than a top-notch clerk.

Describing the Lincoln–Halleck relationship, Secretary of the Navy Gideon Welles noted that Lincoln's 'own convictions and conclusions are infinitely superior to Halleck's – even in military operations more sensible and more correct always – but yet he says, "It being strictly a military question, it is proper I should defer to Halleck, whom I have called here to counsel, advise, and direct in these matters, where he is an expert."'[1]

Unwilling to assert himself, but even more unwilling to let direction of the war continue to slip, Lincoln determined that yet another change was called for and at the beginning of 1864 summoned Grant to Washington to see if this man would accept the awesome responsibilities of overall command, or if he would crumble beneath the burden as had all the others.

The arrival at the White House on the evening of 9 March 1864 of this famous, awkward, 'short, brown, dark-haired man' created quite a stir and the crowd struggled to catch a glimpse of him.[2] Sophisticated easterners were unimpressed with Grant who made a poor initial showing. A party of ladies buttonholed his wife to inquire anxiously if he were up to his new responsibilities. Julia Dent Grant replied that he had succeeded thus far wherever the government had sent him. 'Would he capture Richmond?' they asked. She answered, 'Yes, before he gets through. Mr. Grant always was a very obstinate man.'[3] Only the discerning observer realized that while 'Mr. Grant' was without presence, there was more to him than first met the eye and appreciated his underlying business-like approach to whatever military problem he confronted. To Secretary Welles, this indicated his 'latent power'.[4] To a veteran private of the Army of the Potomac who caught his first glimpse of the general, he looked as though 'he meant it'.[5]

The officers of the Army of the Potomac had reacted to Grant's first victories in the West with an admixture of pleasure and jealousy. In the spring of 1863, when Grant had completed his investment of Vicksburg and Lee had just trounced the Army of the Potomac at Chancellorsville, Meade spoke for many when he wrote to his wife that 'the glorious news from Grant' contrasted sadly 'with our miserable fiasco here'.[6] But many others were purely and simply jealous of Grant's successes. Artillery Colonel Charles Wainwright wrote in his journal how riled it made him to hear people compare the campaigns in the East and West. He observed that the 'whole strength of the rebellion is concentrated on our front', leaving the western Federal armies facing leftovers. Wainwright delighted to note that he had just received a letter from an eastern officer who had transferred to the West, and that this officer confirmed previous reports 'as to the vast inferiority of the Western armies on both sides compared with those here'.[7]

Major General George B. Meade felt much the same. At the end of 1863 Meade had replied to his wife's query about Grant:

'I knew him as a young man in the Mexican war, at which time he was considered a clever young officer, but nothing extraordinary ... I think his great characteristic is indomitable energy and a great tenacity of purpose. He certainly has been very successful, and that is nowadays the measure of reputation. The enemy, however, have never had in any of their Western armies either the generals or the troops they have had in Virginia.'[8]

Many eastern officers and soldiers echoed this refrain: 'let's wait and see how Grant fares against the first team and Bobby Lee'. It was with an almost perverse sense of satisfaction that one of Meade's aides made a diary entry after the first round of fighting at Spotsylvania. Describing some of Grant's staff officers, he wrote that there were 'several very foolish ones, who talked and laughed flippantly about Lee and his army. But they have changed their note now.'[9] Years of failure had induced a sense of psychological inferiority among many officers in the Army of the Potomac. For example, in the autumn of 1863 the army's provost general, General Marsena Patrick, had written in his diary about Lee's pending manoeuvres: 'They are either making a feint, preparatory to an evacuation of our front, or they are preparing to give us our annual Bull Run Flogging.'[10] And this after Gettysburg!

Out west, men who served in Grant's army expected to whip the rebels. He had established a tradition of victory that fed on itself. The Army of the Potomac veterans were understandably sceptical. They 'had seen many military reputations ... melt before the battle fire of the Army of Northern Virginia [and said] "Well, let Grant try what he can accomplish ... He cannot be weaker or more inefficient than the generals who have wasted the lives of our comrades during the past three years."'[11] The soldiers knew that they had fought hard in the past, only to have their efforts thwarted by inferior leadership. A veteran colonel wrote to his father that the army was pleased that Grant had decided personally to lead them in the next campaign, 'but the army can fight no more heroically under General Grant than it did under General McClellan at Antietam, or General Meade at Gettysburg'.[12] Clearly, the new commanding general would have to prove himself to the eastern yankees.

The soldiers' first glimpse of Grant came during a series of formal reviews in late March and April. One of Burnside's Massachusetts soldiers, George Washington Whitman (brother to the poet) reported: 'There was no Grand Review as is generally the case, but the Regiment just fell in line and Grant rode along and looked at them and then went on his business.'[13] Grant's demeanour displeased some officers. A Massachusetts man wrote to his father after this review: 'I was rather disappointed in his looks, as he is anything but an able-looking man.'[14] In contrast to Burnside's command, the Army of the Potomac prided itself upon its ability to look good on parade. In preparation for Grant's inspection they had blackened shoes, polished brass, and cleaned uniforms and rifles. Then they assembled in the fields and awaited the 'great' man's arrival.

As Grant slowly rode along the ranks the regiments cheered in succession, as they had been taught. The general gave no recognition of the compliment. Annoyed, Colonel Rufus Dawes turned to his 6th Wisconsin, one of the old Iron Brigade regiments, and said: 'As General Grant does not seem to think our cheering worth notice, I will not call for cheers.'

When Grant approached, the Wisconsin soldiers stiffly performed the required salutes and then stood motionless. Their conduct briefly startled Grant, who obviously expected more cheering. Recovering quickly, he removed his hat and made a low bow to the men and to their Colours. His action agreeably impressed these veterans. Dawes concluded that Grant's behaviour said, '"I did not come here for a personal ovation." It was genuine Grantism and our men were highly pleased. They said "Grant wants soldiers, not yaupers."' [15]

Grant, on the other hand, well understood the spit-and-polish sensibilities of this army's high-ranking officers. He made the appropriate admiring comments to Meade's staff. One of Meade's volunteer aides, Theodore Lyman, relates that after one of the reviews Grant seemed 'much pleased and says there is nothing of the sort out West, in the way of discipline and organization'.[16]

Not only did Grant have to impress the rank and file, but he would have to prove himself to the Army of the Potomac's generals. Several of them had known him in Mexico and afterwards, and their recollections were poor. In the chatty, club-like way of the Regular service, they shared their impressions with junior officers. Thus a Massachusetts regimental commander learned from his corps commander, John Sedgwick, that the last time Sedgwick has seen Grant, Grant had been 'drunken & dirty to the last extreme'.[17] Artillery Colonel Charles Wainwright wrote that it was difficult to imagine Grant as a Lieutenant General, because those who formerly knew him say that 'he was only distinguished for the mediocrity of his mind, his great good nature, and his insatiable love of whiskey.'[18]

Grant demonstrated his energy, one major component of 'the latent power' that Secretary Welles had detected, the morning after his meeting in the White House. He took the cars south to visit Meade at his headquarters. In the days following Gettysburg, Lincoln had begun to feel that perhaps Meade was not the man for the job. Meade had failed to pursue Lee's crippled army, and this failure prompted Lincoln to say in bitter frustration, 'And that, my God, is the last of this Army of the Potomac.'[19] Yet when Secretary of the Navy Welles suggested removing Meade, Lincoln had refused, saying that there was no one within the army any better. To bring in an outsider would create a new combination of troubles by stirring jealousies and producing awkward subordinates as had been the case with Pope. Half a year later Lincoln willingly dumped this problem in Grant's lap.

On his way to Meade's headquarters, Grant had made up his mind to relieve the Pennsylvania general from command. Instead, he came away from his meeting tremendously impressed by Meade's character, particularly his sense of duty to the cause, and retained Meade in command. As for his own role, Grant told Meade that he would not interfere in the details of managing the Army of the Potomac. It was a very human decision totally in keeping with Grant's personality. From a practical military standpoint, it was a terribly wrongheaded decision. Once Grant decided to take the field with the Army of the Potomac, it meant there would be two parallel headquarters issuing orders to the army. Delay and confusion would be inevitable. Meade's Chief of Staff observed that in effect, two generals would be commanding the same army and there would naturally be some uncertainty as to who was responsible for what. The Army of the Potomac had never been renowned for its flexibility, for rapid, responsive manoeuvre. Repeatedly Lincoln had complained about its leaders' 'imbecility, inefficiency' and their indifference which wasted so many brave men.[20] Now Grant had superimposed upon this hapless army an extremely unwieldy chain of command.

Henceforth, Grant would act in much the same manner as his great opponent, General Lee. He would clearly outline his plan for marches and campaigns to his Adjutant and Chief of Staff and then leave it up to Rawlins to pass on his strategic notions to Meade. Meade, in turn, would apply his own ideas to Grant's strategy, and then order the army's corps commanders to implement it. One reporter explained to his readers that Grant performed the grand strategy while Meade handled the grand tactics. Meade himself agreed with the description written by another reporter: 'The Army of the Potomac, directed by Grant, commanded by Meade, and led by Hancock, Sedgwick, and Warren.'[21]

In making the decision to accompany the Army of the Potomac while continuing to allow Meade to command it, Grant was led astray by his own modesty. He did not appreciate how important his own drive and energy had been in motivating his western subordinates to accomplish difficult feats. Six months ago he had shown these attributes on the very first evening that he had met the leaders of the Army of the Cumberland. He had refused their offer of dry clothes and insisted instead that they immediately begin a detailed strategic analysis of the situation at Chattanooga. At that time he had firmly seized the reins of command from the moment he entered the Army of the Cumberland's headquarters. He had proved that he was a leader who could inspire others to high achievement. In Virginia, his deliberate initial distancing of himself from command cancelled his great ability to inspire officers to get things done.

So Grant's first important decision after coming east was bad on two counts: it created unnecessary complications inherent in maintaining parallel army headquarters, and it deprived the army of one of his great leadership strengths.

Next came the problem of what to do with General Ambrose Burnside. Burnside had once commanded the entire army and Meade – at that time a divisional leader – had served under him. Now Meade commanded the army while Burnside commanded the independent Ninth Corps. These circumstances compelled Grant to retain Burnside's independent status. Burnside would receive orders directly from Grant's headquarters while Meade's headquarters directed the other three infantry corps. It would be most awkward, another potential obstruction in the army's chain of command.

The three important fighting commands in the Army of the Potomac were the infantry corps. The best-known commander was Major General Winfield Scott Hancock who had made the Second Corps into the army's most formidable striking force. In keeping with his illustrious name, Hancock combined magnetic battlefield leadership with tactical aggression, an attribute much lacking in this army. However, his aggression was to bring great trouble. Both in the Wilderness and during the turning operations at Petersburg, he allowed his flanks to become uncovered and witnessed the dismaying spectacle of the veterans of the vaunted Second Corps running for their lives. This disheartening experience would prompt Hancock to leave the army for a rear area command.

Next in seniority was Major General John Sedgwick who led the Sixth Corps. Known throughout his corps as 'Uncle John', Sedgwick was well loved by his men. His leadership qualities were less known. Except for a brief period of independent command during the Chancellorsville campaign, he had not been tested in battle at this high level of command. Sedgwick could be expected to be steadfast in his adherence to duty, but would not display dash or verve. He was killed by a Confederate marksman at Spotsylvania during a foolish display of personal courage.

Like Sedgwick, the commander of the Fifth Corps, Major General Gouverneur K. Warren, was a cautious man. He had received his posting because of one great day at Gettysburg. A pedantic engineer, irritable toward his subordinates, Warren was unproven at this level of command. His command style was to attend personally to all details, which was fine when handling a signals detachment but unworkable when directing a corps. As a staffer observed, he could not 'spread himself over three divisions'.[22] A line soldier complained that Warren's engineering approach to combat enabled him to 'appreciate only the physical advantages & disadvantages & position' while ignoring morale's vital role.[23] Phil Sheridan would find Warren lacking during the Five Forks Campaign and relieve him of command.

The leader of the independent Ninth Corps was a known commodity, and what was known was not necessarily good. Major General Ambrose Burnside had once commanded this army and had exhibited a willingness to see it destroyed in a futile series of frontal attacks at Fredericksburg in 1862. Amiable and well liked, he was an officer of limited ability whose favourite expression was 'trust to luck'.[24] Time and again in the coming campaign his corps would arrive just a little too late to do what it should have done. Burnside lasted through the campaign's opening months. Then, in front of Petersburg, his trust in luck undid him completely when he selected the assault division for the Battle of the Crater by drawing lots and the 'winning' divisional commander proved a coward and a drunkard. Exercising an ugly personal vendetta, Meade relieved Burnside of command after this battle.

Under Grant, the Army of the Potomac would have numerous chances to defeat decisively its outnumbered enemy, but not until after Lee's Army had been fatally weakened by the winter of 1864/5 would this Union army succeed. Somehow it was always just a little late to capitalize on its chances. Over the years the Army of the Potomac had become like Rome's Praetorian Guard – an over-bureaucratized, hidebound, inflexible organization featuring leaders sensitive to rank and privilege. Consequently in large part the impending difficulties and failures can be attributed to a lack of co-operation and mutual trust, magnified by years of failure. An incident during the advance to Spotsylvania Court House highlights this point. Army commander Meade told corps commander Warren that he wanted Warren 'to co-operate' with Sedgwick. Warren replied: 'General Meade, I'll be God d—d if I'll co-operate with Sedgwick or anybody else. You are the commander of this army and can give your orders and I will obey them; or you can put Sedgwick in command and he can give the orders and I will obey them; or you can put me in command and I will give the orders and Sedgwick shall obey them; but I'll be God d—d if I'll *cooperate* with General Sedgwick or anybody else.'[25]

In sum, Grant's infantry advanced against Lee under the command of Meade who held an anomalous position; Hancock, fiery but tactically suspect; Sedgwick, competent but nothing more; Warren, cautious and over his head at this level; and Burnside, inept at best. It was hardly an inspiring or inspired group. Suffering under a tradition of defeat, the Army of the Potomac lacked commanders who were instinctive fighters or who were powerfully aggressive. A handful of junior leaders such as Sprigg Carroll, Alexander Hays and George Custer attacked wherever they got a chance. The more typical leaders obeyed orders but exhibited no offensive initiative.

On 9 March 1864, Lincoln had named Grant supreme commander of 'all armies of the United States' with the rank of Lieutenant General. On the 10th Grant had had his interview with Meade. On the 11th he headed back west to map out a plan of campaign with his soulmate, Major General William T. Sherman, the officer who had succeeded him to command of the Military Division of the Mississippi. Hitherto the Union armies had operated with no plan of action. There were no less than seventeen distinct commanders, each operating independently. This allowed the Confederates to reinforce an active sector from one not engaged. 'I determined to stop this,' Grant later recalled. He strengthened the main armies by reducing the subsidiary forces, devised a simultaneous offensive from the Atlantic to the Mississippi, and ordered those forces assigned to defensive missions to contribute to the whole scheme by joining in the advance. In this way these 'defensive' forces could guard 'their special trusts when advancing from them'.[26] This idea of an active defensive was a novel notion for the Federal armies.

Grant's strategy thus called for simultaneous advances to immobilize Confederate reserves and thereby prevent an enemy concentration as had taken place at Shiloh and Chickamauga. His emphasis had to be on the enemy's two great field armies under Lee and Joseph E. Johnston. To keep Lee from detaching forces to other sectors, he gave Meade the simple order: 'Lee's army will be your objective point. Wherever Lee goes, there you will go also.'[27] Likewise, Sherman's objective was Johnston's army. He had such confidence in this subordinate that he wrote, 'I do not propose to lay down for you a plan of campaign, but simply lay down the work it is desirable to have done and leave you free to execute it in your own way.'[28] This was a far cry from the type of overly detailed instructions with which Halleck had fettered Grant in times past.

No informed individual doubted that the forthcoming campaign would prove decisive. The autumn of 1864 would see another presidential election in the North. Unless the Federal forces made important progress towards winning the war, northern war weariness promised to coalesce into political protest against the Lincoln administration. Generals north and south appreciated this. From his winter quarters in eastern Tennessee, Lee's 'Old War Horse', General James B. Longstreet, explained the stakes:

'If we can ... throw him [the Federal forces] back, he will not be able to recover his position nor his morale until the Presidential election is over, and we shall then have a new President to treat with. If Lincoln has any success early he will be able to get more men and may be able to secure his own re-election. In that event the war must go on for four years longer.'[29]

Longstreet left the obvious unsaid. The ravaged South could not fight for another four years. One way or another, Grant's strategy would lead to the end of the war. This was an enormous command responsibility and one that no other American leader in either part of the divided country had been able to endure as yet.

PART 2. THE ARMY OF THE POTOMAC

Before Grant arrived east, a scheme had been advanced to consolidate the Army of the Potomac by breaking up the First and Third Corps. These formations had suffered terribly at Gettysburg, lost their corps commanders, and seen them replaced by indifferent leaders. Since these corps enjoyed little political backing in Washington, it was easy for the authorities to conclude that they simply no longer carried their weight. Eliminating them would simplify the chain of command, return more men to the ranks – all the corps clerks and many of the support personnel could enter the fighting line – and permit the dismissal of inefficient officers. However, the consolidation was postponed until Grant arrived. Grant was supposedly indoctrinated with the view that eastern Union generals were inferior to those who served in the West. Practically everyone attributed the consolidation to him and consequently saw confirmation of his pro-western bias. Prominent generals who had fought with the Army of the Potomac since its earliest days were relieved of their commands. Gone were George Sykes, William French and John Newton of the infantry and Alfred Pleasonton of the cavalry. Officers and men alike had been taught to acquire a corps pride. The consolidation shattered that pride, and they blamed the 'stumpy, unmilitary, slouchy and western-looking; very ordinary' Grant.[30]

Regimental commanders had a particular reason to be angry with Grant because the consolidation offered fewer opportunities for promotion. The lean pre-war years had made regular officers excessively rank-conscious. Volunteer officers had quickly learned to emulate the regulars' ambitions. It was the reward for good leadership, and in this war good leadership meant leading from the front at great personal risk. Suddenly the consolidation reduced the reward. Many highly qualified colonels had received promotion to brevet general on the strength of their battlefield comportment. The consolidation required them to return to mere regimental command. Faced with this choice some resigned. Others clung on but the experience made them bitter:

'There are few brigades – and many Brigadiers back in the rear that have to be provided for. But these take good care not to get into battle. They leave command at that time to the ranking Colonels. Yet they are always on hand about pay time.'[31]

Even the men in the ranks attributed the loss of something they cherished to the newcomer from the West. The issue was unit identity, a powerful emotion in all Union armies, but particularly in the East where they had been taught a corps-wide *esprit* as exemplified by the corps badges they proudly wore. When Grant arrived, many regiments had to leave the corps with whom they had a long association to enter a new corps. For example, the old 1st Brigade of the 2d Division, Third Corps was broken up, sending half the men to the New Jersey Brigade and half into the Excelsior Brigade. A transferred officer wrote home that his men would defiantly retain their Third Corps diamond badges even though they now belonged the Second Corps.

In sum, the consolidation meant that many corps, divisional and brigade associations ended. Not only did this have a bad effect on morale, but it meant that teamwork among formations that did not know one another would become frayed. Colonel Rufus Dawes of the 6th Wisconsin noted that only six of the army's 41 infantry brigades entered the Wilderness with the same organization they had had less than a year earlier during the Gettysburg Campaign. Only sixteen of these brigades had brigadier generals to lead them. Colonels commanded the remainder. In contrast, brigadier generals led all but four of the infantry brigades in the Army of Northern Virginia. The organizational advantage clearly rested with the rebels.

Then there was the all important matter of individual manpower. The core of the Army of the Potomac resided in the volunteer regiments that had enlisted for three years of service. From the close of 1863 until August 1864, the term of service for 77 of these regiments would expire. When these regiments mustered out, they took with them both experienced veterans and irreplaceable *esprit de corps*.

Consequently, for the 1864 campaign many of the Army of the Potomac's most famous formations existed in name only. The army's élite, the Iron Brigade, had been shattered at Gettysburg. It would not fight well during the 1864 campaign. The 13th Pennsylvania Reserves, the original 'Pennsylvania Bucktails', had earned a fine fighting reputation as skilled marksmen. They proudly demonstrated their sharp-shooting qualities by adorning their caps with jaunty deer tails. Veterans referred to the 1864 unit as the 'Junior Bucktails', wryly noting that apparently the state's deer population had been exterminated because the 'Junior Bucktails' substituted squirrel tails for the genuine articles.

To prepare for the coming campaign, the Army of the Potomac had assembled units from all over the eastern theatre. Some of these were of dubious fighting value. The ranks had been fattened with new recruits, among whose ranks were many bounty jumpers and hapless immigrants signed up for the fight as soon as they disembarked in America. A veteran officer observed how 'It is surprising how poorly the Germans show ... they seem almost idiotic [many were not fluent in English, if they understood it at all] and what is worse, they will plunder and they won't fight.' They were 'miserable', with 'no grit'.[32] These poor immigrants were quite simply cannon-fodder. Under the circumstances it is scarcely surprising that they fought unenthusiastically for a country they barely knew.

Like Grant, Phil Sheridan travelled east towards a new and curious environment. Grant had selected him to command the Army of the Potomac's Cavalry Corps. Sheridan had heard that jealousies and ill-feeling were rampant in the East. He knew no one personally in the Army of the Potomac other than a slight acquaintance with Grant himself. He had to assess his officers and superiors even as they were assessing him. Aged 33, standing a mere five and a half feet tall and weighing only 115 pounds, Sheridan, again like Grant, did not immediately impress anyone with his appearance.

Ordered to the White House, he met Lincoln who told him that to date during the war, the eastern cavalry had not performed well. Lincoln concluded the interview by repeating the old chestnut, 'Who ever saw a dead cavalryman?'

In the field, Sheridan found his new command consisted of three cavalry divisions and twelve horse batteries, numbering in total some 12,000 men. Each of Sheridan's divisional commanders was a veteran officer. At the head of the 1st Cavalry Division was General A. T. Torbert. He had graduated from West Point in 1855 as an infantryman. Indeed, all his service to date had been leading first a foot regiment and then an infantry brigade. Leading the 2d Cavalry Division was another West Point graduate of 1855, General David Gregg, who had seen service with the First Dragoons fighting Indians on the frontier. In the autumn of 1861 he came east to command the 8th Pennsylvania Cavalry, whence he had risen to divisional command. Many considered him one of the best cavalry officers in all the Federal armies. James Wilson, the commander of the 3d Cavalry Division, had graduated from West Point in 1860 as a topographical engineer. He had served out west with Grant, caught Grant's eye, and been promoted for his exploits at Vicksburg and Chattanooga. Sheridan particularly requested Wilson for divisional command and Grant, highly impressed with Wilson's energy and intellect, readily agreed.

Sheridan's nominal chief of artillery was a Mexican War veteran, Captain John M. Robinson. In practice, the guns were not massed, but parcelled out to the divisions in battery and section allotments. Overall, it was a strange group of higher echelon cavalry commanders including only one of three divisional generals with any cavalry experience and a corps commander who had mostly commanded infantry so far during the war and who was virtually unknown to any of the easterners.

The densely wooded terrain of eastern Virginia coupled with an ingrained habit of dismounting and seeking shelter behind hastily improvised barricades meant that there was little opportunity for classic cavalry operations. With the exception of Yellow Tavern, and until they moved to the Shenandoah Valley, the cavalry operated more like mounted infantry. In combat, Sheridan's troopers usually dismounted with three-quarters of the men deploying in an open order skirmish line where they would fight on foot by taking advantage of all the cover they could find. The remaining quarter held the horses under shelter of any convenient woods or folds in the ground.

Sheridan's Cavalry Corps included everything from veteran troopers in excellent regiments like the 1st Vermont to grass green units like the 22d New York who joined Wilson's division because, as Wilson put it, 'it was so green that no one else wanted it'.[33] They were armed with a heterogeneous collection of weapons including Burnside, Smith, Sharps and Colt carbines plus revolvers and sabres. Not until August, when two cavalry divisions returned to Washington to confront Early, did they receive the Spencer magazine carbine.

With the one great exception of Buford's superb delaying action on the first day of Gettysburg, eastern cavalry had avoided fighting enemy infantry. Under Sheridan this would change. He would use his troopers aggressively, frequently seizing important crossroads well in advance of the infantry, and then trying to hold his position against all comers until relieved.

In a typical action on 31 May 1864, Sheridan's troopers fought to hold the crossroads at Cold Harbor. His men dismounted and reversed the Confederate breastworks. Troopers distributed boxes of ammunition along the line. Sheridan relates, 'All this was done in the darkness, and while we were working away at our cover the enemy could be distinctly heard from our skirmish-line giving commands and making preparations to attack.'[34] At dawn rebel infantry charged and

Sheridan's troopers waited until they were within close range before opening fire with horse artillery and their carbines. They managed to repel two charges.

A week later, outside Richmond, his men again confronted enemy infantry. Sheridan's mounted troopers fell back before their advance until reaching the reverse slope of a ridge. Here they dismounted and waited. When the enemy foot reached the crest, the cavalry opened fire at a range of fifteen yards and shredded their line, then pursued them and managed to capture 250 prisoners and two Colours.

A few days after Sheridan's arrival at Brandy Station in the spring of 1864, he held a review of his 12,000 troopers. 'Uncle John' Sedgwick, an old dragoon, attended in order to encourage Sheridan and to tease him about the traditional prejudices the cavalrymen held towards infantry officers. Sheridan saw his command as a body of men in tolerable order but with badly worn horses. It turned out that the cavalry had been on picket duty around the entire army, a perimeter of nearly sixty miles, and the task had greatly reduced the animals. Moreover, to Sheridan's way of thinking, it had been unnecessary.

Sheridan argued to Meade that instead of performing picket duty, creating cordons around encampments, and guarding the trains, the cavalry should be kept in a compact mass in order to fight the enemy cavalry. This concept slightly staggered the conventional Meade. Not only did he wish to retain the cavalry to perform its traditional duties, but he wanted Sheridan himself to remain at Meade's headquarters and to serve essentially as a staff officer. This was not fighting Phil Sheridan's idea of war. So matters stood through the opening of the Wilderness Campaign. To Sheridan's dismay, two-thirds of the cavalry did little more than guard the trains while only Wilson's division scouted in the army's van.

Under the inspired leadership of Henry Hunt, the Army of the Potomac had made strides toward grouping its batteries into a central organization capable of delivering massed firepower. But old habits were hard to overcome. Infantry generals wanted artillery close at hand and they had the command authority – the artillery officers, who nominally controlled the artillery brigades assigned to the infantry corps, only held the rank of colonel – to have their wishes fulfilled. Moreover, since the corps commanders had not come from the artillery branch, they supported their infantry brethren's wishes. Consequently, Warren divided his corps' artillery brigade into separate batteries for the march through the Wilderness. His chief of artillery, Colonel Charles Wainwright, tolerated this because he recognized that a long artillery column would be too vulnerable to surprise enemy attack when confined to the narrow Wilderness roads. However, as the campaign unfolded, Warren continued to distribute the artillery by battery in a direct infantry support role. Likewise, Hancock issued a printed order assigning most of his batteries to the infantry divisions where they would be controlled by the infantry divisional commanders.

This arrangement frustrated the gunners of the Army of the Potomac enormously, but despite their repeated efforts to create the kind of independent artillery command employed by the Army of Northern Virginia, it persisted until the end of the campaign. It was inefficient and went some way to negating the material advantage enjoyed by the army's long arm.

PART 3. INTO THE WILDERNESS

In the winter of 1863/4, efforts to encourage re-enlistment included the promise of a 35-day furlough. Armed with back pay and a cash reward for re-enlisting, young men returned to their small towns and farms only to encounter predators every bit as determined as their opponents in Lee's army. Women found these cash-rich combat veterans irresistible. In some companies up to 50 per cent of the men returned married. Wainwright observed with wry amusement, 'Some four or five hundred dollars cash in hand set the girls wild after the men ... The most steady got married; the others let the women have it [the money] without marrying.'[35]

For the more serious minded there was a religious revival sweeping the Army of the Potomac in the winter of 1864, just as was occurring across the lines in the Confederate camps. When not on drill, many soldiers crowded the churches to listen to preachers and to pray. They sensed that the war was entering a new dark phase. A Massachusetts veteran, Major Henry Livermore Abbott, wrote to his mother that to date, every battle had been more costly than the previous one. He anticipated that the coming campaign would be the worst of all: 'It makes me sad to look on this gallant regiment which I am instructing and disciplining for slaughter, to think that probably 250 or 300 of the 400 which go in, will get bowled out.'[36] Abbott himself would be one those 'bowled out', killed on the second day of the Battle of the Wilderness while leading his 20th Massachusetts.

By mid-April, camp rumours were circulated that outgoing mail would soon be stopped and sutlers and female attendants dismissed. This was an effort by headquarters to plug the leaks that kept Lee so well informed of his enemy's plans. New recruits anxiously prepared for the coming ordeal and received sophisticated guidance from the hardened veterans. A gunner advised:

'Now my lad, do not pick up anything excepting food and tobacco, while you are on the march. Get hold of all the food you can. Cut haversacks from dead men. Steal from the infantry if you can. Let your aim be to secure food and food and still more food, and keep your eyes open for tobacco ... Stick to your gun through thick and thin. Do not straggle. Fill your canteen at every stream we cross and wherever you get a chance elsewhere. Never wash your feet until the day's march is over. If you do, they will surely blister.'[37]

A New Jersey officer commented favourably that in contrast to previous campaigns, he and his men did not know where they were bound because 'Grant has the secret of keeping his own secrets'.[38] However, massing an army, stockpiling supplies, and sending the sick to the rear – this last the habitual final step before beginning active operations – could not be done in hostile territory without alerting the foe.

On 30 March, Lee informed President Davis that Grant had returned from his western visit and was busily preparing for the coming campaign. As yet Lee had not fathomed Grant's specific strategy, but he correctly deduced that he would personally operate with the Army of the Potomac and advance on Richmond. The Army of Northern Virginia's veterans greeted the arrival of a new enemy commander with characteristic aplomb. The Confederate artilleryman Porter Alexander spoke for those in both armies who were sceptical of Grant's abilities when he noted, 'We wanted Grant introduced to Gen. Lee & the army of Northern Virginia, & to let him have a smell of our powder. For we knew that we simply could never be driven off a battle field.'[39] A young and confident Confederate officer boasted that soon the Army of Northern Virginia would whip Grant, just as it had whipped all the others. General Longstreet asked this young man if he knew Grant, and the officer replied 'No.' 'Well, I do,' continued Longstreet, 'and I tell you that we cannot afford to underrate him and the army he now commands. We must make up our minds to get into line of battle and to stay there; for the man will fight us every day and every hour till the end of this war.'[40]

Grant intended to launch the campaign by rapidly crossing the Rapidan River and marching through the closed terrain of the Wilderness before the enemy could react. Lee intended to hit when the Army of the Potomac was in motion. On 5 May 1864, the battle began.

Few military plans survive the shock of first encounter, and the Battle of the Wilderness was no exception. Grant's hopes to pass through the Wilderness before encountering the enemy were naive. His army numbered about 113,000 combat troops supported by 274 artillery pieces. In keeping with his desire to lighten his command's baggage train, Grant had sent back to the rear some 122 of his field guns. But his host still required a huge baggage train including 675 caissons and battery wagons, 835 ambulances and 609 ordinary wagons. Its size placed a tight restrictive limit on how fast the army could advance. Despite Grant and Meade's hard work to reduce the train, there was an irreducible minimum beyond which they could not go. It was largely a matter of draft animals, the overlooked beasts of burden that were fundamental to the army's strategic mobility.

Throughout the war, generals on both sides had their strategic mobility seriously constrained by the limitations of horse-drawn artillery and trains. Authorities in Washington, Lincoln in particular, never understood how the government could keep supplying a field army with terrific numbers of draft animals and yet their generals would plead for more. While cautious commanders could and did use a lack of fit horses as an excuse for inaction, the realities of field operations are well described by James Wilson who commanded Thomas's cavalry during the Nashville campaign:

'Men and horses had suffered all the rigors of winter, snow, rain, frost, mud, and exposure. During the nights, the temperature would fall so as to make ice from half an inch to an inch thick, and this was far too thin to carry horses without breaking through. As a consequence, the roads were worked up into a continuous quagmire. The horses' legs were covered with mud, and this, in turn, was frozen, so that great numbers of the poor animals were entirely disabled, their hoofs softened and the hair of their legs so rubbed off that it was impossible for them to travel. Hundreds lost their hoofs entirely, and in all my experience I have never seen so much suffering.'[41]

To some degree, adverse conditions could be mitigated if the officers paid strict attention to the care of the animals. At the battery level, for example, experience showed that combat efficiency greatly depended on the condition of the horses. Good officers scrupulously supervised their horses' feeding and grooming. Lazy ones did not. Both complained about their superiors' ignorance. These superiors usually came from the infantry or engineering branches. So as not to be caught by surprise by enemy action or by orders from their own field general, divisional and corps generals typically issued alert orders requiring that horses be saddled and in limber ready to march even though the projected movement would not begin for some time. Unable to graze, the horses rapidly consumed the battery's wagon-borne forage.

Simultaneously, most march orders also assigned the men a certain number of days' rations and provided the draft animals with about half that amount since the officers issuing the orders assumed that they could graze to make up the balance. Thus the men entered the Wilderness with sixteen days' worth of rations while the wagons carried only ten days' hay and grain for the horses. As the campaign got under way, the consequences of all of this was that horses and mules weakened from malnutrition and neglect. Weakened teams hauled less forage, completing the vicious circle of equine attrition. It was an overlooked factor that substantially reduced an army's strategic mobility.

Everyone and everything had to be channelled across Germanna and Ely's fords, where the army's 2,276 engineers toiled long and hard to bridge the Rapidan. Grant considered the river crossing to be the most perilous moment. After the Rapidan, the way south led along some poor secondary roads. But the need to regulate the advance to protect the trains prevented the infantry from advancing through the Wilderness. Hancock's advance guard reached the crossroads at Chancellorsville before 10 a.m. on 4 May and encamped for the remainder of the day. The slowness of the advance enabled Lee time to seize the initiative by sending two corps-sized columns along the Orange Turnpike and Orange Plank Road against the flank of the Army of the Potomac. Had Sheridan's 12,000 cavalry been properly utilized, the Federal force would have had ample warning of the rebels' rapid approach. Instead, Meade assigned (and Grant approved) an order of march that put two cavalry divisions on the flank opposite the one exposed to Lee's advance. Wilson, with the 3d Cavalry Division, was assigned to patrol the Orange Turnpike and Plank Road. He left a mere regiment behind for this duty and rode on happily with the rest of his division to engage in a series of meaningless encounters with Stuart's cavalry. Consequently, when the Army of Northern Virginia struck, there were no pickets on the turnpike and only some 600 troopers on the Plank Road.

This colossal failure of reconnaissance and security compounded Grant's habitual unwillingness to consider the enemy's intentions. Coupled with his desire not to reinforce the eastern army's dread of Lee, it led him to ignore what should have been obvious: there would be a battle in the Wilderness. On the other hand, Grant's efforts to deceive the enemy worked to the extent that when Lee struck, he did so before he had concentrated his forces.[42] What unfolded was not the powerful assault that Lee wanted, but rather an episodic series of attacks and counter-attacks which neither leader was able to control.

Any encounter battle taxes a general's abilities, but the problems were much more acute in the baffling woodland known as the Wilderness. This was a terrain of secondary growth timber, 'a dense tangled jungle through which no line can march or keep in order'.[43] With sight lines of fifty paces and less, one seldom saw the enemy. Fighting would erupt unexpectedly and then there was only 'smoke and bushes, and lots of our men tumbling about'.[44] Colonel Theodore Lyman of Meade's staff carried a message to a divisional general who was trying to deploy along the Orange Plank Road. This general told Lyman that the whole of A. P. Hill's Corps was nearby with its skirmishers only 300 yards away. Lyman later wrote: 'For all I could see they might have been in Florida.'[45]

Yet 5 May had the potential to be Grant's day, the day on which the Army of the Potomac could win the war. Lee had miscalculated and as a consequence had only two corps in action to Grant's three. It began when Warren learned of an unknown force advancing on his flank along the Orange Plank Road. At 6.20 a.m. he sent out an infantry reconnaissance and informed his superior. Meade, in turn, received the dispatch and galloped to Fifth Corps headquarters where he told Warren, 'If there is to be any fighting this side of Mine Run, let us to it right off.'[46] Then Meade ordered the trains halted until the situation developed and sent a dispatch reporting everything to Grant. Grant received Meade's dispatch at 7.30. By Grant's lights, Meade's decision was just fine. He encouraged the commander of the Army of the Potomac to fight aggressively, sending a return dispatch at 8.24 that read, in part, 'If any opportunity presents itself for pitching into a part of Lee's army, do so without giving time for disposition.'[47] The careful preparations to pass through the Wilderness had survived less than two hours after first contact with the enemy. One of the many formations to suffer when Meade and Grant improvised an offensive was the brigade of Regulars.

On the second day at Gettysburg, the Regulars had been taken front, flank, and rear during the fighting along the Wheatfield, losing half their officers killed or wounded. In the consolidation of 1864 (which saw the departure of George Sykes, the officer who had always led them) the remaining Regulars merged with the former Zouave Brigade to form Romeyn B. Ayres' Brigade in Charles Griffin's division. There were now five regular regiments, only one of which, the old 2d US Infantry, pre-dated the war. In the early afternoon of 5 May, the Regulars went in for one last great charge.

Advancing through the thick underbrush next to the Orange Turnpike, they emerged into one of the Wilderness's few clearings, an 800-yard-wide, 400-yard-deep rectangle known as Sanders' Field. In the middle of the field was a dry creek bed. The ground rose gradually towards the far end where presumably the enemy held the woodline. Flags flying, the 2,061 Regulars shook out into battle line, and with the 140th New York Volunteers on their left flank, advanced across the field. Observers noted that they marched as if on a parade ground, in straight ranks well formed up. Halfway across they encountered heavy musketry fire from an unseen enemy. Disregarding losses, they continued until nearing the woodline where they received the order to charge. Bayonets flashing, they entered the woods, clambering over a defended line of hastily erected barricades, and sent the defenders, who belonged to Steuart's Brigade, flying.

Meanwhile, the zouave regiment on their left came to a halt under withering fire. Divisional commander Griffin, an old artillery-man, sent Battery D, 1st New York Light Artillery, galloping forward along the pike to help the zouaves. It proved a mistake as Confederate infantry shot down gunners and horses alike, forcing the survivors to abandon two guns. The three remaining zouave regiments charged, made brief headway, and then came to a halt when enemy supports arrived. In fact, although no one realized it, Ayres' brigade was in advance of the entire Army of the Potomac, had both flanks in the air, and was about to receive the attention of two enemy divisions.

Still the Regulars pressed on, breaking a second line held by Walker's famous Stonewall Brigade. Here the three centre regiments became involved in close-range combat and could see nothing of what

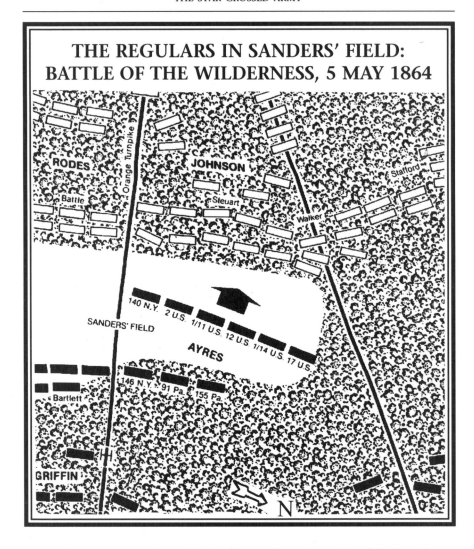

THE REGULARS IN SANDERS' FIELD: BATTLE OF THE WILDERNESS, 5 MAY 1864

was taking place on their flanks. So confused was the fighting that a young English officer who had recently joined from the staff, and wore a gray slouch hat, was shot in the back by a private who mistook him for an enemy. Suddenly, as they began to receive heavy fire from both sides, the men in the centre realized that they were flanked and began to fall back. Unknown to them, elements of three Confederate brigades had struck the left flank of Ayres' brigade while additional enemy forces had lapped the right flank. The brigade collapsed and broke for the rear.

That this had occurred was due to a failure at nearly every command level. The regimental officers in the centre had lost control of their men. A captain in charge of two reserve companies, for example, had committed his men to the front-line fighting during the initially successful advance, and thus his reserve was unavailable for flank protection. The left flank 2d US Infantry and the right flank 17th US Infantry had not pulled their weight and had retreated almost as soon as enemy opposition stiffened. Ayres had committed his brigade into a charge in two lines, and promptly lost control during the advance across the field so that the zouaves never succeeded in tying in with the Regulars. Griffin, in turn, had permitted Ayres to advance before arranging adequate supports. At the topmost level, Meade and Grant had failed to use their cavalry to reconnoitre, so it had devolved upon the Regulars to perform this costly reconnaissance in force.

The losses among the Regulars clearly showed how desperate had been the fight of the three regiments in the centre and how poorly the other two regiments had fought:

Unit	Engaged	Losses	% loss
2d US.	191	1	–
11th US	200	65	32.5
12th US	450	110	24.4
14th US.	530	118	22.4
17th US	690	8	1.0

It was this disaster that led to the celebrated incident, later that afternoon, when Griffin spurred up to army headquarters and began profanely denouncing his fellow officers. Hearing this tirade, Rawlins became angry which prompted Grant to ask Meade, 'Who is the General Gregg? You ought to arrest him!' For once the hot-tempered Meade responded calmly. Reaching forward he gently buttoned Grant's coat and said: 'It's Griffin, not Gregg; and it's only his way of talking.'[48]

It was a depressing débâcle for Ayres. He confided to the corps artillery commander that the loss of two guns was entirely due to 'the bad behavior of his brigade'.[49] The Regulars would refuse to charge on 10 May at Spotsylvania, and then two days later would conduct a most valiant assault. Consolidated and reinforced at Petersburg, they would lose more than half their strength on 19 August during the fight for the Weldon Railroad. By 2 November the survivors had been sent back north and the famous Regular Brigade was no more.

While Warren's Corps and the Regulars were fighting along the Orange Turnpike, an entirely separate conflict was taking place near the intersection of the Orange Plank Road and Brock Road. It was a race to see who could control this vital crossroads. If A. P. Hill's Corps captured it, Grant's army would be cut in two. Fortunately for Grant, his army's survival depended upon Hancock's vaunted Second Corps and its aggressive leader. One of Meade's staff officers provides a picture of Hancock in battle:

'"Report to General Meade that it is very hard to bring up troops in this wood, and that only a part of my Corps is up, but I [Hancock] will do as well as I can." Up rides an officer: "Sir! General Getty is hard pressed and nearly out of ammunition!" "Tell him to hold on and General Gibbon will be up to help him." Another officer: "General Mott's division has broken, sir, and is coming back." "Tell him to stop them, sir!" roared Hancock in a voice of a trumpet. [As Hancock was speaking Mott's men were hurrying by in retreat] Hancock dashed among them. "Halt here! Halt here! Form behind this rifle-pit. Major Mitchell, go to Gibbon and tell him to come up on the double-quick!"'[50]

Hancock's orders brought additional Federal forces up in the nick of time. In a typical flurry, two of the army's most aggressive brigadiers fell within minutes of entering the fight. The very capable General Samuel Carroll brought up his brigade to bolster the hard-pressed defenders at the intersection. Carroll rode at their head, 'as calm as a May morning'.[51] He ordered, 'Left face, prime, forward!' and his brigade disappeared into the woods. There was a tremendous crash of musketry, and stretcher-bearers emerged carrying the wounded brigadier. Then Hays' Brigade came up. General Alexander Hays was a robust, rough-hewn, red-haired officer who always rode at the head of his men shouting and waving his sword. Hays turned to follow in Carroll's wake. Within minutes appeared a riderless white horse soon followed by another group of stretcher-bearers carrying the mortally wounded Hays. He had been shot through the head within minutes of leading his brigade into action.

And so it continued. Units charged, fell back in confusion, reformed, and charged again. After two or three cycles they simply refused to advance any more. Officers waved swords and brandished pistols in an effort to make them go forward again, but to no avail. Having suffered fearful losses, the men were adamant.

The consequences of such relentless attrition for the Army of the Potomac as a whole could be foretold by the sad performance of Mott's Division during the first day in the Wilderness. Two years earlier this had been Hooker's old fighting division, as good a unit as existed in the Army of the Potomac. Following Hooker's elevation to corps command, the division was obliged to endure two commanders of little merit. The division grumbled loudly when the old Third Corps was broken up as part of the reorganization of 1864 and it experienced considerable discontent over re-enlistments. All of these troubles stemmed from the loss of good officers and the consequences emerged in the bullet-swept Wilderness thickets. Mott's division broke badly as soon as it encountered A. P. Hill's men along the Orange Plank Road. On this field, and in subsequent actions, Mott's division proved utterly unreliable. On 12 May, told that Mott's division was to support him, General Wright complained to Meade, 'General, I don't want Mott's men on my left; they are not a support; I would rather have no troops there!'[52] Four days later Meade broke up the division and distributed the men to other formations, thus ending the saga of a once élite unit.

The intense and confused fighting in the Wilderness could easily have unnerved a commanding officer, particularly given the fact that in 1864, Grant's opponent, General Robert E. Lee, had an unmatched reputation for bold, offensive action. Lee enjoyed a moral ascendancy over the eastern generals and this was a psychological obstacle which Grant had to surmount if he were to succeed. At the peak of the battle an excited general approached Grant to warn him that he well understood Lee's methods, the crisis was at hand, and Lee was trying to throw his entire army between the Union army and the Rapidan in order to cut the Federal line of communications. In response, Grant revealed uncharacteristic anger. Rising to his feet he said:

'Oh, I am heartily tired of hearing about what Lee is going to do. Some of you always seem to think he is suddenly going to turn a double somersault, and land in our rear and on both our flanks at the same time. Go back to your command, and try to think what we are going to do ourselves, instead of what Lee is going to do.'[53]

The second day of fighting in the Wilderness, 6 May, featured more of the same. Clever Confederate manoeuvring turned first Grant's left flank and then his right. At nightfall, while the soldiers fell into exhausted stupor, attention turned to the man at the top. Everyone knew that one year ago, under similar circumstances, Hooker had given up and retreated. The leaders of the Army of the Potomac wondered what the man from the West would do. At least one astute junior officer believed he knew. Captain Elisha Rhodes wrote in his diary: 'If we were under any other General except Grant I should expect a retreat, but Grant is not that kind of a soldier.'[54]

The decision would be his alone, because here in the Wilderness Grant was largely without his western comrades, and surrounding by a host of suspicious eastern generals. The results of the first two days had done little to instil confidence in his generalship. Even a stalwart western supporter experienced doubts. Sitting around a smouldering fire in front of Grant's tent, Sylvanus Cadwallader mused that Grant had been forced to fight Lee on ground of the latter's choosing, with the certainty that two Union soldiers would fall for each Confederate until Lee could be dislodged. After two days' bitter fighting the Army of the Potomac had gained scarcely a few yards. Dark anxieties plagued Cadwallader: 'Could it be possible that I had followed Gen. Grant through the Tallahatchie Expedition; the operations against Vicksburg; the campaign of Chattanooga; and finally to the dark and tangled thickets of the Wilderness; to record his defeat and overthrow, as had been recorded of every commander of the Army of the Potomac?'

He looked over to see Grant deep in thought. Then Grant stirred, and as was his wont when he needed to relieve pressure, began a chatty conversation about trivial matters. After thirty minutes of chat the reporter suggested that it was time to go to their tents to get rest. The general agreed, smiled, 'spoke of the sharp work Gen. Lee had been giving us for a couple of days, and entered his tent'. Vastly reassured that Grant was keeping his balance – it was 'the grandest mental sunburst of my life' he later wrote – Cadwallader also went to his tent.[55]

The night march towards Spotsylvania on 7 May revealed to the Army of the Potomac what Cadwallader had detected. It was the campaign's turning-point. Lee's nonpareil army, a force that had won renown on countless fields from Gaines' Mill to Gettysburg by virtue of its punishing attacks, had shot its bolt. Because of Grant's strategy of unrelenting pressure, never again would the Army of Northern Virginia have manoeuvre space to conduct an assault in force. The men in the ranks understood this. Hitherto, on many fields, they had fought equally well only to have their generals lose their nerve. When Grant marched them further south they realized that this time their efforts would not be in vain. Encountering Grant at the road junction from where they continued the march south, soldiers cheered and swung their hats, lit torches and rushed forward to applaud him. 'The demonstration was the emphatic verdict pronounced by the troops upon his first battle in the East.'[56] A New Jersey soldier joked that apparently Grant meant to establish his 'office' in Richmond, and this was just fine by him.

The Wilderness had been another bloody, blundering affair of missed opportunities on both sides. Unknowable at the time was the fact that the battle was a clear strategic victory for the Union. Grant's objective in advancing was to fix Lee's army, and within 48 hours of beginning his campaign he had accomplished this.

Combat Assessment

Grant: By consciously (and unnaturally) distancing himself from command – on the battle's first day he sits on a stump and whittles, an attitude totally at odds with his previous behaviour – Grant ill-serves the army.

Lieutenants: Eager to prove his fighting spirit, Meade attacks at first opportunity without reflecting upon alternatives. Hancock gives sterling service, Warren and Sedgwick are poor. Burnside is late.

Staff: Handles the complex logistics of the river crossing very well, but fails to keep Burnside's Corps well in hand so that it can participate in a timely manner.

Infantry: The last, army-wide, determined fighting effort.

Artillery: Terrain unsuitable for gunnery.

Cavalry: Except for one regiment's delaying action, absent from the fight.

Engineers: A thoroughly professional river assault crossing.

BATTLE OF THE WILDERNESS,[57] 5–7 May 1864
Lieutenant General Ulysses S. Grant commanding
General HQ escort: 5th US Cavalry, Cos. B, F, K

ARMY OF THE POTOMAC: Major General George G. Meade

PROVOST GUARD:
Brigadier General Marsena R. Patrick
1st Massachusetts Cavalry, Cos. C and D
80th New York Infantry (20th Militia)
3d Pennsylvania Cavalry
68th Pennsylvania Infantry
114th Pennsylvania Infantry
ENGINEER TROOPS
50th New York
Battalion United States
GUARDS AND ORDERLIES
Independent Co. Oneida (New York)
  Cavalry

SECOND ARMY CORPS:
Major General Winfield S. Hancock
Staff
1st Vermont Cavalry, Co. M (escort)

First Division:
Brigadier General Francis C. Barlow
FIRST BRIGADE:
Colonel Nelson A. Miles
Staff
26th Michigan
61st New York
81st Pennsylvania
140th Pennsylvania
183d Pennsylvania
SECOND BRIGADE:
Colonel Thomas A. Smyth
Staff
28th Massachusetts
63d New York
69th New York
88th New York
116th Pennsylvania
THIRD BRIGADE:
Colonel Paul Frank
39th New York
52d New York
57th New York
111th New York
125th New York
126th New York
FOURTH BRIGADE:
Colonel John R. Brooke

2d Delaware
64th New York
66th New York
53d Pennsylvania
145th Pennsylvania
148th Pennsylvania

Second Division:
Brigadier General John Gibbon
Provost Guard: 2d Co. Minnesota
  Sharpshooters
FIRST BRIGADE:
Brigadier General Alexander S. Webb
Staff
19th Maine
1st Co. Andrew (Massachusetts)
  Sharpshooters
15th Massachusetts
19th Massachusetts
20th Massachusetts
7th Michigan
42d New York
59th New York
82d New York (2d militia)
SECOND BRIGADE:
Brigadier General Joshua T. Owen
Staff
152d New York
69th Pennsylvania
71st Pennsylvania
72d Pennsylvania
106th Pennsylvania
THIRD BRIGADE:
Colonel Samuel S. Carroll
14th Connecticut
1st Delaware
14th Indiana
12th New Jersey
10th New York Battalion
108th New York
4th Ohio
8th Ohio
7th WV

Third Division:
Major General David B. Birney
FIRST BRIGADE:

Brigadier General J. H. Hobart Ward
20th Indiana
3d Maine
40th New York
86th New York
124th New York
99th Pennsylvania
110th Pennsylvania
141st Pennsylvania
2d US Sharpshooters
SECOND BRIGADE:
Brigadier General Alexander Hays,
    Colonel John S. Crocker
Staff
4th Maine
17th Maine
3d Michigan
5th Michigan
93d New York
57th Pennsylvania
63d Pennsylvania
105th Pennsylvania
1st US Sharpshooters

Fourth Division:
Brigadier General Gershom Mott
FIRST BRIGADE:
Colonel Robert McAllister
1st Massachusetts
16th Massachusetts
5th New Jersey
6th New Jersey
7th New Jersey
8th New Jersey
11th New Jersey
26th Pennsylvania
115th Pennsylvania
SECOND BRIGADE:
Colonel William R. Brewster
11th Massachusetts
70th New York
71st New York
72d New York
73d New York
74th New York
120th New York
84th Pennsylvania
ARTILLERY BRIGADE:
Colonel John C. Tidball
Maine Light, 6th Batt. (F)
Massachusetts Light, 10th Batt.
New Hampshire Light, 1st Batt.
1st New York Light, Batt. G

4th New York Heavy, 3d Bn.
1st Pennsylvania Light, Batt. F
1st Rhode Island Light, Batts. A and B
4th US, Batt. K
5th US, Batts. C and I

FIFTH ARMY CORPS:
Major General Gouverneur K. Warren
Provost Guard: 12th New York Battalion

First Division:
Brigadier General Charles Griffin
FIRST BRIGADE:
Brigadier General Romeyn B. Ayres
Staff
140th New York
146th New York
91st Pennsylvania
155th Pennsylvania
2d US
11th US
12th US
14th US
17th US
SECOND BRIGADE:
Colonel Jacob B. Sweitzer
9th Massachusetts
22d Massachusetts
32d Massachusetts
4th Michigan
62d Pennsylvania
THIRD BRIGADE:
Brigadier General Joseph J. Bartlett
20th Maine
18th Massachusetts
1st Michigan
16th Michigan
44th New York
83d Pennsylvania
118th Pennsylvania

Second Division:
Brigadier General John C. Robinson
FIRST BRIGADE: Colonel Samuel H.
    Leonard, Colonel Peter Lyle
16th Maine
13th Massachusetts
39th Massachusetts
104th New York
SECOND BRIGADE:
Brigadier General Henry Baxter,
    Colonel Richard Coulter

Staff
12th Massachusetts
83d New York (9th Militia)
97th New York
11th Pennsylvania
88th Pennsylvania
90th Pennsylvania
THIRD BRIGADE:
Colonel Andrew W. Denison
1st Maryland
4th Maryland
7th Maryland
8th Maryland

Third Division: Brigadier General
    Samuel W. Crawford
FIRST BRIGADE:
Colonel William McCandless
1st Pennsylvania Reserves
2d Pennsylvania Reserves
6th Pennsylvania Reserves
7th Pennsylvania Reserves
11th Pennsylvania Reserves
13th Pennsylvania Reserves (1st
    Rifles)
THIRD BRIGADE:
Colonel Joseph W. Fisher
5th Pennsylvania Reserves
8th Pennsylvania Reserves
10th Pennsylvania Reserves
12th Pennsylvania Reserves

Fourth Division: Brigadier General
    James S. Wadsworth, Brigadier
    General Lysander Cutler
FIRST BRIGADE:
Brigadier General Lysander Cutler,
    Colonel William W. Robinson
7th Indiana
19th Indiana
24th Michigan
1st New York Battalion Sharpshooters
2d Wisconsin
6th Wisconsin
7th Wisconsin
SECOND BRIGADE:
Brigadier General James C. Rice
76th New York
84th New York
95th New York
147th New York
56th Pennsylvania
THIRD BRIGADE:

Colonel Roy Stone, Colonel Edward S.
    Bragg
121st Pennsylvania
142d Pennsylvania
143d Pennsylvania
149th Pennsylvania
150th Pennsylvania
ARTILLERY BRIGADE:
Colonel Charles S. Wainwright
Massachusetts Light, 3d Batt. (C)
Massachusetts Light, 5th Batt. (E)
1st New York Light, Batt. D
1st New York Light, Batts. E and L
1st New York Light, Batt. H
4th New York Heavy, 2d Battalion
1st Pennsylvania Light, Batt. B
4th US, Batt. B
5th US, Batt. D

SIXTH ARMY CORPS:
Major General John Sedgwick
Escort: 8th Pennsylvania Cavalry, Co. A

First Division:
Brigadier General Horatio G. Wright
FIRST BRIGADE:
Colonel Henry W. Brown
1st New Jersey
2d New Jersey
3d New Jersey
4th New Jersey
10th New Jersey
15th New Jersey
SECOND BRIGADE:
Colonel Emory Upton
5th Maine
121st New York
95th Pennsylvania
96th Pennsylvania
THIRD BRIGADE:
Brigadier General David A. Russell
6th Maine
49th Pennsylvania
119th Pennsylvania
5th Wisconsin
FOURTH BRIGADE:
Brigadier General Alexander Shaler,
    Colonel Nelson Cross
Staff
65th New York
67th New York
122d New York
82d Pennsylvania (det.)

Second Division:
Brigadier General George W. Getty,
    Brigadier General Thomas H. Neill
FIRST BRIGADE:
Brigadier General Frank Wheaton
62d New York
93d Pennsylvania
98th Pennsylvania
102d Pennsylvania
139th Pennsylvania
SECOND BRIGADE:
Colonel Lewis A. Grant
2d Vermont
3d Vermont
4th Vermont
5th Vermont
6th Vermont
THIRD BRIGADE:
Brigadier General Thomas H. Neill,
    Colonel Daniel D. Bidwell
7th Maine
43d New York
49th New York
77th New York
61st Pennsylvania
FOURTH BRIGADE:
Brigadier General Henry L. Eustis
7th Massachusetts
10th Massachusetts
37th Massachusetts
2d Rhode Island

Third Division:
Brigadier General James B. Ricketts
FIRST BRIGADE:
Brigadier General William H. Morris
14th New Jersey
106th New York
151st New York
87th Pennsylvania
10th Vermont
SECOND BRIGADE:
Brigadier General Truman Seymour,
    Colonel Benjamin F. Smith
Staff
6th Maryland
110th Ohio
122d Ohio
126th Ohio
67th Pennsylvania
138th Pennsylvania
ARTILLERY BRIGADE:
Colonel Charles H. Tompkins

Maine Light, 4th Batt. (D)
Massachusetts Light, 1st Batt. (A)
New York Light, 1st Batt.
New York Light, 3d Batt.
4th New York Heavy, 1st Battalion
1st Rhode Island Light, Batt. C
1st Rhode Island Light, Batt. E
1st Rhode Island Light, Batt. G
5th US, Batt. M

CAVALRY CORPS:
Major General Philip H. Sheridan
Escort: 6th US

First Division:
Brigadier General Alfred T. A. Torbert,
    Brigadier General Wesley Merritt
FIRST BRIGADE:
Brigadier General George A. Custer
1st Michigan
5th Michigan
6th Michigan
7th Michigan
SECOND BRIGADE:
Colonel Thomas C. Devin
4th New York
6th New York
9th New York
17th Pennsylvania
RESERVE BRIGADE:
Brigadier General Wesley Merritt,
    Colonel Alfred Gibbs
19th New York (1st Dragoons)
6th Pennsylvania
1st US
2d US
5th US

Second Division:
Brigadier General David McM Gregg
FIRST BRIGADE:
Brigadier General Henry E. Davies, Jr.
1st Massachusetts
1st New Jersey
6th Ohio
1st Pennsylvania
SECOND BRIGADE:
Colonel J. Irvin Gregg
1st Maine
10th New York
2d Pennsylvania
4th Pennsylvania
8th Pennsylvania

16th Pennsylvania

Third Division:
Brigadier General James H. Wilson
Escort: 8th Illinois (det.)
FIRST BRIGADE:
Colonel Timothy M. Bryan, Jr.,
    Colonel John B. McIntosh
1st Connecticut
2d New York
5th New York
18th Pennsylvania
SECOND BRIGADE:
Colonel George H. Chapman
3d Indiana
8th New York
1st Vermont
FIRST BRIGADE HORSE ARTILLERY:
Captain James M. Robertson
New York Light, 6th Batt.
2d US, Batts. B and L
2d US, Batt. D
2d US, Batt. M
4th US, Batt. A
4th US, Batts. C and E

Artillery:
Brigadier General Henry J. Hunt
ARTILLERY RESERVE:
Colonel Henry S. Burton
FIRST BRIGADE: Colonel J. Howard
    Kitching
6th New York Heavy
15th New York Heavy
SECOND BRIGADE:
Major John A. Tompkins
Maine Light, 5th Batt. (E)
1st New Jersey Light, Batt. A
1st New Jersey Light, Batt. B
New York Light, 5th Batt.
New York Light, 12th Batt.
1st New York Light, Batt. B
THIRD BRIGADE:
Major Robert H. Fitzhugh
Massachusetts Light, 9th Batt.
1st New York Light, Batt. C
New York Light, 11th Batt.
New York Light, 15th Batt.
1st Ohio Light, Batt. H
5th US, Batt. E

Horse Artillery:
SECOND BRIGADE:

Captain Dunbar R. Ransom
1st US, Batts. E and G
1st US, Batts. H and I
1st US, Batt. K
2d US, Batt. A
2d US, Batt. G
3d US, Batts. C, F, K

NINTH ARMY CORPS:
Major General Ambrose E. Burnside
Provost Guard: 8th US Infantry

First Division: Brigadier General
    Thomas G. Stevenson
FIRST BRIGADE:
Colonel Sumner Carruth, Colonel
    Jacob P. Gould
35th Massachusetts
56th Massachusetts
57th Massachusetts
59th Massachusetts
4th US
10th US
SECOND BRIGADE:
Colonel Daniel Leasure
3d Maryland
21st Massachusetts
100th Pennsylvania
ARTILLERY:
Maine Light, 2d Batt. (B)
Massachusetts Light, 14th Batt.

Second Division:
Brigadier General Robert B. Potter
FIRST BRIGADE: Colonel Zenas R. Bliss,
    Colonel John I. Curtin
36th Massachusetts
58th Massachusetts
51st New York
45th Pennsylvania
48th Pennsylvania
7th Rhode Island
SECOND BRIGADE:
Colonel Simon G. Griffin
Staff
31st Maine
32d Maine
6th New Hampshire
9th New Hampshire
11th New Hampshire
17th Vermont
ARTILLERY:
Massachusetts Light, 11th Batt.

New York Light, 19th Batt.

Third Division:
Brigadier General Orlando B. Willcox
FIRST BRIGADE:
Colonel John F. Hartranft
2d Michigan
8th Michigan
17th Michigan
27th Michigan
109th New York
51st Pennsylvania
SECOND BRIGADE:
Colonel Benjamin C. Christ
1st Michigan Sharpshooters
20th Michigan
79th New York
60th Ohio (9th and 10th Cos. Ohio
   Sharpshooters att.)
50th Pennsylvania
ARTILLERY:
Maine Light, 7th Batt. (G)
New York Light, 34th Batt.

Fourth Division:
Brigadier General Edward Ferrero
FIRST BRIGADE:
Colonel Joshua K. Sigfried
27th US

30th US
39th US
43d US
30th Connecticut (det.)
19th US
23d US
ARTILLERY:
Pennsylvania Light, Co. D
3d Vermont
CAVALRY:
3d New Jersey
22d New York
2d Ohio
13th Pennsylvania
RESERVE ARTILLERY:
Captain John Edwards, Jr.
New York Light, 27th Batt.
1st Rhode Island Light, Batt. D
1st Rhode Island Light, Batt. H
2d US, Batt. E
3d US, Batt. G
3d US, Batts. L and M
PROVISIONAL BRIGADE:
Colonel Elisha G. Marshall
24th New York Cavalry (dismounted)
14th New York Heavy Artillery
2d Pennsylvania Provisional Heavy
   Artillery

UNION TROOPS AT THE WILDERNESS REGIMENTS BY STATE

72 — Pennsylvania
61 — New York
26 *
41 **
Massachusetts 26
Michigan 18
18
Regulars

* Maryland 6, Indiana 5, Wisconsin 4, Connecticut 3,
New Hampshire 3, Delaware 2, Rhode Island 2, West Virginia 1.
** New Jersey 14, Maine 12, Vermont 8, Ohio 7

1   Gideon Welles, *Diary of Gideon Welles*, vol. 1 (Boston: Houghton Mifflin Co., 1911), p. 364.
2   *Diary of Gideon Welles*, vol. 1, p. 538.
3   Richard Wheeler, *On Fields of Fury. From the Wilderness to the Crater: An Eyewitness History*, (New York: Harper Collins Publishers, 1991), p. 54.
4   *Diary of Gideon Welles*, vol. 1, p. 540.
5   Bruce Catton, *Grant Takes Command*, (Boston, Little, Brown, 1968), p. 159.
6   George Meade, *The Life and Letters of George Gordon Meade*, vol. 1 (New York: Charles Scribner's Sons, 1913), p. 381.
7   Allan Nevins, ed., *A Diary of Battle: The Personal Journals of Colonel Charles S. Wainwright, 1861-1865*, (New York: Harcourt, Brace & World, 1962), p. 210.
8   Meade, vol. 2, p. 162.
9   George R. Agassiz, ed., *Meade's Headquarters 1863-1865: Letters of Colonel Theodore Lyman from the Wilderness to Appomattox*, (Boston: Massachusetts Historical Society, 1922), p. 87.
10 Quoted in Michael C. Adams, *Our Masters the Rebels: Speculations on Union Military Failure in the East, 1861-1865*, (Cambridge, MA: Harvard University Press, 1978), p. 154. Adams' book explores the topic of the Federal psychological inferiority.
11 Wheeler, *On Fields of Fury*, p. 46.
12 Dawes, Rufus R., *Service With the Sixth Wisconsin Volunteers*, (Madison: State Historical Society of Wisconsin, 1962), pp. 239-240.
13 Jerome M. Loving, ed., *Civil War Letters of George Washington Whitman*, (Durham, NC: Duke University Press, 1975), p. 114.
14 Stephen Minot Weld, *War Diary and Letters of Stephen Minot Weld, 1861-1865*, (Boston: Massachusetts Historical Society, 1979), p. 274.
15 Dawes, pp. 241-242.
16 Agassiz, *Meade's Headquarters*, p. 84.
17 Robert Garth Scott, ed., *Fallen Leaves: The Civil War Letters of Major Henry Livermore Abbott*, (Kent, OH: Kent State University Press, 1991), Abbott's letter of March 13, 1864.
18 Nevins, *A Diary of Battle*, p. 329.
19 *Diary of Gideon Welles*, vol. 1, p. 370.
20 For example, see comments of September 21, 1863 reported in *Diary of Gideon Welles*, vol. 1, p. 439.
21 Meade, vol. 2, pp. 197-198.
22 Agassiz, *Meade's Headquarters*, p. 110.
23 *Fallen Leaves*, Abbott's letter of December 6, 1863.
24 John Gibbon, *Personal Recollections of the Civil War*, (Dayton: Morningside Bookshop, 1978), p. 252.
25 James Harrison Wilson, *Under the Old Flag*, vol. 1 (New York: D. Appleton and Co., 1912), p. 396.
26 Ulysses S. Grant, *Personal Memoirs*, (New York: De Capo Press, 1982), pp. 365-366.
27 Grant, *Personal Memoirs*, p. 369.
28 Grant, *Personal Memoirs*, pp. 366-367.
29 *Official Records*, I:32/3, Longstreet to Lawton, March 5, 1864, p. 588.
30 Quoted in Adams, *Our Masters the Rebels*, pp. 173-74.
31 James I. Robertson, ed., *The Civil War Letters of General Robert McAllister*, (New Brunswick, NJ: Rutgers University Press, 1965), p. 404.
32 Agassiz, *Meade's Headquarters*, p. 131.
33 Wilson, *Under the Old Flag*, vol. 1, p. 375.
34 Philip H. Sheridan, *Personal Memoirs of P. H. Sheridan*, vol. 1 (New York: Charles L. Webster & Co., 1888), p. 408.
35 Nevins, *A Diary of Battle*, p. 328.
36 *Fallen Leaves*, Abbott's letter of March 27, 1864.
37 Wheeler, p. 66.
38 *The Civil War Letters of General Robert McAllister*, p. 408.
39 Gary W. Gallagher, ed., *Fighting for the Confederacy: The Personal Recollections of General Edward Porter Alexander*, (Chapel Hill: University of North Carolina Press, 1989), p. 345.

40 Horace Porter, *Campaigning with Grant*, (New York: The Century Co., 1897), p. 47.
41 Wilson, *Under the Old Flag*, vol. 2, p. 143.
42 The maturation of Lee's understanding of the coming blow can be traced in A. L.. Long, ed., *Memoirs of Robert E. Lee*, (Secaucus, NJ: Blue and Grey Press, 1983), Lee to Davis, March 30, April 2, April 5, and April 15, pp. 645-649.
43 Gibbon, *Personal Recollections of the Civil War*, p. 213.
44 Agassiz, *Meade's Headquarters*, p. 101.
45 Agassiz, *Meade's Headquarters*, p. 89.
46 Robert Garth Scott, *Into the Wilderness with the Army of the Potomac*, (Bloomington: Indiana University Press, 1985), pp. 35-36.
47 *Official Records*, I:36/1, Grant to Meade, May 5, 1864, p. 403.
48 Agassiz, *Meade's Headquarters*, p. 91.
49 Nevins, *A Diary of Battle*, p. 351.
50 Agassiz, *Meade's Headquarters*, p. 92.
51 Agassiz, *Meade's Headquarters*, p. 92.
52 Agassiz, *Meade's Headquarters*, p. 110.
53 Porter, *Campaigning with Grant*, p. 70.
54 Robert Hunt Rhodes, ed., *All For the Union: The Civil War Diary and Letters of Elisha Hunt Rhodes*, (New York: Vintage Books, 1992), p. 146.
55 Sylvanus Cadwallader, *Three Years with Grant*, (New York: Alfred A. Knopf, 1956), pp. 180-182.
56 Porter, *Campaigning With Grant*, p. 79.
57 *Official Records*, I:36/1, pp. 119-133; and *Battles and Leaders*, vol. 4, pp. 179-182.

12
'If It Takes All Summer'

PART 1. 'OUR CAVALRY ... DOES WONDERS'

Grant intended that the night march out of the Wilderness bring the Army of the Potomac to the crossroads at Spotsylvania Court House before Lee arrived. To disengage and march across an active enemy's front was a difficult feat that required solid staff work from officers well versed in traffic control. A 4-regiment brigade numbering 2,000 men occupied a good 1,000 yards of road space, and stragglers would further lengthen the column. With the addition of the batteries, baggage wagons, supply vehicles, and ambulances, even a well closed up division on the march occupied nearly two miles of road space. The typical American road nets that brought soldiers to battle were poor affairs featuring narrow, uneven secondary roads, farm lanes and woodland paths. These characteristics made traffic control a nightmare. Faulty staff work that sent a mule train across a unit's line of march could ensure that a combat unit failed to arrive at the battlefield on time. During the early war years, Grant had had to rely on an amateur staff. The Army of the Potomac had the reputation of possessing a much more professional set of staff officers backed by more sophisticated methods.

During the campaign in Virginia, army topographers – trained engineers who specialized in map making, something virtually unknown out West – surveyed the countryside in all directions and returned each evening with their findings. During the night, cartographers collated the information to produce a map of the neighbourhood. If the following day was sunny, photographic copies were made and distributed to the principal commanders. This was enormously helpful because Grant's army was on the offensive and advancing into Confederate territory. It had to feel its way along in the absence of good maps and friendly local people offering themselves as guides.

Despite its reputation, trained personnel, and technical advantages, the army's staff work proved unequal to the challenge of conducting night marches along poor woodland roads during the Wilderness and Spotsylvania Campaigns. Their bungling repeatedly undid Grant's plans. In the march out of the Wilderness, when everyone should have been pulling in harness to beat Lee's army to the vital road junction, the pace was snail-like. One officer recalled moving about one-quarter of a mile per hour along a congested road where men and vehicles had to go in single file to avoid being bogged down in streams.

No staff officer had reconnoitred the district and identified this potential bottleneck.

Matters reached a head on 8 May when Meade complained to Sheridan that his troopers were blocking roads along which the infantry needed to advance, and Sheridan complained that if only Meade would unleash him, he would go out and 'whip' Stuart. Highly irritated, Meade went to Grant and reported this conversation. Grant calmly remarked, 'Did he say so? Then let him go out and do it.'[1] Accordingly, Meade ordered Sheridan to attack Stuart. Delighted, Sheridan told his commanders: 'We going out to fight Stuart's cavalry in consequence of a suggestion from me; we will give him a fair, square fight; we are strong; and I know we can beat him, and in view of my recent representations to General Meade I shall expect nothing but success.'[2]

Sheridan's cockiness seemed to surprise his divisional commanders, for hitherto most missions had been designed to avoid Stuart's vaunted cavaliers. With three days' rations for the men, and one of grain for the horses doled out, – Sheridan intended to travel light – the Cavalry Corps set out. The Battle of Yellow Tavern lay ahead.

Confident as he appeared, in fact Sheridan took one major precaution. Instead of dispersing his corps along parallel roads, the normal practice for a rapid march against the enemy's rear, he concentrated his troops along one route. Consequently, when he began his march on 9 May 1864, he placed his most aggressive brigadier, 24-year-old George Custer, in the lead. Behind Custer came a single, narrow column stretching back over thirteen miles of road. Sheridan accepted this as the price he must pay to avoid being defeated in detail. Also in contrast to past cavalry expeditions, Sheridan insisted that the march be conducted at a steady walk. He wanted his horses fresh when the fighting began. When they halted the troopers made one large camp instead of umpteen small picket camps each with its own sentries as had been the custom on past raids. This relieved more troopers from the strain of all night guard duty.

The next day the advance halted because an unknown enemy force was blocking the road. 'Little Phil' (his troopers had already taken to using this nickname, a sure sign that they were responding to his personal magnetism) rode up to inquire what was wrong. Informed of the presence of an enemy force, he demanded, cavalry or infantry? Told it was cavalry, Sheridan snapped, 'Keep moving, boys. We're going through! There isn't cavalry enough in all the Southern Confederacy to stop us.'[3] The troopers picked up Sheridan's confidence. One recalls that they sang while on the march. Another remembers that Little Phil seemed to be everywhere: 'We saw him daily, whether we were in the advance, at the rear, or the center of the column, and he would as soon borrow a light from the pipe of an enlisted man as from the cigar of an officer. The common soldier's uniform was good enough for him.'[4]

Clearly the eastern troopers were responding to Sheridan's easy-going, egalitarian, western style leadership.

On the 11th, Little Phil found what he had set out to find: Stuart's cavalry offering battle on the outskirts of Richmond. After initial probing, Sheridan made a 2-hour reconnaissance of the enemy position while his own column deployed for battle. He assigned to one brigade the task of protecting his command from a force of Confederate cavalry that had been hounding his rear for the past 24 hours. He sent two brigades to cut Stuart's possible escape route and entered the battle with his remaining four brigades. His troopers holding his centre found themselves under heavy fire from a dismounted line of cavalry and an enfilading artillery section that made 'Yellow Tavern an uncomfortably hot place'.[5] But his personal reconnaissance had convinced him that Stuart's left flank was vulnerable. He ordered Merritt to attack this sector.

Merritt assigned the task to Custer and his brigade of Michigan cavalry. During the course of the war, Custer's command was to run up the highest combat casualty rate of any yankee cavalry unit. At Yellow Tavern, he showed that he was capable of exercising tactical finesse as well as downright aggression. While two regiments dismounted to occupy Confederate attention, Custer led the other two along a covered approach against Stuart's flank. It was a classic cavalry charge. Custer began at a walk, increased the gait to a trot, and then, shouting 'Come on, Wolverines!' (the nickname for Michigan soldiers) charged the final distance at a gallop and overran the two enemy artillery pieces. Custer's attack bowled over the defenders and sent them flying and swept past a party of some 80 rebels who were rallying round a conspicuous caped and plumed, red-bearded Confederate officer.

A Confederate mounted counter-attack sent Custer back the way he had come. Among his retiring troopers was Private John Huff, a hard case soldier. At the age of 43, he had enlisted in an infantry sharpshooter unit for two years and won a prize as his regiment's best marksman. Then he returned to Michigan, and, apparently bored with civilian life, re-enlisted in Custer's cavalry. Now Huff saw the red-bearded enemy officer some 25 feet away, firing his pistol at the passing yankee cavalry. Huff took aim with his own .44-calibre cavalry pistol, fired, and moved on. The swirling battle ended soon after with Sheridan successful, having turned the tables on the enemy brigade attacking his own rear by taking it from behind, while simultaneously charging the force blocking his advance to Richmond in front and flank. The battle left Sheridan with control of the road to Richmond. It also left the red-bearded James Stuart mortally wounded by Huff's shot to his abdomen.

After the action at Yellow Tavern, for one brief, glorious moment Sheridan toyed with the idea of assaulting Richmond. Had he done so he would have faced few trained infantry. Instead, an indifferent militia manned Richmond's fortifications. Had he captured Richmond, it is conceivable that Butler's Army of the James could have joined him there. Lee would have had no choice but to retreat while the Army of the Potomac hounded his rear. But it was not to be. Sheridan chose to bypass Richmond and march on to the James River and the protection of Butler's Army.

Over the next few days, operating in the Chickahominy bottomlands, he faced considerable peril. Converging columns of Stuart's cavalry and the Richmond garrison sought to box him in and destroy his corps, some of whose detachments faced desperate fighting. This was the experience of the 5th US Cavalry, a force comprising about 250 sabres divided into six troops and commanded by Captain A. K. Arnold. Separated from Sheridan's column by intervening Confederate cavalry, the 5th US tried to cut its way to safety. Captain Arnold describes how his unit advanced along a road, spotted an enemy cavalry formation, and 'moved forward with drawn sabres, taking the walk, then the trot, then the gallop'. When within about forty yards of the enemy, Arnold gave the command 'Charge!' A Union officer in the lead heard an enemy officer shout 'Forward, Third Virginia!' and the two bodies of horse collided. For a short time there was 'a general melee, sabres and pistols being used freely'.[6] The mêlée demonstrated once more the superiority of the pistol over the sabre. Arnold's charge failed and his command lost an impressive 68 enlisted men killed, wounded and missing together with two officers captured, a total of 27 per cent of the troopers engaged.

Sheridan, with the majority of his corps in hand, kept his composure and refused to make a hasty escape. Later he would write that he 'wished to demonstrate to the Cavalry Corps the impossibility of the enemy's destroying or capturing so large a body of mounted troops'.[7] He extricated his command to safety and ended his raid on 14 May. At a cost of 625 men killed, wounded, and missing, the cavalry corps had freed 400 Union prisoners, captured about 300 rebels, and while inflicting an unknown number of additional losses at Yellow Tavern, killed the opposing corps commander, and destroyed a large quantity of invaluable Confederate goods including Lee's entire reserve of medical supplies.

On the surface, Sheridan's 16-day absence from Grant's command achieved few concrete results. Sheridan himself was new to independent command and his inexperience led him to be overly cautious. His subordinates were unfamiliar with him and this ignorance impaired vigorous action. As James Wilson wrote, 'neither Sheridan, his generals, nor his command had yet entirely found themselves'.[8] Consequently, the Battle of Yellow Tavern had hardly been a tactical masterpiece. Yet it had important strategic consequences. Stuart's death marked the end of an epoch in the history of the Confederate cavalry. Hereafter, Grant wrote, he never had to concern himself about guarding his trains from Confederate cavalry. Sheridan had demonstrated to friend and foe alike that the Army of the Potomac's mounted arm was henceforth a force to be reckoned with. Even Meade's sardonic staffer, Colonel Theodore Lyman, who was no friend of uncouth westerners like Grant and Sheridan, noted that because of Sheridan's ability to revitalize the cavalry, Lee's cavalry could no longer cope with Sheridan's troopers. Lyman concluded, 'our cavalry is full of confidence and does wonders'.[9]

PART 2. 'ONE GREAT BATTLEFIELD'

While Sheridan was marching on Richmond, Lee's army won the race to Spotsylvania Court House where his men immediately began to construct fieldworks. The terrain was heavily wooded, but there was more open ground than in the Wilderness. The Army of the Potomac gunners found some clearings more suited to their profession. Warren's chief of artillery, Colonel Charles Wainwright, describes a typical artillery duel near the Alsop House on 7 May, before both sides had perfected their works:

'As we came down to this point, the rebel sharpshooters opened a very ugly fire ... especially from the wood to the left of the road where they lay thick behind large fallen trees. [The shooting was from 400 yards' range in controlled volleys directed at individual 'spotted' officers. As previously noted, when Civil War soldiers had a clear field of fire, an infrequent occurrence, they could shoot accurately at great distance.] A couple of batteries of twelve-pounders also opened, from over the open part of the opposite knoll ... a very ugly fire of shrapnel, their guns being entirely hid by the knoll. [The Confederate guns were employing thoroughly modern fire practice using an observer on the knoll to direct their aim.] I immediately put Stewart's leading section in on either side of the road, and the rest of his guns on the right; ordering Walcott in on the right of him. Walcott's men did not behave over well, nor did he push them forward as well he might ... Stewart was as usual himself, also what old men he had left, but his young recruits were inclined to dodge, and once when a couple of fresh limbers came up with ammunition they got quite a scare and attempted to limber up. All this obliged me to keep in the open ground among the guns myself [And thus the prime target for the Confederate marksmen] until I could get them quieted down and firing to please me ...

'The rebel guns ... were, as I have said, quite hid by the knoll behind which they stood; we could only see the puffs of smoke from their explosions. It followed as a matter of course that they fired too high. My own gunners did the same, and it was with great difficulty that I got them down. At last, however, I did so as to make almost every shot strike the top of the knoll just on what was to us the skyline. When I had also got them to burst their shot as they struck, we shut the rebs up in five minutes; probably their guns were withdrawn.'[10] [The duel lasted thirty minutes. Once Wainwright had calmed his men, they had to acquire the range and then set the fusing properly. Once they had done so the enemy battery withdrew speedily.]

Professionally satisfying though it was to Wainwright to best an enemy battery in an artillery duel, in the coming battles artillery would be able to do very little to support the attack. The infantry would have to go it alone. The trenches extended from flank to flank and the ensuing actions at Spotsylvania were a harbinger of the trench warfare attrition of the First World War. One savvy Union veteran exclaimed, 'It is all one great battlefield for miles and miles.'[11]

One federal officer reckoned that he knew how properly defended fieldworks should be charged. Emory Upton was a young colonel who had graduated eighth in the West Point class of 1856, a high ranking that allowed him entrance into the élite engineers. Instead he joined the artillery and then went over to the volunteer service to become colonel of the 121st New York. The previous autumn his divisional commander, General David A. Russell, had conceived a clever surprise assault against a Confederate bridgehead at Rappahannock Station. Upton's brigade had implemented Russell's plan and captured more than 1,000 prisoners. The key to the assault had been the strict orders to the attacking troops not to pause to fire but rather to rush the enemy's works.

Upton was disdainful of the army's lack of tactical leadership and its officers' inability to motivate the troops and let his superiors know that he could do better. On the evening of 10 May he was given a picked force of twelve regiments to see what he could accomplish. The sector he was assigned to attack was formidable. His force would have to pass through a tangled pine wood and then charge uphill over a 200-yard clearing. The main enemy trenchline was solidly built of logs and sloped earth. Head logs, with loopholes cut beneath, allowed the defenders to fire without exposing themselves. Mounds of earth (traverses, one of the Army of Northern Virginia's contributions to the science of warfare) ran back at right angles from the main trenchline to block enfilade fire. One-hundred yards behind the first trench was a second line of works.

With the very able Russell, Upton reconnoitred the enemy position and planned the assault. He arranged his men in four lines of three regiments each. Only the men in the first wave were allowed to put a percussion cap in the breech of their rifles ready for firing. The balance would charge with loaded, but uncapped weapons. Upton knew that speed was essential and he wanted his men to cross the open ground as fast as possible without stopping to engage in a futile firefight. Upton intended that the first wave would mount the enemy's works and then turn left and right to expand the breach. The second wave would occupy the trench, cap their weapons, and prepare to resist the expected counter-attack. The third wave would lie down just outside the works and be available as a close support. The fourth wave would remain on the edge of the wood as a reserve. Upton carefully explained all this to his officers and showed them the ground over which they would charge. He then led them forward:

'Through a terrible front and flank fire the column advanced, quickly gaining the parapet. Here occurred a deadly hand-to-hand conflict. The enemy, sitting in their pits with pieces upright, loaded, and with bayonets fixed, ready to impale the first who should leap over, absolutely refused to yield the ground. The first of our men who tried to surmount the works, fell, pierced through the head with musket balls; others, seeing the fate of their comrades, held their pieces at arm's-length and fired downward; while others, poising their pieces vertically, hurled them down [like spears] upon their enemy, pinning them to the ground... The struggle lasted but a few seconds. Numbers prevailed, and, like a resistless wave, the column poured over the works, quickly putting hors de combat those who resisted, and sending to the rear those who surrendered. Pressing forward and expanding to the right and left, the second line of entrenchments, its line of battle, and the battery, fell into our hands. The column of assault had accomplished its task.'[12]

Upton's men were three-quarters of a mile in front of the Union main line. It was now up to the supports to advance and exploit his success. Unfortunately, the supporting unit on Upton's left was Mott's division which had to cross 400 yards of open ground swept by at least 22 Confederate artillery pieces. The artillery alone broke up Mott's advance. The supports on Upton's right were men who had unsuccessfully charged the works earlier in the day. When ordered forward again they advanced half-heartedly and went to ground when the expected heavy fire began. Out on a limb, badly wounded himself, Upton had to retire. Although he managed to bring back close to 1,000 prisoners from Dole's Georgia brigade, his assault had been a failure.

The affair brought great credit to Upton personally. Grant marked his conduct and, using his authority to promote officers who displayed special gallantry, conferred the rank of brigadier general upon this able officer. He also resolved to find out whether a corps-sized assault could duplicate Upton's feat. The point chosen was the same artillery-studded salient that had repulsed Mott. It would go down in history as the 'Bloody Angle'.

The force chosen for the assault was Hancock's Second Corps. His assault formation derived from the success of the Russell/Upton assault of 10 May, but unlike that attack, which had featured careful reconnaissance and detailed instructions to the regimental officers involved, Hancock's assault substituted mass for tactical subtlety. One of the assault units, Francis Barlow's First Division, advanced in a solid rectangle some forty ranks deep. Emulating Upton's tactic, they had not capped their muskets, and to this extent the Union assault tactic worked.

The Federal troops advanced through the woods in fog at daybreak on the 12th, gave a cheer (a curious aspect of a surprise dawn attack!) received scattered fire from the rebel pickets, and kept coming. Because of a Confederate blunder, the defending artillery was in the process of returning to the salient when the assault struck home. Had it been present, the deep assault formation would have suffered terrible losses. Only two Confederate artillery pieces were in position and each delivered two rounds. The defending infantry fired two or three close-range volleys which wrought terrible punishment among the dense assault formation. Then occurred that rarest of actions, hand-to-hand fighting. Nelson Miles, who had served since the beginning of the war, reported that here he saw for the first time bayonet fighting. But it did not last long. The overwhelming weight of the attacking force overran the works and hundreds of men were taken prisoner including the remnant of the vaunted Stonewall Brigade and most of the returning Confederate artillery before it could fire a shot. Then the flaw in Hancock's assault became apparent. As Meade's chief of staff, General Andrew A. Humphreys later related, 'In the capture of the entrenchments the troops became disordered and mixed, and it was exceedingly difficult to restore order.'[13]

Whereas Upton had carefully separated his units into four distinct waves, given them specific instructions, and kept them well spaced, in the absence of such preparation Hancock's Corps degenerated into an uncontrollable mob. They failed to roll up the exposed Confederate flanks and exploit the gaping hole in Lee's centre. A more prudent assault formation would have ended the war right here. With hindsight, Meade's Chief of Staff concluded that if only the first line had been in attack columns (the Napoleonic-style formation based on a 2-company frontage with the other eight companies arrayed directly behind, making for a 10-rank deep formation) and the second line in a more open formation several hundred yards to the rear, the confusion would have been avoided. Instead came the terrible fighting of the 'Bloody Angle' which pitted inert Union masses against the sacrificial infantry whom Lee sent to hold his centre until his pioneers could complete a new line of works across the base of the salient.

For hour after hour at point-blank range the two forces grappled. A surprising number of valiant men on both sides exhibited berserk frenzy as if they could win the battle by their own efforts:

'Here on both sides of these breastworks, were displayed more individual acts of bravery and heroism than I had yet seen in the war. The graycoats and bluecoats would spring with rifles in hand on top the breastworks, take deadly aim, fire, and then fall across into the trenches below. This I saw repeated again and again.'[14]

Union artillery could contribute little to this conflict. However, at one point a section of Battery C, 5th US Artillery rushed into action to enfilade the defenders at point-blank range. A gunner recalls:

'We were a considerable distance in front of our infantry, and of course artillery could not live long under such a fire as the enemy were putting through there. Our men went down in short order. The left gun fired nine rounds, I fired fourteen with mine ... Our section went into action with 23 men and one officer. The only ones who came out sound were the lieutenant and myself. Every horse was killed, seven of the men were killed outright, sixteen wounded; the gun carriages were so cut with bullets as to be of no further service ... 27 balls passed through the lid of the limber chest while number six was getting out ammunition. The sponge bucket on my gun had 39 holes in it being perforated like a sieve.'[15]

Soldiers of the VIth Corps replaced Hancock's assault troops and continued the battle. By now, after several hours of fighting, most of the soldiers were huddled in the trenches and trying to survive. But a handful of marksmen continued to take deliberate aim before squeezing trigger. An eye-witness recalled one tall private who, 'would load his piece with the greatest care, rise to his full height – which exposed at least half his person – and, after a long, steady aim, deliver his fire. Then he would kneel and reload. Sometimes he would aim, but take down his piece and watch again for his mark, then aim again and fire.'[16]

Although exposed to fearful enemy fire, this private fired more than one hundred times with great precision before being killed at the end of the day. Many regiments recorded that by the end of the battle they had fired the amazing total of 300 rounds per man, all at point-blank range.

The fact that the Confederate trenches included frequent traverses meant that the day's heavy rain could not drain away. The 4-foot deep trenches were like cellars in a flood. They filled with water, adding further to the misery of the living and drowning many of the wounded. After a horrific day's battle that cost the Union army another 6,800 men, Lee retired a short distance to a new line of works.

The fact that Upton had nearly achieved a breakthrough caused his opponents to reflect upon what had taken place. A Confederate officer wrote:

'This affair [Upton's capture of part of the line on 10 May] impressed us with the necessity of strengthening our lines and next morning, May 11, the men fell to work with increased energy, particularly on the abatis, the importance of which in detaining and throwing into confusion an enemy within point-blank range, they now fully appreciated. [Like the barbed wire of the First World War, the abatis served to prolong the attacker's exposure time in the fire zone.] It is a mistake made by non-combatants only to suppose that a slight field breastwork is any material obstacle of itself to a charging enemy, it being a covering only to the men behind it. Indeed, with all its advantages in economizing life, fighting behind such fieldworks has some disadvantages also. Give a man protection for his body and the temptation is very strong to put his head under cover too. My observation during this campaign was that behind works not a few men will crouch down doing nothing, that many will fire above the heads of their assailants ... and few, comparatively, will raise their heads and shoulders fairly above the rampart and level their pieces with effect. [The writer refers to field works only. Given time, defenders converted hastily constructed works into more elaborate trench systems from where the defender could fire with relative impunity.] When the enemy reaches the other side of the work, in perhaps five cases out of six it is carried. [The fact that works could be captured if the attackers had the cohesion to make the final push explains the persistent offensive attitude of Grant and some of his lieutenants. The need for a defender to have a ready reserve to seal off penetrations by delivering sharp counter-attacks explains why even a successful defence was costly in manpower.] Whereas the object and advantage of an abatis is to detain and disorder the assailants, while the defenders, although not firing with accuracy perhaps, yet inflict loss and suffer comparatively little. [If the attacker never advanced through the abatis, the defenders were spared the expense of counter-attacks.] But generally speaking, the result, however favorable to those behind the works, is only a repulse, if a bloody one, and is not followed up with consequences such as attend a victory in the open field.'[17]

The Battle of the Wilderness had started an unprecedented forty days of action during which time the rival armies were always at close quarters. Habitually throughout most of military history and throughout the Civil War, armies paused after a major battle to rest and refit. When the battles around Spotsylvania took place just after the combats in the Wilderness, the contestants realized that they were involved in something altogether different. Among many, Colonel Robert McAllister wrote, 'This campaign beats all the rest in desperation and determination.'[18] He added that prior to the campaign he would not have imagined he could have endured so much combat, fatigue and privation. General Meade doubted that his men would have the physical stamina to fight on such a protracted and fierce scale.

For some the constant fighting proved too much. Earlier in his career General Gershom Mott had been widely considered an able and brave officer, but beginning with the Wilderness, he began to shirk his duties, preferring to stay in the rear while his colonels conducted the fighting. Assistant Secretary of War Charles Dana observed: 'We were disgraced by a retreat of that division [Mott's] without loss and apparently without any considerable force to oppose them. They advanced into the woods with orders to attack, but came out again at once, like cowards.'[19] The army was also featuring poor performances by some of the indifferent units that had no tradition of victory. Meade's aide, Theodore Lyman, noted: 'General Ricketts' division of the 6th Corps, composed of troops from Winchester, known as 'Milroy's weary boys', never has done well. They ran on the Mine Run Campaign, and they have run ever since.'[20] Moreover, many men's terms of service were nearing their end, and they, just like veterans throughout history, proved unwilling to risk all when only days away from discharge and home. One soldier spoke for many when he said the army had suffered '... ruinous waste. With all its losses no appreciable advantage has been gained'.[21]

What motivated the men to endure? To some extent they became physically and mentally hardened. An officer observed his men enjoying a bath at a millpond near the Chickahominy River. They seemed oblivious to the periodic shelling from rebel batteries. Two years before, on nearly the same ground, such shelling had alarmed everyone and occasionally routed entire regiments. Also, they sensed that however awful, they were pressing forward to final victory. McAllister again: 'I am well satisfied that Genl. Grant understands his business and will eventually succeed. Everyone has confidence in him.'[22]

To make up for his losses to date, Grant tapped a special reserve. In the past, Washington authorities, including the man at the top, had displayed a great reluctance to denude the capital of its defenders. Earthworks encircled Washington and manning them required many men and guns. The defence of Washington's fortifications was the particular province of the heavy artillery, trained gunners who guarded Washington's numerous forts. It had been a very comfortable assignment, close to the capital's fleshpots, far from Virginia's battlefields. To their horror all this changed when Grant summoned them to flesh out his depleted ranks. It was a measure of Lincoln's trust in his general that he allowed Grant to strip the capital of its defenders. The arrival of the heavies at the front was immensely pleasing to veteran infantry. At last the rear area warriors would share their risks.

On 19 May a brigade of them went into action for the first time. Jubal Early's veterans were probing for the Union flank one and a half miles north-east of Spotsylvania. Defending the trains in the area of Harris's farm were soldiers of the 1st Maine Heavy Artillery. They had left their heavy guns behind and now, armed with muskets, but still carrying their artillery flags, they were fighting as infantry, something they were not trained to do. An observer noted the consequences:

'First there was Kitching's brigade firing at the enemy; then Tyler's [heavy artillery] men fired into his; up came Birney's division and fired into Tyler's; while the artillery fired at the whole damned lot.'[23]

The 1st Maine Heavy Artillery lost 466 killed, wounded and missing out of 1,789 men in this its first exposure to combat, and this was the beginning of an unmatched lethality rate. Although the regiment had not taken to the field until May 1864, it was to suffer more men killed outright or mortally wounded than any other unit.

Troops forwarded from Department of Washington to the Army of the Potomac, from 1 May 1864

Regiment	Strength	Regiment	Strength
82d and 23d Pennsylvania Volunteers	1,250	Replacements	297
		187th Pennsylvania Volunteers	990
Detachment veteran cavalry	400	3d Delaware and 94th New	
Detachment veteran cavalry	925	York	1,150
1st Vermont Heavy Artillery	1,500	4th Delaware, 5th NY, 157th	
12th United States	85	Pennsylvania	1,050
2d New York Rifles	1,000	21st Pennsylvania Cavalry	
Provisional brigade		(dismounted)	1,038
(replacements)	3,300	Company recruits 16th	
107th Pennsylvania Veteran		Michigan	83
Volunteers	280	2d Pennsylvania Heavy	
67th Pennsylvania Volunteers	250	Artillery	1,233
Provisional brigade		10th New York Heavy Artillery	1,759
(replacements)	425	Purnell (Maryland) Legion	153
Equipped recruits	553	1st Delaware Cavalry	529
8th New York Heavy Artillery	1,500	28th, 29th, 31st Colored	1,154
31st and 32d Maine	402	179th New York	357
7th New York Heavy Artillery	1,835	132d Ohio Volunteer Infantry	829
1st Maine Heavy Artillery	1,789	Company 60th Ohio Volunteer	
2d New York Heavy Artillery	1,679	Infantry	76
1st Massachusetts Heavy		Replacements	1,243
Artillery	1,700	Battalion Minnesota	
Provisional battalion		Volunteers	176
(replacements)	410	Provisional battalion	857
Irish Legion	2,000	23d US Colored Troops	45
36th Wisconsin Volunteers	866	138th Ohio National Guard	840
13th Ohio Cavalry		140th Ohio National Guard	800
(dismounted)	630	Provisional battalion	696
Detachment veteran cavalry	1,150	Provisional battalion	448
2d Connecticut Heavy		155th Ohio National Guard	900
Artillery	1,700	179th New York	
9th New York Heavy Artillery	1,400		85
184th Pennsylvania Volunteers	480	134th Ohio National Guard	800
Provisional battalion		5th New Hampshire Volunteers	467
(replacements)	853		
29th Massachusetts Volunteers	148	TOTAL	48,265
Detachment 184th Pennsylvania	70		
Battalion (replacements)	800	*Official Records*, I:36/3, pp.665–6	

It is interesting to note how Grant and Meade described Tyler's blundering bloodbath. The morning after the engagement, Grant telegraphed Halleck that Tyler and Birney had 'promptly repulsed' Ewell and suffered 'over 600 wounded and about 150 killed and missing'. That evening he corrected the count, stating that losses amounted to '196 killed, 1,090 wounded, and 249 missing', while assuring the Chief of Staff that rebel losses had been suitably severe.[24] There was no mention of the fact that many of these losses had been inflicted by friendly fire. Meade's headquarters went so far as to issue a congratulatory order of the day in which Meade expressed his 'satisfaction with the good conduct' of the heavy artillerymen.[25] What the high command really thought became apparent ten days later when headquarters terminated the experiment of having an entire division composed of heavy artillerymen. Meade broke up Tyler's division and distributed its five regiments to other formations.

Both Lee and Grant realized that the Federal forces held the initiative. Herein lay the significance of Grant's willingness to bull on despite frequent setback. His unrelenting pressure forced the Army of Northern Virginia behind its works, thereby taking away Lee's greatest tool, his mobility. Without mobility, Lee could not give his tactical successes any meaning. At the end of the Spotsylvania Campaign he acknowledged as much in a letter to his commander-in- chief. Lee told Davis that he could not attack Grant's strongly entrenched position 'with any prospect of success without great loss of men'. Worse, while Lee wanted to hit Grant's Army while it was in motion – in part to negate the Army of the Potomac's superior artillery – 'neither the strength of the army nor the condition of our animals will admit it'.[26] Having lost the initiative, Lee was reduced to reacting to Grant's manoeuvres. He concluded by telling Davis all was quiet just now and that he had no hint of anything pending. He was mistaken. The day after he wrote this letter, Grant began a new effort to outflank his enemy.

Spotsylvania was fought in conditions that would be reproduced on a grand scale in the First World War, complete with heavy rains that fouled weapons and rendered movement nearly impossible. The unprecedented extent of the fieldworks that here and henceforth became a routine feature of this campaign marked a change in warfare. Colonel Lyman observed:

'The great feature of this campaign is the extraordinary use made of earthworks. When we arrive on the ground, it takes of course a considerable time to put troops in position for attack, in a wooded country; then skirmishers must be thrown forward and an examination made for the point of attack, and to see if there be any impassable obstacles, such as streams or swamps. Meantime what does the enemy? Hastily forming a line of battle, they then collect rails from fences, stones, logs and all other materials, and pile them along the line; bayonets with a few picks and shovels, in the hands of men who work for their lives, soon suffice to cover this frame with earth and sods; and within one hour, there is a shelter against bullets, high enough to cover a man kneeling, and extending often for a mile or two. When our line advances, there is the line of the enemy, nothing showing but the bayonets, and the battle-flags stuck on the top of the work. It is a rule that, when the Rebels halt, the first day gives them a good riflepit; the second, a regular infantry parapet with artillery in position; and the third a parapet with an abatis in front and entrenched batteries behind. Sometimes they put this three days' work into the first twenty-four hours. Our men can, and do, do the same; but remember, our object is offense – to advance.'[27]

When it came to digging, the Army of the Potomac had the great advantage of more men, more axes, picks and shovels. Typically, the artillery limbers carried the soldiers' entrenching tools. In addition, the superb brigade of engineers provided an expert force capable of designing and building works to required specifications. An envious Confederate brigadier believed that these engineers were worth almost another corps to Grant.[28] Lee himself had been an engineer, although he had specialized in cartography rather than fortifications. His chief engineer, General M. L. Smith, had prior experience fighting Grant. Smith was a distinguished West Point-trained engineer who had served in Mexico. More importantly, he had proven himself during the defence of Vicksburg and was thus well aware of the design and value of modern fieldworks.

None the less, the Confederate works that so dominated Union operations were improvised by soldiers using bayonets and tin cups. What made them so formidable was the wooded terrain. In combination, wooded terrain and extensive fieldworks greatly hampered offensive operations. Too often the only way to detect the Confederate position was by aggressively pushing a brigade forward. Among many, General Gibbon complained how always somewhere ahead of his division 'was the supposed line of entrenchments ... which, however, we were unable to see and the location of which we could judge only by the sound of the musketry from it'.[29] But poor tactics contributed to failure. Too often, Grant's army formed a single long line parallel to the enemy's entrenchments and then charged. Repeated failure taught the soldiers caution. They learned about the overwhelming defensive advantages of fieldworks long before their senior officers absorbed this lesson.

Consequently, during the second series of general assaults at Spotsylvania on 18 May, veterans advanced with a general lack of enthusiasm; when the enemy fire thickened they went to ground. On many sectors, Confederate artillery alone was sufficient to stop the advance. The 2nd Rhode Island, a typical veteran unit, came to a halt under heavy artillery fire 300 yards from the Confederate works. The regiment was too proud to withdraw. It held its ground for two hours and suffered accordingly, losing two captains killed, seven officers wounded, and about 100 rank and file killed and wounded.

Other veteran units advanced with a notable lack of spirit. The Iron Brigade's 6th Wisconsin, committed to a second assault, began its advance by enthusiastically leaping over the breastwork and starting forward through the woods. Soon it encountered 'heavy and destructive fire'. Sensing that there were no supports on either flank and seeing that the men in the first assault wave were lying down in front of the rebel works, the colonel ordered his men to halt, lie down, and open fire. 'After a few minutes of rapid firing, suffering meanwhile severe loss, convinced of the futility of striving without support to advance through the abatis in our front, while to remain longer was wanton sacrifice of life, I ordered my men back.'[30]

Some of the newer regiments initially pressed the assault with more determination. The lieutenant colonel of the 56th Massachusetts, Stephen Weld, relates:

'Received orders to move forward into the woods in my front ... and charge the rebel rifle-pits. Moved forward at 4 a.m. When within about 100 yards of the abatis, I ordered a charge, and going on the double-quick we reached the abatis, a very thick one. Here we were under a very heavy cross fire of canister and musketry, and it was impossible to get the men forward.'

Weld sent back a report to his brigade commander that he could not take the works and asked for instructions. This commander, General James Ledlie – a particularly useless officer who would be cashiered for cowardice at the Crater – offered no assistance so Weld ordered a second charge: 'I ordered the men forward again in vain, and in endeavoring to get up the 35th [Massachusetts] as a support, they ran away.'[31] Weld's men went forward once more, entered the woods, lay down under fire, and then finally received orders to return to their own works.

Experiences like these convinced many that Grant's strategy during the Spotsylvania campaign amounted to nothing more than straightforward pounding. In fact, he tried a variety of approaches in an effort to take his opponent in flank. One of the men who strove mightily to thwart him, Porter Alexander, who commanded the Ist Corps artillery, reflected years afterwards about one of Grant's planned manoeuvres:

'On the 13th he [Grant] devised an attack which would have had a very fair chance of taking us quite by surprise, had he been able to make it. Warren had really moved at dark on the 13th, under orders to pass in rear of the rest of the army & extend its left flank, & at 4 a.m. on the 14th the whole army was to attack us simultaneously. Of course Warren's sudden arrival on our extreme right, where we had as yet no breastworks, would give opportunities of outflanking us & taking us in reverse ... From this danger we were unconsciously delivered by the darkness and the mud ... The head of his column very nearly arrived in time but the rear of it was so scattered & tired out that the whole attack had to be abandoned.'[32]

The Army of the Potomac had prepared carefully for this manoeuvre. Routes of march had been identified, guides assigned, and fires lit along the way to facilitate the march through the woods. Perhaps a thrusting general, a Sheridan, a Logan, or a Hancock, could have prodded the men to overcome the mud and rain. This was beyond Warren and another opportunity was lost.

The period covering the Wilderness and Spotsylvania Court House campaigns cost the Army of the Potomac some 39,791 men killed, wounded and missing. Civil War leadership demanded frontline exposure and the officer casualties underscored this fact. In the trenches at Spotsylvania a rebel sniper mortally wounded 35-year-old Brigadier General James Rice, one of the heroes of Gettysburg. Meade visited Rice as he lay dying. Rice told him, 'Don't you give up this fight! I am willing to lose my life, if it is to be, but don't you give up this fight!'[33] Such leaders could not be replaced.

To date the campaign had killed Sedgwick, Wadsworth, Alexander Hays, Thomas Stephenson, and Rice; wounded Sedgwick's replacement Brigadier General Horatio Wright, divisional commander George W. Getty, and brigade commanders Samuel Carroll, Henry Baxter, William Morris, Gilbert Robinson and Alexander Webb. With the exception of Wadsworth (a dull-witted political general), Stephenson and Carroll, these were very capable generals. In addition, Generals Alexander Shaler and the promising Truman Seymour had been captured during the evening of 6 May in the Wilderness.

Attrition had been equally fearful among the Army of Northern Virginia's highest ranking officers. Whereas five Federal generals had been killed, six Confederate generals had died. In comparison with the Army of the Potomac's seven wounded generals, fifteen Confederate generals had been wounded. Like the Army of the Potomac, two rebel generals had been captured. Because of their losses, the overall combat effectiveness of both armies could only decline.

The fighting around Spotsylvania left Grant's army hurt and dazed. Straggling during the battle reached epic proportions with 'immense numbers of men' quitting the ranks with only 'the slightest pretext or none at all'.[34] Army morale fluctuated according to how recently the men had been ordered to make another bloody assault against entrenchments. James Wilson describes an encounter with an old friend who commanded an infantry company. This captain was an honourable veteran of proven courage. But he appeared changed and asked Wilson a peculiar question. Did Wilson have any part of a musical instrument? Why? asked the puzzled Wilson. The veteran replied, 'Oh, I merely want to be considered as belonging to the band, which, you know, remains behind the fighting line and carries off the wounded. This is the only berth in this army where a man's life is worth a cent. Nearly everybody I know has been killed or wounded, and if this campaign, with its senseless assaults of entrenched positions ... is to continue much longer, my turn is sure to come soon.'[35]

Confronted with such terrible losses, the army could find solace only in the fact that it kept gaining ground. And so it was when Grant's next orders came down calling for another long march. The army could take some satisfaction that their sacrifices were bringing the war closer to an end because, once again, the direction was south.[36]

Combat Assessment

Grant: Still distancing himself and so unable to inspire the army to the extra effort required to overcome tactical changes and a great opponent.
Lieutenants: Sedgwick dies, his replacement must grow into his new position. No high-ranking officer demonstrates particular ability except Sheridan, who proves what a combination of personal leadership and strategic insight ('There isn't cavalry enough in all the Southern Confederacy to stop us.') can accomplish.
Staff: Fearfully bungle the night marches and associated manoeuvres during this phase of the campaign.
Infantry: Valorous men are becoming thin on the ground.
Artillery: Still unable to make a significant contribution.
Cavalry: The coming star of the entire army.
Engineers: Able to construct wonderful defensive works, but the army is having to take the offensive.

SPOTSYLVANIA COURTHOUSE,[37] 8-21 MAY 1864
General HQ escort: 5th US Cavalry, Cos. B, F, K

ARMY OF THE POTOMAC: Major General George G. Meade

PROVOST GUARD:
Brigadier General Marsena R. Patrick
1st Massachusetts. Cavalry, Cos. C
  and D
80th New York Infantry (20th militia)
3d Pennsylvania Cavalry
68th Pennsylvania Infantry
114th Pennsylvania Infantry
ENGINEER TROOPS:
50th New York
Battalion United States
GUARDS AND ORDERLIES:
Independent Co. Oneida (New York)
  Cavalry

SECOND ARMY CORPS:
Major General Winfield S. Hancock
Staff
1st Vermont Cavalry, Co. M (escort)

First Division:
Brigadier General Francis C. Barlow
FIRST BRIGADE: Colonel Nelson A.
  Miles
Staff
26th Michigan
61st New York
81st Pennsylvania
140th Pennsylvania

183d Pennsylvania
SECOND BRIGADE: Colonel Thomas A. Smyth, Colonel Richard Byrnes
28th Massachusetts
63d New York
69th New York
88th New York
116th Pennsylvania
THIRD BRIGADE: Colonel Paul Frank, Colonel Hiram L. Brown, Colonel Clinton D. MacDougall
Staff
39th New York
52d New York
57th New York
111th New York
125th New York
126th New York
FOURTH BRIGADE:
Colonel John R. Brooke
2d Delaware
64th New York
66th New York
53d Pennsylvania
145th Pennsylvania
148th Pennsylvania

Second Division:
Brigadier General John Gibbon
Provost Guard: 2d Co. Minn Sharp-shooters
FIRST BRIGADE:
Brigadier General Alexander S. Webb, Colonel H. Boyd McKeen
Staff
19th Maine
1st Co. Andrew (Massachusetts) Sharpshooters
15th Massachusetts
19th Massachusetts
20th Massachusetts
7th Michigan
42d New York
59th New York
82d New York (2d militia)
36th Wisconsin
SECOND BRIGADE:
Brigadier General Joshua T. Owen
152d New York
69th Pennsylvania
71st Pennsylvania
72d Pennsylvania
106th Pennsylvania

THIRD BRIGADE: Colonel Samuel S. Carroll, Colonel Theodore G. Ellis, Colonel Thomas A. Smyth
14th Connecticut
1st Delaware
14th Indiana
12th New Jersey
10th New York Battalion
108th New York
4th Ohio
8th Ohio
7th West Virginia
FOURTH BRIGADE: Colonel Matthew Murphy, Colonel James P. McIvor
155th New York
164th New York
170th New York
182d New York (69th New York National Guard Artillery)

Third Division: Major General David B. Birney
FIRST BRIGADE:
Brigadier General J. H. Hobart Ward, Colonel Thomas W. Egan
20th Indiana
3d Maine
40th New York
86th New York
124th New York
99th Pennsylvania
110th Pennsylvania
141st Pennsylvania
2d US Sharpshooters
SECOND BRIGADE: Colonel John S. Crocker, Colonel Elijah Walker
4th Maine
17th Maine
3d Michigan
5th Michigan
93d New York
57th Pennsylvania
63d Pennsylvania
105th Pennsylvania
1st US Sharpshooters

Fourth Division: Brigadier General Gershom Mott
FIRST BRIGADE:
Colonel Robert McAllister
Staff
1st Massachusetts
16th Massachusetts

5th New Jersey
6th New Jersey
7th New Jersey
8th New Jersey
11th New Jersey
26th Pennsylvania
115th Pennsylvania
SECOND BRIGADE:
Colonel William R. Brewster
11th Massachusetts
70th New York
71st New York
72d New York
73d New York
74th New York
120th New York
84th Pennsylvania
FOURTH DIVISION (HEAVY ARTILLERY):
Brigadier General Robert O. Tyler
1st Maine
1st Massachusetts
2d New York
7th New York
8th New York
ARTILLERY BRIGADE:
Colonel John C. Tidball
Maine Light, 6th Batt. (F)
Massachusetts Light, 10th Batt.
New Hampshire Light, 1st Batt.
1st New York Light, Batt. G
4th New York Heavy, 3d Bn.
New York Light, 11th Batt.
New York Light, 12th Batt.
1st Pennsylvania Light, Batt. F
1st Rhode Island Light, Batts. A and B
4th US, Batt. K
5th US, Batts. C and I

FIFTH ARMY CORPS:
Major General Gouverneur K. Warren
Provost Guard: 12th New York Battalion

First Division:
Brigadier General Charles Griffin
FIRST BRIGADE:
Brigadier General Romeyn B. Ayres
140th New York
146th New York
91st Pennsylvania
155th Pennsylvania
2d US
11th US

12th US
14th US
17th US
SECOND BRIGADE:
Colonel Jacob B. Sweitzer
9th Massachusetts
22d Massachusetts
32d Massachusetts
4th Michigan
62d Pennsylvania
THIRD BRIGADE:
Brigadier General Joseph J. Bartlett
20th Maine
18th Massachusetts
1st Michigan
16th Michigan
44th New York
83d Pennsylvania
118th Pennsylvania

Second Division:
Brigadier General John C. Robinson,
   Colonel Richard Coulter
FIRST BRIGADE:
Colonel Peter Lyle
16th Maine
13th Massachusetts
39th Massachusetts
104th New York
90th Pennsylvania
107th Pennsylvania
SECOND BRIGADE: Colonel Richard
   Coulter, Colonel James L. Bates
12th Massachusetts
83d New York (9th Militia)
97th New York
11th Pennsylvania
88th Pennsylvania
THIRD BRIGADE:
Colonel Andrew W. Denison, Colonel
   Charles E. Phelps, Colonel Richard
   N. Bowerman
1st Maryland
4th Maryland
7th Maryland
8th Maryland

Third Division: Brigadier General
   Samuel W. Crawford
FIRST BRIGADE:
Colonel William McCandless,
   Colonel William C. Talley,
   Colonel Wellington H. Ent,

Colonel Samuel M. Jackson,
Colonel Martin D. Hardin
1st Pennsylvania Reserves
2d Pennsylvania Reserves
6th Pennsylvania Reserves
7th Pennsylvania Reserves
11th Pennsylvania Reserves
13th Pennsylvania Reserves (1st
Rifles)
THIRD BRIGADE:
Colonel Joseph W. Fisher
5th Pennsylvania Reserves
8th Pennsylvania Reserves
10th Pennsylvania Reserves
12th Pennsylvania Reserves

Fourth Division:
Brigadier General Lysander Cutler
FIRST BRIGADE:
Colonel William W. Robinson
7th Indiana
19th Indiana
24th Michigan
1st Battalion New York Sharpshooters
2d Wisconsin
6th Wisconsin
7th Wisconsin
SECOND BRIGADE:
Brigadier General James C. Rice,
Colonel Edward B. Fowler,
Colonel J. William Hofmann
Staff
76th New York
84th New York (14th Militia)
95th New York
147th New York
56th Pennsylvania
THIRD BRIGADE:
Colonel Edward S. Bragg
121st Pennsylvania
142d Pennsylvania
143d Pennsylvania
149th Pennsylvania
150th Pennsylvania
HEAVY ARTILLERY BRIGADE:
Colonel J. Howard Kitching
6th New York
15th New York (1st and 3d Battalions)
ARTILLERY BRIGADE:
Colonel Charles S. Wainwright
Massachusetts Light, 3d Batt. (C)
Massachusetts Light, 5th Batt. (E)

Massachusetts Light, 9th Batt.
1st New York Light, Batt. B
1st New York Light, Batt. C
1st New York Light, Batt. D
1st New York Light, Batts. E and L
1st New York Light, Batt. H
New York Light, 5th Batt.
New York Light, 15th Batt.
4th New York Heavy, 2d Battalion
1st Pennsylvania Light, Batt. B
4th US, Batt. B
5th US, Batt. D

SIXTH ARMY CORPS:
Major General John Sedgwick,
Brigadier General Horatio G.
Wright
ESCORT: 8th Pennsylvania Cavalry,
Co. A

First Division:
Brigadier General Horatio G. Wright,
Brigadier General David A. Russell
FIRST BRIGADE:
Colonel Henry W. Brown, Colonel
William H. Penrose
Staff
1st New Jersey
2d New Jersey
3d New Jersey
4th New Jersey
10th New Jersey
15th New Jersey
SECOND BRIGADE:
Colonel Emory Upton
5th Maine
121st New York
95th Pennsylvania
96th Pennsylvania
THIRD BRIGADE:
Brigadier General David A. Russell,
Brigadier General Henry L.
Eustis
6th Maine
49th Pennsylvania
119th Pennsylvania
5th Wisconsin
FOURTH BRIGADE:
Colonel Nelson Cross
65th New York
67th New York
122d New York
82d Pennsylvania (det.)

214

Second Division:
Brigadier General Thomas H. Neill
FIRST BRIGADE: Brigadier General
    Frank Wheaton
62d New York
93d Pennsylvania
98th Pennsylvania
102d Pennsylvania
139th Pennsylvania
SECOND BRIGADE:
Brigadier General Lewis A. Grant
1st Vermont (heavy artillery)
2d Vermont
3d Vermont
4th Vermont
5th Vermont
6th Vermont
THIRD BRIGADE:
Colonel Daniel D. Bidwell
Staff
7th Maine
43d New York
49th New York
77th New York
61st Pennsylvania
FOURTH BRIGADE:
Brigadier General Henry L. Eustis,
    Colonel Oliver Edwards
7th Massachusetts
10th Massachusetts
37th Massachusetts
2d Rhode Island

Third Division:
Brigadier General James B. Ricketts
FIRST BRIGADE:
Brigadier General William H. Morris,
    Colonel John W. Schall, Colonel
    William S. Truex
Staff
14th New Jersey
106th New York
151st New York
87th Pennsylvania
10th Vermont

SECOND BRIGADE:
Colonel Benjamin F. Smith
6th Maryland
110th Ohio
122d Ohio
126th Ohio
67th Pennsylvania
138th Pennsylvania
ARTILLERY BRIGADE:
Colonel Charles H. Tompkins
Maine Light, 4th Batt. (D)
Maine Light, 5th Batt. (E)
Massachusetts Light, 1st Batt. (A)
1st New Jersey Light, Batt. A
New York Light, 1st Batt.
New York Light, 3d Batt.
4th New York Heavy, 1st Battalion
1st Ohio Light, Batt. H
1st Rhode Island Light, Batt. C
1st Rhode Island Light, Batt. E
1st Rhode Island Light, Batt. G
5th US, Batt. E
5th US, Batt. M

CAVALRY CORPS (detached):
The Cavalry Corps was absent during
this campaign, so it does not need to
be included here.

ARTILLERY
Brigadier General Henry J. Hunt
SECOND BRIGADE HORSE ARTILLERY:
Captain Dunbar R. Ransom
1st US, Batts. E and G
1st US, Batts. H and I
1st US, Batt. K
2d US, Batt. A
2d US, Batt. G
3d US, Batts. C, F, K
ARTILLERY PARK:
Lieutenant Colonel Freeman
    McGilvery
15th New York Heavy (2d Battalion)
UNATTACHED CAVALRY:
22d New York

NINTH ARMY CORPS: Major General Ambrose E. Burnside
Provost Guard: 8th US Infantry

First Division: Brigadier General
    Thomas G. Stevenson, Colonel
    Daniel Leasure, Major General
    Thomas L. Crittenden
FIRST BRIGADE: Colonel Jacob P.

Gould, Lieutenant Colonel
    Stephen M. Weld, Jr., Brigadier
    General James H. Ledlie
35th Massachusetts
56th Massachusetts

57th Massachusetts
59th Massachusetts
4th US
10th US
SECOND BRIGADE:
Colonel Daniel Leasure, Lieutenant
    Colonel Gilbert P. Robinson
3d Maryland
21st Massachusetts
100th Pennsylvania
PROVISIONAL BRIGADE:
Colonel Elisha G. Marshall
2d New York Mounted Rifles
    (unmounted)
14th New York Heavy Artillery
24th New York Cavalry (dismounted)
2d Pennsylvania Provisional Heavy
    Artillery
ARTILLERY:
    Maine Light, 2d Batt. (B)
Massachusetts Light, 14th Batt.

Second Division:
Brigadier General Robert B. Potter
FIRST BRIGADE: Colonel John I. Curtin
36th Massachusetts
58th Massachusetts
51st New York
45th Pennsylvania
48th Pennsylvania
7th Rhode Island
SECOND BRIGADE:
Colonel Simon G. Griffin
2d Maryland (det.)
31st Maine
32d Maine
6th New Hampshire

9th New Hampshire
11th New Hampshire
17th Vermont
ARTILLERY:
Massachusetts Light, 11th Batt.
New York Light, 19th Batt.

Third Division:
Brigadier General Orlando B. Willcox
FIRST BRIGADE:
Colonel John F. Hartranft
2d Michigan
8th Michigan
17th Michigan
27th Michigan
109th New York
51st Pennsylvania
SECOND BRIGADE:
Colonel Benjamin C. Christ, Colonel
    William Humphrey
1st Michigan Sharpshooters
20th Michigan
79th New York
60th Ohio
50th Pennsylvania
ARTILLERY:
Maine Light, 7th Batt. (G)
New York Light, 34th Batt.

**Fourth Division (in reserve
guarding trains):**
CAVALRY:
3d New Jersey
5th New York
2d Ohio
13th Pennsylvania

1   Philip H. Sheridan, *Personal Memoirs of P.H. Sheridan*, vol. 1 (New York: Charles L. Webster & Co., 1888), p. 369.
2   Sheridan, vol. 1, p. 370.
3   Shelby Foote, *The Civil War*, vol. 3 (New York: Random House, 1963), p. 225.
4   Fletcher Pratt, "Little Phil — Part I," *Coast Artillery Journal* (September-October 1939) p. 440.
5   Sheridan, vol. 1, p. 378.
6   A.K. Arnold, "A War Reminiscence - The Fifth U.S. Regular Cavalry with General Sheridan on Raid Towards Richmond, VA., in 1864," *Journals of the U.S. Cavalry Association*, Vol. II (1889), p. 32.
7   Sheridan, vol. 1, p. 384.
8   James Harrison Wilson, *Under the Old Flag*, vol. 1 (New York: D. Appleton and Co., 1912), p. 420.
9   George R. Agassiz, ed., *Meade's Headquarters 1863-1865: Letters of Colonel Theodore Lyman from the Wilderness to Appomattox*, (Boston: Massachusetts Historical Society, 1922), p. 131.

10 Allan Nevins, ed., *A Diary of Battle: The Personal Journals of Colonel Charles S. Wainwright, 1861-1865*, (New York: Harcourt, Brace & World, 1962), p. 357.

11 James I. Robertson, ed., *The Civil War Letters of General Robert McAllister*, (New Brunswick, NJ: Rutgers University Press, 1965), p. 422.

12 Peter S. Michie, *The Life and Letters of Emory Upton*, (New York: Arno Press, 1979), pp. 97-98.

13 Andrew A. Humphreys, *The Virginia Campaign of '64 and '65*, (New York: Charles Scribner's Sons, 1897), p. 94.

14 *The Civil War Letters of General Robert McAllister*, p. 419.

15 Jack Coggins, *Arms and Equipment of the Civil War*, (New York: Doubleday & Co., 1962), p. 62.

16 Richard Wheeler, *On Fields of Fury. From the Wilderness to the Crater: An Eyewitness History*, (New York: Harper Collins Publishers, 1991), p. 217.

17 McHenry Howard, *Recollections of a Confederate Soldier, 1861-1866*, (Dayton, 1975), pp. 290-291.

18 *The Civil War Letters of General Robert McAllister*, p. 417.

19 Cited in *The Civil War Letters of General Robert McAllister*, p. 417, note 8.

20 Agassiz, *Meade's Headquarters*, p. 98.

21 Cited in *The Civil War Letters of General Robert McAllister*, p. 419, note 13.

22 *The Civil War Letters of General Robert McAllister*, p. 434.

23 *The Civil War Letters of General Robert McAllister*, p. 424, note 24.

24 *Official Records*, I:36/3, p. 3.

25 *Official Records*, I:36/3, p. 6.

26 Douglas Southall Freeman, ed., *Lee's Dispatches to Jefferson Davis*, (New York: G.P Putnam's Sons, 1957), Lee to Davis, May 18, 1864, pp. 183-84.

27 Agassiz, *Meade's Headquarters*, pp. 99-100.

28 Gary W. Gallagher, ed., *Fighting for the Confederacy: The Personal Recollections of General Edward Porter Alexander*, (Chapel Hill: University of North Carolina Press, 1989), p. 370.

29 John Gibbon, *Personal Recollections of the Civil War*, (Dayton: Morningside Bookshop, 1978), p. 218.

30 Rufus R. Dawes, *Service With the Sixth Wisconsin Volunteers*, (Madison: State Historical Society of Wisconsin, 1962), p. 267.

31 Stephen Minot Weld, *War Diary and Letters of Stephen Minot Weld, 1861-1865*, (Boston: Massachusetts Historical Society, 1979), p. 294.

32 *Fighting for the Confederacy: The Personal Recollections of General Edward Porter Alexander*, p. 380.

33 Agassiz, *Meade's Headquarters*, p. 109.

34 Gibbon, p. 223.

35 Wilson , *Under the Old Flag*, vol. 1, p. 427.

36 The soldiers' diaries and letters highlight their fluctuating morale. For a typical example of this attitude, see Nevins, *A Diary of Battle*, p. 381.

37 *Official Records*, I:36/1, pp. 136-149.

13
Stalemate

PART 1. THE RANKS MELT AWAY LIKE SNOW

The war in Virginia had become a meat-grinder, foreshadowing the bloodshed of the First World War. From the start of the campaign until the Battle of Cold Harbor in June, about 28,000 recruits and reinforcements reached Grant's Army, but during that period he lost some 52,700 men on the battlefield and was deprived of the service of many veterans when these surviving volunteers of the early days saw their term of service expire. Nineteen complete regiments mustered out of service. The 2d Rhode Island Infantry saw 265 veteran officers and men depart during its time in the trenches in front of Cold Harbor. An ambitious 22-year-old lieutenant was left in charge of this once proud fighting unit, which had fought in all the army's battles from Bull Run onwards. Henceforth it was a mere ghost of a regiment, numbering a veteran cadre plus a mixed bag of recruits and bounty jumpers. As Colonel McAllister observed: 'Our ranks melt away like snow under an April sun.'[1]

Convalescing officers and men rushed back to the front to replace the fallen. They had no illusions about what they would face. Among them was a pale, emaciated Massachusetts captain who had been wounded virtually fatally three times and had suffered terribly while recovering in hospital. He told a companion on the train to the front that he had regained adequate physical strength to return to the army. But, he said, for the first time he distrusted his courage and feared disgracing himself before his company.[2] Newly enlisted recruits were fed into the fiercest fighting of the war so far, without military discipline or training — and suffered accordingly. Typical was the 36th Wisconsin, a green regiment which went into action alongside the veterans a mere two weeks after reaching the front. They lost their colonel and more than 50 per cent of their numbers at Cold Harbor.

The behaviour of Lysander Cutler's brigade on 23 May underscored the fact that this was not the army it had once been. One year earlier, no unit in the army had stood higher than the Iron Brigade. During the fighting on 23 May: '... one-half of it ran clear across the river without firing a shot, and two-thirds of the other half were brought back with difficulty by their officers to support the batteries'. The brigade's poor performance mirrored Cutler's decline: 'The old man has not been at any time during this campaign what he was last year; he is evidently very much broken, and lost his head entirely when his men behaved so badly.'[3]

Other famous units had simply been ground down to mere shadows of the formations that had begun the campaign. Elisha Rhodes wrote in his diary that he reckoned his division, the 2d Division of the 6th Corps, had lost half its strength by mid-May. More precisely, General Gibbon calculated that his 2d Division, 2d Corps, had lost a staggering 47 per cent of its original strength by the end of May.

The gunners fared much better than the infantry. Like the mechanized soldiers of the future, Civil War gunners looked with some condescension on their foot-slogging brethren. Whereas they were able to take along ample creature comforts on their caissons and limbers, the foot-soldiers were limited by the capacity of their packs. During a march, particularly at the beginning of a campaign, batteries following in the infantry's wake happily picked up the infantry's discarded blankets, knapsacks, pots and pans, and tied them to their horse-drawn transport. It was one of many ways in which life in the artillery or cavalry was far more comfortable than life in the infantry. On the march to Cold Harbor, artilleryman Wainwright noted the grimy state of the infantry officers and observed:

'Almost every day on this campaign I have been obliged to remark ... how superior is the position of a light battery officer to even a colonel of infantry, so far as comfort goes, in times of general discomfort. They have a mechanic and tools always close at hand, and their little cart to carry the mess-chest, a bag each, and the company desk, while either a tent is stuck in on top of the forage wagon, or if their battery is in position, they have their paulins. All these enable them to go through such a month as this last with quite as much comfort as a general officer ... and at times they are better off.'[4]

At about the same time, an infantry colonel described his state: 'We have to march all day and all night, ford rivers, bivouac without blankets or any covering during rain and sunshine, and a good part of the time have been half starved.'[5] An eye-witness reports that since the infantry had no chance to wash or change clothing, even the officers '...were literally encrusted in mud, dirt, dust, perspiration and blood'.[6]

So the army arrived at Cold Harbor, another of those obscure road junctions that became important when rival armies tried to outmanoeuvre each other. Since Lee got there first, Grant's men realized that they would probably have to assault his position. On 2 June, the night before the general assault at Cold Harbor, a sense of doom pervaded the army. By now they knew what to expect when ordered to charge earthworks, and the knowledge depressed them. For the first time, large numbers of infantry wrote name tags and pinned them to their backs so that the survivors would be able to identify their bodies. If anything, the events of the next day surpassed their dreadful fears.

Although it rained during the night, the defenders had heard the sounds of preparation – the tramping of thousands of feet, the muffled orders to align on the Colours and battalion guidons – and knew that the assault was imminent. A Confederate officer tells how the first Union line came on with a rush in a bayonet charge. At the command 'Fire!' the defenders behind the works:

'Raised deliberately, resting their guns upon the works, and fired volley after volley into the rushing but disorganized ranks of the enemy. The first line reeled and attempted to fly the field, but were met by the next column, which halted the retreating troops with the bayonet, butts of guns, and officers' swords ... All this while our sharpshooters and men behind our works were pouring a galling fire into the tangled mass ... The double column, like the first, came with a shout, a huzzah, and a charge. But our men had by this time reloaded their pieces ... the result was telling – men falling on top of men, rear rank pushing forward the first rank, only to be swept away like chaff.'

The rebel artillery 'was not idle, but firing double-shotted canister, and at the distance of one hundred yards was cutting wide swaths through their lines at every fire, literally mowing them down by the dozen, while heads, arms, legs, and muskets were seen flying high in air.'[7]

During this slaughter Grant exercised little battlefield control. Meade told his wife that Grant had visited his headquarters for only about an hour on the day before the battle. On the 3rd, his intentions were sound. In an attempt to control the action he established his headquarters at a central point not too far from the front lines. Here he received a flurry of reports from commanders and staff officers, but the messages 'were rather contradictory, and became more so as the attack proceeded'.[8] As one of Grant's aides observed, the battle was changing more rapidly than could be reported. Some two hours after the initial attack, he instructed Meade to 'suspend the offensive' the moment it became clear that it could not succeed. But he added that if there were success, 'push it vigorously, and if necessary pile in troops at the successful point'.[9]

Grant was grappling with the difficulties of mounting a successful assault in unfamiliar circumstances –– the defence had all the advantages. How can one order an all-out attack with the proviso that it be halted quickly if opposition was too stiff? It was a problem that First World War generals would try to solve with carrier-pigeons and field telegraphs, and subsequent leaders would try to address with radio. In 1864, Grant applied the means at hand and they were inadequate. Command control all but collapsed once the troops entered the killing-ground.

The problems were exacerbated by the absence of skilled, front-line leadership. Emory Upton, who had his horse shot from under him and whose brigade lost about 300 men during its futile assaults at Cold Harbor, wrote to his sister: 'I am very sorry to say I have seen but little generalship during the campaign. Some of our corps commanders are not fit to be corporals. Lazy and indolent, they will not even ride along their lines; yet without hesitancy, they will order us to attack the enemy.'

Because of this poor leadership, Upton continued, 'Our men have ... been foolishly and wantonly sacrificed. Assault after assault has been ordered upon the enemy's entrenchments, when they knew nothing about the strength or position of the enemy.'[10]

The yankees lost 13,153 men killed, wounded and missing from 2 to 10 June. Of these, nearly 6,000 were killed or wounded in the useless general assault on the 3rd, most of them within the first fifteen minutes. Soldiers complained that the sacrifice had been for naught. Their general was bull-headed, stubborn and unskilled. Many noted that by the end of the battle they had merely regained the same ground, at a much higher cost, captured by McClellan in 1862. Richmond newspapers boasted that Grant was floundering in the Chickahominy swamps, the same ground that had undone McClellan, the 'graveyard of Yankee armies'.

The general collapse of morale surprised a veteran officer who joined the Army of the Potomac in August. He listened with astonishment to the gloomy complaints about Grant. He asked, 'But don't you believe in Grant at all?' A colonel replied, 'Yes, we believe in Grant, but we believe a great deal more in Lee and in that Army of Virginia.'[11] Oliver Wendell Holmes, Jr. wrote home that 'many a man has gone crazy since this campaign begun from the terrible pressure on mind & body'.[12]

Meade concluded that the campaign clearly showed that an assault against an entrenched position was doomed to failure. He took some solace from the slaughter by observing that he thought the experience had opened Grant's eyes to the fact that Virginia and Lee were not Tennessee and Bragg. Yet Meade recognized that despite disasters such as Cold Harbor, the Army of the Potomac would triumph because the South could not afford the attrition. He failed to recognize that only Grant, of all of the generals who had commanded this army, had the firmness of purpose to keep going.

There were no more assaults for nine days following the disaster at Cold Harbor. Among many, one veteran wrote thankfully, 'we have not been storming for some days'.[13] But conditions in the front lines were dreadful. The men got little sleep. During the night they had to dig safe approaches leading to their trenches and strengthen the trenches themselves. Then, during the day they had to lie baking beneath a hot Virginia summer sun with only foul surface drainage – this region of Virginia featured many low-lying marshes – to quench their thirst. Because the men could not move freely during the day, such cooking as was done was necessarily of the crudest. To stimulate appetites, there was the stench from the rotting corpses lying between the lines. After a few days the troops began to be rotated, spending 24 hours in the trenches and then going back to the safety of a reserve position. Throughout history this rotation had been common during sieges, but in field operations it was something new. Inexorably, the distinction between field and trench warfare was disappearing as a generation of American citizen soldiers stumbled towards 20th century warfare.

At Cold Harbor there was a constant attrition from snipers and random shellings. The opposing trenchlines were very close, often within 200 yards of one another, sometimes as close as 60 to 80 yards apart. Amid squalid conditions the soldiers endured days of 'bitter sharpshooting and angry artillery practice'.[14]

Because the yankees had more men and tools with which to dig, their trenches offered better protection from sharpshooters. Meanwhile, Union marksmen kept the rebels virtually pinned to their trenches during the day, which denied them easy access to food and water.

A Confederate artillery brigadier, Porter Alexander, describes his daily tour of inspection under these conditions. He walked along the bottom of the trench bent nearly double to keep his head below the parapet. The troops manning the trenches had rigged shelter blankets against the baking sun. Here Alexander had to crawl beneath the improvised tents because stepping over them would have been too risky. The points of maximum danger were where the trenches of adjacent regiments did not join. At these places, federal sharpshooters sighted their rifles and patiently waited until someone moved across the gap. To cross the gap the general followed the soldier's routine of stooping very low and then making a dash for it. When he reached the end of the line, the infantry general who commanded that sector advised him to wait until nightfall before going back.

It was a tedious and tiring process. When Alexander needed to visit an infantry general's headquarters he decided to try a direct approach. This headquarters consisted of an 8-foot by 3-foot hole in the ground about twenty feet behind the main trenchline. By crouching the whole way, Alexander could move up the relatively safe reverse slope leading to headquarters and arrive within 50 yards of his objective. Then, to be safe, he had to crawl the remaining distance. Instead Alexander decided to run across the last danger zone. He dashed the final 50 yards and bounded into a rifle pit where he landed between two dead Texans, each of whom had been shot through the head. A Texas infantryman greeted Alexander sociably, commenting, 'You has to be mighty careful how you shows a head around here, or they'll get you certain! Thars two they got already this morning!'[15]

Sharpshooting made life in the trenches more miserable than it might have been, and contributed nothing to ending the war. Many soldiers understood this and disliked sharpshooters intensely. An Army of the Potomac veteran explained: 'Our sharpshooters were as bad as the Confederates, and neither of them were of any account as far as decisive results ... They could sneak around trees or lurk behind stumps ... and from the safety of their lairs murder a few men ... I hated sharpshooters, both Confederate and Union ... and I was always glad to see them killed.'[16]

In an endeavour to preserve some vestiges of sanity the troops in some sectors arranged unauthorized truces, agreeing with their opponents not to fire at officers or men on foot. By restricting their fire to mounted men they ensured that only the higher-ranking officers would be at risk. It did not quite work out as intended. Unaware of the informal truce, two Union colonels and an orderly rode behind the works to examine the lines. A rebel sharpshooter fired, but the ball passed between the officers and killed the hapless orderly.

Finally, on the night of 12 June, Grant began another powerful outflanking move. His own men had begun to refer to him as 'The

Berdan's Sharpshooters

Two regiments, the 1st and 2nd United States Sharpshooters, killed more enemy soldiers than any other two regiments in the service. These unique units, the famous Berdan's Sharpshooters, were United States troops, but each company came from an individual state. To qualify recruits had to be able to hit a 50-inch target with ten consecutive shots, five from the prone position at 200-yards' range and five standing at 100-yards' range.

Berdan's sharpshooters dominated the siege lines at Yorktown, where they used heavy target rifles fitted with telescope sights to silence Confederate batteries, and again during the 9-month siege of Petersburg.

During the war the 1st USSS suffered 546 killed and wounded while its sister regiment lost 462 killed and wounded, totals reflecting a mortality rate of more than 10 per cent.

State origins of the sharpshooter companies:

1st US Sharpshooters	2nd US Sharpshooters
A. New York	A. Minnesota
B. New York	B. Michigan
C. Michigan	C. Pennsylvania
D. New York	D. Maine
E. New Hampshire	E. Vermont
F. Vermont	F. New Hampshire
G. Wisconsin	G. New Hampshire
H. New York	H. Vermont
I. Michigan	
K. Michigan	

Grand Flanker'. 'He'll flank Lee out of Richmond yet; see if he don't,' said one.[17] The rebels referred to his constant flanking movements as 'elbowing'. This time Grant intended to 'elbow' his way into Petersburg and thereby win the war.

PART 2. 'WE ARE CHARGED OUT'

The movement to Petersburg was Grant's finest combination since the Vicksburg campaign. He planned for a rapid march to the south bank of the James River from where his army would be poised to capture Petersburg. All but one of the railroads supplying Richmond and Lee's army passed through this town. In addition, the capture of Petersburg would outflank the rebel forces who were bottling-up Benjamin Butler's Army of the James in a narrow river bend known as Bermuda Hundred. Having released Butler, Grant intended to turn north against the last railroad line leading to Richmond. Lee would then either have to abandon the capital or stand siege. Grant had been contemplating this masterstroke since 26 May, when he had ordered all available bridging equipment to be assembled to support the crossing of the James River.

The plan was fraught with danger. The army had to be extracted from trenches that were hugging the enemy's line, marched across hostile country where every inhabitant was a potential informant, and then cross the James River in the face of a powerful Confederate ironclad flotilla. Should Lee detect the movement, he could attack Grant's army while it was astride either the Chickahominy or the James, so it had to be conducted with the utmost secrecy.

In the event, the switch from the Richmond front to the far side of the James came as little surprise to many officers and men in the Army of the Potomac. They received news of the impending operation from that oldest and most reliable source, the rear-echelon teamsters who drove the wagons. Here was the time-honoured problem. A major movement required extensive logistical preparation. The Quartermaster Corps had to prepare to switch bases before the infantry set out. Lowly teamsters saw the bustle, asked around, learned what was afoot, and spread the news. Their gossip often undid the most elaborate efforts to deceive the enemy. Thus even while still in the fieldworks facing Lee's trenches at Cold Harbor, and before the corps commanders had been apprised of the plan, an officer who had heard the rumour from the teamsters wrote, 'We are bound for the James River, south side.'[18] The wonder is not that so many knew, but that the man most concerned, Robert E. Lee, was, for once, caught unawares.

The drive on Petersburg began as another long night march, and once again the army's poor march discipline delayed the advance. The column featured more than the usual number of men known as 'coffee-boilers', that is to say, '... men who seldom keep in the ranks, but hang on the rear of the army so long as their rations last ... and always have

Above: To fill the ranks for the 1864 campaign, Union recruiters greeted just-arrived immigrants with handfuls of cash totalling 600 dollars if they enlisted. They did in large numbers, but their services were of dubious value. (Library of Congress)

Below: Grant found the Army of the Potomac to be a spit and polish outfit, as exemplified by these Pennsylvania zouaves, and quite unlike his more casual westerners. (Library of Congress)

Above: The eastern army was justifiably proud of its efficient artillery, but it would contribute little in the coming campaign. (Library of Congress)

Below: Warren and Sedgwick's Corps crossed here at Germanna Ford and entered the Wilderness. (National Park Service)

Above right: Hitherto unpublished Wilderness photograph showing the Orange Plank Road near the key intersection with the Brock Road. (National Park Service)

Below: Grant sat on a stump whittling while his men defiled over the fords and entered the Wilderness. (Author's collection)

Above: Hitherto unpublished view of Sanders' field where the Regulars fought. (National Park Service)

Below: Hastily constructed Confederate works on edge of Wilderness clearing. (National Park Service)

Above: An eye-witness describes the rebels captured at the Wilderness: 'In the lead a stalwart red-whiskered fellow, who carried a patchwork quilt under his arm. Behind him came a youth with a light-gray jacket and trousers, and a gray infantry cap trimmed with light blue. The next one to him wore a striped worsted sailor cap. And the last in order was an old man with long white hair, who was evidently a recruit, for he still wore an old-fashioned stovepipe [hat].' (Library of Congress)

Right: 'Little Phil', one of the war's inspirational frontline leaders. A selection of his utterances: 'Take your men in – make your men fight – push on your column.' 'Go in boys, go in!' 'Ha! the damned rascals are running!' 'The cowardly scoundrels can't fight such brave men as mine.' 'Kill that infernal skulker! Shoot every man down like a dog that tries to skulk from duty.' To a wounded soldier: 'They've hit you have they? Don't give it up just yet. Give the bloody rebels a round or two more to remember you by. Down three or four of the rascals before you go to the hospital.' (Library of Congress)

Above: The Battle of Yellow Tavern; devoid of military results, it was significant because it was here that Jeb Stuart received a mortal wound and during the expedition the eastern cavalry found a new leader. (Library of Congress)

Below: Grant (fourth from left) and his staff in Virginia. Second from right is Ely Parker, whom Wilson wished to unleash against the army's high command. (Library of Congress)

Right: An infantry colonel points the way in the driving rain and close-range action at the Bloody Angle. During this phase of the campaign, the talented General Rice fell badly wounded. He was taken to hospital and his shattered limb was removed. The noise of the fighting could clearly be heard from the field hospital. Rice's pain was intense. 'Turn me over,' he said faintly. 'Which way?' 'Let me die with my face to the enemy.' (Library of Congress)

Above: 'You would be amazed', recalled a soldier, 'to see how this country is intersected with field-works, extending for miles and miles in different directions and marking the different strategic lines taken up by the two armies, as they warily move about each other.' It took a Cold Harbor in Virginia, and a Kennesaw Mountain in Georgia, for Grant and Sherman and their top lieutenants to appreciate the new battlefield environment. They tried to return to a warfare of manoeuvre only to butt up against two fortified positions – the Richmond–Petersburg complex and Atlanta's defences – of unprecedented scale. (National Park Service)

Below: Grant watching his men use bridge and ferry to cross the James River. The movement against Petersburg was one of Grant's finest combinations, but was thwarted by the institutional incapacity of the eastern Union armies. (Author's collection)

Above: The bridge over the James River was an engineering masterpiece. Note the castle badge proudly worn by these Corps of Engineers troops. (Library of Congress)

Below: The investment of Petersburg forced the Federal army to burrow like moles. Lookouts man positions on the skyline while soldiers cook rations on the reverse slope. (Library of Congress)

Above: Over time, Grant's men brought up huge siege cannon, but unlike operations at Vicksburg, they did not dig and blast their way up to the rebel front lines. (Library of Congress)

Below: Despite numerous attempts against Lee's rail communications, the Union cavalry seldom managed to achieve any significant destruction. (Library of Congress)

Above: Abatis (sharpened stakes) served the same purpose as barbed wire during the First World War by channelling attacks into prepared killing zones. (Library of Congress)

Below: Earth and log traverses were one of the Army of Northern Virginia's contributions to the science of war. They prevented the battleline (here facing to the right) from being subjected to enfilade fire. (Library of Congress)

Left: Sheridan's Valley Campaign provided one of the few bright notes during the dismal autumn of 1864. Sheridan and Custer lead a cavalry charge against Confederate works outside Winchester. (Library of Congress)

Below left: Grant's men spent a relatively comfortable winter, with access by water to the North's bounty. His secure riverine communications negated any chance of Lee employing his favourite stroke, a threat against his enemy's line of supply. (Library of Congress)

Below: Extending from this base at City Point, army engineers construct a military railroad to haul supplies to the front. (Library of Congress)

Left: Grant, under shell fire, calmly writes orders to repel Lee's attack against Fort Harrison. It was the Army of Northern Virginia's last offensive. (Author's collection)

Below: By 1865, even the most advanced picket posts were heavily fortified. Here Union soldiers occupy a rebel post captured during Grant's general assault against Petersburg. (Library of Congress)

Right: Confederate soldiers who died while vainly trying to repulse Grant's general assault. (Library of Congress)

Below right: During the splendid Grand Review, a Union regiment wheels before the camera (hence the blur of the mounted officer) and continues along Pennsylvania Avenue. The capitol dome is faintly visible in the background. (Library of Congress)

Left: Black soldiers showed by their battlefield valour that minié balls and cannon shot paid no heed to a man's colour. 'War Episodes: The Veteran', by Thomas Waterman Wood. (The Metropolitan Museum of Art, Gift of Charles Stewart Smith, 1884)

Below: After Champion's Hill, an Ohio soldier wrote: 'Shortly after dark ... a squad of us went out on the field to give our dead comrades some sort of burial. Making a torch, we, by its light, saw some of the awful sights of a battle-field. One, always remembered, was a very large rebel, sitting with his back against a large stump, with more than a deathly pallor, having bled to death; and so many others, lying dead as they fell, friend and foe, now at peace. We soon found our slain com-rades, and having prepared a place, side by side we placed our gallant comrades, shroud-ed in their rubber blankets.' (Library of Congress)

a little tin pail with water in their hands ready to boil coffee half a dozen times a day'.[19] They were part of the hundreds of men who belonged to the army but who never engaged in battle. Joining the shirkers' ranks were the cooks, officers' servants, hospital workers, quartermasters' staff, and the 'present sick', all of whom drew rations, appeared on the army's order of battle, but did not contribute to its fighting strength. Despite the temptation to fall out and linger with these shirkers, the troops closed up on the James where a battalion of Regular engineers built a 2,100-foot-long pontoon bridge. This bridge had to accommodate a 4-foot tidal shift and hold against a strong current. It did both, and ranks as one of the greatest bridges in military history. The men poured across and headed for Petersburg. The unknown factor resolved itself to two questions: when would Lee perceive the threat; would Grant's subordinates see and grasp the opportunity?

On the evening of 15 June, the leading Federal corps commanded by William 'Baldy' Smith – he who had performed so skilfully in an engineering capacity at Chattanooga – displayed extreme caution. Recalling the recent disaster at Cold Harbor, he probed the formidable defences carefully and finally decided that however strong the works, they were held by a mere handful of troops. Smith ordered an assault at 5 p.m. His gunners blundered and delayed the attack for two hours. Finally Brigadier General Edward Hink's division of colored troops spearheaded an attack that overran Petersburg's outer defences: 'At the word of command the colored men stepped out from the woods, and stood before the enemy. They gave a volley, and received one in return. Shells crashed through them, but unheeding the storm, with a yell they started up the slope upon the run. They received one charge of canister, one scathing volley of musketry. Seventy of their number went down, but the living hundreds rushed on.'

Hink's men captured an artillery redoubt and seized several cannon. An officer relates, 'Every soldier of the colored division was two inches taller for that achievement.'[20] Better still, a mile-wide gap invited immediate exploitation. But Smith looked back instead of forward. He expected to see Hancock's Corps arrive at any moment. Indeed it should have been there already, but, by one of those untimely misfortunes that always seemed to afflict the Army of the Potomac, Hancock was late. So Smith postponed further advance until the next day.

It took most of that next day to bring up more troops, but by 6 p.m. something like 48,000 yankees were confronting 14,000 defenders. The assault went in and stubborn fighting ensued. One of Burnside's units employed the new style of assault tactics that was becoming increasing common when facing fieldworks. Stephen Weld relates:

'I made all my men take the caps off their guns. I knew from previous experiences in the campaign that, if we made a charge and the men had the caps on their guns, when we got within a few yards of the works the men would stop to fire and then turn and run, and that would be the end of it. The only chance was to keep on the steady jump and rush them right over the works. I told my men what was to be done, and said, "When you get the order to charge, you let it like the devil. Don't stop for anything, just run as tight as you can."'

Weld's tactics succeeded and his men captured the Confederate works, but the incapacity of his commander, James Ledlie, recently promoted to divisional command and increasingly revealed to be a drunkard, prevented the exploitation of the breach. Ledlie failed to provide supports or ammunition. After a 3-hour fight Weld had to lead his regiment back.

The next day's assault demonstrated that at least some officers had assimilated the accumulated lessons gained from repeated attacks against entrenchments. The tactic of uncapping the musket to prevent the soldiers from stopping to fire was one of them. A surprise attack was another. Brigadier General Simon Griffin resolved to see what would happen by combining the two. During the night Griffin, who was substituting for General Robert Potter, who was on leave, assembled his two brigades in a deep ravine beneath the rebel position. He spent the entire night moving his men through the abatis and carefully positioning them for the assault. He recalls: 'We were so near the enemy that all our movements had to be made with the utmost care and caution; canteens were placed in knapsacks to prevent rattling, and all commands were given in whispers ... My orders were not to fire a shot, but to depend wholly on the bayonet in carrying the lines.'[21] Even the command 'Forward!' was given in a whisper.

The reward for such care was complete surprise. Only one alert Confederate gunner saw the Union line advancing, the remainder of the defenders being asleep in the trenches. Griffin's men captured four guns, five Colours, 1,500 smallarms and 600 prisoners. The remainder of the army did not exhibit such zeal and made minor progress, but by nightfall a long stretch of the high ground shielding Petersburg from attack had been taken. Surely the next day must see final success because some 95,000 Federal soldiers had reached the field to face a mere 20,000 defenders.

At 4 a.m. on 18 June they went forward only to discover that the rebel commander, P. T. Beauregard – who on this field was giving the best performance of his career – had skilfully slipped back to a new line of improvised works one mile closer to Petersburg, and by the time that Grant's columns had sorted themselves out Lee's veterans had arrived to oppose them.

The Union troops launched an assault on the now fully manned Confederate trenchline in an endeavour, as Meade explained, to defeat Lee before his men could fully fortify. The assault smacked of desperation, a recognition in Meade's and Grant's headquarters that a marvellous opportunity had been lost. But the high command was out of touch with frontline reality and the only result was to run up the yankee casualty bill. Colonel McAllister describes the situation:

'This second line of works was built to lead us into a death trap. I halted my Brigade; alone and personally I went to reconnoitre this second line ... I found them very strong – in the form of a half moon with guns planted to enfilade our flanks as we advanced.'

McAllister told a fellow brigade commander who then accompanied him on a second reconnaissance. He confirmed McAllister's impressions and went off to inform headquarters. Time passed and then came the order to charge the defences, with McAllister's brigade in the van:

'The Rebels poured down upon us lead and iron by musketry and cannon that cut our men down like hail cuts the grain and grass. We had to advance a long distance up a cleared plain. Our ranks melted away, and we could not advance further. We dropped down; and those who were not killed or wounded – or who had not fallen back – began digging little pits. We remained there for two or three hours. We were then ordered back and lost many men in retiring.'

McAllister reported to his superior, General Mott, who told him to remain ready because 'we are going to make a charge. You may be needed.'

'"Where is my old 3rd Brigade?" I asked. He replied: "They are going in just where you came out." "God help them!" I exclaimed. "Why?" Mott asked. "It is a death trap," I said. "A brigade can't live in there for five minutes." Just as I said this, an aide rode up. "Move your troops forward to the charge."'[22]

Mott selected the troops of the 1st Maine Heavy Artillery to spearhead the assault on the grounds that they were a fresh and strong unit not yet discouraged by repeated failure. The heavies formed in three lines with one battalion per line and charged across an open field 350 yards in length into the half-moon defences. The plan called for the first line to clear away the abatis and gain the ditch. The second line would follow closely and try to suppress the defender's fire with musketry. Covered by this fire, the first line would make the final charge up the parapet. The third line would follow to provide a close reserve. Meanwhile, when the signal to charge came, the veteran troops who were to charge on the 1st Maine Heavy Artillery's flanks quickly went to ground in the face of the defenders' terrific fire. Not so the men from Maine. The regimental historian, who participated in the attack, describes what transpired:

'The enemy's firing along their whole line was now centred into this field. The earth was literally torn up with iron and lead. The field became a burning, seething, crashing, hissing hell, in which human courage, flesh and bone were struggling with an impossibility, either to succeed or to return with much hope of life. So in ten minutes those who were not slaughtered had returned to the road or were lying prostrate upon that awful field of carnage.'[23]

After losing 632 of 950 men dead or wounded they fell back. This awful total represented the highest number of Union men killed in any one unit in a single engagement. The wounded lay in front of the line crying for water but no relief could be sent. The distressing slaughter even dampened the cheerful McAllister. He wrote that he expected he and his men would charge again, but he hoped not because, he concluded, 'We are charged out.'[24]

The entire sorry episode foreshadowed the repeated ruinous assaults of the First World War, when high-ranking commanders, comfortably ensconced in their châteaux, were totally out of touch with battlefield reality. Like them, some of Grant's commanders blamed the men. Meade complained that the attacks failed because of the soldiers' poor morale. Burnside echoed this sentiment by stating that his heavy gunners were 'worthless, they didn't enlist to fight and it is unreasonable to expect it from them'.[25] Indeed, many assaults had been conducted with little conviction because the soldiers had seen too often the futility of charging defended breastworks.[26] As Theodore Lyman observed, 'The men went in, but not with spirit; received by a withering fire, they sullenly fell back a few paces to a slight crest and lay down, as much as to say, "We can't assault, but we won't run."'[27]

Rufus Dawes, the colonel of the Iron Brigade's Sixth Wisconsin, and as good a patriot as could be found in the army, wrote to his wife, 'Yesterday afternoon in another hopeless assault there was enacted a horrid massacre of our corps ... The suicidal manner in which we are sent against the enemy's entrenchments is discouraging. Our brigade was simply food for powder.'[28] Too many brave officers had become casualties. Gibbon reported that his Second Corps up to the end of July had had seventeen successive brigade commanders, nine of whom had been killed or wounded. Forty of his regimental commanders had become casualties!

Quite simply, this army was spent. For the remainder of the war it would seldom assault enemy works with any drive. When ordered to charge, veterans would typically advance until encountering enemy fire and then go to ground.[29] Only inexperienced, green units continued to attack with élan. This collapse must be attributed to their general's poor tactics. Reflecting on the failed assaults against Petersburg, Colonel Wainwright wrote in his diary:

'The attack this afternoon was a fiasco of the worst kind; I trust it will be the last attempt at this most absurd way of attacking entrenchments by a general advance in line. It has been tried so often now and with such fearful losses that even the stupidest private now knows that it cannot succeed, and the natural consequence follows: the men will not try it. The very sight of a bank of fresh earth now brings them to a halt.'[30] Later he attributed the army's poor morale to the fact that it had been 'fearfully shattered by Grant's brutal attacks'.[31]

The inability of this army to perform adequately thoroughly annoyed Grant. Beginning with the advance over the Rapidan, he had devised combinations which he believed should have triumphed. One day he asked his old staff officer Wilson, 'What is the matter with this army? 'General, there is a great deal the matter with it, but I can tell you much more easily how to cure it.' 'How? 'Send for Parker [one of Grant's aides, a full-blooded Indian] ... after giving him a tomahawk, a scalping knife, and a gallon of the worst whiskey the Commissary Department can supply, send him out with orders to bring in the scalps of major generals.'[32]

Grant laughed but did not disagree with the thrust of Wilson's humour. This army was badly organized and staffed. Burnside's Corps never manoeuvred harmoniously with the Army of the Potomac. During the crossing of the James efforts to co-ordinate with Benjamin Butler's Army of the James had been thwarted by defective staff work. Army group manoeuvring seemed beyond the talents of Grant's staff. Clearly Rawlins' western-style staff habits were not understood by the more formal eastern staff officers. Lastly, in varying proportions, innate caution, jealousy and incompetence prevented Grant's soldiers from capturing Petersburg. Emory Upton understood this clearly. He wrote that there were too many high-ranking officers who 'are stumbling-blocks of too great magnitude to permit a brilliant execution of any movement' in which they were involved.[33] Forty days' of some of the most sustained fighting in history had demonstrated at least this much.

PART 3. 'SO FAIR AN OPPORTUNITY'

'It has got to be this: the Rebels do not and dare not charge on us, and we are not always successful in charging on their works.'[34] This pithy summary by a veteran officer accurately described the situation. Reluctantly Grant came to accept that the most he could do in Virginia would be to keep Lee occupied, and he was not at all certain that he could accomplish this. He realized that a small number of defenders could hold elaborate fortifications against superior numbers and thus free the main body for mobile warfare. Consequently, he feared that Lee would detach forces to reinforce Johnston and deliver a crushing blow against Sherman.

Moreover, Grant could sense the disgruntlement among the troops of the Army of the Potomac. A veteran recalls that when Grant and Meade '... appeared among the troops there was but feeble applause, and the hearty cheers received by some of our former commanders were no longer heard'.[35] Had this veteran and his commanding general been privy to Lee's appraisal of the situation they would have felt more optimistic.

At the beginning of September, Lee described the immensely difficult situation that Grant had forced upon him:

'The enemy's position enables him to move his troops to the right or left without our knowledge until he has reached the point at which he aims, and we are then compelled to hurry our men to meet him ... These rapid and distant movements also fatigue and exhaust our men, greatly impairing their efficiency in battle.'[36]

By Lee's own assessment, Grant had stretched the Confederates to breaking-point. Lee's remaining troops had lost most of their mobility. Although no one yet realized it, Grant's strategy was winning the war. Because of heavy Union pressure against the two main Confederate armies, the rebels, as General Beauregard wrote, had 'no more troops to concentrate'.[37]

The campaign against Petersburg resembled that at Vicksburg but with one crucial difference. Whereas at Vicksburg Grant's army had occupied a solid line around Pemberton's landward front, it never completely cut Petersburg's communications with the rest of the South. Consequently, operations at Petersburg amounted to an investment, not a siege. In places the lines were very close, particularly just south of the Appomattox. In such sectors the works were more extensive than had ever been known. Not only were the front lines incredibly formidable, but rear areas were fortified as well, complete with supporting trenchlines and bombproofs. It was, wrote a soldier, 'one great rabbit warren'.[38]

Farther south, the opposing diverged, with often a mile or more of no man's land between them. This was a tangled region of woods, swamps and streams, and it was here that numerous actions were fought. It was a matter of military geography, and in this war military geography usually boiled down to the location of the railroads. During the Petersburg campaign, Grant concentrated most of his effort to the cutting of Lee's rail communications. As had been the case throughout the campaign, this meant an effort to turn Lee's right flank. It produced a series of fierce encounters that lasted until the onset of winter.

In mid-July a period of intense drought set in, making life miserable for everyone. An officer described his conditions in a letter to his wife: 'Imagine a hole three feet wide and four feet deep in the middle of the street, and a sun perfectly sweltering in its rays and you have our quarters, from which we can not raise our heads.'[39] There was little shade because the woods had quickly disappeared to feed the voracious demand for strengthening and extending the works. In their place were great patches of parched soil that became stifling dust clouds at the slightest movement. Any road march was a particular discomfort. Conditions for the sick and wounded became worse than ever:

'The hospital tents, though pitched in the woods, were like ovens, absorbing and holding the heat of the sun ... Upon the ground lay the sick and wounded, fevered and sore, with energies exhausted, perspiration oozing from their faces, nerves quivering and trembling, pulses faint and feeble, and life ebbing away. Their beds were pine boughs. They lay as they came from the battle-field, wearing their soiled, torn, and bloody garments, and tantalized by myriads of flies.'[40]

The Christian Commission and other relief organizations worked hard to better the men's conditions. The folks back home had given foodstuffs and clothes for the soldiers, and members of the Commission tried to distribute them even-handedly. They gave fruit, onions, pickles, anything to tempt the taste and relieve the otherwise bland diet. Over time, the fact that the army remained static permitted the Federal supply system to bring much better food to the front. Soon regular supplies included potatoes, vegetables and canned fruit. The men could supplement these rations by purchases at the commissary. Now that the men were in fixed positions, the regular delivery of mail resumed. Packages from home often brought baked and canned goods and similar delicacies. By August McAllister could write, 'We have everything that we want on our tables.'[41]

As had been the case at Cold Harbor, static warfare meant daily doses of shelling and sniping. Along many sectors soldiers had to maintain constant vigil from opposing marksmen. Seldom could these sharpshooters be seen. The troops on both sides had learned the art of concealment, even in 'open' ground. One Federal officer went up to the picket line holding a flag of truce. He could see only one rebel sentry. After arranging a truce, 'a line of some seventy-five men rose, as if out of the ground. It was their pickets, who had been concealed in little holes, dug in the slope of a gentle hill.'[42]

From such positions, sharpshooters equipped with heavy rifles and telescopic sights hit Union soldiers as far as three-quarters of a mile from the rebel lines. Particularly vulnerable were the colonels and brigadier generals who had to visit their commands daily. Whereas the front-line troops were generally well protected from sharpshooters by virtue of being stationary behind sophisticated works, these officers were always exposed while going back and forth to different parts of their commands. To silence the sharpshooters in his sector, General David Birney passed word across the lines that if any sharpshooting took place he would bombard everything to his front. For ten days this arrangement held up. Then, Confederate pickets opened fire and Birney responded with a day-long bombardment that expended more than 1,740 rounds. The next day the rebel sharpshooters were quiet.

Not surprisingly, the armies resumed the fraternal behaviour that had characterized other periods of inactivity during the war. Meade observed that if the men were allowed to mingle freely, he was certain they would make permanent peace in about one hour. While informal truces characterized many sectors, such was not the case along the lines held by the 9th Corps. The Confederates hated the black soldiers in Burnside's Corps and consequently maintained a particularly fierce sniping and shelling along this front.

By now everyone from Grant down appreciated the tremendous tactical advantages of defenders sheltered behind breastworks. One veteran colonel estimated that at best the attacker had to accept two-to-one casualties to storm a trench. Even a reconnaissance, intended to determine if Lee had over-thinned his lines, risked high losses for the simple advantage of informing headquarters that 'yes, the greycoats were still there'. Ordered 'to develop the enemy's line', Colonel McAllister hit upon a novel way to conduct a reconnaissance. He ordered his brigade to form a double rank behind its breastworks. Then, in a loud voice intended to be overheard by the enemy, he ordered them to advance. By pre-arrangement his second rank raised their muskets to simulate mens' heads and issued three cheers. When, as expected, the defenders responded by rising and firing, McAllister was able to observe how strongly the Confederates were manning this sector. Too strong to charge, he reported, having accomplished his mission without the loss of a single man.

In times past, Lee had found that he could relieve the yankee pressure on Richmond by threatening Washington. In an effort to return to mobile warfare, he resolved to try this strategy again. He detached a force under Jubal Early and sent it tearing down the Shenandoah Valley towards the Potomac River and Washington. Against a lesser general, or one in whom Lincoln did not have much confidence, Meade for example, it might have worked. Grant, however, responded calmly to the threat and continued business as usual. His adjutant general, Colonel Bowers, reflected his chief's attitude when asked by a reporter what was going on. Bowers replied, 'They are having a little scare at Washington and in the North. It will do them no good.'[43]

Nevertheless, Meade wrote that Lee's bold stroke 'thus far has been successful' because not only did the 6th Corps have to be sent to Washington, but the 19th Corps, scheduled to reinforce the Army of the Potomac, also had to be diverted. Consequently, Meade concluded that no offensive action could take place at Petersburg until Early had been dealt with. Indeed, this was Lee's final strategic triumph over the Army of the Potomac. The detachment of Early with a relatively small force, paid the enormous dividend of prolonging the war into 1865, because, without the 6th and 19th Corps, Grant did not have enough men to pin the Army of Northern Virginia frontally while manoeuvring around the flank. The repeated failures to turn Lee's right flank proved this point. There was to be only one more opportunity to win the war in Virginia in 1864.

It had started with a front-line soldier's comment that the Union army could blow the opposing fort, which stood only 500 feet away, out of existence if a mine were run under it. Lieutenant Colonel Henry Pleasants happened to overhear this comment and he decided to try it. Pleasants' 48th Pennsylvania came from mining country and the colonel himself was an experienced miner. But no high-ranking officer placed much stock in the digging activities of Pleasant's Pennsylvania regiment. When Meade's engineer officer refused to supply a theodolite, an instrument necessary to calculate the distance needed to dig, Pleasants obtained one himself from distant Washington. Refused proper tools and equipment, the men improvised, making hand-barrows from cracker boxes. Finally their progress was such as to attract the attention of Meade himself. Meade inspected Pleasants' work and deemed it poorly situated because of the potential for enemy crossfire to dominate the ground over which assault troops would have to charge. But there was nothing else on the table at the Federal councils, so the work was allowed to continue.

Grant thought up a diversion to draw Lee's attention to the Richmond front. He ordered that an immense train of empty wagons be paraded ostentatiously towards the bridges crossing the James River, to give the impression that supplies were being built-up for an assault on the Richmond front. When Lee responded by marching a large number of men to the north side of the James, the possibilities of piercing the Petersburg lines became manifest. Meade had a meeting to arrange an assault with Burnside and his three divisional generals the day before Pleasants' mine was to be sprung. The key to the operation, Meade impressed upon these officers, was speed. The assault troops had to capitalize upon the mine's explosion, penetrate the enemy's fortifications, and seize a ridge overlooking the place where the mine would explode. Unless they captured the ridge crest, the crater would become a death trap. Burnside selected his assault unit by drawing lots. He ordered the 'winner', General Ledlie, to spearhead the charge and capture the ridge, known as Cemetery Hill. A second divisional wave under Brigadier General Orlando Willcox would follow and exploit the breach to the left. Then Brigadier General Robert Potter's colored division would follow in Ledlie's wake. This was all well and good, but the fact was overlooked that during the campaign to date Ledlie had shown a need to imbibe to fortify his courage.

The mine exploded at 4.45 a.m. on 30 July 1864. Recovering from the stunning explosion after about five minutes (in contrast to a similar event during the siege of Vicksburg where the attackers advanced immediately) Ledlie's division went forward. So poor had been the assault's preparation that no officer had considered the need to remove the obstacles defending the Union lines from in front of the sector where the Federal troops had to pass. Thus there was a totally avoidable delay while the assault troops clambered over their own obstacles. The effort broke their ranks as they advanced. If they had learned one thing, it was that earthworks saved lives, and upon reaching the crater, the site of the mine's explosion, they found the biggest earthwork they had ever encountered. It measured about 50 to 60 yards long, 20 yards wide, and 20 to 25 feet deep. They occupied it pretty promptly and did not budge. Their objective, Cemetery Hill, lay some 500 yards further ahead.

After about an hour, Meade learned that Ledlie's men had not advanced as instructed. The terrible time lag occurred because the divisional general supposedly leading the assault, General Ledlie, was drunk in a bombproof shelter in the rear. The supporting divisional commanders likewise never went forward with their men. Corps commander Burnside apparently did not have the sense to see what was happening. At last, at 5.40 a.m., Meade ordered Burnside to push forward towards the crest with all available troops. The most impetuous men advanced 200 yards beyond the crater, but it was too late. Heavy enemy fire drove them back. Subsequent assault waves just packed the men in more densely. When the Confederates brought up howitzers and 8-inch and 10-inch mortars to open fire against the men in the crater, the attackers' plight became awful. One of Grant's staffers reported that: 'as the enemy rallied from the shock and their fire became hotter our boys huddled together in a confused mass, like cattle awaiting the slaughter.'[44]

At 9.10 a.m. Grant ordered the attack halted. Burnside came to headquarters to complain that if allowed to continue the assault he would capture the heights by nightfall. Unwilling to countenance another Fredericksburg, Grant declined his offer. The Battle of the Crater cost 4,008 men including more than 1,000 men who preferred surrender to the perils of making the short dash back to friendly lines. Included among the prisoners were two brigade commanders. Indicative of the poor morale of the attackers is the fact the they lost 21 Colours during the assault.

Terribly discouraged, Grant wrote to Meade:

'Have you any estimate of our losses in the miserable failure of Saturday? ... So fair an opportunity will probably never occur again for carrying fortifications. Preparations were good, orders ample, and everything, as far as I could see, subsequent to the explosion of the mine, shows that almost without loss the crest beyond the mine could have carried. This would have given us Petersburg with all its artillery and a large part of its Garrison beyond doubt.'[45]

Meade, in turn, blamed Burnside and launched a vendetta against him. The subsequent Court of Inquiry concluded that the troops had been poorly lead. Instead of handy columns of assault, formed and ready before the mine's explosion, the leading assault wave had been indifferently organized. Their own defensive obstacles had not been removed to create lanes for the advance. The 9th Corps' engineers, who surely should have had a prominent role in the attack, had not been assigned any specific tasks. Overall, the inquiry concluded that there was a 'want of a competent head at the scene of assault'.[46] Burnside had had a chequered career and survived a remarkable number of bungles and disasters, but the mismanaged Battle of the Crater put an end to his active career.

Colonel Wainwright spoke for many Army of Potomac veterans when he wrote: 'Never before have I felt that the Army of the Potomac was disgraced; failed it has frequently, and botches its commanding generals have made of more than one piece of work, but the army itself has always come out with honor.'[47]

As Grant observed in his *Memoirs*, the failure at the Crater prolonged the war by another nine months. It also gave the South one last chance to win independence.

Combat Assessment

Grant: Cold Harbor was the war's second, and last, assault that he wished he had never ordered. The concept of the Petersburg campaign shows a return of the strategically dynamic Grant. Tactically, he still exhibits a hands off attitude.

Lieutenants: A dismal chronicle of second-rate performances.

Staff: Shoddy staff work thwarts numerous opportunities.

Infantry: The once gallant infantry of the Army of the Potomac are no more.

Artillery: Now clear of the woods, fortifications prohibit an important role.

Cavalry: A mixed record of success and failure. Not yet clearly ascendant over their southern counterparts.

Engineers: The construction of the James River bridge is a masterpiece.

COLD HARBOR,[48] 3-12 JUNE 1864
The Union Army: Lieutenant General Ulysses S. Grant
(as of 1 June 1864)

ARMY OF THE POTOMAC: Major General George G. Meade

PROVOST GUARD:
Brigadier General Marsena R. Patrick
1st Massachusetts Cavalry, Cos. C
    and D
80th New York Infantry (20th militia)
3d Pennsylvania Cavalry
68th Pennsylvania Infantry
114th Pennsylvania Infantry
VOLUNTEER ENGINEER BRIGADE:
Brigadier General Henry W. Benham
50th New York
Battalion US Engineers

GUARDS AND ORDERLIES:
Oneida (New York) Cavalry

SECOND ARMY CORPS:
Major General Winfield S. Hancock
Escort: 1st Vermont Cavalry, Co. M

First Division:
Brigadier General Francis C. Barlow
FIRST BRIGADE:
Colonel Nelson A. Miles
26th Michigan

2d New York Artillery
61st New York
81st Pennsylvania
140th Pennsylvania
183d Pennsylvania
SECOND BRIGADE:
Colonel Richard Byrnes
28th Massachusetts
63d New York
69th New York
88th New York
116th Pennsylvania
THIRD BRIGADE:
Colonel Clinton D. MacDougall
39th New York
52d New York (with det. of 7th New
  York)
111th New York
125th New York
126th New York
FOURTH BRIGADE:
Colonel John R. Brooke
2d Delaware
7th New York Artillery
64th New York
66th New York
53d Pennsylvania
145th Pennsylvania
148th Pennsylvania

Second Division:
Brigadier General John Gibbon
PROVOST GUARD: 2d Co. Minnesota
  Sharpshooters
FIRST BRIGADE:
Colonel Henry Boyd McKeen
19th Maine
15th Massachusetts
19th Massachusetts
20th Massachusetts
1st Co. Andrew (Massachusetts)
  Sharpshooters
7th Michigan
42d New York
59th New York
82d New York (battalion)
184th Pennsylvania
36th Wisconsin
SECOND BRIGADE:
Brigadier General Joshua T. Owen
152d New York
69th Pennsylvania
71st Pennsylvania

72d Pennsylvania
106th Pennsylvania
THIRD BRIGADE:
Colonel Thomas A. Smyth
14th Connecticut
1st Delaware
14th Indiana
12th New Jersey
10th New York (battalion)
108th New York
4th Ohio
8th Ohio
7th West Virginia (battalion)
FOURTH BRIGADE:
Brigadier General Robert O. Tyler
8th New York Artillery
155th New York
164th New York
170th New York
182d New York (69th New York
  National Guard Artillery)

Third Division:
Major General David B. Birney
FIRST BRIGADE:
Colonel Thomas W. Egan
20th Indiana
3d Maine
40th New York
86th New York
124th New York
99th Pennsylvania
110th Pennsylvania
141st Pennsylvania
2d US Sharpshooters
SECOND BRIGADE:
Colonel Thomas R. Tannatt
4th Maine
17th Maine
1st Massachusetts Artillery
3d Michigan
5th Michigan
93d New York
57th Pennsylvania
63d Pennsylvania
105th Pennsylvania
1st US Sharpshooters
THIRD BRIGADE:
Brigadier General Gershom Mott
1st Maine Artillery
16th Massachusetts
5th New Jersey
6th New Jersey

7th New Jersey
8th New Jersey
11th New Jersey
115th Pennsylvania
FOURTH BRIGADE:
Colonel William R. Brewster
11th Massachusetts
70th New York
71st New York
73d New York
74th New York
120th New York (with three cos. 72d New York)
84th Pennsylvania
ARTILLERY BRIGADE:
Colonel John C. Tidball
Maine Light, 6th Batt.
Massachusetts Light, 10th Batt.
New Hampshire Light, 1st Batt.
2d New Jersey
1st New York Light, Batt. G
4th New York Heavy
New York Light, 11th Batt.
New York Light, 12th Batt.
1st Pennsylvania Light, Batt. F
1st Rhode Island Light, Batts. A and B
4th US, Batt. K
5th US, Batts. C and I

FIFTH ARMY CORPS:
Major General Gouverneur K. Warren
PROVOST GUARD: 12th New York (battalion)

First Division:
Brigadier General Charles Griffin
FIRST BRIGADE:
Brigadier General Romeyn B. Ayres
140th New York
146th New York
91st Pennsylvania
155th Pennsylvania
2d US (six cos.)
11th US (six cos.)
12th US (ten cos.)
14th US (1st Battalion)
17th US (eight cos.)
SECOND BRIGADE:
Colonel Jacob B. Sweitzer
9th Massachusetts
22d Massachusetts (with 2d Co. Sharpshooters)
32d Massachusetts

4th Michigan
62d Pennsylvania
THIRD BRIGADE:
Brigadier General Joseph J. Bartlett
20th Maine
18th Massachusetts
29th Massachusetts
1st Michigan
16th Michigan (with Brady's Co. Sharpshooters)
44th New York
83d Pennsylvania
118th Pennsylvania

Second Division:
Brigadier General Henry H. Lockwood
First Brigade: Colonel Peter Lyle
16th Maine
13th Massachusetts
39th Massachusetts
94th New York
104th New York
90th Pennsylvania
107th Pennsylvania
SECOND BRIGADE:
Colonel James L. Bates
12th Massachusetts
83d New York (9th Militia)
97th New York
11th Pennsylvania
88th Pennsylvania
THIRD BRIGADE:
Colonel Nathan T. Dushane
1st Maryland
4th Maryland
7th Maryland
8th Maryland
Purnell (Md.) Legion

Third Division: Brigadier General Samuel W. Crawford
VETERAN RESERVE BRIGADE: Major William R. Hartshorne
190th Pennsylvania
191st Pennsylvania
INDEPENDENT BRIGADE:
Colonel J. Howard Kitching
6th New York Artillery
15th New York Artillery, (1st and 3d Battalions)

Fourth Division:
Brigadier General Lysander Cutler

Provost Guard: 2d Wisconsin
FIRST BRIGADE:
Colonel William W. Robinson
7th Indiana
19th Indiana
24th Michigan
1st Battalion New York Sharpshooters
6th Wisconsin
7th Wisconsin
SECOND BRIGADE:
Colonel J. William Hofmann
3d Delaware
46th New York
76th New York
95th New York
147th New York
56th Pennsylvania
THIRD BRIGADE:
Colonel Edward S. Bragg
121st Pennsylvania
142d Pennsylvania
143d Pennsylvania
149th Pennsylvania
150th Pennsylvania
ARTILLERY BRIGADE:
Colonel Charles S. Wainwright
Massachusetts Light, 3d Batt.
Massachusetts Light, 5th Batt.
Massachusetts Light, 9th Batt.
1st New York Light, Batt. B
1st New York Light, Batt. C
1st New York Light, Batt. D
1st New York Light, Batts. E and L
1st New York Light, Batt. H
New York Lt, 15th Batt.
1st Pennsylvania Light, Batt. B
4th US, Batt. B
5th US, Batt. D

SIXTH ARMY CORPS:
Major General Horatio G. Wright
Escort: 8th Pennsylvania Cavalry, Co. A

First Division:
Brigadier General David A. Russell
FIRST BRIGADE: Colonel William H.
    Penrose
1st New Jersey
2d New Jersey
3d New Jersey
4th New Jersey
10th New Jersey
15th New Jersey

SECOND BRIGADE:
Colonel Emory Upton
2d Connecticut Artillery
5th Maine
121st New York
95th Pennsylvania
96th Pennsylvania
THIRD BRIGADE:
Brigadier General Henry L. Eustis
6th Maine
49th Pennsylvania
119th Pennsylvania
5th Wisconsin
FOURTH BRIGADE:
Colonel Nelson Cross
65th New York
67th New York
122d New York
23d Pennsylvania
82d Pennsylvania

Second Division:
Brigadier General Thomas H. Neill
FIRST BRIGADE: Brigadier General
    Frank Wheaton
62d New York
93d Pennsylvania
98th Pennsylvania
102d Pennsylvania
139th Pennsylvania
SECOND BRIGADE:
Brigadier General Lewis A. Grant
2d Vermont
3d Vermont
4th Vermont
5th Vermont
6th Vermont
11th Vermont (1st Heavy Artillery)
THIRD BRIGADE:
Colonel Daniel D. Bidwell
7th Maine
43d New York
49th New York
77th New York
61st Pennsylvania
FOURTH BRIGADE:
Colonel Oliver Edwards
7th Massachusetts
10th Massachusetts
37th Massachusetts
2d Rhode Island
Third Division:
Brigadier General James B. Ricketts

FIRST BRIGADE:
Colonel William S. Truex
14th New Jersey
106th New York
151st New York
87th Pennsylvania
10th Vermont
SECOND BRIGADE:
Colonel Benjamin F. Smith
6th Maryland
9th New York Artillery (1st and 3d
    Battalions)
110th Ohio
122d Ohio
126th Ohio
67th Pennsylvania
138th Pennsylvania
ARTILLERY BRIGADE:
Colonel Charles H. Tompkins
Maine Light, 4th Batt.
Maine Light, 5th Batt.
Massachusetts Light, 1st Batt.
1st New Jersey Light
New York Light, 1st Batt.
New York Light, 3d Batt.
9th New York Heavy, 2d Battalion
1st Ohio Light, Batt. H
1st RI Light, Batt. C
1st RI Light, Batt. E
1st RI Light, Batt. G
5th US, Batt. E
5th US, Batt. M

NINTH ARMY CORPS:
Major General Ambrose E. Burnside
Provost Guard: 8th US Infantry

First Division:
Major General Thomas L. Crittenden
FIRST BRIGADE:
Brigadier General James H. Ledlie
56th Massachusetts
57th Massachusetts
59th Massachusetts
4th US
10th US
SECOND BRIGADE:
olonel Joseph M. Sudsburg
3d Maryland
21st Massachusetts
100th Pennsylvania
PROVISIONAL BRIGADE:
Colonel Elisha G. Marshall

2d New York Mounted Rifles (dis-
    mounted)
14th New York Artillery
24th New York Cavalry (dismounted)
2d Pennsylvania Provisional Artillery
ACTING ENGINEERS:
35th Massachusetts
ARTILLERY:
Maine Light, 3d Batt.
Massachusetts Light, 14th Batt.

Second Division:
Brigadier General Robert B. Potter
FIRST BRIGADE: Colonel John I. Curtin
36th Massachusetts
58th Massachusetts
45th Pennsylvania
48th Pennsylvania
7th Rhode Island
SECOND BRIGADE:
Colonel Simon G. Griffin
2d Maryland
31st Maine
32d Maine
6th New Hampshire
9th New Hampshire
11th New Hampshire
17th Vermont
ACTING ENGINEERS:
51st New York
ARTILLERY:
Massachusetts Light, 11th Batt.
New York Light, 19th Batt.

Third Division:
Brigadier General Orlando B. Willcox
FIRST BRIGADE:
Colonel John F. Hartranft
2d Michigan
8th Michigan
27th Michigan (with 1st and 2d Co.
    Sharpshooters)
109th New York
51st Pennsylvania
SECOND BRIGADE:
Colonel Benjamin C. Christ
1st Michigan Sharpshooters
20th Michigan
60th Ohio (with 9th and 10th Co.
    Sharpshooters)
50th Pennsylvania
ACTING ENGINEERS:
17th Michigan

ARTILLERY:
Maine Light, 7th Batt.
New York Light, 34th Batt.

Fourth Division:
Brigadier General Edward Ferrero
FIRST BRIGADE:
Colonel Joshua K. Sigfried
27th US Colored Troops (USCT)
30th USCT
39th USCT
43d USCT
SECOND BRIGADE:
Colonel Henry G. Thomas
19th USCT
23d USCT
31st USCT
ARTILLERY:
Pennsylvania, Co. D
3d Vermont
RESERVE ARTILLERY:
Captain John Edwards, Jr.
27th New York
1st Rhode Island, Batt. D
1st Rhode Island, Batt. H
2d US, Batt. E

CAVALRY CORPS:
Major General Philip H. Sheridan
Escort: 6th US

First Division:
Brigadier General Alfred T. A. Torbert
FIRST BRIGADE:
Brigadier General George A. Custer
1st Michigan
5th Michigan
6th Michigan
7th Michigan
SECOND BRIGADE:
Colonel Thomas C. Devin
4th New York
6th New York
9th New York
17th Pennsylvania
RESERVE BRIGADE:
Brigadier General Wesley Merritt
19th New York (1st Dragoons)
6th Pennsylvania
1st US
2d US
5th US

Second Division:
Brigadier General David McM. Gregg
FIRST BRIGADE:
Brigadier General Henry E. Davies, Jr.
1st Massachusetts
1st New Jersey
10th New York
6th Ohio
1st Pennsylvania
SECOND BRIGADE:
Colonel J. Irvin Gregg
1st Maine
2d Pennsylvania
4th Pennsylvania
8th Pennsylvania
13th Pennsylvania
16th Pennsylvania

Third Division:
Brigadier General James H. Wilson
Escort: 8th Illinois (det.)
FIRST BRIGADE:
Colonel John B. McIntosh
1st Connecticut
3d New Jersey
2d New York
5th New York
2d Ohio
18th Pennsylvania
SECOND BRIGADE:
Colonel George H. Chapman
3d Indiana
8th New York
1st Vermont
FIRST BRIGADE HORSE ARTILLERY:
Captain James M. Robertson
New York Light, 6th Batt.
2d US, Batts. B and L
2d US, Batt. D
2d US, Batt. M
4th US, Batt. A
4th US, Batts. C and E

Artillery:
Brigadier General Henry J. Hunt
HORSE ARTILLERY:
SECOND BRIGADE:
Captain Dunbar R. Ransom
1st US, Batts. E and G
1st US, Batts. H and I
1st US, Batt. K
2d US, Batt. A
2d US, Batt. G

3d US, Batts. C, F, K
ARTILLERY PARK: 15th New York (2d
    Battalion)

EIGHTEENTH ARMY CORPS:
Major General William F. Smith

First Division: Brigadier General
    William T. H. Brooks
FIRST BRIGADE:
Brigadier General Gilman Marston
81st New York
96th New York
98th New York
139th New York
SECOND BRIGADE:
Brigadier General Hiram Burnham
8th Connecticut
10th New Hampshire
13th New Hampshire
118th New York
THIRD BRIGADE: Colonel Guy V. Henry
21st Connecticut
40th Massachusetts
92d New York
58th Pennsylvania
188th Pennsylvania

Second Division:
Brigadier General John H. Martindale
FIRST BRIGADE:
Brigadier General George J. Stannard
23d Massachusetts
25th Massachusetts
27th Massachusetts
9th New Jersey

89th New York
55th Pennsylvania
SECOND BRIGADE:
Colonel Griffin A. Stedman
11th Connecticut
8th Maine
2d New Hampshire
12th New Hampshire
148th New York

Third Division:
Brigadier General Charles Devens, Jr.
FIRST BRIGADE:
Colonel William B. Barton
47th New York
48th New York
115th New York
76th Pennsylvania
SECOND BRIGADE:
Colonel Jeremiah C. Drake
13th Indiana
9th Maine
112th New York
169th New York
THIRD BRIGADE:
Brigadier General Adelbert Ames
4th New Hampshire
3d New York
117th New York
142d New York
97th Pennsylvania
ARTILLERY BRIGADE:
Captain Samuel S. Elder
1st US, Batt. B
4th US, Batt. L
5th US, Batt. A

1 James I. Robertson, ed., *The Civil War Letters of General Robert McAllister*, (New Brunswick, NJ: Rutgers University Press, 1965), p. 427.
2 For a moving description of this man, see Sylvanus Cadwallader, *Three Years With Grant*, (New York: ALfred A. Knopf, 1956), pp. 224-225.
3 Allan Nevins, ed., *A Diary of Battle: The Personal Journals of Colonel Charles S. Wainwright, 1861-1865*, (New York: Harcourt, Brace & World, 1962), p. 386.
4 Nevins, *A Diary of Battle*, p. 408.
5 Stephen Minot Weld, *War Diary and Letters of Stephen Minot Weld, 1861-1865*, (Boston: Massachusetts Historical Society, 1979), p. 302.
6 Cadwallader, p. 215.
7 Richard Wheeler, *On Fields of Fury. From the Wilderness to the Crater: An Eyewitness History*, (New York: Harper Collins Publishers, 1991), p. 259.
8 Horace Porter, *Campaigning with Grant* (New York: The Century Co., 1897), p. 177.
9 Porter, pp. 176-177.
10 Peter S. Michie, *The Life and Letters of Emory Upton*, (New York: Arno Press, 1979), pp. 108-109.
11 Cited in Michael C. Adams, *Our Masters the Rebels: Speculations on Union Military Fail-*

ure in the East, 1861-1865, (Cambridge, MA: Harvard University Press, 1978), p. 172.

12 Quoted in Adams, p. 171.

13 *Civil War Letters of General Robert McAllister*, p. 437.

14 Gary W. Gallagher, ed., *Fighting for the Confederacy: The Personal Recollections of General Edward Porter Alexander*, (Chapel Hill: University of North Carolina Press, 1989), p. 373. He is specifically referring to Spotsylvania, but the description applies equally to Cold Harbor.

15 *Personal Recollections of General Edward Porter Alexander*, p. 412.

16 Wheeler, *On Fields of Fury*, p. 236.

17 Charles Carleton Coffin, *The Boys of '61*, (Boston: Dana Estes & Co., 1896), p. 305.

18 Nevins, *A Diary of Battle*, p. 413.

19 Nevins, *A Diary of Battle*, p. 415.

20 Coffin, *The Boys of '61*, p. 316.

21 Andrew A. Humphreys, *The Virginia Campaign of '64 and '65*, (New York: Charles Scribner's Sons, 1897), p. 217.

22 *Civil War Letters of General Robert McAllister*, pp. 443-444.

23 Horace H. Shaw, *The First Maine Heavy Artillery, 1892-1865*, (Portland, ME: 1903), p. 122.

24 *Civil War Letters of General Robert McAllister*, p. 445.

25 George R. Agassiz, ed., *Meade's Headquarters 1863-1865: Letters of Colonel Theodore Lyman from the Wilderness to Appomattox*, (Boston: Massachusetts Historical Society, 1922), p. 168.

26 In *A Diary of Battle*, p. 425, Wainwright, observes, "I cannot say that our men went in well."

27 Agassiz, *Meade's Headquarters*, p. 170.

28 Rufus R. Dawes, *Service With the Sixth Wisconsin Volunteers*, (Madison: State Historical Society of Wisconsin, 1962), pp. 290-291.

29 See John Gibbon, *Personal Recollections of the Civil War*, (Dayton: Morningside Bookshop, 1978), p. 229.

30 *A Diary of Battle*, p. 425.

31 *A Diary of Battle*, p. 471.

32 James Harrison Wilson, *Under the Old Flag*, vol. 1 (New York: D. Appleton and Co., 1912), p. 400.

33 *Life and Letters of Emory Upton*, pp. 123-124.

34 *Civil War Letters of General Robert McAllister*, p. 445.

35 Augustus Meyers, *Ten Years in the Ranks, U.S. Army*, (New York: The Stirling Press, 1914), p. 320.

36 A.L. Long, ed., *Memoirs of Robert E. Lee*, (Secaucus, NJ: Blue and Grey Press, 1983), p. 658.

37 Thomas Lawrence Connelly and Archer Jones, *The Politics of Command: Factions and Ideas in Confederate Strategy*, (Baton Rouge: Louisiana State University Press, 1973), p. 181.

38 *A Diary of Battle*, p. 441.

39 Dawes, *Sixth Wisconsin*, p. 292.

40 Coffin, *The Boys of '61*, p. 324.

41 *Civil War Letters of General Robert McAllister*, p. 477.

42 Agassiz, *Meade's Headquarters*, p. 172.

43 Coffin, *The Boys of '61*, p. 341.

44 "Samuel H. Beckwith: "Grant's Shadow," in John Y. Simon and David L. Wilson, eds., *Ulysses S. Grant: Essays, Documents*, (Carbondale IL: Southern Illinois University Press, 1981), p. 107.

45 "Samuel H. Beckwith: "Grant's Shadow," in *Ulysses S. Grant: Essays, Documents*, p. 108.

46 George Meade, *The Life and Letters of George Gordon Meade*, vol. 2 (New York: Charles Scribner's Sons, 1913), Appendix T, p. 347.

47 *A Diary of Battle*, p. 443.

48 *Battles & Leaders of the Civil War*, vol. 4, pp. 185-187.

A Regiment on Campaign

In the autumn of 1863 volunteer enlistments throughout the North continued to dwindle, and this was a source of great anxiety for the Lincoln Administration. More clearly than most, Lincoln saw that the war could not be won without a great deal of additional bloody fighting and he was concerned as to how to find the manpower. The institution of the national draft, which allowed the rich to avoid service by hiring substitutes, had engendered even greater resentment among a war-weary people. The city of Fitchburg, Massachusetts, was typical. It had contributed a large number of enthusiastic men back in 1861. By the end of 1863 few could be found who would willingly join the army. The draft quota called for 241 men from Fitchburg. Only four entered the service. In addition to the usual exemptions, 181 townsmen received certificates from the town's obliging physician, exempting them on the basis of physical disabilities. Fitchburg was scarcely a fertile recruiting ground for the new 57th Massachusetts Volunteers.

To encourage recruits, the town paid a $100 bounty to new enlistees. Added to the Federal $300 and the state's $325 bounty, this made an attractive sum. Then, for two solid weeks the town hall featured recruiting meetings complete with patriotic speeches, music, and suchlike. By the end of February Fitchburg had raised its quota, men who would become Company F. Each recruit received his bounty, one greatcoat, one nine-button dress frock-coat, one four-button sack coat, a pair of infantry trousers, forage cap, and one woollen and one rubber blanket. Thus equipped, they were sent to Camp John E. Wool at nearby Worcester to learn how to be

soldiers. One of the reasons why military service had become so unappealing became immediately apparent when the recruits had their first sight of their quarters: large, company-sized barracks built from rough green pine which had split and cracked so that gaping holes gave little protection from the cold New England winter.

The 1,038 officers and men who served in the 57th Massachusetts were a typical cross-section of a New England regiment. Fewer than 50 per cent were native Massachusetts men. The remainder had come from eighteen states and thirteen foreign countries. One in ten was a Canadian. About one in five was Irish. Even in this, one of the more industrialized parts of the country, most of the men had been farmers. The second most common occupation had been boot- and shoe-making. They ranged in age from 15 to 45, most being in their mid-20s. Because the bounty had been the major factor in luring them into service, the regiment had more pickpockets, thieves, scoundrels and cowards than had been the case when the region sent off soldiers to war in 1861. Nominally, the 57th was to be a 'Veteran Volunteer' unit composed of a plurality of experienced soldiers. In fact, only about 20 per cent of its numbers were veterans and most of these were corporals and sergeants.

At Camp Wool the men received the rest of their equipment: two gray or blue flannel shirts, two sets of flannel long underwear, the unpopular Hardee hat, and, on 5 March, the model 1863 Springfield .58 calibre rifled musket made in the nearby Springfield Arsenal. In time, Company K, which had been designated a sharpshooter company, would receive the Spencer magazine rifle. Everyone was issued with the standard leather accoutrements – waist belt with brass buckle, cap box, cartridge box with brass plate, shoulder-strap with brass eagle, triangular bayonet and scabbard, haversack, wool-covered tin canteen, and a black canvas knapsack bearing the stencilled legend in 2-inch lettering: '57 MVM' (57th Massachusetts Volunteer Militia).

Although the war had been going on for three years, the 57th practised a drill that was little changed from that in use at the beginning. Lessons learned on countless bloody battlefields had made no impact on the parade ground. Squad drill (the school of the soldier) for one hour and a half every morning and company drill (the school of the company) for two hours every afternoon was performed according to Casey's *System of Infantry Tactics* whereby the recruits were taught to stand erect, dress ranks, salute, and march in various directions. They learned the formal procedure for loading their weapons (in nine separate movements) and a more rapid sequence in four movements. They practised firing while standing, kneeling or prone, and learned bayonet drill. What they did not learn was how to survive on the battlefield.

The regiment was fortunate to have a true combat veteran for colonel. William Francis Bartlett, a Boston blue-blood and graduate of Harvard College, had entered the service as a captain in 1861. He had seen action at Ball's Bluff in the autumn of 1861 and went on the Peninsula campaign in the spring of 1862. At Yorktown he had received a serious leg wound that necessitated amputation. Fitted with a cork leg, he returned to service at Port Hudson on the Mississippi, where he was wounded twice more. Having recovered, the state governor offered him command of the 57th Massachusetts.

On 16 April, while Meade and Grant were perfecting the pending crossing of the Rapidan River, the men received their bounty money and the news that they would be leaving for the front in two days' time. An enormous wave of desertion occurred led by those professional bounty jumpers; men who joined under an alias, received the bounty, deserted, enlisted and repeated the process. In two days 100 men deserted, almost 10 per cent of the regiment. The remainder travelled by rail and ship to Annapolis, Maryland, to become part of Ambrose Burnside's IX Corps. The regiment joined three veteran units – the 35th Massachusetts and the 4th and 10th United States Regular Infantry Regiments - and two new Massachusetts units to compose Brigadier General Thomas G. Stevenson's 1st Brigade, 1st Division.

At Annapolis the men exchanged their dress uniforms – the Hardee hats and nine-button frock-coats – for shelter tent halves and other equipment including the promised Spencer repeaters for the sharpshooter company. At 4 a.m. on Saturday, 23 April, the entire corps set off for the front. Their march looked very similar to the march of the men who went to Bull Run. In poor condition, the overburdened men quickly became fatigued, straggled badly and began discarding equipment. Each night's camp featured a steady trickle of desertions, each morning's roll call saw increasing numbers of men reporting sick. Unknown to the men, their colonel wrote in his diary that his regiment '... was in no condition to take into action'.[1] A bit belatedly, Bartlett realized that his men had received very little battalion and regimental drill. None the less, on 5 May they heard for the first time the sounds of battle where Grant's army had entered the Wilderness, and on the 6th they participated in Burnside's assault against the centre of Lee's army.

Had Burnside launched his attack in a timely fashion, Grant would have achieved a great victory because there was a large gap in Lee's line just where he was supposed to strike. Delayed for a variety of reasons – not least of which being Grant's poor command and control arrangements whereby IX Corps was retained as an independent command and the consequent problems of issuing orders smoothly and having them obeyed promptly – by the time Burnside advanced he found himself confronting The Army of Northern Virginia's veterans head on. The 548 frightened soldiers of the 57th Massachusetts charged as they had been taught. The veterans who served as file closers kept them in close ranks, the men standing erect with fixed bayonets. They strode forward over the ranks of a prone regiment of Yankee veterans who told them to lie down or they would get their heads shot off. Led by their colonel on his horse, the three standard-bearers, one for each of the national Colour, state flag, and IX Corps Colour, and the Colour guard, they advanced 'in perfect line' into the dense woods.[2] Here they were slaughtered.

In about one hour's fighting the 57th Massachusetts lost 262 of their men. This total included 54 men killed outright, 29 mortally wounded, ten missing and presumably killed, 156 wounded including twenty who were left behind and captured, and another twelve unwounded men who were captured. Included in the casualties were nearly 60 per cent of Fitchburg's Company F. The regiment's casualties included their colonel who received a glancing head wound.

On 12 May the regiment, now with a strength of 333 officers and men, delivered a spirited charge against the right side of the Confederate breastworks at Spotsylvania to support Hancock's attack against the Bloody Angle. They lost twelve killed, five mortally wounded, 56 wounded, one missing and four men taken prisoner.

On 18 May the regiment, now with a strength of about 250 officers and men, was in the second wave of another assault against the enemy works. This time they merely advanced to the line of abatis and lost three killed, six mortally wounded, thirteen wounded and one prisoner.

In twelve days, the 57th Massachusetts had lost about two-thirds of their strength. The only result of significance to the survivors was that now the brigade's other veteran units treated them like fellow soldiers instead of contemptible bounty men.

Next day, one of the regiment's wounded soldiers wrote home and concluded his letter, 'may you never see the sights I have seen for the last week'.[3]

The regiment fought along the North Anna River, entering the fight with 237 men and losing 38 of them. It sent 184 survivors into an assault at Petersburg on 17 June and lost 52 more. Now with a mere 98 men, the 57th Massachusetts went into action at the Crater, losing 51 men, more than half their strength. Forty-five survivors fought at the Weldon Railroad where fifteen became casualties. Reinforced to 93 men, nine of them fell at Poplar Grove Church on 30 September. On the same field eight days later, the regiment went in with 90 men and suffered fourteen casualties.

Strengthened to 212 men for the 1865 campaign, and armed with Spencer breech-loaders, the regiment fought at Fort Stedman on 25 March where 93 men became casualties. A total of eleven men survived to fight in every one of the regiment's battles.

1   Warren Wilkinson, *Mother, May You Never See the sights I have seen: the Fifty-Seventh Massechusetts Veteran Volunteers in the Army of the Potomac, 1864–1865* (New York: Harper & Row, 1990), p. 70.
2   Wilkinson, p.73.
3   Wilkinson, p.121.

14
To Win a War

PART 1. AUTUMN OF FUTILITY

The autumn of 1864 saw the terrible attrition claim the army's best known fighting general, Winfield Scott Hancock. He and his corps had spearheaded numerous efforts to work around Lee's flank and cut his communications. The results had been decidedly unhappy for 'Hancock the superb'. Back on 22 June, along Hatcher's Run, one of Lee's aggressive generals, William 'Little Billy' Mahone, had discovered a gap between Hancock's 2d Corps and the adjacent unit. Mahone had promptly exploited this Union bungle with a howling counter-attack that captured 1,600 prisoners, four artillery pieces, and eight stands of Colours. One yankee officer declared it the corps' most humiliating experience since its formation.

What was happening to the 2d Corps was happening army wide. Consistently poor fighting in the Army of the Potomac compelled Meade's Adjutant General to order that any battery or regiment that lost its Colour through battlefield misconduct would not receive a replacement Colour until it retrieved its 'tarnished honor.'[1] The loss of veterans through casualties and expiration of terms of service depleted what was left of the 2d Corps' fighting spirit. A surgeon in the 105th Pennsylvania wrote, 'some fearful fatality has pursued all our Senior Officers in this Campaign. We have lost our Col., Major, Lieut. Col., five Senior Captains and a proportionable amount Lieuts. and privates. It has been a splendid Regt. – but I fear its days of glorious deeds have passed.'[2] The loss of enthusiasm among the surviving veterans and the poor quality of the replacements all combined to reduce the once mighty Army of the Potomac to a pale shadow of its former self. And General Hancock could barely stand the humiliation.

Worse was to follow. Towards the end of August, Hancock led his corps around Lee's flank again with the objective of destroying the Weldon Railroad. For two days his men happily tore up rails. Then, on 25 August, a vicious Confederate assault from troops commanded by A. P. Hill and Wade Hampton surprised and sent the corps reeling. Caught by fire front and rear, Gibbon's division 'seemed suddenly to go to pieces'.[3] At a cost of 720 casualties, the rebels inflicted losses amounting to 2,742 men, nineteen cannon and twelve stands of Colours. Of the Federal losses, 2,150 were captured, a figure underscoring the fact that the corps had not fought well. It was another terribly depressing experience. Hancock slumped over an aide's shoulder and cried out, 'I pray God I may never leave this field!'[4] In the event, Hancock did leave the field and shortly afterwards left the army for good. He pleaded incapacity because of an old wound, and indeed fragments of bone from his Gettysburg wound had worked to the surface to cause intense suffering. But the surpassing wound was to his pride.

Many officers in the army censured Grant for his repetitive and unimaginative flanking tactics. Two years earlier, such repeated failures would have prompted popular and political outcry, but by 1864, so firmly had the Lincoln administration seized control of the news – a typical northern newspaper described the disaster of 25 August as 'Another great victory by Gen. Hancock' – and so inured had the public become to the war's casualties, that few people could be bothered to complain.[5]

Much had changed in the relationship between the military and the press since the war had begun. Before the war, newspapers concentrated on local news and ignored most events elsewhere. Their front pages featured advertisements to the extent that even local news was relegated to the inside pages. Then came the war, the biggest thing that had ever happened in the lives of most Americans. Battle accounts appeared on the front page, elbowing aside the advertisements, and were written in a lively style complete with headlines. People avidly digested the latest reports from the field. To meet this demand, publishers hired a string of correspondents and sent them into the field to follow the armies. Because competition among reporters was quite cutthroat, the correspondent who could provide the latest, most accurate information had a great advantage when it came to demanding payment from tight-fisted editors. Thus, conflict between reporters, who cited the prerogative of 'freedom of the press', and generals, who demanded military security, was inevitable.

In fact, generals on both sides relied heavily upon newspapers for intelligence about their enemy's plans. In August 1861, the Lincoln administration revived an article from the military code of 1806 that promised 'death or other such punishment' for anyone convicted of corresponding with or providing intelligence for the enemy. As signed by Lincoln, General Order 67 added to the 1806 list of violations by stating that 'all correspondence and communication, verbally, or by writing, printing, or telegraphing' about military activities had to be approved by the field general in command. This Draconian order did not work, of course.

The simplest way for correspondents to outmanoeuvre military censorship was by befriending high-ranking officers who were not averse to a surreptitious glass of fine brandy together with an approving mention of their names in the papers. When military authorities tried to limit reporters' access to the telegraphs, the correspondents established a very efficient courier line to carry their dispatches to the nearest telegraph office outside military control. When banned altogether from an army, reporters wore disguises so that they could accompany the troops, or bribed their way past the guards. Throughout the war, Grant's armies suffered from serious and frequent breaches of security. In 1864, for example, a northern newspaper published the number of sick in the Army of the Potomac and mentioned the proportion this represented of total army strength. Within days Lee had this paper and by simple arithmetic calculated accurately his opponent's strength.

Newspapers also had a impact on both army and public morale. Then as now, soldiers liked to read about their battles and particularly sought out any reference to their own units. Knowing that promotion required political connections, valorous officers eagerly scanned their local papers to see if their conduct had received favorable notice. Although Grant himself cared very little about a favorable press, when dispatches from Fort Donelson informed the public that his initials stood for 'Unconditional Surrender Grant', it went a long way towards securing his future. Likewise, when a reporter picked up a phrase in his dispatch to Washington from the field at Spotsylvania saying that he proposed to 'fight it out if it took all summer' it went far towards maintaining public morale in the face of heavy casualties.

During the war, no one fell more foul of the press than Grant's great lieutenant, William T. Sherman. On 29 December 1862, Sherman ordered the ill-conceived assault against the bluffs north of Vicksburg. Having already acquired a considerable distaste for 'the gentlemen of the press', he had barred all reporters from his expedition and prohibited the sending of any dispatch until he had censored it. When he realized that reporters were ignoring these orders, he had his staffers search the mailbags for letters from newspaper correspondents. The press retaliated twenty days later when the *New York Herald* described Sherman's battle and told its readers: 'Insanity and inefficiency have brought their result: let us have them no more.' The *New York Times* added that had Sherman and his officers spent more time preparing for the campaign and less time 'bullying correspondents, overhauling mailbags, and prying into private correspondence', the disgraceful assault would not have taken place.[6]

This, of course, was too much for the sour-tempered Sherman. He had an offending reporter named Thomas Knox of the *New York Herald* arrested and court-martialled on three counts: providing intelligence to the enemy; violation of General Order 67 (meaning that Knox would be tried as a spy); and wilfully disobeying Sherman's orders regarding the transmission of reports. Sherman proposed only one witness against the reporter, himself! During the ensuing trial, Knox was found not guilty of the first two charges and guilty, although not criminally culpable, of the third charge. Thus Sherman was able to banish Knox from the theatre. Sherman tried to make the other two charges stick and even appealed to Grant, explaining that freedom of the press 'has lost us millions of money, thousands of lives, and will continue to defeat us to the end of time, unless some remedy be devised'.[7]

Sherman's partial triumph over Knox validated a principle that was to continue into modern times. Namely, a correspondent could not work in the field without permission from the commanding general. In later wars this would lead to formal press accreditation. For the immediate future, Sherman's efforts put a scare into reporters, and for the remainder of the war those who followed his army were very circumspect in what they wrote. Many Union generals achieved a favourable press by toadying to newspaper correspondents. Sherman reached the same end in his own unique style.

During the 1864 campaign in Virginia, General Meade too ran into conflict with the press, in particular with *New York Times* correspondent William Swinton (after the war he wrote a popular history of the Army of the Potomac). Swinton was an unsavoury fellow who lurked about headquarters and several times had to be ejected by Grant's staff when he tried to eavesdrop on important secret discussions. After Meade expelled Swinton from the army, all the correspondents joined in a conspiracy of silence. Henceforth, when describing the battles in Virginia, they always omitted to mention Meade's name. This greatly bothered the vain, thin-skinned Meade and left the public ignorant of the fact that he had had anything to do with the Virginia campaign.

The war was to herald several important changes regarding the role of the press in American life. The demand for war news promoted mechanical innovation involving stereotyping processes to mould type cylinders, and steam-powered presses which increased output. After the war publishers had to find new topics to justify the hefty capital investments that had been made in wartime. Ahead lay a future of lurid journalism dedicated to crime, corruption, scandal and sin, topics deemed sufficiently entertaining to replace war news. Lastly, prior to the conflict there had been no Sunday papers, but because there was no pause in the fighting on Sundays, people had demanded newspapers seven days a week. So among many consequences flowing from the war came a new national institution — the regular Sunday newspaper.

The South's last hope for independence hinged on the autumn presidential election in the North. With his armies stalemated before Richmond and Atlanta, no less a sage politician than Abraham Lincoln predicted that he would fail to be re-elected. To ensure this result the Democratic Party decided to base its campaign on an appeal to the nation's war weariness. It nominated General George B. McClellan, in large part because of his reputed continued popularity among the soldiers. Indeed, McClellan had been the parent figure of the Army of the Potomac during its crucial formative days. Although the rank and file had lionized him in 1862, their attitudes had changed by 1864. Despite the dreadful losses incurred during the advance to the Petersburg lines, most soldiers did not welcome news of McClellan's nomination.

In large measure this attitude stemmed from the fact that the army had begun to appreciate the fact that under Grant they had accomplished something important. Common soldiers had long been more interested in results rather than appearances, and the obvious result of Grant's manoeuvres was that they had advanced to the gates of the enemy capital. There they had pinned Lee and his army to a defensive line. They perceived that under Grant's leadership they would eventually win. To elect McClellan would be to throw all of this away. Their officers had always been more sceptical of Grant's talents. Many had resented the slovenly westerner and still considered themselves McClellan men. Yet they too were learning to accept Grant. On 2 September a keen-eyed officer wrote to his family: 'Grant, too, is rising daily in the opinion of the officers who were ill-affected toward him when he took command.'[8]

Indeed, during army-wide electioneering one political observer said that it appeared the men were six to one in favour of Lincoln. Only recent immigrants seemed to support the democratic candidate, an unsurprising finding given that their introduction to the United States was to be recruited for a civil war as soon as they came ashore. In the 1860s, however, men who left their state lost their vote. This meant that soldiers could not participate in the coming election. Several states rectified this shortcoming by empowering soldiers to vote in the field. Other states such as New Jersey, by virtue of heavy lobbying by local Democrats, continued to deny soldiers the vote. To get around this obstacle, Union armies released many men on furlough and sick leave so that they could return home to vote.

In the weeks before the election, Sheridan's victories in the Shenandoah Valley, Farragut's victory at Mobile Bay, and Sherman's timely capture of Atlanta convinced a healthy majority of voters that victory was near. Accordingly they re-elected Lincoln. In the Army of the Potomac, the soldiers voted in favour of Lincoln by about a four to one ratio. Notably, 75 per cent of the McClellan voters were in Pennsylvania regiments.

PART 2. WINTER QUARTERS

Slowly a subtle change in army management had taken place. Whereas at the start of the campaign, Grant had only drafted broad instructions and left most details up to Meade, by October he was personally directing the action, leaving Meade with little to do. Taking advantage of the fact that entrenchments worked both ways, Grant left a mere 14,000 men in the line facing Petersburg and sent 43,000 others to cut the plank road and the Southside Railroad, two vital arteries supplying Lee's army. To ensure success he accompanied them. It was the first time in the East that he faced heavy personal risk. On 27 October 1864 he remained mounted throughout the day under heavy shellfire while issuing orders. His presence did not help.

In a textbook example of Army of the Potomac mismanagement, two wings of the advance became lost in swampy, timbered country. Although separated by a mere mile, these wings failed to link up. The Confederates had no trouble finding the gap and delivered a punishing assault. Ruefully, a Union officer reflected, 'It is touching a tiger's cubs to get on that road.'[9]

It was the familiar problem of trying to maintain order while manoeuvring in thick woodland. Theodore Lyman explained that the divisions involved '... lost connection, they cannot cover the ground designated [by the higher command], their wing is in the air, their skirmish line has lost its direction'.[10] Meade came up to try to rearrange the lines and was unable to get anything accomplished beyond losing his temper. Divisional generals had to use compasses to align their command and hours had elapsed before they were finally ready. When the Union counter-attack went in, it struck the rebels already secure behind fieldworks. The result was another repulse.

Following one of the bungled attempts to cut the Weldon Railroad, Union solders had an opportunity to comb the field for discarded weapons. They retrieved about 1,500 rifles, muskets and carbines, half of which had been left by the opposition. A soldier assigned to the ordnance depot at the army's great base at City Point, described what he found while making an inventory:

'I found that the ram-rods were missing from a considerable number of discharged guns, and a greater number had failed to be discharged on account of defective caps, or a befouled nipple. Some were doubly charged, and an occasional one had three, or even four, cartridges in the barrel, indicating that the soldier continued to load without noticing that his piece had not been discharged. Others were bursted at the muzzle, showing that the tompion had not been removed before firing ... It has been said that it takes a man's weight in lead for every soldier killed in battle. I am inclined to almost believe that, from my own observations [he had previously served in a line regiment] and from the amount of ammunition I knew to be expended on the battlefield of the Weldon Railroad, where I noticed innumerable bullet marks on trees standing on level ground, at height that could only endanger birds.'[11]

Even though Civil War battles now involved mostly veteran troops, the same behaviour as was exhibited early in the war by green troops persisted. In the confusion and terror of combat many soldiers were still failing to load their weapons properly, and a greater number were continuing to fire too high.

But sufficient enemy soldiers had fired accurately enough to inflict enormous losses on the Army of the Potomac. Before Grant's arrival, during the period April 1862 to December 1863, it had lost about 100,000 men. The 1864 campaign from May to December had cost 90,000 more. The bulk of these casualties were sustained by enthusiastic volunteers, but few of these were left, their places having been taken by poorly motivated recruits, generally either recent immigrants or hired substitutes lured by a bounty paid on signing up. After receiving the money many deserted. The 11th New Jersey Regiment, once a proud fighting regiment, lost 341 deserters in the summer and autumn of 1864. It was demoralizing for the remaining stalwart veterans to know that fresh recruits received hefty bounties and yet could not be relied upon in combat. Meade commented that in Lincoln's July call for another 500,000 men, only 120,000 showed up. Of these, 60,000 actually joined the field armies, while the Army of the Potomac received a mere 15,000, most of whom were foreigners who had a tendency to desert.

After repeated failures to turn Lee's flank, the army began settling in to winter quarters. By now Union troops had rendered their position virtually impregnable. The physical aspects of their lines had grown in sophistication. Most sectors featured a layered defence beginning with thick abatis linked with wire strung six inches off the ground. Behind these obstacles stood fortified outposts to provide warning of any attack. Then came multiple trenchlines with firesteps and headlogs. Regular earthen traverses offered protection from enfilade fire and could seal off any sector in the event of an enemy penetration. Connecting communication trenches enabled troops to move rapidly while completely protected. The reserve troops were housed in bombproof shelters. The artillery had pre-registered killing zones with interlocking fields of fire. The generals had virtually instantaneous communication with headquarters via the field telegraphs. The men practised defensive drill tactics to the extent that the well-trained regiments could respond to an alert, find their allotted positions – the works had signposts noting each company's sector – and man the firing step within two minutes.

There were intermittent flurries of action. Although the Confederates lacked the strength to challenge seriously the Union trenchline, occasionally they mounted what in the First World War would be called a trench raid. On the night of 5 November Confederate General Bushrod Johnson's division tried to capture a yankee picket line that had advanced a bit too close for comfort. In a well-prepared plan, the initial surprise attack overran about 40 rifle pits. The second Confederate wave carried picks and shovels and a large cross-cut saw with which it was intended to re-align the captured breastworks so as to face the Union line. But a prompt Union counter-attack foiled the endeavour at the cost of 60 casualties.

Thanksgiving Dinner inside the Federal lines was a time of plenty. The army itself provided a basic supper, a typical brigade receiving three-quarters of a pound of poultry per man together with three doughnuts, some pies and four or five apples. A well-stuffed Rhode Island soldier reported that he had eaten stewed oysters, canned roast turkey, bread pudding, tapioca pudding, apple pie from the camp bakers, washed it all down with lemonade, and enjoyed after-dinner cigars. Many private groups organized food drives. A prominent New York publisher suggested that the people of New York City give the soldiers 'a grand Thanksgiving dinner', and New Yorkers responded generously. A New Jersey lady sent a turkey to her state's soldiers with the note that it had been raised and fed by an anti-war Copperhead but purchased by a loyal lady 'who gives it freely to the soldiers of her country'.[12] In a tremendous outpouring of support, the folks back home rallied to their soldiers, sending them many holiday supplements including turkeys, chickens, pies, preserves, doughnuts, dried beef, pound cake, sponge cake, apples, ginger snaps, tobacco and cigars. Meanwhile, Lee's hungry soldiers slowly wasted away on scanty rations of foul beef, old bacon, and hard bread.

On 7 December a last assault against Lee's communications began. It was notable for what did not happen. Previous efforts to wreck the Weldon Railroad had provoked punishing counter-strokes. This time an entire corps marched to within nine miles of the North Carolina border, tore up the railroad lines, and returned without opposition. There was time for one brigadier to line up his men in single file along the track and give 'an order not known in tactics and not taught at West Point: "Take hold!"' The men stooped to seize the crossties. 'Turn over!'[13] Soon the rails were bent, twisted and unusable and there was one less supply artery leading to Petersburg.

The onset of winter brought a long period of inactivity and, as always, a general decline in discipline. In part, this was a consequence of the appalling losses that had taken many of the best officers. Too often now majors led brigades, captains commanded regiments, and corporals headed companies. The incidents of disobedience to orders, careless performance of duties, self-inflicted wounds and desertions soared. Along one sector some men who went over to the enemy were found to have entered Confederate service. When they were recaptured and court-martialled, a veteran described how his division formed hollow square to witness their execution:

'At half past eleven we heard the brass band strike up the dead march ... The Gallows was already and the graves dug ... First came the band then the three cowardly devils and then a file of twelve men before and twelve behind – They was led up one under each rope. Then the priest (for they were Catholics) went to them and pow wayed a while and the ropes was tied around the neck and a white cap was then drawn down over the head to the shoulder, arms tied behind them and legs tied together. While this was going on you could hear the boys talking in this way, desert us will you, fight against us will you ... a little bit sorry for what you have done ain't you. I will bet the little fellow dies game. I know by the way he stands, that big one, says another, is such a calf he can hardly stand ... I wish they would hurry and not keep us waiting here all day gaping at them ... Now a fellow stands under with a big wooden mallet ready to Knock out the stanchion at 12 o'clock, he gets the signal, out goes the prop and down goes three poor fellows about three feet but they stop suddenly and commence to struggle. It is an awful sight ... As the word is attention, right face – forward – file right – march. And off we go, I think no more of it until we get our dinners.'[14]

Such punishment seemed to have little effect. Indeed, that night seven more soldiers deserted.

John Gibbon, newly assigned to command the Twenty-fourth Army Corps, tried to stop the haemorrhage of deserters by instituting a furlough system designed to reward the best soldiers. It featured a strict meritocracy beginning with each company sending forward its best soldier to regimental headquarters where a select few would pass up the chain of command until they competed at divisional level for the precious right to go home for a few days. Many soldiers vied for this privilege because it was the only way to get home. Gibbon's simple programme immediately improved his corps' discipline.

The end of operations allowed the men to prepare semi-permanent winter quarters. An officer described his home for three months:

'My log hut is very comfortable with its fireplace made of sticks and mud with a barrel for a chimney. On the walls are numerous pictures of Generals and battles taken from *Harpers Weekly*, while a carbine and my sabre and spurs hang on the wall. My Library is not extensive, only some dozen books on a shelf with a rude table beneath. Several chairs made of cracker box boards with a bed of poles and boughs complete the furniture ... In the rear of our quarters we have an office, cook house and a tent for our servants. Besides we have a hut where three times a day we meet to try the quality of Uncle Sam's hardtack.'[15]

The end of the year tried Grant's patience mightily. Lincoln had charged him with directing the entire war effort. What was clear after the fact, that the Confederacy was played out, was not clear in December 1864. Sherman had disappeared somewhere in Georgia while Hood had invaded Tennessee. No less a strategist than George Meade was worried that Hood's movements could entirely undo what Sherman had accomplished. Defending Tennessee against Hood was George Thomas and it was not apparent that he was the man for the job. Grant repeatedly and futilely urged Thomas to seek battle and send Hood packing. Exasperated at Thomas's continued procrastination (in fact, Thomas, although slow, had good cause for delay) he prepared orders to relieve 'the Rock of Chickamauga' from command. Then, at the proverbial last minute, on 15-16 December, Thomas delivered a crushing attack against Hood at Nashville and knocked his army out of the war.

The Richmond–Petersburg front continued to be static, and boredom set in among the men in the trenches. Enticing the rebels to desert, something that was growing ever easier, was a cheap entertainment. Saint Patrick's Day 1865 came and a fortunate handful received invitations for a typical drunken binge hosted by the remnant of the Irish Brigade. The day featured hurdle races and ditch jumping. After seeing one colonel and several enlisted men badly injured when thrown from their horses, a guest wrote in his diary, 'I returned to camp satisfied that Irish celebrations are dangerous amusements.'[16]

Dress parades and formal reviews — at which the Army of the Potomac had always excelled – relieved the monotony in part, but mostly the men waited for the onset of spring and what they hoped would be one last campaign.

THE PERFECTED MACHINE: WILSON'S LIGHTNING CAMPAIGN

When Grant was drawing up his final plans to 'close down' the Confederacy in 1865, one element featured a cavalry expedition that would begin in north-west Alabama. Under the command of General James Wilson, whom Grant had detached from Sheridan and sent west to reorganize the Union cavalry, the objective was to demolish the important ordnance works at Selma and Tuscaloosa. Hitherto cavalry had proved themselves notoriously incapable of accomplishing anything of any significance during deep penetration raids. Wilson himself had seen this for himself while serving under Sheridan and operating against the railroad lines serving Richmond. His campaign of 1865 was to change this state of affairs. Its combination of mobility and firepower foreshadowed the mechanized tactics of the Second World War and is a case study of the perfection of Grant's military machine.

Wilson gathered his force on the Tennessee River at the end of February 1865. There they reorganized, re-equipped and trained. Wilson was blessed with confident, experienced divisional and brigade generals, many of whom had volunteered when the war was young and risen by merit. Among them were O. H. LaGrange – a cool martinet in camp who performed like a berserker on the battlefield; R. H. Minty, a dandified son of a British officer who brought a keen intelligence and prickly personality to the command; A. O. Miller, an intrepid leader who commanded a mounted infantry brigade that once had been Wilder's famous 'Lightning Brigade'; and Edward Hatch, a former lumberman who had never seen a company of uniformed soldiers until he volunteered for the army and never thereafter declined any assignment no matter how risky. Other officers, most notably the brilliant Emory Upton of Spotsylvania fame, who had come west to round out his military education by serving with the cavalry after having already commanded artillery and infantry, were West Point educated. Like Napoleon's cavaliers and Guderian's panzer leaders, these were aggressive men accustomed to making quick decisions without recourse to formal orders from their superiors.

Wilson's corps comprised about 12,500 horsemen, both cavalry and mounted infantry, divided into three divisions. He assigned a four-gun horse battery to each division and 1,500 dismounted train guards whom he intended to mount on captured horses. By stripping every command in the region of its Spencer rifles and carbines, Wilson managed to equip his entire force with this superb weapon. It was the first time in the history of warfare that an entire corps took the field armed with magazine weapons. In order to travel fast, every trooper carried in his haversacks five days' light rations, 24 pounds of grain, 100 rounds of ammunition, and two extra horseshoes. Wilson ruthlessly cut down the number of wagons he would take. The resultant 250-wagon supply train carried 80 rounds of extra ammunition per man while pack animals toted five days' hard bread rations, ten of coffee, twenty of sugar, and fifteen of salt. Because he would be operating in a region criss-crossed by rivers, Wilson took along a light pontoon train of 39 canvas boats hauled by fifty 6-mule teams. On 22 March the corps set off through a barren land that had been thoroughly stripped of supplies. Wilson had little information about the defenders he would confront, but one enemy personage towered over every other consideration. Wilson proposed entering Nathan Bedford Forrest's domain, and many yankee expeditions had failed ignominiously against the legendary Forrest.

In order to acquire as much information about his enemy as possible, Wilson employed the familiar combination of scouts, spies, civilian interrogations, and news of the area brought by fleeing slaves. He also arranged several meetings under a flag of truce, ostensibly to discuss prisoner exchange, but the officers involved were ordered to talk to Forrest in the hope of learning something of his intentions. Forrest seemed as interested in Wilson, of whom he knew little, as Wilson was in Forrest. He wanted to know such things as Wilson's age and whether he was a volunteer or regular. Forrest concluded the discussion with a challenge: 'Captain, you can tell General Wilson that I have picked out a first-rate place for a cavalry battle down here and if he'll come down with any force he pleases, I'll meet him with the same number and agree to whip the fight.'[17] From anyone else these words might have seemed an empty boast. From Forrest, they were a warning to be ignored at peril.

When the Union column set off, a period of heavy rain had turned the roads into cloying mud paths and swollen the numerous streams and rivers of north-western Alabama into serious obstacles, conditions that had foiled many raids in the past. Undeterred, Wilson pressed on. Meanwhile, the same conditions kept Forrest from gathering his own forces to oppose his advance. The Confederate commanders in the region confidently assured one another that a mounted force represented little threat and could easily be seen off by the usual expedient of home guards and local security detachments protected by fortifications and artillery.

The first indication that Wilson's cavalry expedition would be unlike those of the past came on 30 March when the Federal column destroyed a concentration of iron forges and then emerged from the town of Montevallo to encounter Confederate cavalry. The yankee horse charged, routed the Confederates, pursued them vigorously and captured hundreds of prisoners and three field pieces. Perhaps this could be blamed on the poor morale of the rebels. What occurred at Selma could not.

Selma, with its arsenals, workshops and foundries, was the most important city in the Confederate south-west. Here Forrest and four other generals massed 1,500 of his finest troops together with thousands of foot soldiers backed by a considerable artillery to man the sophisticated earthworks. Experience had shown that a force behind earthworks could outface a far larger attacking force. Moreover, cavalry never charged fortifications.

Arriving in mid-afternoon on 2 April, Wilson quickly prepared to shatter this notion. He had the advantage of having received detailed information about Selma's defences from an Englishman who had worked on them and then deserted. The works were formidable; strongly constructed, double bastioned, covered by a continuous stockade and deep ditch buttressed by many guns. Wilson decided to attack on two sectors. Long's division went in dismounted, the troopers fanning out in open order, a yard between each man. Covered by the Chicago Board of Trade Battery, Long's men advanced implacably, 'pumping out a sheet of lead with each discharge' from their magazine rifles.[18] The troopers advanced to the glacis, where they vied with one another and with their regimental and brigade officers, including British-born Minty, to be first over the works.

So sudden and unexpected was their charge that within 25 minutes the first defence collapsed. Long immediately committed his mounted sabre battalion into the breach and their charge routed their opponents and nearly bagged Forrest himself. Meanwhile Upton's troopers charged across an 'impassable' swamp, overran the works, and kept going into the heart of the rebel position. Confronting another set of field works complete with a thick slashing of trees and a commanding two-gun redoubt, Upton and Long — 'without delaying to reconnoitre the enemy's position, to count his numbers, or to ask for instructions' — improvised another assault. Fixing the enemy frontally with the usual open order skirmish line, Upton sent two mounted regiments against the flank. Wilson later wrote that his command's 'instinct for the flank had led it to the vital spot at the vital time'.[19] His men captured 2,700 men and 96 artillery pieces together with Selma's considerable resources. The combination of mobility, startling shock action — cavalry simply did not charge fortifications — fire discipline – Wilson's troopers did not use up ammunition while mounted, but waited to close the enemy on foot and then used their rapid-firing Spencers — and tactical surprise – Upton's charge through the swamp – made Selma an amazing affair. More was to come.

Having crossing the swollen 870-foot-wide Alabama River, Wilson destroyed his heavy wooden boats and half his canvas boats and marched east along muddy roads to the outskirts of Columbus, Georgia, another important rebel arsenal, well-protected by elaborate earthworks. His approach was so rapid that a mere 2,000 defenders had arrived before the yankee spearhead, the 1st Ohio Cavalry, surprised them and overran a series of bridges before they could be destroyed. It was nightfall before Wilson had assembles half his corps on the field, and most commanders would have waited until all their forces were present. Not so Wilson; he decided on a night attack.

Behind a thick skirmish line, six companies of the 3d Iowa Cavalry dismounted and advanced quietly to within 200 yards of the enemy's line. Behind them at a distance of 400 yards came the 10th Missouri Cavalry who remained mounted. On a sheltered side road, 200 yards farther to the rear, was another mounted regiment'. Opposing this force, directly in front of the Federal cavalry, was a well-manned fort with four 12-pounders. A second line of works lay behind this position. The initial Federal charge overran the 4-gun fort and a mounted charge swirled through the resultant gap; its objective, the bridge leading to Columbus. The spearheading cavalry surprised the bridge guard, captured a battery at the far end, and found itself surrounded by the aroused defenders. The lead Union cavalry retired in disorder. Up came a reserve regiment which dismounted and charged, capturing a formidable redoubt housing 250 infantry and ten artillery pieces before pressing on across another bridge into Columbus. Up came a mounted reserve which swept through the streets, dispersed the organized knots of defenders, and in general spread panic and confusion. At the cost of only ten killed and twenty wounded, Wilson's troopers captured the Confederacy's last important manufacturing centre together with 1,500 defenders and 27 artillery pieces.

In 28 days, Wilson's corps marched 528 miles through enemy territory. Neither poor weather, frequent natural barriers, nor the activities of the defenders had seriously impaired the march. Wilson surmounted logistical and natural obstacles that would have thwarted a corps belonging to any other nation in the world in 1865. The speed of his advance always kept the Confederate defenders several steps behind.

By operating in mass (a lesson learned from Sheridan) Wilson ensured that he had a substantial numerical edge at the point of decision. His horses allowed both strategic mobility and the ability on the battlefield to exploit Confederate errors. When manoeuvre was impossible, Wilson relied on direct shock action backed by the Spencer's firepower. All of which meant that the Confederates were never able to regain their balance once his campaign had begun. The entire expedition had been conducted with energy and enterprise.

In sum, Wilson and his lieutenants exhibited a modern style of warfare. Hitherto, because of the musket's inefficiencies, tactics had demanded packing men in close ranks in order to achieve adequate firepower. The new breed of American general recognized that the Spencer's firepower permitted a thinning of the front line. Upton observed that there was no longer much need of a second rank because one man armed with a Spencer was at least the equal of two armed with rifled muskets.[20] The future would show that too few military men paid attention to the lessons of the American Civil War. The style of Wilson's 1865 campaign was not seen again until the Germans' tank/aircraft campaign in France 74 years later. In the intervening years would come the slaughter of trench warfare during the First World War, a slaughter wholly predictable to any Civil War combat veteran.

'WE WILL GO ON.'

As reports of Sheridan's, Sherman's and then Thomas's successes reached the soldiers of the Army of the Potomac, some of them wondered if they were pulling their weight. But their general had resolved that tying Lee to his defensive works was task enough, for it enabled the other Union armies to march at will across the South.

At the end of March 1865, active operations began anew in Virginia, but by an entirely different army from the one that had begun the campaign by crossing the Rapidan River one year earlier. Gone were many veterans and many familiar leaders. Now, except for Grant, the army was led by West Point's élite, the engineers. Meade and all his corps commanders were engineer officers. Intelligent and capable as they were, none knew that this would be the final campaign. The men closer to the front better understood how played out were their opponents. Ever increasing numbers of Confederates deserted to the Union lines and, most notably, their ranks began to include not just the obvious misfits and shirkers, but combat-hardened veterans who had simply decided that they could not win.

Grant's relentless pressure had changed the Army of Northern Virginia into a mere husk of its former self. Lee had been forced to respond to the Federal turning efforts by extending his own line east to protect his line of communications. The defenders of Richmond and Petersburg were now stretched perilously thin:

Sector and Command	Infantry per defended mile[21]
North of the James:	
Field's and Kershaw's divisions (Longstreet)	1,360
Virginia Reserves, local defences troops, siege artillery (Ewell)	740
Howlett Line:	
Mahone's division	740
From the Appomattox to Lieutenant Run:	
Gordon's Corps	1,350
From Lieutenant Run to Burgess' Mill:	
Wilcox's division minus McGowan (Hill's Corps)	888
Heth's division plus McGowan (Hill's Corps)	1,550
Beyond Burgess's Mill:	
Anderson's Corps	1,600

On the weakest sector there was a defender every 2½ yards. The strongest sector featured a defender every yard. Even given the fact that many Confederate riflemen in the trenches had several loaded weapons, this was more akin to a picket line than a battle line, but by now no one expected to charge successfully defended works and Grant did not intend to try. Instead he would again manoeuvre out around his left flank and try once more to cut the Southside Railroad. To oppose him the only reserve Lee could muster was Pickett's infantry division numbering about 5,000 men and 4,200 cavalry led by Rooney Lee and Tom Rosser. Pickett's division had never recovered from Gettysburg. The number of deserters from its ranks, a sure sign of poor morale, exceeded almost every other rebel formation. Sheridan had repeatedly given Rosser's cavalry a drubbing during the Shenandoah Campaign. Grant's grand strategy, formulated one year ago, had come to this: the men Lee could summon for the crisis were few and in poor condition.

The man Grant charged with turning Lee's right flank was Phil Sheridan. 'Little Phil' had risen greatly in esteem among soldiers of the Army of the Potomac. As with any general, it had taken him some time to find himself. On the battlefield he had exhibited no particular tactical flair. Instead he provided high energy, high visibility frontline leadership that prodded the army's mounted arm into a confident, aggressive force. In the Shenandoah Valley he had taken on independent command of a combined arms force. Although by 1864 jaded soldiers had given up the habit of cheering their generals, there was something about Sheridan that created a special enthusiasm. When the issue hung in the balance during Sheridan's first field battle in the Valley, he had coursed the field to inspire his soldiers, and although few of his infantry had ever seen him in battle, his appearance caused them to cheer themselves hoarse. Sheridan had piled success upon success and now, in the spring of 1865, Grant considered him the most able general in Virginia. Accordingly, Grant gave Sheridan the lead role in his plan to close out the Confederacy. In modern terms, Sheridan had risen to become a task force commander of the army's shock troops.

Sheridan's Cavalry Corps spearheaded the movement to turn Lee's right. It began on 30 March and quickly threatened to bog down under the heavy deluges that soaked the ground and become, like Burnside's abortive 1863 campaign, another ignominious 'Mud March'. Grant seriously considered suspending the movement, a course of action pressed upon him by numerous subordinates. Sheridan disagreed and explained that his cavalry was advancing despite all obstacles. Grant considered and then firmly declared, 'We will go on.'[22]

Sheridan's report that a major element of Lee's army had ventured out from their entrenchments (these were Pickett's troops) inspired Meade to send the following message at 9.45 p.m. on 31 March 31: 'Would it not be well for Warren to go down with his whole corps and smash up the force in front of Sheridan?'[23] This aggressive proposition is another example of how a man who is overly cautious when in charge of an army can become bold when he serves in a subordinate capacity. In the event Grant authorized the movement. Sheridan, in turn, hoped to receive the 6th Corps because he was familiar with its officers. Together in the Shenandoah Valley they had formed a seamless combined-arms force. But Wright's 6th Corps was too distant to support Sheridan, so on came the 5th Corps and its leader General Warren.

On 29 March on the Quaker Road, and again two days later at Dinwiddie Court House, the rival forces collided in battle. In the latter action Sheridan's cavalry managed to hold off the Confederate infantry and cavalry only with difficulty. Even though his command could no longer maintain contact with the balance of Grant's army, Sheridan sensed that Pickett's isolated force lay vulnerable. When one of Grant's aides galloped to Sheridan to indicate just how isolated he was, 'Little Phil' replied, 'the enemy is in more danger than I am. If I am cut off from the Army of the Potomac, it is cut off from Lee's army, and not a man in it ought ever be allowed to get back to Lee. We at last have drawn the enemy infantry out of its fortifications, and this is our chance to attack it.'[24]

The chance came on the first day of April 1865. Lee had ordered Pickett to hold the important crossroads at Five Forks 'at all hazards'.[25] Rooney Lee's cavalry division were holding Pickett's right flank. Pickett's five infantry brigades were manning field works along the White Oak Road, a line extending east past Five Forks and then making a short

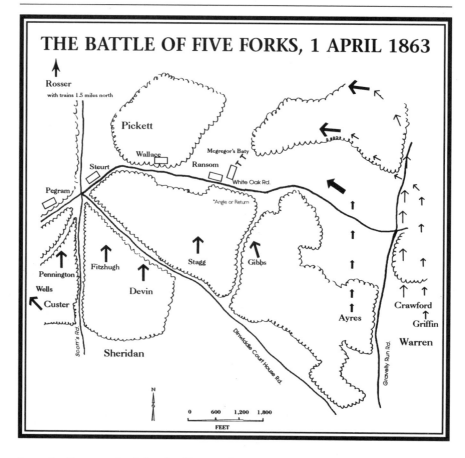

THE BATTLE OF FIVE FORKS, 1 APRIL 1863

Rosser
with trains 1.5 miles north

Pickett

Wallace

Mcgregor's Baty

Steurt

Ransom

White Oak Rd.

Pegram

"Angle or Return"

Pennington

Fitzhugh

Stagg

Gibbs

Wells

Devin

Custer

Crawford

Ayres

Griffin

Warren

Scott's Rd.

Sheridan

Dinwiddle Court House Rd.

Gravelly Run Rd.

N

0   600   1,200   1,800

FEET

turn to the north. Munford's cavalry were guarding the open flank at this 'angle of return'. The entire infantry front ran about one and three-quarter miles. Ten Confederate artillery pieces were in the front line wherever they could find an adequate field of fire. In Pickett's rear were Rosser's cavalry, guarding the trains and serving as a reserve.

On the morning of 1 April Sheridan's cavalry carefully probed through the woods toward Five Forks. Along a stream in front of the Confederate position, Thomas Devin's cavalry encountered an infantry outpost line. Through most of the war, the presence of opposing infantry was enough to stop cavalry cold. But during the Shenandoah Valley campaign, Sheridan's troopers had learned how to fight rebel foot soldiers. In a textbook manoeuvre, Devin ordered a brigade to dismount and charge across the stream. As soon it gained a toehold, Devin committed a mounted brigade to expand the bridgehead. Additional troopers crossed the stream to take up positions guarding both flanks of the bridgehead. Then, after the crossing had been secured, the troopers pressed on towards Five Forks.

There, Devin's troopers 'developed a strong line of breast-works ... filled with masses of infantry'.[26] But, they were not done yet. Mounted combat patrols advanced to within twenty yards of the enemy position in an aggressive reconnaissance in force. In places dismounted troopers crossed the breastworks, captured some prisoners and dragged them back to Federal lines for interrogation. Sheridan used the information acquired by his cavalry to formulate a battle plan. He would use two cavalry divisions in a frontal holding attack, feint against the Confederate right, and assail the opposite flank with Warren's infantry, thereby severing Pickett's contact with Lee's Army. Danger lay in the fact that Lee's right flank was only some three miles off and should he emerge with characteristic vigour, he could attack Sheridan's flank while Sheridan was operating against Pickett's flank.

Sheridan galloped to Warren to explain in detail what he expected the infantry to accomplish. He wanted them to take time to form properly so as the deliver a crushing blow. To that end he expected 'that the formation was to be oblique to the road, with the right advanced, with two divisions in front, and the third in reserve behind the right division'. He left further details up to Warren. The Fifth Corps commander instructed his two leading divisions each to deploy two brigades in front in two regimental lines, and hold their third brigades in reserve. Warren posted his third division in columns of battalions behind his right assault division. Thus, Warren's 12,000 men extended over a 1,000-yard front. Because the terrain was rough, wooded and cut by numerous ravines, it took three hours for Warren to complete these dispositions. To the impatient Sheridan, this seemed excessive.

Warren was clearly troubled by his open right flank and remarked that, 'Bobby Lee was always getting people into trouble.'[27] Warren's time-consuming deployment seemed more alarming when Sheridan received a report from Meade that the nearest Federal units of the main army had pulled back, thereby isolating Sheridan even more. Concerned that Lee could sortie against Warren's right flank, Sheridan assigned 25-year-old Ranald Mackenzie's cavalry division of the Army of the James to protect this flank.

Grant regarded Mackenzie as 'the most promising young officer in the army', a man who had risen high on his own merits, without any political influence.[28] Eager for action, Mackenzie hustled his troopers forward until he encountered enemy infantry. Driving in their outposts, the yankee troopers developed a line of rifle pits along the edge of a wood manned by a brigade of North Carolina infantry. Dismounted troopers of the 11th Pennsylvania Cavalry pinned the Carolina infantry to their pits with their rapid-firing Spencer carbines. Seeing the defending infantry ducking low, Mackenzie placed himself at the head of a mounted battalion and charged in column of fours. Shifting direction in mid career, Mackenzie closed in on the infantry's flank which threw the defenders into disorder. The dismounted troopers charged from the front and completed the rout. Spirited Federal frontline leadership was evident in this charge. Although Mackenzie survived unscathed, three other intrepid officers died at the head of their men. This success was extremely important. Mackenzie had driven off Lee's nearest infantry and interposed his force between him and Pickett. Now Sheridan felt comfortable enough to turn his entire attention to Pickett's men at Five Forks.

Initially, Sheridan's holding attack went in as intended. The veteran dismounted cavalry worked up close to the rebel entrenchments and opened a heavy fire. But as Warren's deployment took longer than Sheridan had planned, things began to go sour. Custer's men retired before the defenders' heavy fire while Devin just barely managed to hold. Knowing that his prized cavalry were having a stiff fight irritated the always short-tempered Sheridan and he urged Warren to hurry. Finally, at about 4.15 p.m., Warren's assault began, but the entire effort spun out of control. The problem was that the defenders were not quite where Warren had expected them to be. He thought that the Confederate's mainline was on the White Oak Road. When his assault divisions crossed that road unopposed, he assumed that the line lay just a little farther along, somewhere in the woods ahead. Only Ayres' division, the leftmost of the two assault units, encountered fire and it all came in against his left flank. Although none of the Union officers realized it, this fire was coming from the approximately 140-yard-long 'return' entrenchment protecting Pickett's left flank. Ayres immediately faced front to the left and charged.

Too often in the past had Ayres' men faced this situation and their assault lacked enthusiasm. An observer says that Sheridan 'put spurs to his horse, and dashed along in front of the line of battle from left to right, shouting encouragement ... "Come on, men ... go at 'em with a will! Move on at a clean jump, or you'll not catch one of 'em. They're all getting ready to run now, and if you don't get on to them in five minutes they'll every one get away from you! Now go for them!" A bullet hit the neck of a nearby soldier, who exclaimed as blood spurted from his jugular, "I'm killed." "You're not hurt a bit!" cried Sheridan. "Pick up your gun, man, and move right on to the front."[29] The man grabbed his weapon, got up and staggered a few paces then fell dead.

Ayres' men continued to waver. Sheridan called for his battle-flag, a crimson and white standard. Waving it furiously he rode through a hail of bullets that pierced the flag, killed his Colour sergeant, wounded his quartermaster and brought down two or three horses of his staff. Sheridan's conduct inspired Ayres himself to draw his sword and lead his men forward. Until now, Ayres' veterans had performed like the combat weary men they were. They had obeyed the order to advance without enthusiasm and had then withdrawn or gone to ground when the enemy opened fire. But their officers' amazing performance caused them to behave like the volunteers of 1862. With a cheer they charged. The Colour-bearer of the 190th Pennsylvania surpassed all others and was the first to plant his standard on the enemy works.

Since the 'return' entrenchment was a mere 140 yards long, the attackers' ranks lapped around the defenders' flank. In truth, some of the defenders (of Ransom's North Carolina brigade) had already begun to waver. Sensing disaster, their supporting battery limbered up to withdraw. When Ayres' men turned their flank, those who remained either died at their posts or surrendered. Ayres' division scooped up more than 1,000 prisoners here.

Sheridan's orders had massed his strength on his own right, and accordingly Warren expected to turn the Confederate flank with his right assault division. Instead, Warren's left assault division commanded by Ayres achieved this so Warren tried to countermarch his other two divisions towards the scene of the fighting. But this recall was difficult in the wooded terrain, particularly since Crawford's and Griffin's men had happily surged straight forward across the White Oak road towards a thin screen of dismounted cavalry.

Hearing the sounds of Ayres' engagement, Griffin, whose division was Warren's reserve, on his own initiative galloped to Ayres to ask what was happening. Ayres replied that it was 'nothing new. The same old story, Crawford has gone off and left me to fight alone.'[30] Griffin promised support and took off to find his men, a task which at this point was preoccupying not only Warren and Sheridan, but numerous staff officers. The defenders took quick advantage of the gap in the Federal line to deliver a punishing counter-attack. Furious, Sheridan tried to correct this error. Whereas Warren was nowhere to be found, General Griffin, on his own initiative, followed up his conversation with Ayres by countermarching to seal the gap. Ayres' men returned to the attack and together with Devin's cavalry division overran the line of breastworks. This breakthrough proved decisive. The yankees rolled up Pickett's flank and sent his force fleeing after capturing guns, Colours and men. It had been a well-planned, but extraordinary fight, featuring cavalry attacking the works frontally while infantry turned their flank.[31] Warren's Corps had lived up to Meade's hopes by truly 'smashing' Pickett, but Warren himself did not enjoy the victory. Thoroughly exasperated by Warren's lacklustre leadership, when he finally found him Sheridan relieved the hero of Little Roundtop from command.

The fighting on 1-2 April deducted some 5,000 men from Lee's army. For the Confederates, Five Forks had been a more costly day than any since the Bloody Angle of 12 May 1864. Grant's relentless attrition had worn them down and on this field they did not fight with their customary valour. A Union officer observed that the prisoners did not march to the rear exhibiting their usual sullen attitude. Instead, they joked, 'We are coming back into the Union, boys, we are coming back into the Union.'[32]

It had been, wrote one Federal officer, 'The most momentous day of the war so far.'[33]

When Grant heard of Sheridan's victory he ordered a general assault for 2 April. Along some of the front generals had their men prepare carefully for a surprise dawn assault. The Sixth Corps took all the usual steps to ensure secrecy. The soldiers discarded noisy equipment, non-commissioned officers patrolled the ranks to keep everyone quiet and prevent anyone from sneaking a smoke. Volunteers crept forward stealthily, axes in hand, to be ready to chop through the abatis. In the pre-dawn light on the 2nd, the men advanced with uncapped muskets. Then a Pioneer Corps mule loaded with picks and shovels broke loose and stampeded towards the Confederate lines. Awakened, the defenders opened fire. Just in case there was any remaining doubt that an attack was imminent, the troops, although having been ordered to remain silent, cheered loudly before advancing!

Despite the noise the 2d Rhode Island, still with uncapped muskets, managed to overrun the Confederate picket line.They found that the rebels were only too eager to surrender. As the yankee colonel reformed his men for the main advance, an idiotic corporal called for three cheers for the colonel and the resultant noise pinpointed the regiment's position to the fully alerted enemy artillery which opened a crossfire as the regiment closed its objective.

All along the line the Federal soldiers surged forward. In places the attackers easily overran the fortifications. More typically they ran into heavy initial opposition. A brigade commander recalls sending his men forward into 'a terrific fire of musketry, canister, and shell.'[34] Although his assault units suffered losses, still they advanced. Then it became apparent that the fight had gone out of many of the defenders. His brigade scooped up 165 rebels in the forward picket line and then advanced to capture a redoubt from which were hanging many white sheets in token of surrender and despair. It was a glorious triumph. Grant's men had finally seized the trenches that had defied them for nine long months.

But the assault on Fort Gregg, a last bastion protecting Lee's escape route, showed yet again the enormous advantage enjoyed by even badly depleted defenders protected by fortifications. General Gibbon, whose men led the assault, describes the scene:

'The line moved rapidly and steadily forward to [the fort's] deep, wide ditch half filled with water from the recent rains. Now a most desperate struggle took place. Our men gathering around the fort, jumped into the ditch and assisting each other clambered upon the exterior slope, receiving the fire in their very faces. First one regimental color and then another was planted on the parapet as rallying points for the gathering men, now separated from the enemy only by the width of the parapet. Again and again did these gallant fellows rise up and deliver their fire upon the garrison within, only to be forced back and down by the withering fire, but men gathered thicker every moment and at last the wave, with increased effort surged forward, swept over the parapet, and finished the work with the bayonet.'[35]

The capture of Fort Gregg and its two guns cost Gibbon's men about 500 killed and wounded. They captured 300 defenders and found another 55 bodies in a heap inside the fort.

A LAST STAIR TO CLIMB

'If the thing is pressed, I think Lee will surrender,' Sheridan wrote to Grant. Grant replied, 'Let the thing be pressed.'

The result was a week-long whirlwind campaign featuring a driving, relentless pursuit. Key to the Federal success was Grant's ability to anticipate where Lee was headed and march to intercept him. Like so many campaigns during the war, this one was about railroads. Lee had to find supplies somewhere along the Richmond and Danville Railroad. His line of march described an arc leading to Amelia Court House, a station on the railroad that Lee had designated as a rallying point. Instead of following directly in his wake, Grant marched to cut the chord of this arc and thereby saved nineteen miles. When Lee arrived at Amelia Court House on 4 April he found yankee infantry and cavalry sitting squarely athwart the railroad, his intended line of retreat, some eight miles away. He had no choice but to conduct another killing night march.

The pursuit wore heavily on Grant's men as well. After months of static warfare, men and horses alike had lost their condition. Many broke down under the strain of repeated forced marches. Hundreds pressed on although barefoot and bleeding. They knew that the end was near and knew too that it was Grant who had brought it about. No longer were they reticent to cheer their commanding general. A soldier recalls how his marching column parted to permit Meade and Grant to pass: 'I thought the boys would split open they hallowed, cheered and made such a noise.'[36]

Grant conducted the chase with such skill that Lee was never able to break contact. He used Ord's Army of the James, Griffin's Fifth Corps and Sheridan's Cavalry Corps to head off Lee's van while the balance of the Army of the Potomac maintained constant pressure on his rear. Consequently Lee could not confront one opponent without risking attack from the other.

The end came with startling suddenness. During the pursuit of Lee there had been little opportunity for the far-flung Union columns to exchange news, so they were unaware that they were closing in to trap the remnant of the Army of Northern Virginia at a place called Appomattox Court House. Here Sheridan's troopers captured the Confederate supply train on 8 April and then blocked the rebels' line of march. Meanwhile Meade was boring in against Lee's rear.

On 9 April Major General George B. Meade made one last great contribution to the war. He had Lee's demoralized army at bay, his own troops well positioned for a decisive assault. It was his decision to make because Grant was nowhere to be found (he was riding cross-country between the Union columns). Here was the chance to disprove his critics who claimed that he had blundered by letting Lee escape after Gettysburg. Here was the chance to return to the newspapers' headlines, to win everlasting renown as the general who commanded the war-ending assault. Instead Meade ordered a halt to see if a truce could be arranged.

When Grant arrived at headquarters he caught up on events and exchanged notes with Lee about a proposed meeting. Grant's staff, and Rawlins in particular, detected cunning behind Lee's apparent prevarication and they were right. Lee was simultaneously making plans for a breakout attack while writing notes about a proposed meeting with Grant, the subject of which could only be terms of surrender. But Grant did not see it that way. He reassured his staff by saying: 'Some allowance must be made for the trying position in which Gen. Lee is placed,'[37] and that if he met Lee, the latter would surrender. And so it transpired.

When Ulysses S. Grant climbed the stairs in Wilmer McLean's home to meet Robert E. Lee, the contrast between the two generals could not have been more striking. Grant was of humble origins, having endured a hardscrabble upbringing in the Midwest. Lee, the son of a Revolutionary War hero, had lived the life of a Virginia patrician. At the time when Grant had been a captain and forced to resign because of drunkenness, Lee had been superintendent of West Point. And on 9 April 1865, because he had been riding hard and his baggage had not been able to keep up, Grant was wearing a muddy, travel-stained uniform. Lee was wearing an immaculate full-dress uniform. Yet it was Grant, aged 42, who entered the McClean parlour to negotiate terms of surrender for the third time with an enemy general whom he had defeated.

Overlooking an initial snub from Lee, Grant proposed exceedingly generous terms. He asked only that the rebels pledge not to take up arms against the United States again. He allowed officers to retain their sidearms and any man who owned a horse to take it home with him to help with the spring planting.

The preparation of the surrender documents ironically underscored the interdependency of the two divided sections. Lee's aide, Charles Marshall, had to ask to borrow ink from Union officers to pen the South's portion. Grant's designated clerk proved too nervous to write and so he asked Ely Parker, the Seneca Indian, to write in his stead. Parker had no paper and asked Marshall to lend him some. So it was that a non-citizen (at this time Indians were not legal American citizens) finalized Lee's surrender by writing with Union ink on Confederate paper.

The surrender also featured one last 'breach' of security by the press, although it turned out to be harmless. Knowing that the press would not be invited into Wilmer McLean's home while Grant and Lee negotiated terms of surrender, an enterprising correspondent for the *New York Tribune* arranged to 'scoop' the opposition. In mid-afternoon, while the generals were still conferring, a Federal officer emerged on to McLean's porch and took off his hat and wiped his brow. It was a coded signal indicating that Lee had agreed to surrender. Correspondent Henry E. Wing jumped on his horse and galloped to the nearest telegraph station to transmit the news to his paper. By 11 p.m. that evening bulletins outside the *Tribune*'s office in New York City announced the news before it was known by any other newspaper.

Many Union soldiers heard the news from General Meade himself. Normally a restrained individual, he galloped from the McLean house towards his men, '... bare-headed, with his hair streaming in the wind and wildly waving his cap ... Every man was quickly on his feet.' Meade drew near and cried out: 'Lee has surrendered! Lee has surrendered!'[38]

The release of tension among the soldiers was enormous. They had anticipated one last desperate fight. Instead, they had the rest of their lives to look forward to. Quickly the former enemies began to fraternize. A Union soldier recorded his impressions in his diary on the day after Lee's surrender:

'We have stacked arms a few yards apart. The boys in the Blue and in the gray are trading, everything that is tradable. Hats, Caps, Penknives, Coffee, Sugar, Tobacco ... It looks like a fair ... The late hostile armies seem to have forgotten they were enemies yesterday morning, and are mixing and chatting the hours away in a very friendly manner ... I look over our thinned ranks and miss the boys that stood side by side with us ... If we could only have them here to day to see what they helped to make possible; but alas! they are sleeping that long last sleep that knows no waking, scattered in unknown graves among the battlefields of Virginia or absent in the Hospital with shattered Health, wounds or amputated limbs.

'The Blue and the Gray are all glad it seems to me that the cruel war is over – what a change a few short hours has made. The Shades of night come on, all is quiet, all quiet on the lines, all quiet, and we shall try to sleep but cannot for the war is over and we feel so glad, so proud of ourselves, and so sorry for our comrades that have fallen by the wayside.'[39]

CAVALRY CORPS, Military Division of the Mississippi
Major General James H. Wilson, Commanding
Escort: 4th US. Cavalry

First Division:
Brigadier General Edward McCook
(128 officers, 3,568 men)
FIRST BRIGADE:
Brigadier General John H. Crouton
8th Iowa Cavalry
4th Kentucky Infantry (mounted)
6th Kentucky Cavalry
2d Michigan Cavalry
SECOND BRIGADE:
Colonel Oscar LaGrange
2nd Indiana Cavalry (battalion)
4th Indiana Cavalry
4th Kentucky Cavalry
7th Kentucky Cavalry
1st Wisconsin Cavalry
ARTILLERY: Indiana Light, 18th Battery

Second Division: Brigadier General
Eli Long (172 officers, 4,586 men)
FIRST BRIGADE (MOUNTED INFANTRY):
Colonel Abram Miller
98th Illinois
123d Illinois
17th Indiana

72d Indiana
SECOND BRIGADE:
Colonel Robert Minty
4th Michigan Cavalry
3d Ohio Cavalry
4th Ohio Cavalry
7th Pennsylvania Cavalry
ARTILLERY:
Chicago Board of Trade Battery

Fourth Division:
Brevet Major General Emory Upton
(113 officers, 3,180 men)
FIRST BRIGADE: Brevet Brigadier General Edward F. Winslow
3d Iowa Cavalry
4th Iowa Cavalry
10th Missouri Cavalry
SECOND BRIGADE: Brevet Brigadier
General Andrew J. Alexander
5th Iowa Cavalry
1st Ohio Cavalry
7th Ohio Cavalry
ARTILLERY: 4th US, Battery I

1   John Gibbon, *Personal Recollections of the Civil War,* (Dayton: Morningside Bookshop, 1978), p. 270.
2   William Watson, *Letters of a Civil War Surgeon,* (W. Lafayette, IN: Purdue Research Fdn., 1961), p. 87.
3   Gibbon, p. 257.
4   James I. Robertson, ed., *The Civil War Letters of General Robert McAllister,* (New Brunswick, NJ: Rutgers University Press, 1965), cited in footnote 49, p. 489.
5   Cited by Gibbon, p. 259.
6   See Brayton Harris, "The Role of the Press in the Civil War," *Civil War,* Vol. XV (December 1988), p. 34.
7   Ibid., p. 34.
8   Peter S. Michie, *The Life and Letters of Emory Upton,* (New York: Arno Press, 1979), p. 123.
9   George R. Agassiz, ed., *Meade's Headquarters 1863-1865: Letters of Colonel Theodore Lyman from the Wilderness to Appomattox,* (Boston: Massachusetts Historical Society, 1922), p. 217.
10 Agassiz, *Meade's Headquarters,* p. 173.
11 Augustus Meyers, *Ten Years in the Ranks, U.S. Army,* (New York: The Stirling Press, 1914), p. 334.
12 *Civil War Letters of General Robert McAllister,* p. 546.
13 *Civil War Letters of General Robert McAllister,* p. 554.
14 W. Springer Menge and J. August Shimrak, eds., *The Civil War Notebook of Daniel Chisholm,* (New York: Orion Books, 1989), p. 55.
15 Robert Hunt Rhodes, ed., *All For the Union: The Civil War Diary and Letters of Elisha Hunt Rhodes,* (New York: Vintage Books, 1992), p. 202.

16 Rhodes, p. 220.
17 James Harrison Wilson, *Under the Old Flag*, vol. 2 (New York: D. Appleton and Co., 1912), p. 185.
18 Wilson, *Under the Old Flag*, vol. 2, p. 216.
19 Wilson, *Under the Old Flag*, vol. 2, p. 218.
20 *Life and Letters of Emory Upton*, p. 192.
21 Edwin C. Bearss and Chris Caulkins, *Battle of Five Forks*, (Lynchburg, VA: H. E. Howard, 1985), p. 124.
22 Philip H. Sheridan, *Personal Memoirs of P. H. Sheridan*, vol. 2 (New York: Charles L. Webster & Co., 1888), p. 145.
23 Sheridan, vol. 2, p. 154.
24 Horace Porter, *Campaigning With Grant*, (New York: The Century Co., 1897), p. 432.
25 Bearss and Caulkins, *Battle of Five Forks*, p. 76.
26 Bearss and Caulkins, *Battle of Five Forks*, pp. 84-85.
27 Sheridan, vol. 2, p. 161.
28 Ulysses S. Grant, *Personal Memoirs*, (New York: De Capo Press, 1982), p. 583.
29 Porter, *Campaigning With Grant*, p. 437.
30 Bearss and Caulkins, *Battle of Five Forks*, p. 96.
31 See Allan Nevins, ed., *A Diary of Battle: The Personal Journals of Colonel Charles S. Wainwright, 1861-1865*, (New York: Harcourt, Brace & World, 1962), p. 515.
32 Nevins, *A Diary of Battle*, p. 512.
33 Nevins, *A Diary of Battle*, p. 510.
34 *Civil War Letters of General Robert McAllister*, p. 603.
35 Gibbon, p. 301.
36 *Civil War Notebook of Daniel Chisholm*, p. 75.
37 Sylvanus Cadwallader, *Three Years With Grant*, (New York: Alfred A. Knopf, 1956), p. 319.
38 Cited in *Civil War Letters of General Robert McAllister*, footnote 46, p. 607.
39 *Civil War Notebook of Daniel Chisholm*, p. 79.

Epilogue:
Pass In Review

TWO GLORIOUS DAYS, 23 AND 24 MAY 1865, WITNESSED THE triumphal Grand Review of Grant's armies in the nation's capital. For one last time the Army of the Potomac, the most spit and polish of American armies, worked hard to put on a good show. The soldiers cleaned their equipment, groomed horses, and blackened harness. Many received new uniforms for the affair. At 9 a.m. on the 23rd they marched along Pennsylvania Avenue in one long, grand column.

General George B. Meade proudly led the procession accompanied by his staff. Then came the Cavalry Corps led by Major General Wesley Merritt. (Sheridan, to his dismay, had been sent to the Rio Grande to take charge of a force intended to overawe the French in Mexico.) Behind the cavalry marched Brevet Brigadier General Macey's Provost Marshals Brigade followed by Brigadier General Benham's Engineer Brigade. And then came the line corps.

First, the Ninth Army Corps commanded by Major General Parke. A handful of these soldiers, including Parke himself, had participated in Grant's Vicksburg campaign. Attached to this corps was Dwight's division of the Nineteenth Corps. Then came Brevet Major General Griffin and the Fifth Corps. Last in line marched the famous Second Army Corps, now led by Meade's one-time Chief of Staff, Major-General Andrew Humphreys. Up Pennsylvania Avenue towards the Capitol they marched in closed columns, infantry companies limited to a 20-man front so as to hide their losses and present a more uniform appearance. They marched in the formal step taught on countless drill fields, looking straight ahead, resplendent in the new uniforms and white gloves. Young girls threw garlands at their feet. Many in the enormous crowd searched their programmes to identify passing units and cheered them by name. In front of the White House was a reviewing stand where President Andrew Johnson and his cabinet received the army's salutes. It had all been meticulously arranged and professionally presented in keeping with the image this army had of itself.

The next day saw a different spectacle. It was Sherman's turn, and his western veterans neither looked nor acted like the men in the eastern armies. They were bigger men and looked healthier, not having suffered the privations of the soldiers who had fought in Virginia. Sherman, recognizing the futility of trying to compete with the Army of the Potomac in formal drill, let them be themselves. At the head of each division came a corps of black pioneers armed with picks and spades, marching in double ranks, keeping perfect dress and step. Then came the line soldiers who marched in the western style with a loose-limbed, long-striding gait.

To the crowd's delight, and unlike the soldiers on the previous day, the westerners cheerfully acknowledged the repeated ovations. Six ambulances followed each division to represent the baggage train. They came complete with goats, milch-cows and pack mules, as they would have been on campaign. Attached to wagons and mules were the normal accoutrements of an army on the march including game-cocks, poultry and hams. Families of freed slaves – men, women and children – trailed along. It was a scene that had struck terror in the hearts of the people in the South during Sherman's march to the sea and subsequent march north through the Carolinas. Here in the capital of the newly reunited nation, it produced delighted laughter.

A woman explained to Colonel Wainwright why so many preferred the second day's review: 'The Army of the Potomac marched past just like its commander [Meade], looking neither to the right nor the left, and only intent on passing the reviewing officer properly; while Sherman's officers and men were bowing on all sides and not half so stiff.' Wainwright replied that 'she had paid the greatest compliment to the Army of the Potomac I had heard'.[1]

In all, some 150,000 soldiers passed in review during the two-day parade. Then, in keeping with American tradition, the volunteer army disbanded and the veterans headed north and west to resume civilian life.

The fact that this review took place at all is attributable to the political leadership of Abraham Lincoln and the military leadership of Lieutenant General Ulysses S. Grant. Grant gave the North what hitherto it had lacked: systematic direction so that its superior force could be brought to bear against the South's main armies. He was the strategic architect who designed and implemented a war-winning campaign. Grant was the only general, North or South, who could endure the strain of continental war management. If his confrontation with Lee lacked flair, it should not detract from his surpassing achievements.

In examining what made Grant a success, certain attributes stand out. He was possessed of what Napoleon called 2 a.m. courage, by which the Emperor understood the ability to make a positive decision under the most adverse circumstances. Unlike nearly all his contemporaries, Grant experienced no sudden self-doubts about what the enemy was up to. Regardless of their unknown manoeuvring, he continued with his plan of operation. He did not wait until he had more men or supplies or better intelligence. From Belmont through the Wilderness, he went into action with what he had at hand. Once he began he did not pause because of anxiety as to enemy intentions.

Grant defined the art of war simply: find your enemy, fight him, fight him again, and move on. He thereby exerted his own will over that of his opponents. At the beginning of the war he was secure in the knowledge that his enemies were plagued by all the problems that beset his own forces and that they would take counsel of their fears while he would not. By 1864 his security was buttressed by the knowledge that the enemy simply did not have enough troops to stop the Union forces if their advance were co-ordinated on a strategic scale. Unlike every other Union general who served in the East, Grant did not pause to worry about what Lee would do to him, but concentrated on what he would do to Lee, thereby negating one of Lee's own great weapons, the Virginian's iron will.

Grant lacked the education, ambition and perhaps the intellect to become a 'Great Captain'. James Wilson observed that he 'never became what regular officers regarded as a first-class technical or theoretical soldier'.[2] However, Grant above all others, understood with crystal clarity that this war was different from previous wars: the objective was to subdue a whole people and this could only be accomplished by wasting the enemy armies and breaking civilian morale. Napoleon once observed that typical generals 'see too many things; as for me, I see only one: masses. I seek to destroy them, knowing well that the accessories will then fall of their own accord.'[3] Most Civil War-era generals saw 'too many things'. Not Grant. He exhibited true Napoleonic strategy, particularly in 1864, by focusing on the enemy's main armies and ignoring all other distractions.

Long after his death the US Army College continued to perpetuate the Grant way. On the eve of the Second World War, Field Manual 100-5, a document that articulated operational strategy, stated: 'An objective may sometimes be gained through maneuver alone; ordinarily, it must be gained through battle.' A commentator writing in the journal of the Command and General Staff School, used Grant-like words to elaborate on this theme: 'It should be remembered that the price of victory is hard fighting and that no matter what maneuver is employed, ultimately the fighting is frontal ... Blood is the price of victory. One must accept the formula or not wage war.'[4] This was Grant's military legacy.

Much like his great rival Lee, Grant's preferred command style was to design a campaign's broad outlines and then leave it up to trusted subordinates to implement his strategy. To this end he wrote clear and simple orders. This approach worked in the West and failed in Virginia. It took Grant four weeks or so of combat association with the Army of the Potomac to appreciate that the spirit of co-operation that characterized his western armies was entirely absent in the East.

Grant had an outstanding ability to develop his lieutenants' skills. Consider his relationship with Sherman. Although talented, widely read in military science and military history, Sherman's unstable personality would have undone him but for Grant's firm support. His careful nurturing enabled Sherman to grow into the responsibility of independent command. Grant had great faith in selected lieutenants such as Sherman and McPherson and left them to go about their duties in their own way. Although he had a West Pointer's scepticism about the ability of civilian officers, he showed greater flexibility than any other army leader in letting competent civilians rise to their level. Thus he promoted Logan, Crocker, John E. Smith, Morgan L. Smith and Ransom – civilians all – to high rank because their performance merited it.

He never inspired his soldiers in the dynamic fashion exhibited by leaders such as Sheridan, Logan, Ransom or Custer. But the common soldier appreciated that Grant did not order a countermarch unless it could not be avoided and did not change their destination unless a change became clearly necessary. His leadership style flowed from his personality. His impact on his officers and men was uncalculated. Yet his battlefield record created a tradition of victory that helped see his western soldiers through to victory in numerous trying circumstances. His character gave, by the narrowest of margins, his eastern soldiers enough confidence to persevere.

During Grant's time in Virginia, Meade had had a long opportunity to study this man up close. He concluded: 'Grant is not a mighty genius,' but he was upright and honest with great force of character. His 'unflinching tenacity' was an outstanding quality, but it required judgement to control it lest it become costly bull-headed stubbornness. Meade thought that Grant was occasionally overly sanguine, too confident for his own and the army's good. Moreover, he was guileless and therefore vulnerable to influence seekers. Here Meade had accurately measured his man. Grant's guilelessness would greatly impair his presidency. Meade saw Grant warts and all, and, even while the investment of Petersburg remained unresolved, concluded, that of all the federal commanders, he was 'the best man the war has yet produced'.[5]

When then and thereafter people delved into Grant's character in an effort to understand how this man had won the war, they often went astray, making him out to be more complex than he was. General John M. Schofield summed it up well: 'The greatest of all the traits of Grant's character was that which lay always on the surface, visible to all who had eyes to see.'[6] Grant was a simple man who dealt with the facts as he found them. While his contemporaries saw war in all its complexities and too often took counsel of their fears, from Belmont to Appomattox Grant saw the main chance, stuck to it, and thus led his armies to victory.

1   Allan Nevins, ed., *A Diary of Battle: The Personal Journals of Colonel Charles S. Wainwright, 1861-1865*, (New York: Harcourt, Brace & World, 1962), p. 530.
2   James Harrison Wilson, *Under the Old Flag*, vol. 1 (New York: D. Appleton and Co., 1912), p. 322.
3   US. Military Academy, *A Military History and Atlas of the Napoleonic Wars*, (New York: Frederick A. Praeger Publishers, 1964), text facing Map 45.
4   Russell F. Weigley, *Eisenhower's Lieutenants*, (Bloomington: Indiana University Press, 1981), p. 7.
5   George Meade, *The Life and Letters of George Gordon Meade*, vol. 2 (New York: Charles Scribner's Sons, 1913), p. 246.
6   Cited in E. B. Long, "Ulysses S. Grant for Today" in *Ulysses S. Grant: Essays, Documents*, (Carbondale: Southern Illinois University Press, 1981), p. 24.

Bibliography

Students of the Civil War are fortunate in that the conflict featured a happy confluence of a highly literate soldiery and the absence of censorship.

PRIMARY SOURCES

Archives, Fort Donelson National Battlefield, Dover, Tennessee

Abernethy, Byron R. (ed.). *Private Elisha Stockwell, Jr. Sees the Civil War*. Norman: University of Oklahoma Press, 1958

Agassiz, George R. (ed.). *Meade's Headquarters 1863–1865: Letters of Colonel Theodore Lyman from the Wilderness to Appomattox*. Boston: Massachusetts Historical Society, 1922

Arnold, A. K. 'A War Reminiscence – The Fifth U. S. Regular Cavalry with General Sheridan on Raid Towards Richmond, VA., in 1864', in *Journals of the U. S. Cavalry Association*, vol. II (1889) 28-33

Baumgartner, Richard A. and Strayer, Larry M. (eds.). *Ralsa C. Rice: Yankee Tigers: Through the Civil War with the 125th Ohio*. Huntington, WV: Blue Acorn Press, 1992

Cadwallader, Sylvanus. *Three Years with Grant*. New York: Alfred A. Knopf, 1956

Coffin, Charles Carleton. *The Boys of '61*. Boston: Dana Estes & Co., 1896

Dana, Charles A. *Recollections of the Civil War*. New York: Appleton & Co., 1899

Dawes, Rufus R. *Service With the Sixth Wisconsin Volunteers*. Madison: State Historical Society of Wisconsin, 1962

DeForest, John William. *A Volunteer's Adventures: A Union Captain's Record of the Civil War*. New Haven: Yale University Press, 1946

Fitch, Michael Hendrick. *The Chattanooga Campaign, with especial reference to Wisconsin's participation therein*. Wisconsin History Commission, 1911

Force, Manning F. *Personal Recollections of the Vicksburg Campaign*. Cincinnati: Henry C. Sherick, 1885

Freeman, Douglas Southall (ed.). *Lee's Dispatches to Jefferson Davis*. New York: G. P Putnam's Sons, 1957

Gallagher, Gary W. (ed.). *Fighting for the Confederacy: The Personal Recollections of General Edward Porter Alexander*. Chapel Hill: University of North Carolina Press, 1989

Gibbon, John. *Personal Recollections of the Civil War*. Dayton: Morningside Bookshop, 1978

Grant, Ulysses S. *Personal Memoirs*. New York: De Capo Press, 1982 (Written during his race against death, here is the great man's life in his own words.)

Hazen, W. B. *A Narrative of Military Service*. Boston: Ticknor & Co., 1885

Howard, McHenry. *Recollections of a Confederate Soldier, 1861–1866*. Dayton, 1975

Humphreys, Andrew A. *The Virginia Campaign of '64 and '65*. New York: Charles Scribner's Sons, 1897

Kimbell, Charles B. *History of Battery 'A' First Illinois Light Artillery Volunteers*. Chicago: Cushing Printing Co., 1899

Long, A. L. (ed.). *Memoirs of Robert E. Lee*. Secaucus, NJ: Blue and Grey Press, 1983

Lord, Walter (ed.). *The Fremantle*

Diary. Boston: Little, Brown and Co., 1954

Loving, Jerome M. (ed.). *Civil War Letters of George Washington Whitman.* Durham, NC: Duke University Press, 1975

Marcus, Edward (ed.). *A New Canaan Private in the Civil War: Letters of Justus M. Silliman, 17th Connecticut Volunteers.* New Canaan, CT: New Canaan Historical Society, 1984

Meade, George. *The Life and Letters of George Gordon Meade.* 2 vols. New York: Charles Scribner's Sons, 1913

Menge, W. Springer and Shimrak, J. August (eds.). *The Civil War Notebook of Daniel Chisholm.* New York: Orion Books, 1989

Meyers, Augustus. *Ten Years in the Ranks, U. S. Army.* New York: The Stirling Press, 1914

Michie, Peter S. *The Life and Letters of Emory Upton.* New York: Arno Press, 1979

Nevins, Allan (ed.). *A Diary of Battle: The Personal Journals of Colonel Charles S. Wainwright, 1861–1865.* New York: Harcourt, Brace & World, 1962. (One of the most comprehensive contemporary accounts of the Army of the Potomac's trials and tribulations.)

Porter, Horace. *Campaigning With Grant.* New York: The Century Co., 1897

Rhodes, Robert Hunt (ed.). *All For the Union: The Civil War Diary and Letters of Elisha Hunt Rhodes.* New York: Vintage Books, 1992

Robertson, James I. (ed.). *The Civil War Letters of General Robert McAllister.* New Brunswick, NJ: Rutgers University Press, 1965. (McAllister took pride in the Army of the Potomac's New Jersey units, but his graphic account shows soldier life warts and all in this most frustrating of Union armies.)

Roth, Margaret Brobst (ed.). *Well Mary: Civil War Letters of a Wisconsin Volunteer.* Madison: University of Wisconsin Press, 1960

Scott, Robert Garth (ed.). *Fallen Leaves: The Civil War Letters of Major Henry Livermore Abbott.* Kent, OH: Kent State University Press, 1991

Sears, Stephen W. (ed.) *For Country, Cause & Leader: The Civil War Journal of Charles B. Haydon.* New York: Ticknor & Fields, 1993

Shaw, Horace H. *The First Maine Heavy Artillery, 1892–1865.* Portland, ME: 1903

Sheridan, Philip H. *Personal Memoirs of P. H. Sheridan.* 2 vols. New York: Charles L. Webster & Co., 1888. (Self-serving but informative.)

Sherman, William Tecumseh. *Memoirs of General W. T. Sherman.* New York: Library of America, 1990

Simon, John Y. (ed.) *The Papers of Ulysses S. Grant.* Carbondale: Southern Illinois University Press, 1970

Simon, John Y. and Wilson, David L. (eds.) *Ulysses S. Grant: Essays, Documents.* Carbondale: Southern Illinois University Press, 1981

Smith, William Farrar. *From Chattanooga to Petersburg Under Generals Grant and Butler.* Boston: Houghton Mifflin, 1893

Smith, William Wrenshall. 'Holocaust Holiday', in *Civil War Times Illustrated,* vol. XVIII (October 1979) 28–40

Sparks, David S. (ed.) *Inside Lincoln's Army: The Diary of General Patrick.* New York, Thomas Yoseloff, 1964

Stillwell, Leander. *The Story of a Common Soldier of Army Life in the Civil War 1861–1865.* Franklin Hudson Publishing Co., 1920

US Government. *War of the Rebellion: Official Records of the Union and Confederate Armies.* Washington, 1890. (The indispensable source for Civil War history, containing the correspondence leading up to battle and the post-action reports of the participants. A word of warning. What is bungled on the field can be won back by shrewd report writing!)

Villard, Henry. *Memoirs of Henry Villard.* 2 vols. Boston: Houghton,

Mifflin Co., 1904. (Villard, a newspaper correspondent, never quite understood how a man like Grant could rise to the top. He didn't much like him and it shows. However, Villard was an eye-witness of many notable events.)

Watson, William. *Letters of a Civil War Surgeon.* W. Lafayette, IN: Purdue Research Fdn., 1961

Weld, Stephen Minot. *War Diary and Letters of Stephen Minot Weld, 1861–1865.* Boston: Massachusetts Historical Society, 1979

Welles, Gideon. *Diary of Gideon Welles.* 3 vols. Boston: Houghton Mifflin Co., 1911. (Secretary of the Navy Welles offers pointed commentary on the Lincoln administration's views of the war's progress. Grant's steady rise in Lincoln's esteem contrasts with the commander-in-chief's frustrations over the commanders of the Army of the Potomac.)

Wilson, James Harrison. *Under the Old Flag.* 2 vols. New York: D. Appleton and Co., 1912. (Fascinating, gossipy account by an intelligent man who, so he says, never made any battlefield errors and whose advice prompted many of Grant's greatest manoeuvres.)

Woodward, E. M. *Our Campaigns.* Philadelphia: John E. Potter & Co., 1865

SECONDARY SOURCES

Adams, Michael C. *Our Masters the Rebels: Speculations on Union Military Failure in the East, 1861–1865.* Cambridge, MA: Harvard University Press, 1978. (Exploration of the Federal psychological inferiority.)

Anders, Leslie. *The Twenty-First Missouri: From Home Guard to Union Regiment.* Westport, CT: Greenwood Press, 1975

Arnold, James R. *Chickamauga 1863: The River of Death.* London: Osprey Publishing, 1992

Bauer, Dan. 'Who Knows the Truth About the Big Bender?', in *Civil War Times Illustrated* (December 1988), 36-43

Bearss, Edwin C. *The Campaign for Vicksburg.* 4 vols. Dayton: Morningside, 1986

— *Hardluck Ironclad: The Sinking and Salvage of the Cairo.* Baton Rouge: Louisiana State University Press, 1966

— *Unconditional Surrender: The Fall of Fort Donelson.* Eastern National Park and Monument Assoc., 1991

— and Calkins, Chris. *Battle of Five Forks.* Lynchburg, VA: H. E. Howard, 1985

Boatner, Mark Mayo, III. *The Civil War Dictionary.* New York: David McKay Co., 1959

Catton, Bruce. *Grant Takes Command.* Boston: Little, Brown, 1968

Cisco, Walter Brian. 'Galvanized Rebels', in *Civil War*, VII:5 (September–October 1990), 48-54

Coggins, Jack. *Arms and Equipment of the Civil War.* New York: Doubleday & Co., 1962

Connelly, Thomas Lawrence and Jones, Archer. *The Politics of Command: Factions and Ideas in Confederate Strategy.* Baton Rouge: Louisiana State University Press, 1973

Cooling, Benjamin Franklin. *Forts Henry and Donelson: The Key to the Confederate Heartland.* Knoxville: University of Tennessee Press, 1987. (Good account of the strategic situation, naval actions, and Confederate high command. Less good for Grant and land battles.)

Farnum, George R. 'John A. Rawlins: Country Lawyer and Grant's Lieutenant' in *American Bar Association Journal*, vol. 29 (November 1943)

Foote, Shelby. *The Civil War.* 3 vols. New York: Random House, 1963

Foster, G. Allen. *The Eyes and Ears of the Civil War.* New York: Criterion Books, 1963

Fox, William F. *Regimental Losses in the American Civil War.* New York: Brandow, 1898, repr. by Morningside Bookshop, 1974. (A statistical compilation of Federal losses.)

Frank, Joseph Allan and Reaves, George A. *'Seeing the Elephant': Raw Recruits at the Battle of Shiloh*. New York: Greenwood Press, 1989. (A fine compilation of eye-witness accounts coupled with interesting commentary.)

Glover, Edwin A. *Bucktailed Wildcats: A Regiment of Civil War Volunteers*. New York: Thomas Yoseloff, 1960

Griffith, Paddy. *Battle Tactics of the Civil War*. New Haven, CT: Yale University Press, 1989

Harris, Brayton, 'The Role of the Press in the Civil War', in *Civil War*, vol. XV (December 1988)

Huffstodt, Jim. *Hard Dying Men: The Story of General W. H. L. Wallace, General T. E. G. Ransom, and their 'Old Eleventh' Illinois Infantry in the American Civil War (1861–1865)*. Bowie, MD: Heritage Books, 1991

Hughes, Nathaniel C. *The Battle of Belmont*. Chapel Hill: University of North Carolina Press, 1991. (A fine account of Grant's first battle.)

Lewis, Lloyd. *Captain Sam Grant*. Boston: Little, Brown and Co., 1950. (An entertaining account of Grant's early years through to the time he becomes colonel of an Illinois regiment in 1861.)

Lord, Francis A. *They Fought for the Union*. New York: Bonanza Books, 1960. (An excellent one-volume account of military life.)

McDonough, James Lee. *Chattanooga: A Death Grip on the Confederacy*. Knoxville: University of Tennessee Press, 1984

Miers, Earl S. *The Web of Victory: Grant at Vicksburg*. Baton Rouge: Louisiana State University Press, 1955

Military Analysis of the Civil War: An Anthology by the Editors of Military Affairs. Millwood, NY: KTO Press, 1977

Mullins, Michael A. *The Fremont Rifles: A History of the 37th Illinois Veteran Volunteer Infantry*. Wilmington, NC: Broadfoot Publishing, 1990

Pratt, Fletcher. 'Little Phil – Part I', in *Coast Artillery Journal*, September–October 1939

Reed, Rowena. *Combined Operations in the Civil War*. Annapolis: Naval Institute Press, 1978. (A thorough recapitulation of amphibious operations. The author is unimpressed by the genius of Grant's improvisational efforts during the Vicksburg campaign. Her critique, based upon modern staff principles, is unpersuasive given the reality of the situation in 1863.)

Reese, Timothy J. *Sykes' Regular Infantry Division, 1861–1864*. Jefferson, NC: McFarland & Co., 1990

Scott, Robert Garth. *Into the Wilderness with the Army of the Potomac*. Bloomington: Indiana University Press, 1985

Starr, Stephen Z. *The Union Cavalry in the Civil War*. 2 vols. Baton Rouge: Louisiana State University Press, 1985

Sword, Wiley. *Shiloh: Bloody April*. Dayton: Morningside Bookshop, 1988. (Still the most detailed account. Well written and interesting.)

US Military Academy. *The West Point Atlas of American Wars, Volume I, 1689–1900*. New York: Frederick A. Praeger Publishers, 1959

— *A Military History and Atlas of the Napoleonic Wars*. New York: Frederick A. Praeger Publishers, 1964

Wheeler, Richard. *On Fields of Fury. From the Wilderness to the Crater: An Eyewitness History*. New York: Harper Collins Publishers, 1991

Weigley, Russell F. *Eisenhower's Lieutenants*. Bloomington: Indiana University Press, 1981

Wilkinson, Warren. *Mother, May You Never See the Sights I Have Seen: The Fifty-seventh Massachusetts Veteran Volunteers in the Army of the Potomac, 1864–1865*. New York: Harper & Row, 1990

Index